Study Guide

Fundamentals of Financial Management Concise Edition

Seventh Edition

Eugene F. Brigham & Joel F. Houston

SOUTH-WESTERN
CENGAGE Learning™

Australia • Brazil • Japan • Korea • Mexico • Singapore • Spain • United Kingdom • United States

ISBN-13: 978-0-538-48152-6
ISBN-10: 0-538-48152-8

South-Western Cengage Learning
Cengage Learning
2640 Eagan Woods Drive Suite 220
Eagan, MN 55121

Cengage Learning is a leading provider of customized learning solutions with office locations around the globe, including Singapore, the United Kingdom, Australia, Mexico, Brazil, and Japan. Locate your local office at: **international.cengage.com/region**.

Cengage Learning products are represented in Canada by Nelson Education, Ltd.

For your course and learning solutions, visit **www.cengage.com**.

Purchase any of our products at your local college store or at our preferred online store **www.CengageBrain.com**.

TABLE OF CONTENTS

PREFACE   iv

HOW TO USE THIS STUDY GUIDE   v

WANT TO DO WELL ON EXAMS? THEN READ THIS!   vi

<u>CHAPTER</u>

1. AN OVERVIEW OF FINANCIAL MANAGEMENT   1
2. FINANCIAL MARKETS AND INSTITUTIONS   11
3. FINANCIAL STATEMENTS, CASH FLOW, AND TAXES   21
4. ANALYSIS OF FINANCIAL STATEMENTS   37
5. TIME VALUE OF MONEY   63
6. INTEREST RATES   99
7. BONDS AND THEIR VALUATION   115
8. RISK AND RATES OF RETURN   143
9. STOCKS AND THEIR VALUATION   169
10. THE COST OF CAPITAL   191
11. THE BASICS OF CAPITAL BUDGETING   211
12. CASH FLOW ESTIMATION AND RISK ANALYSIS   231
13. CAPITAL STRUCTURE AND LEVERAGE   253
14. DISTRIBUTIONS TO SHAREHOLDERS: DIVIDENDS AND SHARE REPURCHASES   275
15. WORKING CAPITAL MANAGEMENT   295
16. FINANCIAL PLANNING AND FORECASTING   319
17. MULTINATIONAL FINANCIAL MANAGEMENT   341

PREFACE

This *Study Guide* is designed primarily to help you develop a working knowledge of the concepts and principles of financial management. Additionally, it will familiarize you with the types of true/false and multiple-choice test questions that are being used with increasing frequency in introductory finance courses.

The *Study Guide* follows the outline of *Fundamentals of Financial Management: Concise Seventh Edition.* You should read carefully the next section, "How to Use This Study Guide," to familiarize yourself with its specific contents and to gain some insights into how it can be used most effectively.

We would like to thank Susan Whitman for her considerable assistance in the preparation of this edition, and Lou Gapenski and Bob LeClair for their helpful ideas in prior editions that we carried over to this one.

We have tried to make the *Study Guide* as clear and error-free as possible. However, some mistakes may have crept in, and there are almost certainly some sections that could be clarified. Any suggestions for improving the *Study Guide* would be greatly appreciated and should be addressed to Joel Houston at the e-mail address below. Since instructors almost never read study guides, we address this call for help to students!

Eugene F. Brigham
Joel F. Houston
Dana Aberwald Clark

Houston & Associates
4723 N.W. 53rd Ave., Suite A
Gainesville, FL 32653-4804
email address: concise@joelhouston.com

February, 2011

HOW TO USE THIS STUDY GUIDE

Different people will tend to use the *Study Guide* in somewhat different ways. This is natural because both introductory finance courses and individual students' needs vary widely. However, the tips contained in this section should help all students use the *Study Guide* more effectively, regardless of these differences.

Each chapter contains (1) a list of learning objectives, (2) an overview, (3) an outline, (4) definitional self-test questions, (5) conceptual self-test questions, (6) self-test problems, and (7) answers and solutions to the self-test questions and problems. You should begin your study by reading the list of learning objectives and the overview; they will give you an idea of what is contained in the chapter and how this material fits into the overall scheme of things in financial management.

Next, read over the outline to get a better fix on the specific topics covered in the chapter. It is important to realize that the outline does not list every facet of every topic covered in the textbook. The *Study Guide* is intended to highlight and summarize the textbook, not to supplant it. Also, note that web appendix material is clearly marked as such within the outline. Thus, if your instructor does not assign a particular web appendix, you may not want to study that portion of the outline.

The definitional self-test questions are intended to test your knowledge of, and also to reinforce your ability to work with, the terms and concepts introduced in the chapter. If you do not understand the definitions thoroughly, review the outline prior to going on to the conceptual self-test questions and problems.

The conceptual self-test questions focus on the same kinds of ideas that the textbook end-of-chapter questions address, but in the *Study Guide*, the questions are set out in a true/false or multiple-choice format. Thus, for many students these questions can be used to practice for the types of tests that are being used with increasing frequency. However, regardless of the types of tests you must take, working through the conceptual questions will help drive home the key concepts of financial management.

The numeric problems are also written in a multiple-choice format. Generally, the problems are arranged in order of increasing difficulty. Also, note that some of the *Study Guide* problems are convoluted in the sense that information normally available to financial managers is withheld and information normally unknown is given. Such problems are designed to test your knowledge of a subject, and you must work "backwards" to solve them. Furthermore, such problems are included in the *Study Guide* in part because they provide a good test of how well you understand the material.

Finally, each *Study Guide* chapter provides the answers and solutions to the self-test questions and problems. The rationale behind a question's correct answer is explained where necessary, but the problem solutions are always complete. Note that the problems generally provide "financial calculator" solutions.

Of course, each student must decide how to incorporate the *Study Guide* in his or her overall study program. Many students begin an assignment by reading the *Study Guide's* learning objectives, overview, and outline to get the "big picture." Then, they go on to read the chapter in the textbook. Naturally, the *Study Guide* overview and outline are also used extensively to review for exams. Most students work the textbook questions and problems, using the latter as a self-test and review tool. However, if you are stumped by a text problem, try the *Study Guide* problems first because their detailed solutions can get you over stumbling blocks.

WANT TO DO WELL ON EXAMS? THEN READ THIS!

The goals of a good testing system are (1) to give students direction as to the most important material, (2) to motivate them to study properly, and (3) to determine how much they have learned. In finance, it is easy to construct a combination problem/essay exam that accomplishes these goals, but if essay questions are ruled out by class size, then instructors have a more difficult job. They must then develop complex, unambiguous questions and problems that require students to think through the issues and determine which of several plausible-looking statements is most correct. A good exam will require students to recall how to use a number of equations, graphs, and problem set-ups, to actually set up examples or draw graphs to determine the required answers, and to understand how the results are used in the decision-making process. It is not easy to accomplish these goals in a multiple-choice exam, but it can be done.

Many students in the introductory finance course have never faced this type of an exam, and they are "thrown for a loop" by our questions. Eventually, they catch on to our examination process, and when they do, they think it is both fair and reasonable. Still, learning how to take multiple-choice finance exams can be traumatic and stressful. *The purpose of this section is to try to reduce your stress if you will be faced with multiple-choice exams.* If you will be taking "regular" problem/essay exams, the section will still be useful, but if you will be taking multiple-choice exams, you simply cannot afford to skip it!

How to Take Multiple-Choice Finance Tests

Like it or not, testing is inherently competitive—students compete against one another and also against the instructor. Of course, the instructor wants the students to do well, but he or she also wants to challenge students and to see just how well they understand the material.

You should understand how your instructor makes up his or her exams because this will help you to prepare for them. Obviously, we don't know how your specific instructor will construct exams, but chances are that he or she will do something similar to what we and most other instructors do. So, here are some pointers that will help you as you study finance and prepare for exams.

1. Recognize that finance is inherently quantitative—it deals with numbers and relationships between numbers. It is less intuitive than management or marketing but more intuitive than accounting or statistics. For example, accountants are primarily interested in reporting *historical* data, but in finance we want to know how different actions will affect *future* data. Therefore, as they write out exams, instructors will ask you to do many calculations, but to do more than just crank out numerical answers. They will also expect you to know how your answer would tend to change if the data were changed and how the very possibility of such changes might influence actual decisions.

2. You will probably have to answer two types of questions on finance exams: (1) numerical problems and (2) conceptual true/false or multiple-choice questions. You are probably used to taking courses where you can cram just before the exams, memorize some equations and facts, then regurgitate them on the exam and do fine. That won't work in finance—you obviously will need to learn some facts, but you must also learn how to set up and solve relatively complex problems and reason out difficult conceptual multiple-choice questions.

vi

3. You can study for problems in two ways: work all the problems you can find and hope you will get recognizably similar ones on the exam, or, preferably, think about the various types of problems in a generic sense, and try to understand what each type of problem is all about; that is, think about why the particular problem is important, what type of decision it deals with, and why the solution is laid out as it is.

4. The worst way to study homework problems is to just work on each problem until you get the right answer, pat yourself on the back for getting it, and then move on to the next problem. The best way to study problems is to go consciously and systematically through these four steps: (1) Begin by asking yourself what the purpose of the problem is. For example, if the problem deals with a ratio analysis by a banker considering whether or not to make a loan to a company, make note of that fact. (2) Next, ask yourself what formula, table set-up, or what-have-you is necessary to obtain a solution. In a ratio analysis, you might at this point list the ratios that would be most relevant. (3) Then insert the data to arrive at the required answer. (4) Finally, conclude by asking yourself two sets of questions:

    a. If my instructor were to give us a problem like this on the exam, how might he or she change it to make up a good exam problem? Obviously the numbers could be changed, but could we be required to solve for a different variable? For example, if the problem gave us balance sheet data and then required us to determine the current ratio, could we be given the current ratio plus some balance sheet data and then be required to complete the balance sheet?

    b. If our instructor wants to see if we understand the implications of the answer for decision making, what kind of conceptual question might we be asked? For example, if we calculated a current ratio of 2.3×, how could we tell if that ratio was good, bad, or indifferent, and who might use the current ratio, and for what purposes?

    We let our students bring to the exams one 8½" by 11" sheet of paper with as much written on the two sides as they can squeeze on it. We do this partly to reduce their tendency to try to memorize things, but we also want them to think about problems generically, and having them list formulas and prototype examples of each type of problem on their "cheat sheet" helps in this regard.

5. Except for a few definitional questions, most non-numeric (conceptual) exam questions are actually based on problems. When we and most other finance professors make up regular problem/essay exams as opposed to multiple-choice exams, we often ask for the solution to a problem and then ask for an essay explanation of how changes in various factors would affect the answer. Or, we might just skip the numerical problem part and simply ask you to explain how changes in different input variables would affect some output variable.

    For example, we might give you the following partial balance sheet and then ask you to calculate the current ratio:

Inventory	$ 50	Accounts payable	$ 50
Other current assets	45	Short-term bank loans	50
Total current assets	$ 95	Total current liabilities	$100

You would find the current ratio to be 95/100 = 0.95. Then, on an essay exam, we might ask you three additional questions:

a. Would the current ratio be improved (increased) if the company took out a 6-month loan for $100 and used the proceeds to increase inventory?

b. Would your answer in Part a have been the same if the company's original current ratio had been 1.5 rather than 0.95? Explain.

c. What general conclusions can you reach regarding the effects on the current ratio of adding equal dollar amounts to both current assets and current liabilities?

To answer Part a, you would make the necessary changes in the balance sheet, calculate the new current ratio of ($95 + $100)/($100 + $100) = $195/$200 = 0.975, and answer, "Yes, the current ratio would be improved—it would increase from 0.95 to 0.975." To answer Part b, you would increase Other current assets (or Inventory) by $55 to produce a situation where the original current ratio was 1.5, then add $100 to both inventories and bank loans, and calculate this new current ratio:

$$\text{Current ratio} = (\$150 + \$100)/(\$100 + \$100) = \$250/\$200 = 1.25.$$

Then you would answer Part b as follows: "No. In this case, adding an equal amount to both current assets and current liabilities will cause the current ratio to decrease from 1.5 to 1.25."

To answer Part c, you should first suspect that whether the current ratio increases or decreases depends on whether or not the initial current ratio is above or below 1.0. You might then go back to the original data, add $5 to other current assets to bring the current ratio up to 1.0, and then add $100 to both inventories and bank loans to confirm your hunch. Then you would answer Part c as follows: "If the current ratio is initially below 1.0, then adding equal dollar amounts to current assets and current liabilities will improve the current ratio, while if the initial ratio is greater than 1.0, the current ratio will be reduced. If the initial current ratio is 1.0, then the change will have no effect on the current ratio—it will remain constant at 1.0."

6. The essay questions in Point 5 were derived directly from the problem, and we answered the questions by modifying the data in the problem. Thus, the questions were based on the problem. *Now note that we could have skipped the problem and gone directly to the conceptual questions.* For example, we could have given you a question like this:

> If a company whose current ratio is 0.95 takes out a 6-month loan from its bank and uses the cash to increase inventory, how would this affect its current ratio?

Now you would probably approach the question by writing out the formula for the current ratio, making up some data where the current ratio is 0.95, then adding some amount to current assets and current liabilities, and finally calculating a new current ratio. Some people can think such questions through abstractly, but most of us find it easier to work out some numbers, get the picture of what's happening, and then reach general conclusions. *Therefore, for most of us it is most efficient to approach conceptual questions that test our knowledge of relationships by first asking what generic problem the question is based on by thinking about the question within the framework of a problem,* in this case the calculation of a current ratio.

7. When we make up multiple-choice exams, we put several false statements plus one true statement into a question and then ask you to identify the correct statement. For example, we might ask you the following question:

If a firm takes out a 6-month loan and uses the proceeds to build inventory, then, other things held constant, its current ratio will

   a. Increase.
   b. Decrease.
   c. Remain constant.
   d. Fluctuate.
   e. Increase, decrease, or remain constant, depending on the level of the initial current ratio.

As we saw above, the correct answer is "e," but if we had not just gone through the example, how would you have approached the question? You could try guessing, but a better approach would be to set up a partial balance sheet, put some numbers in, and see what happens to the current ratio. That is the best way for most of us to attack many of the conceptual questions you will face.

8. You should realize that when professors make up conceptual questions, they often start with numerical problems and then frame "word" questions as they look at the details of a problem. For example, we might be looking at a balance sheet and the calculations for the current ratio and then come up with the question posed in Point 7.

9. To take this a step further, many professors write a multiple-choice exam problem and then ask a multiple-choice conceptual question that is related to the problem, *but do not tie the two together* physically on the exam. Thus, you might be asked to calculate some ratios as a problem and then, separately, be asked to answer a conceptual question about ratios that would be easier to answer if you make the connection between the problem and the question.

10. At Florida, we generally give two midterms plus a final exam, and each is a 2-hour exam. We have about 10 multiple-choice conceptual questions first, then about 10 multiple-choice problems. Initially, most students worked straight through the exam, front to back. However, some of the more astute students figured out that if they worked the problems first, they would get some clues that would help with the questions. Now our students generally work the problems first, regardless of their order of appearance on the exams. Note, though, that we and many other instructors include a number of relatively easy questions and problems, along with some difficult ones designed to separate the best students from the rest. Further, the most difficult problems are placed toward the end of the problem set. We warn our students not to spend too much time on any one problem and, if they don't have a clue as to how to handle it, to go on and then to come back to it later if they have time.

11. One final comment about studying is appropriate. Some of our less astute students tend to tackle a given problem, not see how to work it, look up the solution or have someone to explain it to them, and then say to themselves, "Oh yes, I see how to work it, and I could work one like it on the exam. Now let's finish the rest of the problems." Too often, this is pure self-deceit: The student really doesn't understand the problem and could not work one like it unless it was virtually identical. Slowing down and going through our checklist will help you avoid this problem.

1

AN OVERVIEW OF FINANCIAL MANAGEMENT

Learning Objectives

1. Explain the role of finance and the different types of jobs in finance.

2. Identify the advantages and disadvantages of different forms of business organization.

3. Explain the links between stock price, intrinsic value, and executive compensation.

4. Discuss the importance of business ethics and the consequences of unethical behavior.

5. Identify the potential conflicts that arise within the firm between stockholders and managers and between stockholders and bondholders, and discuss the techniques that firms can use to mitigate these potential conflicts.

Overview

This chapter provides an overview of financial management and should give you a better understanding of the following: (1) how finance fits into the structure of a firm's organization, (2) how businesses are organized, (3) what the goals of a firm are and how financial managers can contribute to the attainment of these goals, (4) important business trends, (5) business ethics: what companies are doing and the consequences of unethical behavior, and (6) conflicts that arise between managers, stockholders, and bondholders.

Outline

I. **Finance grew out of economics and accounting and it is divided into three areas: (1) financial management, (2) capital markets, and (3) investments.**

    A. *Financial management* is also called corporate finance.

        1. It focuses on:

            a. decisions relating to how much and what types of assets to acquire,

            b. how to raise the capital needed to buy assets, and

            c. how to run the firm so as to maximize its value.

1

B. *Capital markets* relate to the markets where interest rates, along with stock and bond prices, are determined.

   1. Financial institutions that supply capital to businesses are studied here.

   2. Governmental organizations such as the Federal Reserve System, which regulates banks and controls the supply of money, and the SEC, which regulates the trading of stocks and bonds in public markets, are also studied as part of capital markets.

C. *Investments* relate to decisions concerning stocks and bonds. It includes a number of activities.

   1. *Security analysis* deals with finding the proper values of individual securities.

   2. *Portfolio theory* deals with the best way to structure individual/institution portfolios.

      a. A properly balanced portfolio is necessary to limit risk.

   3. *Market analysis* deals with the issue of whether stock and bond markets at any given time are too high, too low, or just right.

      a. *Behavioral finance* examines investor psychology in an effort to determine if stock prices have been bid up to unreasonable heights or driven down to unreasonable lows.

II. **The legal structure of a firm affects some aspects of a firm's operations and thus must be recognized. The four main forms of business organization are sole proprietorships, partnerships, corporations, and limited liability corporations/partnerships. About 80% of businesses operate as sole proprietorships, but when based on dollar value of sales, 80% of all business is conducted by corporations.**

A. A *proprietorship* is an unincorporated business owned by one individual.

   1. Its advantages are:

      a. it is easily and inexpensively formed,

      b. it is subject to few government regulations, and

      c. it is subject to lower income taxes than are corporations.

   2. Its disadvantages are:

      a. the proprietor has unlimited personal liability for business debts, which can result in losses that exceed the money they have invested in the company,

      b. it has a life limited to the life of the individual who created it, and

      c. it is limited in its ability to raise large sums of capital.

   3. Proprietorships are used primarily for small businesses, but they are converted to corporations when their disadvantages outweigh their advantages.

B. A *partnership* is a legal arrangement between two or more persons who decide to do business together.

   1. Its advantages are:

      a. its low cost and ease of formation, and

      b. its income is allocated on a pro rata basis to partners and taxed on an individual basis.

2. Its disadvantages are:

   a. unlimited personal liability,

   b. limited life,

   c. difficulty of transferring ownership, and

   d. difficulty of raising large amounts of capital.

C. A *corporation* is a legal entity created by a state, and it is separate and distinct from its owners and managers.

   1. Its advantages are:

      a. unlimited life,

      b. ownership that is easily transferred through the exchange of stock,

      c. limited liability, and

      d. ease of raising large amounts of capital to operate large businesses.

   2. Its disadvantages are:

      a. corporate earnings may be subject to double taxation and

      b. setting up a corporation and filing required state and federal reports are more complex and time-consuming than for a proprietorship or partnership.

   3. A drawback to corporations is taxes because most corporations' earnings are subject to double taxation.

      a. As an aid to small business, Congress created *S Corporations* that are taxed as if they were a proprietorship or a partnership rather than a corporation.

      b. S status is retained until stock is sold to the public, at which time they become C corporations.

D. A *limited liability corporation (LLC)* is a hybrid between a partnership and a corporation.

   1. LLCs have limited liability like corporations.

   2. LLCs are taxed like partnerships.

   3. *Limited liability partnerships* are similar to LLCs, but are used for professional firms in such fields as accounting, law, and architecture.

E. The value of any business other than a very small one will probably be maximized if it is organized as a corporation for three reasons.

   1. Limited liability reduces the risks borne by investors, and the lower the firm's risk, the higher its value.

   2. A firm's value is dependent on its growth opportunities, which are dependent on the firm's ability to attract capital. Corporations are better able to take advantage of growth opportunities.

   3. The value of an asset also depends on its liquidity, which means the ease of selling the asset and converting it to cash at a "fair market value." Corporate investments are more liquid than similar investments in proprietorships or partnerships, and this enhances their value.

3

III.   **Management's primary goal is stockholder wealth maximization; however, managers have an obligation to behave ethically. They must follow the laws and other society-imposed constraints.**

    A.   Most managers recognize that being socially responsible is not inconsistent with maximizing shareholder value.

        1.   Society can impose a wide range of costs on a company that doesn't follow laws or other socially-imposed constraints.

        2.   These costs would ultimately lead to a reduction in shareholder value.

    B.   The finance department's principal task is to evaluate proposed decisions and judge how they will affect the stock price and therefore shareholder wealth.

    C.   Stock prices change over time as conditions change and as investors obtain new information about companies' prospects.

        1.   A firm's investment decisions determine its future profits, investors' cash flows, and its stock price.

IV.   **Stock price maximization requires us to take a long-run view of operations. However, in recent years the focus for many companies shifted to the short run.**

    A.   Prior to the recent financial crisis, many Wall Street executives received huge bonuses for engaging in risky transactions that generated short-term profits.

    B.   In trying to reform the system, regulators are looking for ways to insure that financial institutions once again focus on their firms' long-run values.

    C.   Academics and practitioners stress the important role that executive compensation plays in encouraging managers to focus on the proper objectives.

        1.   Stock and stock options have been used increasingly as a key part of executive pay.

        2.   The hope is that structuring compensation in this manner, managers will think more like stockholders and continually work to increase shareholder value.

    D.   Stock options, given to managers as an incentive to focus on stock prices, led many managers to try to maximize the stock price on the option exercise date—not over the long run.

    E.   Managerial actions, combined with taxes and economic and political conditions, determine investors' cash flows.

        1.   Expected and realized cash flows are quite different.

        2.   Investors like high cash flows but dislike risk, so the larger the expected cash flows and the lower the perceived risk, the higher the stock price.

    F.   There are differences between "true" expected cash flows and risk versus "perceived" cash flows and risk.

        1.   By "true" we mean the cash flows and risk that investors would expect if they had all the information that exists about a company.

        2.   "Perceived" means what investors expect, given the limited information that they actually have.

    G.   Each stock has an *intrinsic value*, which is an estimate of its true value as calculated by a competent analyst who has the best available data, and a *market price*, which is the actual market price based on perceived but possibly incorrect information as seen by the marginal investor.

1. The *marginal investor* determines the actual price.

2. The stock is said to be in *equilibrium* when there is no pressure for a change in the stock's price. Actual market price and intrinsic value will converge.

3. Intrinsic values are strictly estimates, and estimating intrinsic values is what security analysis is all about and is what distinguishes successful from unsuccessful investors.

4. A firm's managers have the best information about the company's future prospects, so managers' estimates of intrinsic value are generally better than the estimates of outside investors.

H. Intrinsic value is a long-run concept.

1. Management's goal should be to take actions designed to maximize the firm's intrinsic value, not its current market price.

2. Maximizing the intrinsic value will maximize the average price over the long run.

3. Management should provide information that helps investors make accurate estimates of the firm's true intrinsic value, which will keep the stock price closer to its equilibrium level. However, there may be times when management cannot divulge the true situation because doing so would provide helpful information to its competitors.

V. **Three important business trends should be noted.**

A. There is increased globalization of business.

1. Developments in communications technology have made this possible.

2. The trend toward globalization is likely to continue, and companies that resist it will have difficulty competing in the 21st century.

B. Ever-improving information technology is having a profound effect on financial management.

C. *Corporate governance*, or the way the top managers operate and interface with stockholders, is changing the way things are done within firms.

VI. **As a result of recent scandals, there has been a strong push to improve business ethics. Business ethics can be thought of as a company's attitude and conduct toward its employees, customers, community, and stockholders.**

A. A firm's commitment to business ethics can be measured by the tendency of its employees to adhere to laws, regulations, and moral standards relating to product safety and quality, fair employment practices, fair marketing and selling practices, the use of confidential information for personal gain, community involvement, and illegal payments to obtain business.

B. Most firms today have in place strong written codes of ethical behavior and conduct training programs to ensure that employees understand proper behavior in different situations.

1. Unethical actions can have consequences far beyond the companies that perpetrate them.

a. Many investors lost faith in American business and turned away from the stock market, which made it difficult for firms to raise the capital they needed to grow, create jobs, and stimulate the economy.

5

2. Far too often the desire for stock options, bonuses, and promotions drive managers to take unethical actions.

3. Ethics is an important consideration in both business and business schools.

VII. **It has long been recognized that managers' personal goals may compete with shareholder wealth maximization. Managers might be more interested in maximizing their own wealth rather than their stockholders' wealth.**

A. Good executive compensation plans can motivate managers to act in their stockholders' best interests.

1. Useful motivational tools include (a) reasonable compensation packages; (b) firing managers who don't perform well; and (c) the threat of hostile takeovers.

2. The compensation package should be sufficient to attract and retain able managers but not go beyond what is needed.

3. The compensation package should be structured so that managers are rewarded on the basis of the stock's performance over the long run, not the stock's price on an option exercise date.

4. Options, or direct stock awards, should be phased in over a number of years, so managers will have an incentive to keep the stock price high over time.

B. Stockholders can intervene directly with managers.

1. Institutional money managers have the clout to exercise considerable influence over firms' operations.

   a. They can speak with managers and make suggestions about how the business should be run.

   b. They act as lobbyists for the body of stockholders.

2. Any shareholder who has owned $2,000 of a company's stock for one year can sponsor a proposal that must be voted on at the annual stockholders' meeting, even if management opposes the proposal.

   a. Shareholder proposals are nonbinding; however, the results of such votes are clearly heard by top management.

C. If a firm's stock is undervalued, then corporate raiders will see it to be a bargain and will attempt to capture the firm in a hostile takeover.

1. A *corporate raider* is an individual who targets a corporation for takeover because it is undervalued.

2. A *hostile takeover* is the acquisition of a company over the opposition of its management.

3. Managers should try to maximize their stock's intrinsic value and then communicate effectively with stockholders. That will cause the intrinsic value to be high and the actual stock price to remain close to the intrinsic value over time.

D. Conflicts can also arise between stockholders and bondholders.

1. Bondholders generally receive fixed payment regardless of how the firm does, while stockholders do better when the firm does better. This situation leads to conflicts between these two groups.

6

a. Investments in risky ventures that have great payoffs to stockholders if successful, but threaten bankruptcy if they fail creates a conflict between a firm's bondholders and stockholders.

2. Another type of bondholder/stockholder conflict arises over the use of additional debt.

3. Bondholders attempt to protect themselves by including *covenants* in bond agreements that limit firms' use of additional debt and constrain managers' actions.

Self-Test

Definitional Questions

1. Proprietorships are easily formed, but often have difficulty raising _____, they subject proprietors to unlimited _____, and they have a limited _____.

2. A partnership is dissolved upon the withdrawal or _____ of any one of the partners. In addition, the difficulty in _____ ownership is a major disadvantage of the partnership form of business organization.

3. A(n) _____ is a legal entity created by a state, and it is separate from its owners and managers.

4. A(n) _____ _____ _____ is a hybrid between a partnership and a corporation.

5. The concept of _____ liability means that a firm's stockholders are not personally liable for the debts of the business.

6. Management's primary goal is the _____ of shareholder _____.

7. Business _____ can be thought of as a company's attitude and conduct towards its employees, customers, community, and stockholders.

8. A hostile _____ is the acquisition of a company over the opposition of its management.

9. A majority of businesses operate as _____, but when based on dollar value of sales, the majority of all business is conducted by _____.

10. The _____ structure of a firm affects some aspects of a firm's operations and thus must be recognized.

11. Stock price maximization requires us to take a _____-_____ view of operations.

12. _____ actions, combined with taxes and economic and political conditions, determine investors' cash flows.

13. Investors like high cash flows but dislike risk, so the _____ the expected cash flows and the _____ the perceived risk, the higher the stock price.

14. Each stock has a(n) _____ value, which is an estimate of its true value as calculated by a competent analyst who has the best available data.

15. The _____ investor determines the actual price of a stock.

16. A stock is said to be in _____ when there is no pressure for a change in the stock's price and the actual market price and the intrinsic value converge.

7

17. Good executive _____ plans can motivate managers to act in their stockholders' best interests.

18. A corporate _____ is an individual who targets a corporation for takeover because it is undervalued.

19. Bondholders attempt to protect themselves by including _____ in bond agreements that limit firms' use of additional debt and constrain managers' actions.

20. _____ _____ is the way the top managers operate and interface with stockholders, and it is changing the way things are done within firms.

Conceptual Questions

1. The primary objective of the firm is to maximize EPS.

   a. True
   b. False

2. There are factors that influence stock price over which managers have virtually no control.

   a. True
   b. False

3. Which of the following factors tend to encourage management to act in their stockholders' best interests?

   a. A reasonable compensation package sufficient to attract and retain able managers.
   b. Direct intervention by shareholders.
   c. Firing managers who do not perform well.
   d. Threat of a hostile takeover.
   e. All of the above encourage management to act in shareholders' best interests.

4. Which of the following represents a significant *disadvantage* to the corporate form of organization?

   a. Difficulty in transferring ownership.
   b. Exposure to taxation of corporate earnings and stockholder dividend income.
   c. Degree of liability to which corporate owners and managers are exposed.
   d. Level of difficulty corporations' face in obtaining large amounts of capital in financial markets.
   e. All of the above are disadvantages to the corporate form of organization.

Answers

Definitional Questions

1. capital; liability; life
2. death; transferring
3. corporation
4. limited liability corporation (LLC)
5. limited
6. maximization; wealth
7. ethics
8. takeover
9. proprietorships; corporations
10. legal

8

11. long-run
12. Managerial
13. larger; lower
14. intrinsic
15. marginal

16. equilibrium
17. compensation
18. raider
19. covenants
20. Corporate governance

Conceptual Questions

1. b. The primary objective is stockholder wealth maximization, which is the maximization of stock price.

2. a. Managers have no control over factors such as (1) external constraints, (2) the general level of economic activity, (3) taxes, (4) interest rates, and (5) conditions in the stock market.

3. e. All of these statements should encourage management to act in shareholders' best interests.

4. b. Corporations' earnings are taxed, and then earnings paid out as dividends to shareholders are taxed again, generally at a rate of 15%.

2

FINANCIAL MARKETS AND INSTITUTIONS

Learning Objectives

1. Identify the different types of financial markets and financial institutions, and explain how these markets and institutions enhance capital allocation.

2. Explain how the stock market operates, and list the distinctions between the different types of stock markets.

3. Explain how the stock market has performed in recent years.

4. Discuss the importance of market efficiency, and explain why some markets are more efficient than others.

Overview

It is critical that financial managers understand the environment and markets within which they operate. In this chapter, we examine the markets in which capital is raised, securities are traded, and stock prices are established. We examine the institutions that operate in these markets and through which securities transactions are conducted. Finally, we discuss market efficiency, what that means, why some people believe markets are efficient and others do not, and the conclusions reached about market efficiency.

Outline

I. **In a well-functioning economy, capital will flow efficiently from those who supply capital to those who demand it. Transfers of capital between savers and borrowers take place in three different ways.**

   A. *Direct transfers* of money and securities occur when a business sells its stocks or bonds directly to savers, without going through any type of financial institution.

   B. Transfers through an *investment bank* occur when it underwrites the issue serving as a middleman and facilitating the issuance of securities.

11

C. Transfers through a *financial intermediary* occur when a bank, insurance company, or mutual fund obtains funds from savers in exchange for its own securities, and then uses these funds to purchase other businesses' securities.

1. Intermediaries literally create new forms of capital.

2. The existence of intermediaries greatly increases the efficiency of money and capital markets.

D. In a global context, economic development is highly correlated with the level and efficiency of financial markets and institutions.

1. It is difficult for an economy to reach its full potential if it doesn't have access to a well-functioning financial system.

2. In a well-developed economy, an extensive set of markets and institutions have evolved over time to facilitate the efficient allocation of capital.

3. To raise capital efficiently, managers must understand how these markets and institutions work; and individuals need to know how the markets and institutions work to earn high rates of return on their savings.

II. **Financial markets bring together people and organizations wanting to borrow money with those having surplus funds.**

A. There are many different financial markets in a developed economy. Each deals with a different type of instrument, serves a different set of customers, or operates in a different part of the country.

B. The major types of financial markets include:

1. *Physical asset markets* (also called "tangible" or "real" asset markets) are the markets for products such as wheat, autos, real estate, computers, and machinery.

2. *Financial asset markets* deal with stocks, bonds, notes, mortgages, and derivative securities.

3. *Spot markets* are markets in which assets are bought or sold for "on-the-spot" delivery.

4. *Futures markets* are markets in which participants agree today to buy or sell an asset at some future date.

5. *Money markets* are the markets for short-term, highly liquid debt securities, those securities that mature in less than one year.

6. *Capital markets* are the markets for intermediate- or long-term debt and corporate stocks.

7. *Primary markets* are the markets in which corporations raise new capital.

8. *Secondary markets* are the markets in which existing, already outstanding securities are traded among investors.

9. *Private markets* are the markets where transactions are negotiated directly between two parties.

10. *Public markets* are the markets where standardized contracts are traded on organized exchanges.

C. Other classifications could be made, and the distinctions among markets are often blurred and unimportant except as a general point of reference.

D. A healthy economy is dependent on efficient funds transfers from people who are net savers to firms and individuals who need capital.

    1. Without efficient transfers, the economy could not function.

E. Financial markets have experienced many changes in recent years.

    1. Technological advances in computers and telecommunications, along with the globalization of banking and commerce, have led to deregulation, which has increased competition throughout the world.

    2. As a result, there are much more efficient, internationally linked markets, which are far more complex than what existed a few years ago.

        a. With globalization has come the need for greater cooperation among regulators at the international level.

        b. Complicating coordination are: (1) the different structures in nations' banking and securities industries, (2) the trend toward financial services conglomerates, and (3) the reluctance of individual countries to give up control over their national monetary policies.

F. Another important trend in recent years has been the increased use of derivatives.

    1. A *derivative* is any security whose value is derived from the price of some other "underlying" asset.

    2. The market for derivatives has grown faster than any other market in recent years, providing investors with new opportunities but also exposing them to new risks.

    3. Derivatives can be used either to manage risks or to speculate.

        a. *Credit default swaps* are examples of derivatives.

            (1.) They are contracts that offer protection against the default of a particular security.

            (2.) A bank agrees to make regular payments to another financial institution. In return, the financial institution agrees to insure the bank against losses that would occur if the borrower defaulted.

        b. Purchasing derivatives to reduce a company's risk of a decline in an asset's value is a *hedging operation*.

        c. *Speculation* is done in the hope of high returns, but it raises risk exposure.

    4. According to former Fed Chairperson Greenspan, in theory derivatives should allow companies to manage risk better, but it is not clear whether recent innovations have "increased or decreased the inherent stability of the financial system."

III. **In the U.S. and other developed nations, a set of highly efficient financial intermediaries has evolved. Their original roles were quite specific, and regulation prevented them from diversifying. In recent years regulations against diversification have been largely removed; and today the differences between institutions have become blurred. Still, there remains a degree of institutional identity, so a description of the major categories follows.**

A. *Investment banks* underwrite and distribute new investment securities and help businesses obtain financing.

    1. They help corporations design securities with features that are attractive to investors.

2. They then buy these securities from the corporation.

3. They then resell them to savers.

B. *Commercial banks* are the traditional department stores of finance serving a variety of savers and borrowers.

1. Historically, they were the major institutions that handled checking accounts and through which the Federal Reserve System expanded or contracted the money supply.

2. Several other institutions also provide checking services and significantly influence the money supply.

C. *Financial services corporations* are large conglomerates that combine many different financial institutions within a single corporation.

1. They offer a wide range of financial services, including investment banking, brokerage operations, insurance, and commercial banking.

D. *Credit unions* are cooperative associations whose members are supposed to have a common bond.

1. They are often the cheapest source of funds available to individual borrowers.

E. *Pension funds* are retirement plans funded by corporations or government agencies for their workers and administered primarily by the trust departments of commercial banks or by life insurance companies.

F. *Life insurance companies* take savings in the form of annual premiums; invest these funds in stocks, bonds, real estate, and mortgages; and make payments to the beneficiaries of the insured parties.

G. *Mutual funds* are corporations that accept money from savers and use these funds to buy stocks, long-term bonds, or short-term debt instruments issued by business or government units.

1. These organizations pool funds and thus reduce risks by diversification.

2. They also achieve economies of scale in analyzing securities, managing portfolios, and buying and selling securities.

3. They have grown more rapidly than most other institutions in recent years, in large part because of a change in the way corporations provide for employees' retirement. Most workers turn their retirement funds over to a mutual fund.

H. *Exchange Traded Funds (ETFs)* are similar to regular mutual funds and are often operated by mutual fund companies.

1. These funds buy a portfolio of stocks of a certain type and then sell their own shares to the public.

2. ETF shares are generally traded in the public markets.

I. *Hedge funds* are similar to mutual funds because they accept money from savers and use the funds to buy various securities, but there are some important differences.

1. Hedge funds are largely unregulated.

2. Hedge funds typically have large minimum investments (often exceeding $1 million) that are marketed primarily to institutions and individuals with high net worths.

3. Hedge funds received their name because they were traditionally used when an individual was trying to hedge risks.

4. Some hedge funds take on risks that are considerably higher than that of an average individual stock or mutual fund.

5. As hedge funds have become more popular, many of them have begun to lower their minimum investment requirements. Their rapid growth and shift toward smaller investors have also led to a call for more regulations.

J. *Private equity companies* are organizations that operate much like hedge funds; but rather than buying some of the stock of a firm, private equity players buy and then manage entire firms.

1. Most of the money used to buy the target company is borrowed.

IV. **The most active secondary market, and the most important one to financial managers, is the stock market because it is here where prices of firms' stocks are established. Because the primary goal of financial managers is to maximize their firms' stock prices, knowledge of the stock market is important to anyone involved in managing a business. There are two basic types of stock markets.**

A. The *physical location exchanges,* typified by the New York Stock Exchange (NYSE) and the American Stock Exchange (AMEX), are tangible, physical entities.

1. They are formal organizations that have tangible physical locations and conduct auction markets in designated "listed" securities.

2. Each of these larger exchanges occupies its own building, has a limited number of members, and has an elected governing body, its board of governors.

3. Like other markets, security exchanges facilitate communication between buyers and sellers.

4. Exchange members with sell orders offer the shares for sale, and they are bid for by the members with buy orders. Thus, the exchanges operate as *auction markets*.

B. The *electronic dealer-based markets* include the Nasdaq stock market, the less formal over-the-counter market, and the recently developed electronic communications networks (ECNs).

1. The *dealer market* includes all facilities that are needed to conduct security transactions not conducted on the physical location exchanges.

2. Traditionally referred to as the *over-the-counter (OTC) market*, which is a large collection of brokers and dealers, connected electronically by telephones and computers, it provides for trading in unlisted securities.

3. Brokers and dealers who participate in the over-the-counter market are members of a self-regulatory body known as the *National Association of Securities Dealers (NASD)*, which licenses brokers and oversees trading practices.

4. Over the past decade the competition between the NYSE and Nasdaq has become increasingly fierce. Nasdaq has grown to become an organized securities market with its own listing requirements.

5. Since most of the largest companies trade on the NYSE, the market capitalization of NYSE-traded stocks is much higher than for stocks traded on Nasdaq. However, reported volume (number of shares traded) is often larger on Nasdaq, and more companies are listed on Nasdaq.

a. One transaction on Nasdaq generally shows up as two separate trades (the buy and the sell). This "double counting" makes it difficult to compare the volume between stock markets.

V. **Closely held corporations are those owned by a few individuals who are typically associated with the firm's management. Publicly owned corporations are those owned by a relatively large number of individuals who are not actively involved in its management. Institutional investors have a significant influence on the prices of individual stocks.**

A. Stock market transactions can be classified into three distinct categories.

1. Trading in the outstanding shares of established, publicly owned companies occurs in the *secondary market*.

a. Companies receive no new money when sales occur in this market.

2. Additional new shares are sold by established, publicly owned companies in the *primary market*.

3. *Initial public offerings (IPOs)* by privately held firms in the process of going public comprise the *IPO market*.

a. *Going public* is the act of selling stock to the public at large by a closely held corporation or its principal stockholders.

b. It is often difficult to purchase shares in the initial offering because they are generally *oversubscribed*, which means the demand for shares at the offering price exceeds the number of shares issued.

c. IPOs often underperform the overall market over the long run.

d. In a *Dutch auction*, individual investors place bids for shares directly. The actual transaction price is set at the highest price (the clearing price) that causes all of the offered shares to be sold.

e. Firms can go public without raising any additional capital. For example, the Ford Foundation sold Ford stock to the public, but Ford itself raised no capital in the transaction.

VI. **There generally are large differences between expected and realized prices and returns. A stock's expected return as estimated by investors at the margin is always positive, for otherwise investors would not purchase the stock. However, in some years actual returns turn out to be negative.**

A. Besides newspapers, it is now possible to obtain quotes from a wide variety of internet sources. However, unlike newspapers, it's possible to obtain quotes all during the day from these internet sources.

1. A great deal of information is often contained in these quotes.

B. Since 1968 the market trend has been strongly up, but by no means does it go up every year.

1. Even in bad years some individual companies do well, so "the name of the game" in security analysis is to pick the winners.

VII. **When markets are efficient, investors can buy and sell stocks and be confident that they are getting good prices. When markets are inefficient, investors may be afraid to invest which will lead to a poor allocation of capital and economic stagnation. From an economic standpoint, market efficiency is good.**

16

A. There is an "efficiency continuum" with the market for some companies' stocks being highly efficient and the market for other stocks being highly inefficient.

1. The key factor is the size of the company. The larger the firm, the more analysts tend to follow it and thus the faster new information is likely to be reflected in the stock's price.

2. Different companies communicate better with analysts and investors; and the better the communications, the more efficient the market for the stock.

B. If the stock market is efficient, it is a waste of time for most people to seek bargains by analyzing published data on stocks. If stock prices already reflect all publicly available information, they will be fairly priced; and a person can beat the market only with luck or inside information.

1. In this situation, it would be better to buy an index fund designed to match the overall market as reflected in an index such as the S&P 500.

C. Markets are more efficient for individual stocks than for entire companies; so for investors with enough capital, it does make sense to seek out badly managed companies that can be acquired and improved.

D. Even if markets are efficient and all stocks and companies are fairly priced, an investor should still be careful when selecting stocks for his or her portfolio.

1. Most importantly, the portfolio should be diversified, with a mix of stocks from various industries along with some bonds and other fixed-income securities.

Self-Test

Definitional Questions

1. Markets for short-term debt securities are called _____ markets, while markets for intermediate- or long-term debt and corporate stocks are called _____ markets.

2. Firms raise capital by selling newly issued securities in the _____ markets, while existing, already outstanding securities are traded in the _____ markets.

3. An institution that issues its own securities in exchange for funds and then uses these funds to purchase other businesses' securities is called a financial _____.

4. A(n) _____ bank facilitates the transfer of capital between savers and borrowers by acting as a middleman.

5. The two basic types of stock markets are the _____ location exchanges, such as the NYSE, and the electronic _____-_____ or _____-_____-_____ market.

6. _____ markets bring together people and organizations wanting to borrow money with those having surplus funds.

7. _____ transfers of money and securities occur when a business sells its stock or bonds to savers, without going through any type of financial institution.

8. A(n) _____ is any security whose value is derived from the price of some other "underlying" asset.

9. The result of ongoing regulatory changes has been a blurring of the distinctions between the different types of financial institutions. As a result, in the U.S. the trend has been toward huge _____ services corporations, large conglomerates that combine many different financial institutions within a single corporation.

10. The _____ market is one of the most important markets to financial managers because it is here where the prices of firms' stocks are established.

11. The initial _____ offering market is the market in which firms "go public" by offering shares to the public for the first time.

12. _____ markets are markets in which transactions are negotiated directly between two parties.

13. _____ markets are markets in which standardized contracts are traded on organized exchanges.

14. _____ markets are the markets in which assets are bought or sold for "on-the-spot" delivery.

15. _____ markets are the markets in which participants agree today to buy or sell an asset at some future date.

16. _____ asset markets are the markets for products such as wheat, autos, real estate, computers, and machinery.

17. _____ asset markets deal with stocks, bonds, notes, mortgages, and derivative securities.

18. In a global context, _____ development is highly correlated with the level and efficiency of financial markets and institutions.

19. _____ banks are the traditional department stores of finance serving a variety of savers and borrowers.

20. _____ unions are cooperative associations whose members are supposed to have a common bond.

21. _____ funds are retirement plans funded by corporations or government agencies for their workers and administered primarily by the trust departments of commercial banks or by life insurance companies.

22. Life _____ companies take savings in the form of annual premiums; invest these funds in stocks, bonds, real estate, and mortgages; and make payments to beneficiaries.

23. _____ funds are regulated corporations that accept money from savers, pool these funds to reduce risks by diversification, and use the funds to buy stocks, long-term bonds, or short-term debt instruments issued by businesses or government units.

24. _____ funds are similar to mutual funds except that they are largely unregulated; typically have large minimum investments that are marketed primarily to institutions and individuals with high net worths.

25. _____ held corporations are those owned by a few individuals who are typically associated with the firm's management.

26. _____ owned corporations are those owned by a relatively large number of individuals who are not actively involved in its management.

27. Going _____ is the act of selling stock to the public at large by a closely held corporation or its principal stockholders.

28. Initial offerings are often _____, which means that the demand for shares at the offering price exceeds the number of shares issued.

18

29. If the stock market is _____, it is a waste of time for most people to seek bargains by analyzing published data on stocks.

30. In a(n) _____ _____, individual investors place bids for shares directly. The actual transaction price is set at the highest price (the clearing price) that causes all of the offered shares to be sold.

Conceptual Questions

1. Which of the following statements is *not correct*?

   a. One of the major benefits of well-developed stock markets is that they increase liquidity, which makes it easier for firms to raise capital.
   b. In the United States, we have a number of specialized financial institutions, but, according to the text, the trend is toward larger, more diversified institutions that offer broad arrays of financial services.
   c. The dealer market is a formal organization that has a tangible physical location and conducts auction markets in designated listed securities.
   d. A healthy economy is dependent on efficient transfers of funds from people who are net savers to firms and individuals who need capital.
   e. Technological advances in computers and telecommunications, along with the globalization of banking and commerce, have led to deregulation, and this has increased competition throughout the world.

2. Which of the following statements is *not correct*?

   a. Firms can go public without raising any additional capital.
   b. Additional new shares are sold by established, publicly owned companies in the secondary market.
   c. Going public is the act of selling stock to the public at large by a closely held corporation or its principal stockholders.
   d. A stock's expected return as estimated by investors at the margin is always positive, for otherwise investors would not purchase the stock.
   e. Besides newspapers, it is now possible to obtain quotes from a wide variety of internet sources.

3. Which of the following statements is correct?

   a. In theory, derivatives should allow companies to manage risk better, but it is not clear whether recent innovations have increased or decreased the inherent stability of the financial system.
   b. Financial intermediaries do not create new forms of capital.
   c. A derivative is an example of an asset traded in the physical asset or tangible asset market.
   d. Stocks, bonds, and mortgages are all examples of the types of securities traded in the money markets.
   e. Standardized contracts are traded in private markets.

4. Which of the following statements is correct?

   a. Short-term, highly liquid debt securities are traded in the capital markets.
   b. Wheat, autos, and real estate are all examples of the type of assets traded in the financial asset markets.
   c. Globalization of the financial markets has resulted in a much more efficient, internationally linked market, and one that is less complex and easily coordinated with the structures of the different nations' banking and securities industries.

d. Hedge funds are similar to mutual funds except they are largely unregulated, typically have large minimum investments marketed primarily to institutions and individuals with high net worths, and some hedges take on risks that are considerably higher than that of an average individual stock or mutual fund.

e. Pension funds take savings in the form of annual premiums; invest these funds in stocks, bonds, real estate, and mortgages; and then make payments to the beneficiaries of the insured parties.

Answers

Definitional Questions

1. money; capital
2. primary; secondary
3. intermediary
4. investment
5. physical; dealer-based; over-the-counter (OTC)
6. Financial
7. Direct
8. derivative
9. financial
10. stock
11. public
12. Private
13. Public
14. Spot
15. Futures
16. Physical
17. Financial
18. economic
19. Commercial
20. Credit
21. Pension
22. insurance
23. Mutual
24. Hedge
25. Closely
26. Publicly
27. public
28. oversubscribed
29. efficient
30. Dutch auction

Conceptual Questions

1. c. This statement is false. This is the definition for a physical location exchange.

2. b. This statement is false. Trading in the outstanding shares of established, publicly owned companies occurs in the secondary market.

3. a. This statement is true. Derivatives can be used either to reduce risks as in a hedging operation or for speculation in the hope of high returns but which raises risk exposure.

4. d. This statement is true. Mutual funds are registered and regulated by the SEC, typically target small investors, and charge very small fees.

3

FINANCIAL STATEMENTS, CASH FLOW, AND TAXES

Learning Objectives

1. List each of the key financial statements and identify the kinds of information they provide to corporate managers and investors.

2. Estimate a firm's free cash flow and explain why free cash flow has such an important effect on firm value.

3. Discuss the major features of the federal income tax system.

Overview

Financial management requires the consideration of the types of financial statements firms must provide to investors. Thus, this chapter begins with a discussion of the basic financial statements, how they are used, and what kinds of financial information users need. The value of any asset depends on the usable, or after-tax, cash flows the asset is expected to produce, so the chapter also explains the difference between net income versus free cash flow. Finally, because the firm's after-tax cash flow impacts its value, the chapter provides an overview of the federal income tax system.

Outline

I. **A firm's annual report is the most important report that corporations issue to shareholders and it contains two types of information.**

   A. The first is a verbal statement of the company's recent operating results during the past year and discusses new developments that will affect future operations.

   B. The second is a set of quantitative financial statements that report what actually happened to the firm's financial position, earnings, cash flow, and stockholders' equity over the past few years.

      1. The *balance sheet* shows what assets the company owns and who has claims on those assets as of a given date.

      2. The *income statement* shows the firm's sales, costs, and profit over a period of time.

21

3. The *statement of cash flows* shows how much cash the firm began the year with, how much cash it ended up with, and what it did to increase or decrease its cash.

4. The *statement of stockholders' equity* shows the amount of equity the stockholders had at the start of the year, the items that increase or decreased equity, and the equity at the end of the year.

C. The information contained in an annual report can be used to help forecast future earnings and dividends.

II. **The balance sheet is a statement of the firm's financial position at a specific point in time. It shows the firm's assets and the claims against those assets.**

A. Assets, found on the left-hand side of the balance sheet, are typically shown in the order of their liquidity.

1. The balance sheet may be thought of as a snapshot of the firm's financial position at a point in time (for example, the end of the year). The balance sheet changes every day as inventory is increased or decreased, as fixed assets are added or retired, as bank loans are increased or decreased, and so on.

2. Assets are divided into two major categories: current assets and long-term assets.

3. *Current assets* include cash and equivalents, accounts receivable, and inventory. Only cash and equivalents represent actual spendable money.

   a. Current assets are often called *working capital* because these assets "turn over." They are used and then replaced throughout the year.

   b. *Net working capital* is the difference between current assets and current liabilities.

   c. *Net operating working capital* distinguishes between "free" liabilities and interest-bearing notes payable. It is calculated as current assets less the difference between current liabilities and notes payable.

4. *Long-term assets* are those whose useful lives exceed one year, and they include physical assets such as plant and equipment and intellectual property such as patents and copyrights.

B. Claims, found on the right-hand side, are generally listed in the order in which they must be paid.

1. Claims against the assets consist of liabilities and stockholders' equity:

   Assets – Liabilities – Preferred stock = Common stockholders' equity (Net worth)

2. Liabilities are further divided into current liabilities and long-term debt.

   a. *Current liabilities* are obligations that are due to be paid off within a year, and include accounts payable, accruals (total of accrued wages and accrued taxes), and notes payable to banks that are due within one year.

   b. *Long-term debt* includes bonds that mature in more than one year.

3. *Common stockholders' equity*, or *net worth*, is capital supplied by common stockholders and represents ownership. The common equity section of the balance sheet is divided into two accounts: common stock and retained earnings.

   a. The *common stock* account arises from the issuance of stock to raise capital.

      b. *Retained earnings* are built up over time as the firm "saves" a part of its earnings rather than paying all earnings out as dividends.

    4. *Preferred stock* is a hybrid, or a cross between common stock and debt.

C. Companies use generally accepted accounting principles (GAAP) to determine the values reported on their balance sheets.

    1. In most cases, these accounting numbers (referred to as *book values*) are different from the corresponding *market values*.

III. The income statement summarizes the firm's revenues and expenses during a reporting period (generally a quarter or a year).

A. *Earnings per share (EPS)* is called "the bottom line," denoting that of all the items on the income statement, EPS is the most important. A typical stockholder focuses on reported EPS.

    1. To compare companies' operating performances, it is essential to focus on their earnings before deducting taxes and interest payments.

        a. This is called *EBIT* and is often referred to as *operating income*.

        b. Operating income is derived from the firm's regular core business.

    2. *Depreciation* is an annual noncash charge against income that reflects the estimated dollar cost of the capital equipment and other tangible assets that were used up in the production process.

        a. *Amortization* is similar to depreciation except that it applies to *intangible assets*, such as patents, copyrights, trademarks, and good will.

        b. Because depreciation and amortization are so similar, they are often lumped together on the income statement.

    3. *EBITDA* represents earnings before interest, taxes, depreciation, and amortization.

        a. Managers, security analysts, and bank loan officers who are concerned with the amount of cash a company is generating often calculate EBITDA.

B. Management generally prepares monthly, quarterly, and annual income statements.

    1. The quarterly and annual statements are released to investors, while the monthly statements are used internally for planning and control purposes.

C. The income statement is tied to the balance sheet through the retained earnings account on the balance sheet.

    1. Net income, as reported on the income statement, less dividends paid is the retained earnings for the year.

    2. Those retained earnings are added to the cumulative retained earnings from prior years to obtain the year-end balance for retained earnings.

    3. The retained earnings for the year are also reported in the statement of stockholders' equity.

IV. Management's goal is to maximize the price of the firm's stock; and the value of any asset, including a share of stock, is based on the cash flows the asset is expected to produce. Therefore, managers strive to maximize the cash flows available to investors. The Statement of Cash Flows reports the impact of a firm's operating, investing, and financing activities on cash flows the firm is generating over an accounting period.

A. The company's cash position as reported on the balance sheet is affected by many factors, including income, changes in working capital, fixed assets, security transactions, and dividend payments.

B. The statement can be separated into four parts:

1. *Operating activities*, which includes net income, depreciation, and changes in working capital other than cash and short-term debt.

2. *Investing activities*, which includes purchases or sales of fixed assets.

3. *Financing activities*, which includes raising cash by issuing short-term debt, long-term debt, or stock, or using cash to pay dividends or to buy back outstanding stock or retiring bonds.

4. *Summary*, shows the net decrease (increase) in cash from the three activities above, shows the cash at the beginning of the year, and then calculates the cash at the end of the year.

C. Financial managers generally use this statement, along with the cash budget, when forecasting their companies' cash positions.

V. **The Statement of Stockholders' Equity reports changes in the equity accounts between balance sheet dates and why these changes occurred.**

A. The balance sheet account "retained earnings" represents a claim against assets, not assets per se.

1. Retained earnings as reported on the balance sheet do not represent cash and are not "available" for the payment of dividends or anything else.

2. Retained earnings represent funds that have already been reinvested in the firm's operating assets.

VI. **Financial statements provide a great deal of useful information. At the same time, investors need to be cautious when they review financial statements.**

A. Companies are required to follow generally accepted accounting principles (GAAP) when reporting financial statements; however, managers still have a lot of discretion in deciding how and when to report certain transactions.

1. Two firms in exactly the same situation may report financial statements that convey different impressions about their financial strength.

2. As long as the financial statements follow GAAP, such actions are legal, but these differences make it difficult for investors to compare companies and gauge their true performances.

B. After the Enron and WorldCom scandals, Congress passed the Sarbanes-Oxley Act (SOX).

1. It required companies to improve their internal auditing standards.

2. It required the CEO and CFO to certify that the financial statements were properly prepared.

3. It also created a new watchdog organization to help make sure that the outside accounting firms were doing their jobs.

C. Recently, a serious debate has arisen regarding the appropriate accounting for complicated investments held by financial institutions.

    1. Currently, regulators and other policy makers are struggling to come up with the best way to account for and regulate many of these "toxic assets."

D. Even if investors receive accurate accounting data, it is cash flow, not accounting income, that matters most.

VII. The traditional financial statements are designed primarily for use by creditors and tax collectors, not for managers and stock analysts. Therefore, corporate decision makers and security analysts often modify accounting data to meet their needs.

A. Management is not completely free to use the available cash flow however it pleases. The value of a company's operations depends on all the future expected free cash flows.

    1. *Free cash flow* is defined as "the amount of cash that could be withdrawn without harming a firm's ability to operate and to produce future cash flows."

    2. *Free cash flow* is the cash flow actually available for payments to all investors (stockholders and debtholders) after the company has made the investments in fixed assets, new products, and working capital required to sustain ongoing operations.

        a. Free cash flow is defined as after-tax operating income minus the investments in working capital and fixed assets necessary to sustain the business.

$$FCF = \left[EBIT(1-T) + \begin{array}{c} \text{Depreciation and} \\ \text{amortization} \end{array} \right] - \left[\begin{array}{c} \text{Capital} \\ \text{expenditures} \end{array} + \begin{array}{c} \Delta \text{ Net operating} \\ \text{working capital} \end{array} \right]$$

        b. Free cash flow can also be calculated as net operating profit after taxes (NOPAT) less net investment in operating capital.

    3. A positive FCF indicates that the firm is generating more than enough cash to finance its current investments in fixed assets and working capital.

    4. Negative FCF means that the company does not have sufficient internal funds to finance its investments in fixed assets and working capital, and that it will have to raise new money in the capital markets in order to pay for these investments.

    5. Negative free cash flow is not always bad. If free cash flow is negative because after-tax operating income is negative, this is bad, because the company is probably experiencing operating problems.

        a. Exceptions to this might be startup companies; companies that are incurring significant current expenses to launch a new product line; or high-growth companies, which will have large investments in capital that cause low current free cash flow, but that will increase future free cash flow.

        b. Eventually new investments must be profitable and contribute to free cash flow.

    6. Many analysts regard FCF as being the single and most important number that can be developed from accounting statements, even more important than net income.

        a. FCF shows how much cash the firm can distribute to its investors.

VIII. The accounting statements do not reflect market values, so they are not sufficient for purposes of evaluating managers' performance. To help fill this void, financial analysts have developed two additional performance measures, *Market Value Added (MVA)* and *Economic Value Added (EVA)*.

25

A. Shareholders' wealth is maximized by maximizing the difference between the market value of a firm's common equity and the book value as shown on the balance sheet. This difference is called the Market Value Added (MVA).

$$MVA = \text{Market value of common equity} - \text{Book value of common equity}$$
$$= (\text{Shares outstanding})(\text{Stock price}) - \text{Total common equity}$$

1. This amount represents the difference between the money a firm's stockholders have invested in the corporation since its founding (including retained earnings) versus the cash they could receive if they sold the business.

2. The higher its MVA, the better the job management is doing for the firm's shareholders.

3. Note though, that most firms' stock prices rise in a rising stock market, so a positive MVA may not be entirely attributable to management.

4. MVA is applied to the entire firm.

B. Economic Value Added (EVA), sometimes called "economic profit," is closely related to MVA.

$$EVA = NOPAT - \text{After-tax dollar cost of capital}$$

$$= EBIT(1-T) - \left(\begin{array}{c}\text{Total investor-supplied}\\\text{operating capital}\end{array}\right)\left(\begin{array}{c}\text{After-tax percentage}\\\text{cost of capital}\end{array}\right)$$

1. Total investor-supplied operating capital equals the sum of net fixed assets and net operating working capital.

2. EVA is an estimate of a business' true economic profit for a given year.

3. EVA differs sharply from accounting net income. Accounting income has no deduction for the cost of equity whereas this cost is deducted when calculating EVA.

4. If EVA is positive, then after-tax operating income exceeds the cost of the capital needed to produce that income, and management's actions are adding value for stockholders.

5. Positive EVA on an annual basis will help ensure that MVA is also positive.

6. EVA can be determined for divisions as well as for the company as a whole, so it is useful as a guide to "reasonable" compensation for divisional as well as top corporate managers.

IX. **Corporations must pay out a significant portion of their income as taxes, and individuals are also taxed on their income.**

A. Individuals pay taxes on wages and salaries, on investment income, and on the profits of proprietorships and partnerships.

1. Tax rates are *progressive* where tax rates are higher on higher income.

   a. Rates begin at 10% and rise to 35% on taxable incomes over $372,950.

2. The *marginal tax rate* is the tax rate applicable to the last unit of a person's income.

3. The *average tax rate* is calculated as taxes paid divided by taxable income.

4. *Capital gain (loss)* is the profit (loss) from the sale of a capital asset (one not normally bought and sold in the course of business) for more (less) than its purchase price.

   a. A short-term capital gain is added to ordinary income, such as wages and interest, and then is taxed at the same rate as ordinary income.

    b.   A long-term capital gain is taxed at a lower rate than an individual's ordinary income. The top rate on long-term capital gains in 2010 is 15%. The asset must be held for more than one year to qualify as long term.

    c.   On December 17, 2010, President Obama signed a bill extending the lower capital gains tax rate through 2012.

5.   Interest earned is taxable income.

    a.   An important exception is that interest on most state and local government debt is exempt from federal taxes.

    b.   State and local bonds are often called "*munis*," or municipal bonds, and individuals in high tax brackets generally purchase them.

6.   Dividends received by an individual are taxed at the same rate as capital gains, 15%.

    a.   This rate has also been extended through 2012.

7.   Generally, individuals cannot deduct interest payments. However, interest on home loans is deductible within limits.

8.   *Alternative minimum tax (AMT)* was created by Congress to make it more difficult for wealthy individuals to avoid paying taxes through the use of various deductions.

B. Corporate income is generally taxed at rates that begin at 15% and increase to 38% on income between $15 million and $18.33 million and then decline to 35% on taxable income over $18.33 million.

1.   Interest income received by a corporation is taxed as ordinary income at regular corporate tax rates.

2.   Dividend income received by corporations is taxed more favorably.

    a.   A corporation that receives dividend income can exclude some of the dividends from its taxable income. This provision in the Tax Code minimizes the amount of triple taxation that would otherwise occur.

    b.   The dividend exclusion depends on the percentage of the paying company's stock the receiving company owns. If it owns less than 20%, 70% of the dividend will be excluded.

    c.   Other factors might lead a corporation to invest in bonds, but the tax factor favors stock investments by a corporation.

3.   For a business, interest payments are regarded as an expense, and they may be deducted when calculating taxable income.

4.   Corporations pay dividends, and dividends paid are generally not deductible for tax purposes.

    a.   There is a double tax on dividend income—the corporation that paid the dividend is first taxed, and then the individual who receives it is taxed again.

    b.   Our tax system encourages debt financing over equity financing because interest paid is tax deductible while dividends paid are not.

    c.   Higher interest charges mean lower taxable income, lower taxes, and higher cash flow.

5. The Tax Code allows firms to carry losses back to offset profits in prior years, and if losses haven't been offset by past profits then they are carried forward to offset future profits, which causes taxes over time to reflect average income.

6. If a corporation owns 80% or more of another corporation's stock, it can aggregate income and file one *consolidated tax return*.

7. An *S corporation* enjoys the advantages of the corporate form of organization yet still receives the tax advantages of a proprietorship or partnership.

8. Depreciation plays an important role in income tax calculations—the larger the depreciation, the lower the taxable income, the lower the tax bill, and thus the higher the operating cash flow.

Self-Test

Definitional Questions

1. Of all its communications with shareholders, a firm's _____ report is generally the most important.

2. The income statement reports the results of operations during the past year, the most important item being _____ per share.

3. The _____ sheet lists the firm's assets as well as claims against those assets.

4. Typically, assets are listed in order of their _____, while liabilities are listed in the order in which they must be paid.

5. Assets are divided into two major categories: _____ assets and _____-_____ assets.

6. Claims against assets consist of _____ and stockholders' _____.

7. _____ liabilities are obligations that are due to be paid off within a year, and include accounts payable, accruals (the total of accrued wages and accrued taxes), and notes payable to banks that are due within one year.

8. Assets – Liabilities – Preferred stock = _____ worth, or common _____ equity.

9. _____ stock is a hybrid, or a cross between common stock and debt.

10. The two accounts that normally make up the common equity section of the balance sheet are common _____ and retained _____.

11. _____ earnings as reported on the balance sheet represent income earned by the firm in past years that has not been paid out as dividends.

12. Retained earnings are generally reinvested in operating _____ and are not held in the form of cash.

13. Companies use generally accepted _____ principles to determine the values reported on their balance sheets.

14. The accounting numbers on the balance sheet are referred to as _____ values and, in most cases are different from the corresponding _____ values.

15. The Statement of _____ Flows reports the impact of a firm's operating, investing, and financing activities on cash flows the firm is generating over an accounting period.

16. The four parts of the Statement of Cash Flows are cash flows associated with _____ activities, _____ activities, _____ activities, and summary.

17. The _____ stock account arises from the issuance of stock to raise capital.

18. The Statement of _____ Equity reports changes in the equity accounts between balance sheet dates and why these changes occurred.

19. The traditional financial statements are designed primarily for use by _____ and tax collectors, not for _____ and stock analysts.

20. _____ cash flow is the cash flow actually available for payments to all investors (stockholders and debtholders) after the company has made the investments in fixed assets, new products, and working capital required to sustain ongoing operations.

21. A(n) _____ tax system is one in which tax rates are higher at higher levels of income.

22. Interest received on _____ bonds is generally not subject to federal income taxes. This feature makes them particularly attractive to investors in _____ tax brackets.

23. _____ received by an individual are taxed at the same rate as long-term capital gains to help reduce the effects of the double taxation on them.

24. In order to qualify as a long-term capital gain or loss, _____ not normally bought and sold in the course of business must be held for more than _____ year(s).

25. Interest payments paid by a corporation are tax _____, while dividend payments are not.

26. The Tax Code permits a corporation (that meets certain restrictions) to be taxed at the owners' personal tax rates. This type of corporation is called a(n) ____ corporation.

27. The _____ tax rate is the tax rate applicable to the last unit of a person's income.

28. A long-term capital gain is taxed at a _____ tax rate than an individual's ordinary income.

29. Generally, individuals _____ deduct interest from taxable income; however, an exception is interest on _____ loans.

30. If a corporation owns 80% or more of another corporation's stock, it can aggregate income and file one _____ tax return.

31. Shareholders' wealth is maximized by maximizing the difference between the market value of a firm's common equity and the book value as shown on the balance sheet. This difference is called _____ Value Added.

32. _____ Value Added is an estimate of a business' true economic profit for a given year.

33. If EVA is positive, then after-tax operating income exceeds the cost of the _____ needed to produce that income, and management's actions are adding _____ for stockholders.

34. _____ can be determined for divisions as well as for the company as a whole, while _____ must be applied to the entire corporation.

35. EVA differs sharply from accounting ____ _____ because the cost of equity is deducted when calculating EVA.

Conceptual Questions

1. The fact that some intercorporate dividends received by a corporation are excluded from taxable income has encouraged debt financing over equity financing.

    a. True
    b. False

2. Which of the following statements is correct?

    a. In order to avoid double taxation and to escape the frequently higher tax rate applied to capital gains, stockholders generally prefer to have corporations pay dividends rather than to retain their earnings and reinvest the money in the business. Thus, earnings should be retained only if the firm needs capital very badly and would have difficulty raising it from external sources.
    b. Under our current tax laws, when investors pay taxes on their dividend income, they are being subjected to a form of double taxation.
    c. The fact that a percentage of the interest received by one corporation, which is paid by another corporation, is excluded from taxable income has encouraged firms to use more debt financing relative to equity financing.
    d. If the tax laws stated that $0.50 out of every $1.00 of interest paid by a corporation was allowed as a tax-deductible expense, this would probably encourage companies to use more debt financing than they presently do, other things held constant.
    e. A corporation's payments for capital—interest and dividend payments—are tax deductible; therefore, the government does not encourage companies to use one form of financing over the other.

Problems

1. Ryngaert & Sons, Inc. has operating income (EBIT) of $2,250,000. The company's depreciation expense is $450,000, its interest expense is $120,000, and it faces a 40% tax rate. Assume the firm has no amortization expense. What is its net income?

    a. $1,008,000
    b. $1,278,000
    c. $1,475,000
    d. $1,728,000
    e. $1,800,000

Exhibit 3-1

Smith Brothers Corporation
Income Statements for Year Ending December 31
(Millions of Dollars)

	2011	2010
Sales	$360	$300
Operating costs excluding depreciation	306	255
EBITDA	$ 54	$ 45
Depreciation	9	7
EBIT	$ 45	$ 38
Interest	7	6
EBT	$ 38	$ 32
Taxes (40%)	15	13
NI available to common stockholders	$ 23	$ 19
Common dividends	$ 16	$ 10

Smith Brothers Corporation
Balance Sheets as of December 31
(Millions of Dollars)

Assets	2011	2010
Cash	$ 4	$ 3
Accounts receivable	54	45
Inventories	54	60
Total CA	$112	$108
Net plant & equipment	90	75
Total assets	$202	$183

Liabilities and Equity	2011	2010
Accounts payable	$ 32	$ 28
Notes payable	20	16
Accrued liabilities	22	18
Total CL	$ 74	$ 62
Long-term bonds	45	45
Total debt	$119	$107
Common stock (50,000,000 shares)	15	15
Retained earnings	68	61
Common equity	$ 83	$ 76
Total liabilities and equity	$202	$183

2. Given the financial information in Exhibit 3-1, what is the 2011 NOPAT (net operating profit after taxes) in millions of dollars?

   a. $18
   b. $27
   c. $34
   d. $40
   e. $45

3. Given the financial information in Exhibit 3-1, what is the 2011 net operating working capital (NOWC) in millions of dollars?

   a. $ 38
   b. $ 54
   c. $ 58
   d. $ 87
   e. $112

4. Given the financial information in Exhibit 3-1, what is the 2011 free cash flow in millions of dollars?

   a. $11
   b. $16
   c. $20
   d. $25
   e. $27

5. In its recent income statement Tyler Toys Inc. reported $72.5 million of net income, and in its year-end balance sheet it reported $1,174 million of retained earnings. The previous year its balance sheet showed $1,131 million of retained earnings. What were the total dividends (in millions of dollars) paid to shareholders during the most recent year?

   a. $10.5
   b. $17.7
   c. $24.6
   d. $29.5
   e. $33.0

6. Peterson Manufacturing recently reported EBITDA of $18.75 million and $4.5 million of net income. It has $5 million of interest expense and its corporate tax rate is 40%. What was its depreciation and amortization expense (in millions of dollars)?

   a. $6.25
   b. $3.75
   c. $1.50
   d. $2.25
   e. $8.50

7. GPD Corporation has operating income (EBIT) of $300,000, total assets of $1,500,000, and its capital structure consists of 40% debt and 60% common equity. Total assets equal total operating capital. The firm's after-tax cost of capital is 10.5% and its tax rate is 40%. The firm has 50,000 shares of common stock currently outstanding and the current price of a share of common stock is $27.00. What is the firm's Market Value Added (MVA)?

   a. $ 22,500
   b. $ 87,575
   c. $187,740
   d. $450,000
   e. $575,000

8. GPD Corporation has operating income (EBIT) of $300,000, total assets of $1,500,000, and its capital structure consists of 40% debt and 60% common equity. Total assets equal total operating capital. The firm's after-tax cost of capital is 10.5% and its tax rate is 40%. The firm has 50,000 shares of common stock currently outstanding and the current price of a share of common stock is $27.00. What is the firm's Economic Value Added (EVA)?

   a. $ 22,500
   b. $ 87,575
   c. $187,740
   d. $450,000
   e. $575,000

9. Wayne Corporation had income from operations of $385,000, it received interest payments of $15,000, it paid interest of $20,000, it received dividends from another corporation of $10,000, and it paid $40,000 in dividends to its common stockholders. What is Wayne's federal income tax?

   a. $122,760
   b. $130,220
   c. $141,700
   d. $155,200
   e. $163,500

10. The Carter Company's taxable income and income tax payments are shown below for 2008 through 2011:

Year	Taxable Income	Tax Payment
2008	$10,000	$1,500
2009	5,000	750
2010	12,000	1,800
2011	8,000	1,200

   Assume that Carter's tax rate for all 4 years was a flat 15%, that is, each dollar of taxable income was taxed at 15%. In 2012, Carter incurred a loss of $17,000. Using corporate loss carry-back, what is Carter's adjusted tax payment for 2011?

   a. $850
   b. $750
   c. $610
   d. $550
   e. $450

Answers

Definitional Questions

1. annual
2. earnings
3. balance
4. liquidity
5. current; long-term

6. liabilities; equity
7. Current
8. Net; stockholders'
9. Preferred
10. stock; earnings

11. Retained
12. assets
13. accounting
14. book; market
15. Cash
16. operating; investing; financing
17. common
18. stockholders'
19. creditors; managers
20. Free
21. progressive
22. municipal; high
23. Dividends

24. assets; one
25. deductible
26. S
27. marginal
28. lower
29. cannot; home
30. consolidated
31. Market
32. Economic
33. capital; value
34. EVA; MVA
35. net income

Conceptual Questions

1. b. Debt financing is encouraged by the fact that interest payments paid by corporations are tax deductible while dividend payments are not.

2. b. To avoid double taxation, stockholders would prefer that corporations retain more earnings because long-term capital gains are generally taxed at a maximum rate of 15% and are paid only when the stock is sold.

Solutions

Problems

1. b.

EBIT	$2,250,000
Interest	120,000
EBT	$2,130,000
Taxes (40%)	852,000
Net income	$1,278,000

2. b. $\text{EBIT}(1 - T) = \$45(0.6)$
   $= \$27$

3. c. Net operating working capital$_{11}$ = Current assets − (Current liabilities − Notes payable)
   $= (\$4 + \$54 + \$54) - (\$74 - \$20)$
   $= \$112 - \$54 = \$58$

4. b. $FCF_{11} = EBIT(1 - T) + Depreciation - (Capital\ expenditures + \Delta NOWC)$
$$= \$27 + \$9 - (\$24 + (-\$4))$$
$$= \$16$$

Note that capital expenditures = Net PPE + Depreciation and NOWC declines from 2010 to 2011, so there is a reduction in NOWC investment.

5. d. $NI = \$72,500,000$; $R/E_{Y/E} = \$1,174,000,000$; $R/E_{B/Y} = \$1,131,000,000$; Dividends = ?
$R/E_{B/Y} + NI - Div = R/E_{Y/E}$

$$\$1,131,000,000 + \$72,500,000 - Div = \$1,174,000,000$$
$$\$1,203,500,000 - Div = \$1,174,000,000$$
$$\$29,500,000 = Div$$

6. a. $EBITDA = \$18,750,000$; $NI = \$4,500,000$; $Int = \$5,000,000$; $T = 40\%$; $DA = ?$

EBITDA	$18,750,000	
DA	6,250,000	EBITDA – DA = EBIT; DA = EBITDA – EBIT
EBIT	$12,500,000	EBIT = EBT + Int = $7,500,000 + $5,000,000
Int	5,000,000	(Given)
EBT	$ 7,500,000	$\dfrac{\$4,500,000}{(1-T)} = \dfrac{\$4,500,000}{0.6}$
Taxes (40%)	3,000,000	
NI	$ 4,500,000	(Given)

7. d.   Market value added = (Shares outstanding)(P_0) – Total book value of common equity
$$= 50,000(\$27.00) - (0.6)(\$1,500,000)$$
$$= \$1,350,000 - \$900,000$$
$$= \$450,000$$

8. a. $EVA = EBIT(1 - T) - (Total\ operating\ capital)(AT\ percentage\ cost\ of\ capital)$
$$= \$300,000(0.6) - (\$1,500,000)(0.105)$$
$$= \$180,000 - \$157,500$$
$$= \$22,500$$

9. b.   The first step is to determine taxable income:

Income from operations	$385,000
Interest income (fully taxable)	15,000
Interest expense (fully deductible)	(20,000)
Dividend income (30% taxable)	3,000
Taxable income	$383,000

(Note that dividends are paid from after-tax income and do not affect taxable income.)

35

Based on the current corporate tax table, the tax calculation is as follows:

Tax = $113,900 + 0.34($383,000 − $335,000) = $113,900 + $16,320 = $130,220.

10. e.

Year	Taxable Income	Tax Payment	Adjusted Taxable Income	Adjusted Tax Payment
2008	$10,000	$1,500	$10,000	$1,500
2009	5,000	750	5,000	750
2010	12,000	1,800	0	0
2011	8,000	1,200	3,000	450

The carry-back can go back only 2 years. Thus, there were no adjustments made in 2008 and 2009. After a $12,000 adjustment in 2010, there was a $5,000 loss remaining to apply to 2011. The 2011 adjusted tax payment is $3,000(0.15) = $450. Thus, Carter received a total of $2,550 in tax refunds after the adjustment.

4

ANALYSIS OF FINANCIAL STATEMENTS

Learning Objectives

1. Explain what ratio analysis is.

2. List the five groups of ratios and identify, calculate, and interpret the key ratios in each group.

3. Discuss each ratio's relationship to the balance sheet and income statement.

4. Discuss why ROE is the key ratio under management's control, how the other ratios impact ROE, and explain how to use the DuPont equation for improving ROE.

5. Compare a firm's ratios with those of other firms (benchmarking) and analyze a given firm's ratios over time (trend analysis).

6. Discuss the tendency of ratios to fluctuate over time (which may or may not be problematic), explain how they can be influenced by accounting practices as well as other factors, and why they must be used with care.

Overview

Financial analysis is designed to determine the relative strengths and weaknesses of a company. Investors need this information to estimate both future cash flows from the firm and the risk of those cash flows. Financial managers need the information provided by analysis both to evaluate the firm's past performance and to map future plans.

Financial statement analysis highlights the key aspects of a firm's operations. It involves a study of the relationships between income statement and balance sheet accounts, how these relationships change over time (trend analysis), how a particular firm's ratios compare with industry averages, and how a particular firm compares with other firms in its industry (benchmarking). Although financial analysis has limitations, when used with care and judgment, it can provide some very useful insights into a company's operations.

Outline

I. **Financial statements are used to help predict the firm's future earnings and dividends. From an investor's standpoint, predicting the future is what financial statement analysis is all about. From management's standpoint, financial statement analysis is useful both to help anticipate future conditions and, more important, as a starting point for planning actions that will improve the firm's future performance.**

   A. Financial ratios are designed to help one evaluate a firm's financial statements.

      1. Evaluations of firms and comparisons among firms are made from *ratio analysis*.

II. **A liquid asset is an asset that trades in an active market, and thus can be converted to cash quickly at the going market price.**

   A. *Liquidity ratios* are used to measure a firm's ability to meet its current obligations as they come due.

      1. A full liquidity analysis requires the use of cash budgets, but by relating cash and other current assets to current liabilities, ratio analysis provides a quick and easy-to-use measure of liquidity.

      2. Two of the most commonly used liquidity ratios are the current ratio and the quick ratio.

   B. The *current ratio* measures the extent to which current liabilities are covered by current assets, those assets expected to be converted to cash in the near future.

      1. It is calculated by dividing current assets by current liabilities.

      2. It is the most commonly used measure of short-term solvency.

   C. The *quick ratio* is a measure of a firm's ability to pay off short-term obligations without relying on the sale of inventories.

      1. It is calculated by deducting inventories from current assets and then dividing the remainder by current liabilities.

      2. Inventories are typically the least liquid of a firm's current assets, hence they are the assets on which losses are most likely to occur in the event of liquidation.

III. **Asset management ratios measure how effectively a firm is managing its assets and whether the level of those assets is properly related to the level of operations as measured by sales.**

   A. The *inventory turnover ratio* is defined as sales divided by inventories.

      1. It is often necessary to use average inventories rather than year-end inventories, especially if a firm's business is highly seasonal, or if there has been a strong upward or downward sales trend during the year.

      2. Excess inventory is unproductive and represents an investment with a low or zero rate of return.

   B. *Days sales outstanding (DSO)*, also called the "average collection period" (ACP), is used to appraise accounts receivable, and it is calculated by dividing accounts receivable by average daily sales to find the number of days' sales tied up in receivables.

      1. The DSO represents the average length of time that the firm must wait after making a sale before receiving cash.

2. The DSO can also be evaluated by comparison with the terms on which the firm sells its goods.

3. If the trend in DSO over the past few years has been rising, but the credit policy has not been changed, this would be strong evidence that steps should be taken to expedite the collection of accounts receivable.

C. The *fixed assets turnover ratio* is the ratio of sales to net fixed assets.

1. It measures how effectively the firm uses its plant and equipment.

2. A potential problem can exist when interpreting the fixed assets turnover ratio of a firm with older, lower-cost fixed assets compared to one with recently acquired, higher-cost fixed assets.

   a. Financial analysts recognize that a problem exists and deal with it judgmentally.

   b. The older firm will probably have the higher fixed assets turnover ratio.

D. The *total assets turnover ratio* is calculated by dividing sales by total assets.

1. It measures the utilization, or turnover, of all the firm's assets.

2. It measures whether the firm generates enough sales given its total assets.

IV. **Debt management ratios measure the extent to which a firm is using debt financing, or financial leverage, and the degree of safety afforded to creditors.**

A. Debt has a leveraging effect on ROE for two reasons.

1. Interest is tax deductible, so the use of debt lowers the tax bill and leaves more of the firm's operating income available to its investors.

2. If the rate of return on assets exceeds the interest rate on debt, a company can use debt to acquire assets, pay interest on the debt, and have something left over as a bonus for its stockholders.

   a. Firms with relatively high debt ratios have higher expected returns when the economy is normal but lower returns and possibly bankruptcy if the economy goes into a recession.

   b. Decisions about the use of debt require firms to balance higher expected returns against increased risk.

B. Analysts use two procedures to examine the firm's debt: (1) They check the balance sheet to determine the proportion of total funds represented by debt, and (2) they review the income statement to see the extent to which interest is covered by operating profits.

C. The *debt ratio*, or ratio of total debt to total assets, measures the percentage of funds provided by creditors. Total debt includes both current liabilities and long-term debt.

1. The lower the ratio, the greater the protection afforded creditors (cushion against creditors' losses) in the event of liquidation.

2. Stockholders, on the other hand, may want more leverage because it can magnify expected earnings.

3. A debt ratio that exceeds the industry average raises a red flag and may make it costly for a firm to borrow additional funds without first raising more equity capital.

   a. Creditors will be reluctant to lend the firm more money.

      b. Management would probably be subjecting the firm to too high a risk of bankruptcy if it sought to borrow a substantial amount of additional funds.

  D. The *times-interest-earned (TIE) ratio* is determined by dividing earnings before interest and taxes (EBIT) by interest charges.

     1. The TIE measures the extent to which operating income can decline before the firm is unable to meet its annual interest costs. It's a measure of the firm's ability to meet its annual interest payments.

     2. Note that EBIT, rather than net income, is used in the numerator. Because interest is paid with pretax dollars, the firm's ability to pay current interest is not affected by taxes.

V.   Profitability ratios show the combined effects of liquidity, asset management, and debt on operating results. Profitability ratios reflect the net result of all of the firm's financing policies and operating decisions.

  A. The *operating margin* is calculated by dividing operating income (EBIT) by sales.

     1. It measures operating income (EBIT) per dollar of sales.

     2. This ratio will show whether operating costs are too high.

  B. The *profit margin* is calculated by dividing net income by sales.

     1. It gives the profit per dollar of sales.

     2. This ratio looks at both operating efficiency and impact of leverage on profit.

     3. In addition to return, we must also be concerned with turnover. So, a high profit margin may still not be optimal if total sales are low.

  C. The *return on total assets (ROA)* is the ratio of net income to total assets.

     1. It measures the return on all the firm's assets after interest and taxes.

  D. The *basic earning power (BEP) ratio* is calculated by dividing earnings before interest and taxes (EBIT) by total assets.

     1. It shows the raw earning power of the firm's assets, before the influence of taxes and debt.

     2. It is useful for comparing firms with different debt and tax situations.

  E. The *return on investors' capital (ROIC)* is defined as after-tax operating income divided by total investor capital.

     1. The numerator shows the after-tax operating income the firm generates for its investors, while the denominator shows the money investors have supplied.

     2. It measures the rate of return on the total capital supplied to the firm by investors.

  F. The *return on common equity (ROE)* measures the rate of return on stockholders' investment.

     1. It is equal to net income divided by common equity.

     2. Stockholders invest to receive a return on their money, and this ratio tells how well they are doing in an accounting sense.

VI.   Market value ratios relate the firm's stock price to its earnings and book value per share, and thus give management an indication of what investors think of the company's risk and future prospects. If the liquidity, asset management, debt management, and profitability

ratios all look good, and if investors think these ratios will continue to look good in the future, the market value ratios will be high, the stock price will be as high as can be expected, and management will be judged to have been doing a good job.

    A. The market value ratios are used in three primary ways.

        1. By investors when they're deciding to buy or sell stock.

        2. By investment bankers when they're setting the share price for a new stock issue (an IPO).

        3. By firms when they're deciding how much to offer for another firm in a potential merger.

    B. The *price/earnings (P/E) ratio*, or price per share divided by earnings per share, shows how much investors are willing to pay per dollar of current earnings.

        1. P/E ratios are higher for firms with strong growth prospects and relatively little risk but low for slowly growing and risky firms.

        2. There is no "correct" P/E ratio. The S&P 500's historical average is 15.9×, and it has ranged from 7.1× to 48.1× over the last 30 years.

    C. The *market/book (M/B) ratio*, defined as market price per share divided by book value per share, gives another indication of how investors regard the company.

        1. Companies with safe and growing earnings and cash flows sell at higher multiples of book value than those with low returns.

        2. M/B ratios greater than 1.0 mean that investors are willing to pay more for stocks than their accounting book values.

            a. This situation occurs primarily because asset values, as reported by accountants on corporate balance sheets, do not reflect either inflation or goodwill.

VII. The DuPont equation shows how return on equity is affected by assets turnover, profit margin, and leverage.

    A. The profit margin times the total assets turnover gives the rate of return on assets (ROA):

$$\text{ROA} = \text{Profit margin} \times \text{Total assets turnover}$$

    B. The ROA times the *equity multiplier* (total assets divided by common equity) yields the return on equity (ROE).

$$\text{ROE} = \text{Profit margin} \times \text{Total assets turnover} \times \text{Equity multiplier}$$

        1. Management can use the DuPont equation to analyze ways of improving the firm's performance.

        2. If a company is financed only with common equity, the return on assets (ROA) and the return on equity (ROE) are the same because total assets will equal common equity. This equality holds only if the company uses no debt.

VIII. Despite its widespread use and the fact that ROE and shareholder wealth are often highly correlated, some problems can arise when firms use ROE as the sole measure of performance.

    A. ROE does not consider risk.

        1. Financial leverage can increase expected ROE but at the cost of higher risk, so raising ROE through greater use of leverage may not be good.

    B. ROE does not consider the amount of invested capital.

        1. A project with a high ROE but involving a small amount of capital will do little to enhance shareholder wealth.

    C. A focus on ROE can cause managers to turn down profitable projects.

    D. A project's return, risk, and size combine to determine its impact on shareholder value.

IX. **Ratio analysis involves comparisons because a company's ratios are compared with those of other firms in the same industry, that is, to industry average figures.**

    A. Comparative ratios are available from a number of sources including *ValueLine*, Dun & Bradstreet, Yahoo! Finance, MSN Money, and Risk Management Associates.

        1. When you select a comparative data source, be sure that your emphasis is similar to that of the organization whose ratios you plan to use.

        2. There are often definitional differences in the ratios presented by different sources, so before using a source, be sure to verify the exact definitions of the ratios to ensure consistency.

    B. *Benchmarking* is the process of comparing the ratios of a particular company with those of a smaller group of "benchmark" companies, rather than with the entire industry.

        1. Benchmarking makes it easy for a firm to see exactly where the company stands relative to its closest competition.

    C. It is important to analyze trends in ratios as well as their absolute levels.

        1. Trend analysis can provide clues as to whether the firm's financial condition is likely to improve or to deteriorate.

        2. Trend analysis involves plotting a firm's ratios on a graph over time.

X. **There are some inherent problems and limitations to ratio analysis that necessitate care and judgment.**

    A. Ratio analysis conducted in a mechanical, unthinking manner is dangerous, but used intelligently and with good judgment, it can provide useful insights into a firm's operations.

    B. Financial ratios are used by three main groups:

        1. Managers, who use ratios to help analyze, control, and thus improve their firm's operations.

        2. Credit analysts, such as bank loan officers or bond rating analysts, who analyze ratios to help judge a company's ability to repay its debts.

        3. Stock analysts, who are interested in a company's efficiency, risk, and growth prospects.

    C. Ratios are often not useful for analyzing the operations of large firms that operate in many different industries because it is difficult to develop a meaningful set of industry averages.

    D. The use of industry averages may not provide a very challenging target for high-level performance. It is best to focus on industry leaders' ratios, and benchmarking is useful for this.

    E. Inflation affects depreciation charges, inventory costs, and therefore, the value of both balance sheet items and net income. For this reason, the analysis of a firm over time, or a comparative analysis of firms of different ages, can be misleading.

F. Ratios may be distorted by seasonal factors, or manipulated by management to give the impression of a sound financial condition (*window dressing techniques*).

G. Different operating policies and accounting practices, such as the decision to lease rather than to purchase equipment, can distort comparisons.

H. Many ratios can be interpreted in different ways, and whether a particular ratio is good or bad should be based upon a complete financial analysis rather than the level of a single ratio at a single point in time.

I. Firms often have some ratios that look good and others that look bad, which makes it difficult to tell whether the company is, on balance, strong or weak. To deal with this, statistical procedures to analyze the net effects of a set of ratios are used and, on the basis of this analysis, firms are classified according to their probability of getting into financial trouble.

XI. **While it is important to understand and interpret financial statements, sound financial analysis involves more than just calculating and interpreting numbers.**

A. Good analysis requires that certain qualitative factors be considered when evaluating a company. Some of these factors are:

1. The extent to which the company's revenues are tied to one key customer.

2. The extent to which the company's revenues are tied to one key product.

3. The extent to which the company relies on a single supplier.

4. The percentage of the company's business generated overseas.

5. The level of competition faced by the firm.

6. The success of future products in the pipeline.

7. The impact of the legal and regulatory environment on the firm.

XII. **Web Appendix 4A discusses common size analysis and percent change analysis, two other techniques that can be used to identify trends in financial statements.**

A. In a common size analysis, all income statement items are divided by sales, and all balance sheet items are divided by total assets.

1. Common size analysis facilitates comparisons of balance sheets and income statements over time and across companies.

B. In a percent change analysis, growth rates are calculated for all income statement items and balance sheet accounts.

1. Analyzing percentages makes comparisons among firms easier than analyzing dollar amounts.

C. The conclusions reached in common size and percent change analyses generally parallel those derived from ratio analysis.

1. Occasionally a serious deficiency is highlighted by only one of the three analytical techniques: ratio analysis, common size analysis, and percent change analysis.

2. It is often helpful to use all three techniques and to drive home to management, in slightly different ways, the need to take corrective actions.

Self-Test

Definitional Questions

1. _____ ratios are the category of ratios used to measure a firm's ability to meet its current obligations as they come due.

2. The _____ ratio measures the extent to which current liabilities are covered by current assets.

3. The _____ ratio is a measure of a firm's ability to pay off short-term obligations without relying on the sale of inventories.

4. _____ management ratios measure how effectively a firm is managing its assets and whether the level of those assets is properly related to the level of operations as measured by sales.

5. The days sales outstanding (DSO) ratio is found by dividing average sales per day into accounts _____. The DSO is the length of time that a firm must wait after making a sale before it receives _____.

6. The _____ assets turnover ratio measures how effectively the firm uses its plant and equipment.

7. The _____ assets turnover ratio measures the utilization of all the firm's assets.

8. Debt management ratios are used to evaluate a firm's use of financial _____.

9. Analysts use two procedures to examine the firm's debt: (1) They check the _____ sheet to determine the proportion of total funds represented by debt, and (2) they review the _____ statement to see the extent to which interest is covered by operating profits.

10. The debt ratio, which is the ratio of total _____ to total _____, measures the percentage of funds provided by creditors.

11. The _____-_____-_____ ratio is calculated by dividing earnings before interest and taxes by the amount of interest charges.

12. The combined effects of liquidity, asset management, and debt on operating results are measured by _____ ratios.

13. Dividing net income by sales gives the _____ margin.

14. The basic _____ power ratio is useful for comparing firms with different debt and tax situations.

15. The _____/_____ ratio measures how much investors are willing to pay for each dollar of a firm's current earnings.

16. The _____ equation shows how return on equity is affected by assets turnover, profit margin, and leverage.

17. _____ makes it easy for a firm to see exactly where the company stands relative to its closest competition.

18. Return on assets is a function of two variables, the profit _____ and total _____ turnover.

19. Analyzing a particular ratio over time for an individual firm is known as _____ analysis.

20. Financial ratios are used by three main groups: (1) _____, who employ ratios to help analyze, control, and thus improve their firm's operations; (2) _____ analysts, who analyze ratios to help judge a company's ability to pay its debts; and (3) _____ analysts, who are interested in a company's efficiency, risk, and growth prospects.

Conceptual Questions

1. The equity multiplier can be expressed as 1 − (Debt/Assets).

    a. True
    b. False

2. A high current ratio is *always* a good indication of a well-managed liquidity position.

    a. True
    b. False

3. International Appliances Inc. has a current ratio of 0.5. Which of the following actions would improve (increase) this ratio?

    a. Use cash to pay off current liabilities.
    b. Collect some of the current accounts receivable.
    c. Use cash to pay off some long-term debt.
    d. Purchase additional inventory on credit (accounts payable).
    e. Sell some of the existing inventory at cost.

4. International Appliances has a current ratio of 1.2. Which of the following actions would improve (increase) this ratio?

    a. Use cash to pay off current liabilities.
    b. Collect some of the current accounts receivable.
    c. Use cash to pay off some long-term debt.
    d. Purchase additional inventory on credit (accounts payable).
    e. Use cash to pay for some fixed assets.

5. Examining the ratios of a particular firm against the same measures for a small group of firms from the same industry, at a point in time, is an example of

    a. Trend analysis.
    b. Benchmarking.
    c. DuPont analysis.
    d. Simple ratio analysis.
    e. Industry analysis.

6. Which of the following statements is correct?

    a. Having a high current ratio is always a good indication that a firm is managing its liquidity position well.
    b. A decline in the inventory turnover ratio suggests that the firm's liquidity position is improving.
    c. A high times-interest-earned ratio is one indication that the firm should be able to meet its debt obligations.
    d. Since ROA measures the firm's effective utilization of assets (without considering how these assets are financed), two firms with the same EBIT must have the same ROA.
    e. If, through specific managerial actions, a firm has been able to increase its ROA, then, because of the fixed mathematical relationship between ROA and ROE, it must also have increased its ROE.

7. Which of the following statements is correct?

   a. Suppose two firms with the same amount of assets pay the same interest rate on their debt and earn the same rate of return on their assets and that ROA is positive. However, one firm has a higher debt ratio. Under these conditions, the firm with the higher debt ratio will also have a higher rate of return on common equity.
   b. One of the problems of ratio analysis is that the relationships are subject to manipulation. For example, we know that if we use some cash to pay off some of our current liabilities, the current ratio will always increase, especially if the current ratio is weak initially, for example, below 1.0.
   c. Generally, firms with high profit margins have high asset turnover ratios and firms with low profit margins have low turnover ratios; this result is exactly as predicted by the DuPont equation.
   d. Firms A and B have identical earnings and identical dividend payout ratios. If Firm A's growth rate is higher than Firm B's, then Firm A's P/E ratio must be greater than Firm B's P/E ratio.
   e. Each of the above statements is false.

8. Which of the following statements is *not correct*?

   a. Profitability ratios reflect the net result of all of the firm's financing policies and operating decisions.
   b. Companies with safe and growing earnings and cash flows sell at higher multiples of book value than those with low returns.
   c. Management can use the DuPont equation to analyze ways of improving the firm's performance.
   d. Financial leverage can increase expected ROE without increasing risk, so raising ROE through greater use of leverage is always good.
   e. Trend analysis can provide clues as to whether the firm's financial situation is likely to improve or to deteriorate.

Problems

1. Info Technics Inc. has an equity multiplier of 2.75. The company's assets are financed with some combination of long-term debt and common equity. What is the company's debt ratio?

   a. 25.00%
   b. 36.36%
   c. 52.48%
   d. 63.64%
   e. 75.00%

2. Info Technics Inc. has an equity multiplier of 2.75. The company's assets are financed with some combination of long-term debt and common equity. What is the company's common equity ratio?

   a. 25.00%
   b. 36.36%
   c. 52.48%
   d. 63.64%
   e. 75.00%

3. Cutler Enterprises has current assets equal to $4.5 million. The company's current ratio is 1.25. What is the firm's level of current liabilities (in millions)?

    a. $0.8
    b. $1.8
    c. $2.4
    d. $2.9
    e. $3.6

4. Jericho Motors has $4 billion in total assets. The other side of its balance sheet consists of $0.4 billion in current liabilities, $1.2 billion in long-term debt, and $2.4 billion in common equity. The company has 500 million shares of common stock outstanding, and its stock price is $25 per share. What is Jericho's market-to-book ratio?

    a. 2.00
    b. 4.27
    c. 5.21
    d. 3.57
    e. 1.42

5. Taylor Toys Inc. has $6 billion in assets, and its tax rate is 35%. The company's basic earning power (BEP) is 10%, and its return on assets (ROA) is 2.5%. What is Taylor's times-interest-earned (TIE) ratio?

    a. 1.625
    b. 2.000
    c. 2.433
    d. 2.750
    e. 3.000

Exhibit 4-1

Roberts Manufacturing Balance Sheet
December 31, 2011
(Dollars in Thousands)

Cash	$ 200	Accounts payable	$ 205
Receivables	245	Notes payable	425
Inventory	625	Other current liabilities	115
Total current assets	$1,070	Total current liabilities	$ 745
Net fixed assets	1,200	Long-term debt	420
		Common equity	1,105
Total assets	$2,270	Total liabilities and equity	$2,270

Roberts Manufacturing Income Statement
for Year Ended December 31, 2011
(Dollars in Thousands)

Sales		$2,400
Cost of goods sold:		
Materials	$1,000	
Labor	600	
Heat, light, and power	89	
Indirect labor	65	
Depreciation	80	1,834
Gross profit		$ 566
Selling expenses		175
General and administrative expenses		216
Earnings before interest and taxes (EBIT)		$ 175
Interest expense		35
Earnings before taxes (EBT)		$ 140
Taxes (40%)		56
Net income (NI)		$ 84

6. From the financial statements given in Exhibit 4-1, calculate the current ratio.

   a. 1.20
   b. 1.33
   c. 1.44
   d. 1.51
   e. 1.60

7. From the financial statements given in Exhibit 4-1, calculate the asset management ratios, that is, the inventory turnover ratio, fixed assets turnover, total assets turnover, and days sales outstanding. Assume a 365-day year.

   a. 3.84; 2.00; 1.06; 37.26 days
   b. 3.84; 2.00; 1.06; 35.25 days
   c. 3.84; 2.00; 1.06; 34.10 days
   d. 3.84; 2.00; 1.24; 34.10 days
   e. 3.84; 2.20; 1.48; 34.10 days

8. From the financial statements given in Exhibit 4-1, calculate the debt and times-interest-earned ratios.

   a. 0.39; 3.16
   b. 0.39; 5.00
   c. 0.51; 3.16
   d. 0.51; 5.00
   e. 0.73; 3.16

9. From the financial statements given in Exhibit 4-1, calculate the profitability ratios, that is, the operating margin, the profit margin, return on total assets, return on common equity, and basic earning power of assets.

    a. 7.29%; 3.50%; 4.25%; 7.60%; 8.00%
    b. 7.29%; 3.50%; 3.70%; 7.60%; 7.71%
    c. 7.29%; 3.70%; 3.50%; 7.60%; 7.71%
    d. 7.50%; 3.70%; 3.50%; 8.00%; 8.00%
    e. 7.50%; 4.25%; 3.70%; 7.60%; 8.00%

10. From the financial statements given in Exhibit 4-1, calculate the market value ratios, that is, the price/earnings ratio and the market/book value ratio. Roberts had an average of 10,000 shares outstanding during 2011, and the stock price on December 31, 2011, was $40.00.

    a. 4.21; 0.36
    b. 3.20; 1.54
    c. 3.20; 0.36
    d. 4.76; 1.54
    e. 4.76; 0.36

11. From the financial statements given in Exhibit 4-1, use the DuPont equation to determine Roberts' return on equity.

    a. 6.90%
    b. 7.24%
    c. 7.47%
    d. 7.60%
    e. 8.41%

12. Lewis Inc. has sales of $2 million per year, all of which are credit sales. Its days sales outstanding is 42 days. What is its average accounts receivable balance? Assume a 365-day year.

    a. $230,137
    b. $266,667
    c. $333,333
    d. $350,000
    e. $366,750

13. Southeast Jewelers Inc. sells only on credit. Its days sales outstanding is 73 days, and its average accounts receivable balance is $500,000. What are its sales for the year? Assume a 365-day year.

    a. $1,500,000
    b. $2,500,000
    c. $2,000,000
    d. $2,750,000
    e. $3,000,000

14. A firm has total interest charges of $20,000 per year, sales of $2 million, a tax rate of 40%, and a profit margin of 6%. What is the firm's times-interest-earned ratio?

    a. 10
    b. 11
    c. 12
    d. 13
    e. 14

15. A firm has total interest charges of $20,000 per year, sales of $2 million, a tax rate of 40%, and a profit margin of 6%. What is the firm's TIE, if its profit margin decreases to 3% and its interest charges double to $40,000 per year?

    a. 3.0
    b. 2.5
    c. 3.5
    d. 4.2
    e. 3.7

16. A fire has destroyed many of the financial records at Anderson Associates. You are assigned to piece together information to prepare a financial report. You have found that the firm's return on equity is 12% and its debt ratio is 0.40. What is its return on assets?

    a. 4.90%
    b. 5.35%
    c. 6.60%
    d. 7.20%
    e. 8.40%

17. A fire has destroyed many of the financial records at Anderson Associates. You are assigned to piece together information to prepare a financial report. You have found that the firm's return on equity is 12% and its debt ratio is 0.40. What is the firm's debt ratio if its ROE is 15% and its ROA is 10%?

    a. 67%
    b. 50%
    c. 25%
    d. 33%
    e. 45%

18. Rowe and Company has a debt ratio of 0.50, a total assets turnover of 0.25, and a profit margin of 10%. The president is unhappy with the current return on equity, and he thinks it could be doubled. This could be accomplished (1) by increasing the profit margin to 14% and (2) by increasing debt utilization. Total assets turnover will not change. What new debt ratio, along with the 14% profit margin, is required to double the return on equity?

    a. 0.55
    b. 0.60
    c. 0.65
    d. 0.70
    e. 0.75

19. Altman Corporation has $1,000,000 of debt outstanding, and it pays an interest rate of 12% annually. Altman's annual sales are $4 million, its federal-plus-state tax rate is 40%, and its profit margin is 10%. If the company does not maintain a TIE ratio of at least 5 times, its bank will refuse to renew the loan, and bankruptcy will result. What is Altman's TIE ratio?

a. 9.33
b. 4.44
c. 2.50
d. 4.00
e. 6.56

20. Altman Corporation has $1,000,000 of debt outstanding, and it pays an interest rate of 12% annually. Altman's annual sales are $4 million, its federal-plus-state tax rate is 40%, and its profit margin is 10%. If the company does not maintain a TIE ratio of at least 5 times, its bank will refuse to renew the loan, and bankruptcy will result. What is the maximum amount Altman's EBIT could decrease and its bank still renew its loan?

a. $186,667
b. $ 45,432
c. $ 66,767
d. $ 47,898
e. $143,925

21. Pinkerton Packaging's ROE last year was 2.5%, but its management has developed a new operating plan designed to improve its financial position. The new plan calls for a total debt ratio of 50%, which will result in interest charges of $240 per year. Management projects an EBIT of $800 on sales of $8,000, and it expects to have a total assets turnover ratio of 1.6. Under these conditions, the federal-plus-state tax rate will be 40%. If the changes are made, what return on equity will Pinkerton earn?

a.   2.50%
b. 13.44%
c. 13.00%
d. 14.02%
e. 14.57%

Exhibit 4-2

Baker Corporation Balance Sheet
December 31, 2011

Cash and marketable securities	$ 50	Accounts payable	$ 250
Accounts receivable	200	Accrued liabilities	250
Inventory	250	Notes payable	500
Total current assets	$ 500	Total current liabilities	$1,000
Net fixed assets	1,500	Long-term debt	250
		Common stock	400
		Retained earnings	350
Total assets	$2,000	Total liabilities and equity	$2,000

22. From the balance sheet given in Exhibit 4-2, what is Baker Corporation's current ratio as of December 31, 2011?

    a. 0.35
    b. 0.65
    c. 0.50
    d. 0.25
    e. 0.75

23. Baker Corporation's balance sheet is given in Exhibit 4-2. If Baker uses $50 of cash to pay off $50 of its accounts payable, what is its new current ratio after this action?

    a. 0.47
    b. 0.44
    c. 0.54
    d. 0.33
    e. 0.62

24. Baker Corporation's balance sheet is given in Exhibit 4-2. If Baker uses its $50 cash balance to pay off $50 of its long-term debt, what will be its new current ratio?

    a. 0.35
    b. 0.50
    c. 0.55
    d. 0.60
    e. 0.45

25. Given these financial statements, what are Whitney's basic earning power and ROA ratios?

Whitney Inc. Balance Sheet
December 31, 2011

		Total current liabilities	$100
		Long-term debt	250
		Common stockholders' equity	400
Total assets	$750	Total liabilities and equity	$750

Whitney Inc. Income Statement
for Year Ended December 31, 2011

Sales		$1,000
Cost of goods sold (excluding depreciation)	$550	
Other operating expenses	100	
Depreciation	50	
Total operating costs		700
Earnings before interest and taxes (EBIT)		$ 300
Interest expense		25
Earnings before taxes (EBT)		$ 275
Taxes (40%)		110
Net income		$ 165

a. 30%; 22%
b. 40%; 30%
c. 50%; 22%
d. 40%; 22%
e. 40%; 40%

26. Given these financial statements, what are Cotner Enterprise's basic earning power and ROA ratios?

Cotner Enterprises Balance Sheet
December 31, 2011

		Total current liabilities	$ 300
		Long-term debt	500
		Common stockholders' equity	450
Total assets	$1,250	Total liabilities and equity	$1,250

Cotner Enterprises Income Statement
for Year Ended December 31, 2011

Sales		$1,700
Cost of goods sold (excluding depreciation)	$1,190	
Other operating expenses	135	
Depreciation	75	
Total operating costs		1,400
Earnings before interest and taxes (EBIT)		$ 300
Interest expense		54
Earnings before taxes (EBT)		$ 246
Taxes (35%)		86
Net income		$ 160

a. 20.0%; 12.8%
b. 24.0%; 12.8%
c. 24.0%; 15.8%
d. 17.5%; 12.8%
e. 24.0%; 10.5%

27. Dauten Enterprises is just being formed. It will need $2 million of assets, and it expects to have an EBIT of $400,000. Dauten will own no securities, so all of its income will be operating income. If it chooses to, Dauten can finance up to 50% of its assets with debt that will have a 9% interest rate. Dauten has no other liabilities. Assuming a 40% federal-plus-state tax rate on all taxable income, what is the difference between the expected ROE if Dauten finances with 50% debt versus the expected ROE if it finances entirely with common stock?

a. 7.2%
b. 6.6%
c. 6.0%
d. 5.8%
e. 9.0%

53

28. Helen's Fashion Designs recently reported net income of $3,500,000. The company has 700,000 shares of common stock, and it currently trades at $25 a share. The company continues to expand and anticipates that one year from now its net income will be $4,500,000. Over the next year the company also anticipates issuing an additional 100,000 shares of stock, so that one year from now the company will have 800,000 shares of common stock. Assuming the company's price/earnings ratio remains at its current level, what will be the company's stock price one year from now?

    a. $25.255
    b. $27.500
    c. $28.125
    d. $31.000
    e. $33.000

29. Henderson Chemical Company has $5 million in sales. Its ROE is 10% and its total assets turnover is 2.5×. The company is 60% equity financed. What is the company's net income?

    a. $ 95,750
    b. $105,300
    c. $110,250
    d. $120,000
    e. $145,000

30. Bradberry Bolts' net income is $750,000, its interest expense is $210,000, and its return on assets is 6%. The company's tax rate is 35%. What is the company's basic earning power (BEP) ratio?

    a. 7.25%
    b. 8.33%
    c. 9.45%
    d. 10.00%
    e. 10.91%

Answers

Definitional Questions

1. Liquidity
2. current
3. quick
4. Asset
5. receivable; cash
6. fixed
7. total
8. leverage
9. balance; income
10. debt; assets
11. times-interest-earned (TIE)
12. profitability
13. profit
14. earning
15. price/earnings
16. DuPont
17. Benchmarking
18. margin; assets
19. trend
20. managers; credit; stock

Conceptual Questions

1. b. The result of this expression is Equity/Assets, which is the reciprocal of the equity multiplier. The equity multiplier is equal to Assets/Equity.

2. b. Excess cash, receivables, and inventory resulting from poor management could produce a high current ratio.

3. d. This question is best analyzed using numbers. For example, assume current assets equal $50 and current liabilities equal $100. Assume a $10 purchase of inventory is made on credit (accounts payable). The new current ratio would be $60/$110 = 0.55, which is an increase over the old current ratio of 0.5

4. a. This question is best analyzed using numbers. For example, assume current assets equal $120 and current liabilities equal $100. Assume $5 in cash is used to pay off $5 in current liabilities. The new current ratio would be $115/$95 = 1.21, which is an increase over the old current ratio of 1.2.

5. b. The correct answer is benchmarking. A trend analysis compares the firm's ratios over time, while a DuPont analysis shows how return on equity is affected by assets turnover, profit margin, and leverage.

6. c. The TIE ratio is used to measure whether the firm can meet its debt obligation, and a high TIE ratio would indicate this is so.

7. a. From the information given in statement a, one can determine that the two firms' net incomes are equal; thus, the firm with the higher debt ratio (lower equity ratio) will indeed have a higher ROE.

8. d. Financial leverage can increase expected ROE but at the cost of higher risk, so raising ROE through greater use of leverage may not be good.

Solutions

Problems

1. d. 2.75 = A/E
       E/A = 1/2.75
       E/A = 36.36%

       D/A = 1 – E/A
            = 1 – 36.36%
            = 63.64%

2. b. $2.75 = A/E$
$E/A = 1/2.75$
$E/A = 36.36\%$

3. e. CA = \$4.5 million; CA/CL = 1.25

$$\$4.5/CL = 1.25$$
$$1.25(CL) = \$4.5$$
$$CL = \$3.6 \text{ million}$$

4. c. TA = \$4,000,000,000; CL = \$400,000,000; LT debt = \$1,200,000,000; CE = \$2,400,000,000;
Shares outstanding = 500,000,000; P_0 = \$25; M/B = ?

$$\text{Book value} = \frac{\$2,400,000,000}{500,000,000} = \$4.80$$

$$M/B = \frac{\$25.00}{\$4.80} = 5.2083 \approx 5.21$$

5. a. TA = \$6,000,000,000; T = 35%; EBIT/TA = 10%; ROA = 2.5%; TIE = ?

$$\frac{EBIT}{\$6,000,000,000} = 0.10$$
$$EBIT = \$600,000,000$$

$$\frac{NI}{\$6,000,000,000} = 0.025$$
$$NI = \$150,000,000$$

Now use the income statement format to determine interest so you can calculate the firm's TIE ratio.

EBIT	\$600,000,000	See above.	INT = EBIT – EBT
INT	369,230,769		= \$600,000,000 – \$230,769,231
EBT	\$230,769,231	EBT = \$150,000,000/0.65	
Taxes (35%)	80,769,231		
NI	\$150,000,000	See above.	

TIE = EBIT/INT
= \$600,000,000/\$369,230,769
= 1.625×

6. c. $$\text{Current ratio} = \frac{\text{Current assets}}{\text{Current liabilities}} = \frac{\$1,070}{\$745} = 1.44\times$$

7. a. $\text{Inventory turnover} = \dfrac{\text{Sales}}{\text{Inventory}} = \dfrac{\$2,400}{\$625} = 3.84\times$

$\text{Fixed assets turnover} = \dfrac{\text{Sales}}{\text{Net fixed assets}} = \dfrac{\$2,400}{\$1,200} = 2.00\times$

$\text{Total assets turnover} = \dfrac{\text{Sales}}{\text{Total assets}} = \dfrac{\$2,400}{\$2,270} = 1.06\times$

$\text{DSO} = \dfrac{\text{Accounts receivable}}{\text{Sales}/365} = \dfrac{\$245}{\$2,400/365} = 37.26 \text{ days}$

8. d. Debt ratio = Total debt/Total assets = $1,165/$2,270 = 0.51 = 51%

TIE ratio = EBIT/Interest = $175/$35 = 5.00×

9. b. $\text{Operating margin} = \dfrac{\text{EBIT}}{\text{Sales}} = \dfrac{\$175}{\$2,400} = 0.0729 = 7.29\%$

$\text{Profit margin} = \dfrac{\text{Net income}}{\text{Sales}} = \dfrac{\$84}{\$2,400} = 0.0350 = 3.50\%$

$\text{ROA} = \dfrac{\text{Net income}}{\text{Total assets}} = \dfrac{\$84}{\$2,270} = 0.0370 = 3.70\%$

$\text{ROE} = \dfrac{\text{Net income}}{\text{Common equity}} = \dfrac{\$84}{\$1,105} = 0.0760 = 7.60\%$

$\text{BEP} = \dfrac{\text{EBIT}}{\text{Total assets}} = \dfrac{\$175}{\$2,270} = 0.0771 = 7.71\%$

10. e. $\text{EPS} = \dfrac{\text{Net income}}{\text{Number of shares outstanding}} = \dfrac{\$84,000}{10,000} = \$8.40$

$\text{P/E ratio} = \dfrac{\text{Price}}{\text{EPS}} = \dfrac{\$40.00}{\$8.40} = 4.76\times$

$\text{Market/Book value} = \dfrac{\text{Market price}}{\text{Book value}} = \dfrac{\$40(10,000)}{\$1,105,000} = 0.36\times$

11. d.   ROE= Profit margin × Total assets turnover × Equity multiplier

$$= \frac{\$84}{\$2,400} \times \frac{\$2,400}{\$2,270} \times \frac{\$2,270}{\$1,105} = 0.035 \times 1.057 \times 2.054$$

$$= 0.0760 = 7.60\%$$

12. a. $$DSO = \frac{\text{Accounts receivable}}{\text{Sales}/365}$$

$$42 \text{ days} = \frac{AR}{\$2,000,000/365}$$

$$AR = \$230,137$$

13. b.   DSO = Accounts receivable/(Sales/365)
          73 days = $500,000/(Sales/365)
     73(Sales/365) = $500,000
          Sales = $2,500,000

14. b.   Net income = $2,000,000(0.06) = $120,000

Earnings before taxes = $120,000/(1 − 0.4) = $200,000

EBIT = $200,000 + $20,000 = $220,000

TIE = EBIT/Interest = $220,000/$20,000 = 11×

15. c.   Net income = $2,000,000(0.03) = $60,000

Earnings before taxes = $60,000/(1 − 0.4) = $100,000

EBIT = $100,000 + $40,000 = $140,000

TIE = EBIT/Interest = $140,000/$40,000 = 3.5×

16. d.   If Total debt/Total assets = 0.40, then Total equity/Total assets = 0.60, and the equity multiplier (Assets/Equity) = 1/0.60 = 1.667

$$\frac{NI}{E} = \frac{NI}{A} \times \frac{A}{E}$$
ROE = ROA × EM
12% = ROA × 1.667
ROA = 7.20%

17. d. ROE = ROA × Equity multiplier

    15% = 10% × TA/Equity

      1.5 = TA/Equity

    Debt/TA = 1 − Equity/TA = 1 − 0.67 = 0.33 = 33%

18. c. If Total debt/Total assets = 0.50, then Total equity/Total assets = 0.50 and the equity multiplier (Assets/Equity) = 1/0.50 = 2.0

    ROE = PM × Total assets turnover × EM

    Before: ROE = 10% × 0.25 × 2.00 = 5.00%

    After: 10.00% = 14% × 0.25 × EM; thus EM = 2.8571

$$\text{Equity multiplier} = \frac{\text{Assets}}{\text{Equity}}$$

$$2.8571 = \frac{1}{\text{Equity/Assets}}$$

$$0.35 = \text{Equity/Assets}$$

    Debt/TA = 1 − Equity/TA = 100% − 35% = 65%

19. e. TIE = EBIT/Interest, so find EBIT and Interest

    Interest = $1,000,000(0.12) = $120,000

    Net income = $4,000,000(0.10) = $400,000

    Pretax income = $400,000/(1 − T) = $400,000/0.6 = $666,667

    EBIT = $666,667 + $120,000 = $786,667

    TIE = $786,667/$120,000 = 6.56×

20. a. Interest = $1,000,000(0.12) = $120,000

    Net income = $4,000,000(0.10) = $400,000

    EBT = $400,000/0.6 = $666,667

    EBIT = $666,667 + $120,000 = $786,667

    TIE = EBIT/INT

      5 = EBIT/$120,000

    EBIT = $600,000

    EBIT could decrease by $786,667 − $600,000 = $186,667

21. b. ROE = Profit margin × Total assets turnover × Equity multiplier
   = NI/Sales × Sales/TA × TA/Equity

Now we need to determine the inputs for the equation from the data that were given. On the left we set up an income statement, and we put numbers in it on the right:

Sales (given)	$8,000
Cost	NA
EBIT (given)	$ 800
Interest (given)	240
EBT	$ 560
Taxes (40%)	224
Net income	$ 336

Now we can use some ratios to get some more data:

Total assets turnover = S/TA = 1.6× (given)

D/A = 50%, so E/A = 50%, and therefore TA/E = 1/(E/A) = 1/0.5 = 2.00×

Now we can complete the DuPont equation to determine ROE

ROE = $336/$8,000 × 1.6 × 2.0 = 13.44%

22. c. Current ratio = Current assets/Current liabilities = $500/$1,000 = 0.50×

23. a. New current ratio = ($500 – $50)/($1,000 – $50) = $450/$950 = 0.47×

24. e. Only the current assets balance is affected by this action. Baker's new current ratio = ($500 – $50)/$1,000 = $450/$1,000 = 0.45×

25. d. BEP = EBIT/Total assets = $300/$750 = 40%

   ROA = Net income/Total assets = $165/$750 = 22%

26. b. BEP ratio = EBIT/Total assets = $300/$1,250 = 24.0%

   ROA = Net income/Total assets = $160/$1,250 = 12.8%

27. b.   Known data: Total assets = $2,000,000; EBIT = $400,000; r_d = 9%, T = 40%

D/A = 0.5 = 50%, so Equity = 0.5($2,000,000) = $1,000,000

	D/A = 0%	D/A = 50%
EBIT	$400,000	$400,000
Interest	0	90,000*
Taxable income	$400,000	$310,000
Taxes (40%)	160,000	124,000
Net income (NI)	$240,000	$186,000

*If D/A = 50%, then half of assets are financed by debt, so Debt = 0.5($2,000,000) = $1,000,000. At a 9% interest rate, INT = 0.09($1,000,000) = $90,000.

For D/A = 0%, ROE = NI/Equity = $240,000/$2,000,000 = 12%. For D/A = 50%, ROE = $186,000/$1,000,000 = 18.6%. Difference = 18.6% – 12.0% = 6.6%.

28. c.   The current EPS is $3,500,000/700,000 shares or $5.00. The current P/E ratio is then $25/$5 = 5.00×. The new number of shares outstanding will be 800,000. Thus, the new EPS = $4,500,000/800,000 = $5.625. If the shares are selling for 5 times EPS, then they must be selling for $5.625(5) = $28.125.

29. d.   Step 1:   Calculate total assets from information given.
Sales = $5 million

$$2.5\times = \text{Sales/TA}$$
$$2.5\times = \frac{\$5,000,000}{\text{Assets}}$$
$$\text{Assets} = \$2,000,000$$

Step 2:   Calculate net income.
There is 40% debt and 60% equity, so Equity = $2,000,000 × 0.6 = $1,200,000.

$$\text{ROE} = \text{NI/S} \times \text{S/TA} \times \text{TA/E}$$
$$0.10 = \text{NI}/\$5,000,000 \times 2.5 \times \$2,000,000/\$1,200,000$$
$$0.10 = \frac{4.1667(\text{NI})}{\$5,000,000}$$
$$\$500,000 = 4.1667(\text{NI})$$
$$\$120,000 = \text{NI}$$

30. e.   ROA = 6%; Net income = $750,000

$$ROA = \frac{NI}{TA}$$

$$6\% = \frac{\$750,000}{TA}$$

$$TA = \$12,500,000$$

To calculate BEP, we still need EBIT. To calculate EBIT construct a partial income statement:

EBIT	$1,363,846	($210,000 + $1,153,846)
Interest	210,000	(Given)
EBT	$1,153,846	$750,000/0.65
Taxes (35%)	403,846	
NI	$ 750,000	(Given)

$$BEP = \frac{EBIT}{TA}$$

$$= \frac{\$1,363,846}{\$12,500,000}$$

$$= 0.1091 = 10.91\%$$

5

TIME VALUE OF MONEY

Learning Objectives

1. Explain how the time value of money works and discuss why it is such an important concept in finance.

2. Calculate the present value and future value of lump sums.

3. Identify the different types of annuities, calculate the present value and future value of both an ordinary annuity and an annuity due, and calculate the relevant annuity payments.

4. Calculate the present value and future value of an uneven cash flow stream. You will use this knowledge in later chapters that show how to value common stocks and corporate projects.

5. Explain the difference between nominal, periodic, and effective interest rates. An understanding of these concepts is necessary when comparing rates of returns on alternative investments.

6. Discuss the basics of loan amortization and develop a loan amortization schedule that you might use when considering an auto loan or home mortgage loan.

Overview

A dollar in the hand today is worth more than a dollar to be received in the future because, if you had it now, you could invest that dollar and earn interest. Of all the techniques used in finance, none is more important than the concept of time value of money, also called discounted cash flow (DCF) analysis. It is essential for financial managers to have a clear understanding of the time value of money and its impact on stock prices.

Future value and present value techniques can be applied to a single cash flow (lump sum), ordinary annuities, annuities due, and uneven cash flow streams. Future and present values can be calculated using a regular calculator, a calculator with financial functions, or a computer spreadsheet program. The principles of time value analysis have many applications, ranging from setting up schedules for paying off loans to decisions about whether to acquire new equipment.

Outline

I.   **The time line is one of the most important tools in time value of money calculations.**

    A. Time lines help visualize what is happening in a particular problem.

1. Cash flows are placed directly below the tick marks, and interest rates are shown directly above the time line; unknown cash flows are indicated by question marks.

2. To find the future value of $100 after 5 years at 5% interest, the following time line can be set up as follows:

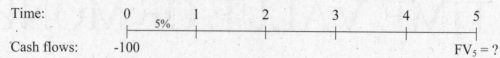

B. Time lines are essential when you are first learning time value concepts, but even experts use them to analyze complex finance problems.

   1. Begin each problem by setting up a time line to show what's happening, then determine the equation(s) that must be solved to find the answer.

II.   **Finding the future value (FV), or compounding, is the process of going from today's values (or present values) to future amounts (or future values). The future value is calculated as: $FV_N = PV(1 + I)^N$ where PV = present value, or beginning amount; I = interest rate per year; and N = number of periods involved in the analysis. This equation can be solved in one of three ways: numerically, with a financial calculator, or with a computer spreadsheet program. For calculations, assume the data that were presented in the time line above: present value (PV) = $100, interest rate (I) = 5%, and number of years (N) = 5.**

   A. To solve numerically, use a regular calculator to find $1 + I = 1.05$ raised to the fifth power, $(1.05)^5$, which equals 1.2763. Multiply this figure by PV = $100 to obtain the final answer of $FV_5 = \$127.63$.

   B. With a financial calculator, the future value can be found by using the time value of money (TVM) input keys, where N = number of periods, I/YR = interest rate per period, PV = present value, PMT = payment, and FV = future value. By entering N = 5, I/YR = 5, PV = -100, and PMT = 0, and then pressing the FV key, the answer 127.63 is displayed.

      1. Some financial calculators require that all cash flows be designated as either inflows or outflows, thus an outflow must be entered as a negative number (for example, PV = -100 instead of PV = 100).

      2. When PMT is zero, it doesn't matter what sign you enter for PV as your calculator will automatically assign the opposite sign to FV when it is calculated.

   C. Spreadsheet programs are ideally suited for solving many financial problems, including time value of money problems. With very little effort, the spreadsheet itself becomes a time line.

      1. The format of Excel's FV function is FV(rate,nper,pmt,[pv],[type]).

      2. "Type" indicates whether cash flows occur at the beginning of the period or at the end of the period.

         a. Type is used only if PMT is a nonzero number.

         b. Zero indicates that cash flows occur at the end, while 1 indicates that cash flows occur at the beginning. If type is left blank, cash flows are assumed to occur at the end.

   D. A graph of the compounding process shows how any sum grows over time at various interest rates. The greater the interest rate, the faster the growth rate.

      1. Time value concepts can be applied to anything that grows—sales, population, earnings per share, or your future salary.

III. **Finding present values is called discounting, and it is simply the reverse of compounding.**

A. The present value of a cash flow due N years in the future is the amount which, if it were on hand today, would grow to equal the future amount. By solving for PV in the future value equation, the present value, or discounting, equation can be developed and written as follows:

$$PV = \frac{FV_N}{(1+I)^N} = FV_N \left(\frac{1}{1+I}\right)^N$$

1. To solve for the present value of $127.63 discounted back 5 years at a 5% *opportunity cost rate,* which is the rate of return that could be earned on an alternative investment of similar risk, one can utilize any of the three solution methods:

   a. Numerical solution: Divide $127.63 by 1.05 five times to get PV = $100.

   b. Financial calculator solution: Enter N = 5, I/YR = 5, PMT = 0, and FV = 127.63, and then press the PV key to get PV = -100.

   c. With Excel, you can use the built-in spreadsheet PV function to solve for PV = 100. The format for this function is PV(rate,nper,pmt,[fv],[type]).

B. A graph of the *discounting process* shows how the present value of any sum to be received in the future diminishes as the years to receipt increases.

1. At relatively high interest rates, funds due in the future are worth very little today.

2. Even at a relatively low discount rate, the present value of a sum due in the very distant future is quite small.

C. The fundamental goal of financial management is to maximize the firm's value.

1. The value of a business (or any asset, including stocks and bonds) is the present value of its expected future cash flows.

2. Present value lies at the heart of the valuation process.

IV. **There are four variables used in the future value and present value equations: PV, FV, I, and N. If three of the four variables are known, you can find the value of the fourth variable. Note that the PMT variable in these two equations is zero.**

A. If we are given PV, FV, and N, we can determine I by substituting the known values into either the present value or future value equations, and then solving for I. Thus, if you can buy a security at a price of $78.35 that will pay you $100 after 5 years, what is the interest rate earned on the investment?

1. This is the numerical solution, and it requires a bit more algebra to solve for I.

$$\$100 = \$78.35(1+I)^5$$
$$1.2763 = (1+I)^5$$
$$1.2763^{1/5} = (1+I)$$
$$1.05 = 1+I$$
$$I = 5\%$$

2. Financial calculator solution: Enter N = 5, PV = -78.35, PMT = 0, and FV = 100, then press the I/YR key, and I/YR = 5 is displayed.

3. Computer spreadsheet program: Most spreadsheets have a built-in function to find the interest rate.

65

    a. The format for Excel's function is RATE(nper,pmt,pv,[fv],[type],[guess]). In many cases, you do not have to enter a guess for the interest rate.

B. Likewise, if we are given PV, FV, and I, we can determine N by substituting the known values into either the present value or future value equations, and then solving for N. Thus, if you can buy a security with a 5% interest rate at a price of $78.35 today, how long will it take for your investment to return $100?

    1. Numerical solution: We cannot use a simple formula—the situation is like that with interest rates.

    2. Financial calculator solution: Enter I/YR = 5, PV = -78.35, PMT = 0, and FV = 100, then press the N key, and N = 5 is displayed.

    3. Computer spreadsheet program: The format of Excel's built-in function is NPER(rate,pmt,pv,[fv],[type]).

V.   An annuity is a series of equal payments made at fixed intervals for a specified number of periods.

A. If the payments occur at the end of each period, as they typically do, the annuity is an *ordinary* (or *deferred*) *annuity*.

B. If the payments occur at the beginning of each period, it is called an *annuity due*.

C. Annuities must have constant payments at fixed intervals for a fixed number of periods. If these conditions don't hold, then those cash flows don't constitute an annuity.

VI.   The future value of an annuity, FVA$_N$, is the total amount one would have at the end of the annuity period if each payment were invested at a given interest rate and held to the end of the annuity period.

A. FVA$_N$ is the compound sum of an ordinary annuity of N years and PMT is the periodic payment. The second line of the equation is a streamlined version of the first line.

$$FVA_N = PMT\sum_{t=1}^{N}(1+I)^{N-t}$$

$$= PMT\left[\frac{(1+I)^N - 1}{I}\right]$$

    1. If PMT = 100, I = 0.05, and N = 3, we can solve for FVA$_N$ as follows:

$$FVA_N = \$100\left[\frac{(1.05)^3 - 1}{0.05}\right]$$

$$= \$100\left(\frac{0.1576}{0.05}\right)$$

$$= \$100(3.1525) = \$315.25$$

B. With a financial calculator, the future value of an ordinary annuity can be found as follows: Enter N = 3, I/YR = 5, PV = 0, and PMT = -100. Then press the FV key, and 315.25 is displayed.

C. Most spreadsheets have a built-in function to find the future value of an annuity. The format of Excel's built-in function is FV(rate,nper,pmt,[pv],[type]).

1. The function allows you to specify the annuity "type," that is, whether the annuity is an ordinary annuity or an annuity due.

2. A zero indicates an ordinary annuity, while 1 indicates an annuity due. If type is left blank, it is assumed that the annuity is an ordinary annuity.

VII. **Each payment of an annuity due is compounded for one additional period, so the future value of the entire annuity is equal to the future value of an ordinary annuity compounded for one additional period.**

A. Each payment of an annuity due occurs one period earlier than the payments of an ordinary annuity, so the formula to calculate the future value of an annuity due is

$$\text{FVA}_{\text{due}} = \text{FVA}_{\text{ordinary}}(1 + \text{I})$$

B. Most financial calculators have a switch, or key, marked "DUE" or "BEG" that permits you to switch from end-of-period payments (an ordinary annuity) to beginning-of-period payments (an annuity due).

1. Switch your calculator to "BEG" mode, and calculate the future value of an annuity due as you would an ordinary annuity.

2. Do not forget to switch your calculator back to "END" mode when you are finished.

VIII. **The present value of an annuity is the single (lump sum) payment today that would be equivalent to the annuity payments received at fixed intervals over the annuity period.**

A. It is the amount today that would permit withdrawals of an equal amount (PMT) at the end (or beginning for an annuity due) of each period (must be same fixed interval) for N periods.

B. Defining PVA_N as the present value of an ordinary annuity of N years and PMT as the periodic payment, we can write

$$\text{PVA}_N = \text{PMT} \sum_{t=1}^{N} \left(\frac{1}{1+\text{I}} \right)^t$$

$$= \text{PMT} \left[\frac{1 - \dfrac{1}{(1+\text{I})^N}}{\text{I}} \right]$$

1. If PMT = 100, I = 0.05, and N = 3, we can solve for PVA_N as follows:

$$\text{PVA}_N = \$100 \left[\frac{1 - \dfrac{1}{(1.05)^3}}{0.05} \right]$$

$$= \$100 \left(\frac{0.1362}{0.05} \right)$$

$$= \$100(2.7232) = \$272.32$$

C. Using a financial calculator, enter N = 3, I/YR = 5, PMT = -100, and FV = 0, and then press the PV key, for an answer of $272.32.

D. Most spreadsheets have a built-in function to find the present value of an annuity. The format of Excel's built-in function is PV(rate,nper,pmt,[fv],[type]).

1. The function allows you to specify the annuity "type," that is, whether the annuity is an ordinary annuity or an annuity due. A zero indicates an ordinary annuity, while 1 indicates an annuity due. If you leave type blank, it is assumed that the annuity is an ordinary annuity.

2. For an annuity due, each payment is discounted for one less period, so the present value of the entire annuity is equal to the present value of an ordinary annuity multiplied by $(1 + I)$. Solving for PVA_{due}:

$$PVA_{due} = PVA_{ordinary}(1 + I)$$
$$= \$272.32(1.05) = \$285.94$$

3. Using a financial calculator, switch to the "BEG" mode, and then enter N = 3, I/YR = 5, PMT = -100, and FV = 0, and then press PV to get the answer, $285.94. Again, do not forget to switch your calculator back to "END" mode when you are finished.

IX. **We can find payments, periods, and interest rates for annuities. Here five variables come into play: N, I, PMT, FV, and PV. If we know any four variables, we can find the value of the fifth variable.**

A. Suppose you need to accumulate $10,000 in 5 years and you can earn a return of 6% on the savings, which are currently zero. What is the annual deposit that you need to make?

1. End Mode: N = 5, I/YR = 6, PV = 0, and FV = 10000. Solve for PMT = -$1,773.96.

2. Begin Mode: N = 5, I/YR = 6, PV = 0, and FV = 10000. Solve for PMT = -$1,673.55.

a. Because payments occur at the beginning of the period, the deposit is smaller than if they were made at the end of the period. Payments received at the beginning earn interest for one additional year.

3. The format of Excel's built-in function is PMT(rate,nper,pv,[fv],[type]).

a. "Type" indicates whether the annuity is an ordinary annuity or an annuity due. A zero indicates an ordinary annuity, while a 1 indicates an annuity due. If you leave type blank, it is assumed that the annuity is an ordinary annuity.

B. Suppose you still need to accumulate $10,000 and you can earn a return of 6% on the savings, which are currently zero. If you can only make deposits of $1,200, how long will it take you to reach your $10,000 goal?

1. End Mode: I/YR = 6, PV = 0, PMT = -1200, and FV = 10000. Solve for N = 6.96.

2. Begin Mode: I/YR = 6, PV = 0, PMT = -1200, and FV = 10000. Solve for N = 6.63.

a. Because payments occur at the beginning of the period, it takes less time to reach your goal than if payments were made at the end of the period. Payments received at the beginning earn interest for one additional year.

3. The format of Excel's built-in function is NPER(rate,pmt,pv,[fv],[type]).

a. "Type" indicates whether the annuity is an ordinary annuity or an annuity due. A zero indicates an ordinary annuity, while a 1 indicates an annuity due. If you leave type blank, it is assumed that the annuity is an ordinary annuity.

C. Suppose you still need to accumulate $10,000 in 5 years, you can save only $1,200 annually, and your current savings are zero. What rate of return would enable you to achieve your goal?

1. End Mode: N = 5, PV = 0, PMT = -1200, and FV = 10000. Solve for I/YR = 25.78%.

2. Begin Mode: N = 5, PV = 0, PMT = -1200, and FV = 10000. Solve for I/YR = 17.54%.

    a. Because payments occur at the beginning of the period, it takes a lower rate of return to reach your goal than if payments were made at the end of the period. Payments received at the beginning earn interest for one additional year.

3. The format of Excel's built-in function is RATE(nper,pmt,pv,[fv],[type],[guess]).

    a. "Type" indicates whether the annuity is an ordinary annuity or an annuity due. A zero indicates an ordinary annuity, while a 1 indicates an annuity due. If you leave type blank, it is assumed that the annuity is an ordinary annuity.

X. **An annuity that goes on indefinitely is called a perpetuity. The payments of a perpetuity constitute an infinite series.**

A. The present value of a perpetuity is:

$$PV(\text{Perpetuity}) = \frac{\text{Payment}}{\text{Interest rate}} = \frac{PMT}{I}$$

B. For example, if the interest rate were 12%, a perpetuity of $1,000 a year would have a present value of $1,000/0.12 = $8,333.33.

XI. **Many financial decisions require the analysis of uneven, or nonconstant, cash flows rather than a stream of fixed payments. Dividends on common stocks typically increase over time, and investments in capital equipment almost always generate uneven cash flows.**

A. The present value of an uneven stream of income is the sum of the PVs of the individual cash flow components. Similarly, the future value of an uneven stream of income is the sum of the FVs of the individual cash flow components.

1. *PMT (payment)* is the term designated for equal cash flows coming at regular intervals, while *CF (cash flow)* is the term designated for uneven cash flows.

2. With a financial calculator, enter each cash flow (beginning with the t = 0 cash flow) into the cash flow register, CF_j, enter the appropriate interest rate, and then press the NPV key to obtain the PV of the cash flow stream.

3. Some calculators have a net future value (NFV) key that allows you to obtain the FV of an uneven cash flow stream.

    a. Even if your calculator doesn't have the NFV feature, you can use the cash flow stream's net present value to find its net future value:

$$NFV = NPV(1 + I)^N$$

4. Spreadsheets are especially useful for solving problems with uneven cash flows. Just as with a financial calculator, you must enter the cash flows in the spreadsheet. To find the PV of an uneven cash flow stream, you can use Excel's NPV function.

B. If one knows the relevant cash flows, the effective interest rate can be calculated efficiently with a financial calculator.

1. Enter each cash flow (beginning with the t = 0 cash flow) into the cash flow register, CF$_j$, and then press the IRR key to obtain the interest rate of an uneven cash flow stream.

2. Excel has an IRR function that can be used to obtain the interest rate of an uneven cash flow stream.

XII. **Semiannual, quarterly, and other compounding periods more frequent than an annual basis are often used in financial transactions. Compounding on a nonannual basis requires an adjustment to both the compounding and discounting procedures discussed previously.**

A. Whenever payments occur more than once a year, you must make two conversions: (1) convert the stated interest rate into a "periodic rate," and (2) convert the number of years into "number of periods."

1. Periodic rate = Stated annual rate/Number of payments per year = I/M.

2. Number of periods = Number of years × Periods per year = N × M.

XIII. **Different compounding periods are used for different types of investments. If we are to compare investments or loans with different compounding periods properly, we need to put them on a common basis.**

A. The *nominal rate* is the rate that is quoted by borrowers and lenders. Nominal rates can only be compared with one another if the instruments being compared use the same number of compounding periods per year.

1. The nominal rate is never shown on a time line, or used as an input in a financial calculator, unless compounding occurs only once a year. In general, nonannual compounding can be handled one of two ways:

   a. State everything on a periodic rather than on an annual basis. Thus, N = 6 periods rather than N = 3 years and I = 3% instead of I = 6% with semiannual compounding.

   b. Find the effective annual rate (EAR) with the equation below and then use the EAR as the rate over the given number of years.

$$\text{EAR} = \left(1 + \frac{I_{NOM}}{M}\right)^M - 1$$

B. The *effective annual rate (EAR or EFF%)* is the rate that would have produced the same future value under annual compounding as would more frequent compounding at a given nominal rate.

1. The effective annual percentage rate is given by the following formula:

$$\text{Effective annual rate (EAR)} = \text{EFF\%} = \left(1 + \frac{I_{NOM}}{M}\right)^M - 1$$

   a. I$_{NOM}$ is the *nominal, or quoted, interest rate* and M is the number of compounding periods per year.

2. The format of Excel's built-in function to calculate the effective annual rate is EFFECT(nominal_rate,npery). Here, npery corresponds to the number of payments per year.

3. The EAR is useful in comparing securities with different compounding periods.

4. If a loan or investment uses annual compounding, then the nominal annual rate is also its effective annual rate.

    a. However, if compounding occurs more than once a year, the EFF% is higher than I_{NOM}.

C. The *annual percentage rate (APR)* is the periodic rate times the number of periods per year:

$$APR = I_{PER} \times M$$

XIV. **Fractional time periods are used when payments occur within periods, instead of either at the beginning or at the end of periods.**

A. Solving these problems requires using the fraction of the time period for N, number of periods, and then solving numerically, with a financial calculator, or with a computer spreadsheet program. (Some older calculators will produce incorrect answers because of their internal "solution" programs.)

XV. **An important application of compound interest involves amortized loans, which are paid off in equal installments over time.**

A. With a financial calculator, enter N (number of years), I/YR (interest rate), PV (amount borrowed), and FV = 0, and then press the PMT key to find the periodic payment.

B. Each payment consists partly of interest and partly of the repayment of principal. This breakdown is often developed in a *loan amortization schedule*.

    1. The interest component is largest in the first period, and it declines over the life of the loan.

    2. The repayment of principal is smallest in the first period, and it increases thereafter.

C. Financial calculators are programmed to calculate amortization tables.

D. Spreadsheets are ideal for developing amortization tables.

XVI. **Web Appendix 5A discusses the formulas necessary for continuous compounding and discounting.**

A. The equation for continuous compounding is $FV_N = PV(e^{IN})$, where e is the approximate value 2.7183.

B. The equation for continuous discounting is $PV = FV_N(e^{-IN})$.

XVII. **Web Appendix 5B discusses growing annuities, which are defined as a series of payments that are growing at a constant rate.**

A. These types of problems can be solved two ways.

    1. Use a financial calculator and calculate the real rate of return. The real rate of return is the nominal rate adjusted for inflation. This adjusted number is then used for I/YR.

        a. Real rate = $[(1 + r_{NOM})/(1 + Inflation)] - 1$.

    2. Use a spreadsheet model similar to an amortization table. You can then use Excel's goal seek function to find the inflation-adjusted withdrawal that produces a zero balance at the end of the growing annuity's term.

    3. If you need to solve for constant real income with end-of-year withdrawals, the initial withdrawal amount needs to be multiplied by 1 + inflation. This calculated amount would be the first withdrawal.

4. If you're calculating the initial deposit to accumulate a future sum, you must first calculate the purchasing power of the target sum as

$$\frac{\text{Target}}{(1+\text{Inflation})^N}$$

The purchasing power amount is entered as the FV, N = term, PV = 0, and I/YR = the real rate, and then solve for PMT.

Self-Test

Definitional Questions

1. The beginning value of an account or investment in a project is known as its _____ value.

2. The difference between a savings account's present value and its future value at the end of the period is due to _____ earned during the period.

3. The process of finding present values is often referred to as _____ and is the reverse of the _____ process.

4. A series of payments of a constant amount at fixed intervals for a specified number of periods is a(n) _____. If the payments occur at the end of each period it is a(n) _____ annuity, while if the payments occur at the beginning of each period it is an annuity _____.

5. The present value of an uneven stream of future payments is the _____ of the PVs of the individual payments.

6. Since different types of investments use different compounding periods, it is important to distinguish between the quoted, or _____, rate and the _____ annual interest rate.

7. The time _____ is one of the most important tools in time value of money calculations; it helps visualize what is happening in the situation at hand.

8. An annuity that goes on indefinitely is called a(n) _____.

9. _____ loans are those that are paid off in equal installments over time.

10. The breakdown of each loan payment as partly interest and partly principal is developed in a loan _____ schedule.

11. The _____ cost rate is the rate of return that could be earned on an alternative investment of similar risk.

12. _____ is the term designated for equal cash flows coming at regular intervals, while _____ is the term designated for uneven cash flows.

13. The _____ annual rate is that rate that would have produced the same future value under annual compounding as would more frequent compounding at a given nominal rate.

14. The _____ percentage rate is the periodic rate times the number of periods per year.

15. The value of a business (or any asset, including stocks and bonds) is the _____ value of its expected future cash flows.

16. Whenever payments occur more than once a year, you must make two conversions: (1) convert the stated interest rate into a(n) _____ rate, and (2) convert the number of years into number of _____.

17. If a loan or investment uses _____ compounding, then its nominal rate is also its effective rate.

18. _____ time periods are used when payments occur within periods, instead of either at the beginning or at the end of periods.

19. A(n) _____ _____ is defined as a series of payments that increase at a constant rate.

20. The _____ rate of return is equal to the nominal rate adjusted for inflation.

Conceptual Questions

1. If a bank uses quarterly compounding for savings accounts, the nominal rate will be greater than the effective annual rate (EAR).

    a. True
    b. False

2. If money has time value (that is, I > 0), the future value of some amount of money will always be more than the amount invested. The present value of some amount to be received in the future is always less than the amount to be received.

    a. True
    b. False

3. You have determined the profitability of a planned project by finding the present value of all the cash flows from that project. Which of the following would cause the project to look *less* appealing, that is, have a *lower* present value?

    a. The discount rate decreases.
    b. The cash flows are extended over a longer period of time.
    c. The discount rate increases.
    d. Statements b and c are correct.
    e. Statements a and b are correct.

4. As the discount rate increases without limit, the present value of a future cash inflow

    a. Gets larger without limit.
    b. Stays unchanged.
    c. Approaches zero.
    d. Gets smaller without limit; that is, approaches minus infinity.
    e. Goes to e^{IN}.

5. Which of the following statements is correct?

    a. Except in situations where compounding occurs annually, the periodic interest rate exceeds the nominal interest rate.
    b. The effective annual rate always exceeds the nominal rate, no matter how few or many compounding periods occur each year.

c. If compounding occurs more frequently than once a year, and if payments are made at times other than at the end of compounding periods, it is impossible to determine present or future values, even with a financial calculator. The reason is that under these conditions, the basic assumptions of discounted cash flow analysis are not met.

d. Assume that compounding occurs quarterly, that the nominal interest rate is 8%, and that you need to find the present value of $1,000 due 6 months from today. You could get the correct answer by discounting the $1,000 at 2% for 2 periods.

e. All of the above statements are false.

Problems

Note: In working these problems, you may get an answer that differs from ours by a few cents due to rounding differences. This should not concern you; just pick the closest answer.

1. Assume that you purchase a 6-year, 8% savings certificate for $1,000. If interest is compounded annually, what will be the value of the certificate when it matures?

   a. $ 630.17
   b. $1,469.33
   c. $1,677.10
   d. $1,586.87
   e. $1,766.33

2. Assume that you purchase a 6-year, 8% savings certificate for $1,000. What is the difference between the ending value of the savings certificate if it were compounded semiannually and if it were compounded annually?

   a. The semiannual is worth $14.16 more than the annual.
   b. The semiannual is worth $14.16 less than the annual.
   c. The semiannual is worth $21.54 more than the annual.
   d. The semiannual is worth $21.54 less than the annual.
   e. The semiannual is worth the same as the annual.

3. A friend promises to pay you $600 two years from now if you loan him $500 today. What annual interest rate is your friend offering?

   a.   7.5%
   b.   8.5%
   c.   9.5%
   d. 10.5%
   e. 11.5%

4. At an inflation rate of 9%, the purchasing power of $1 would be cut in half in just over 8 years (some calculators round to 9 years). How long, to the nearest year, would it take for the purchasing power of $1 to be cut in half if the inflation rate were only 4%?

   a. 12 years
   b. 15 years
   c. 18 years
   d. 20 years
   e. 23 years

5. Jane Smith has $20,000 in a brokerage account, and she plans to contribute an additional $7,500 to the account at the end of every year. The brokerage account has an expected annual return of 8%. If Jane's goal is to accumulate $375,000 in the account, how many years will it take for Jane to reach her goal?

   a. 5.20
   b. 10.00
   c. 12.50
   d. 16.33
   e. 18.40

6. You are offered an investment opportunity with the "guarantee" that your investment will double in 5 years. Assuming annual compounding, what annual rate of return would this investment provide?

   a. 40.00%
   b. 100.00%
   c. 14.87%
   d. 20.00%
   e. 18.74%

7. You decide to begin saving towards the purchase of a new car in 5 years. If you put $1,000 at the end of each of the next 5 years in a savings account paying 6% compounded annually, how much will you accumulate after 5 years?

   a. $6,691.13
   b. $5,637.09
   c. $1,338.23
   d. $5,975.32
   e. $5,731.94

8. Suppose you make 5 annual deposits of $1,000 in a savings account paying 6% compounded annually. The deposits are made at the beginning of each year. What amount would be in your account in Year 5?

   a. $6,691.13
   b. $5,637.09
   c. $1,338.23
   d. $5,975.32
   e. $5,731.94

9. What would be the ending amount if you deposit $500 in an account at the end of each 6-month period for 5 years and the account paid 6% compounded semiannually?

   a. $6,691.13
   b. $5,637.09
   c. $1,338.23
   d. $5,975.32
   e. $5,731.94

10. Calculate the present value of $1,000 to be received at the end of 8 years. Assume an annual interest rate of 7%.

    a. $ 582.01
    b. $1,718.19
    c. $ 531.82
    d. $5,971.30
    e. $ 649.37

11. How much would you be willing to pay today for an investment that would return $800 each year at the end of each of the next 6 years? Assume an annual interest rate of 5%.

    a. $5,441.53
    b. $4,800.00
    c. $3,369.89
    d. $4,060.55
    e. $4,632.37

12. You have applied for a mortgage of $60,000 to finance the purchase of a new home. The bank will require you to make annual payments of $7,047.55 at the end of each of the next 20 years. Determine the interest rate in effect on this mortgage.

    a. 8.0%
    b. 9.8%
    c. 10.0%
    d. 10.5%
    e. 11.2%

13. If you would like to accumulate $7,500 over the next 5 years, how much must you deposit each six months, starting six months from now, given a 6% interest rate and semiannual compounding?

    a. $1,330.47
    b. $ 879.23
    c. $ 654.23
    d. $ 569.00
    e. $ 732.67

14. A company is offering bonds that pay $100 per year indefinitely. If you require a 12% return on these bonds—that is, the discount rate is 12%—what is the value of each bond?

    a. $1,000.00
    b. $ 962.00
    c. $ 904.67
    d. $ 866.67
    e. $ 833.33

15. What is the present value (t = 0) of the following cash flows if the discount rate is 12%?

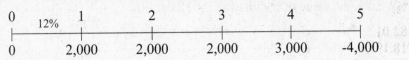

a. $4,782.43
b. $4,440.51
c. $4,221.79
d. $4,041.23
e. $3,997.98

16. What is the effective annual rate (EAR) of 12% compounded monthly?

   a. 12.00%
   b. 12.55%
   c. 12.68%
   d. 12.75%
   e. 13.00%

17. Martha Mills, manager of Plaza Gold Emporium, wants to sell on credit, giving customers 4 months in which to pay. However, Martha will have to borrow from her bank to carry the accounts receivable. The bank will charge a nominal 18%, but with monthly compounding. Martha wants to quote a nominal rate to her customers (all of whom are expected to pay on time at the end of 4 months) *that will exactly cover her financing costs*. What nominal annual rate should she quote to her credit customers?

   a. 15.44%
   b. 19.56%
   c. 17.11%
   d. 18.41%
   e. 16.88%

18. How much *principal* will be repaid in the *second* year on a 20-year, $60,000 mortgage requiring annual payments and a 10% annual interest rate?

   a. $1,152.34
   b. $1,725.70
   c. $5,895.24
   d. $7,047.58
   e. $1,047.58

19. You have $1,000 invested in an account that pays 16% compounded annually. A commission agent (called a "finder") can locate for you an equally safe deposit that will pay 16%, compounded quarterly, for 2 years. What is the maximum amount you should be willing to pay him now as a fee for locating the new account?

   a. $10.92
   b. $13.78
   c. $16.14
   d. $16.78
   e. $21.13

20. The present value (t = 0) of the following cash flow stream is $11,958.20 when discounted at 12% annually. What is the value of the missing t = 2 cash flow?

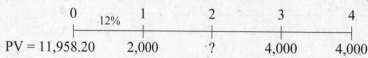

a. $4,000.00
b. $4,500.00
c. $5,000.33
d. $5,500.50
e. $6,000.16

21. Today is your birthday, and you decide to start saving for your college education. You will begin college on your 18th birthday and will need $4,000 per year at the *end* of each of the following 4 years. You will make a deposit 1 year from today in an account paying 12% annually and continue to make an identical deposit each year up to and including the year you begin college. If a deposit amount of $2,542.05 will allow you to reach your goal, what birthday are you celebrating today?

a. 13
b. 14
c. 15
d. 16
e. 17

22. Assume that your aunt sold her house on December 31 and that she took a mortgage in the amount of $50,000 as part of the payment. The mortgage has a stated (or nominal) interest rate of 8%, but it calls for payments every 6 months, beginning on June 30, and the mortgage is to be amortized over 20 years. Now, one year later, your aunt must file Schedule B of her tax return with the IRS informing them of the interest that was included in the two payments made during the year. (This interest will be income to your aunt and a deduction to the buyer of the house.) What is the *total* amount of *interest* that was paid during the *first* year?

a. $1,978.95
b. $ 526.17
c. $3,978.95
d. $2,000.00
e. $ 750.02

23. Assume that you inherited some money. A friend of yours is working as an unpaid intern at a local brokerage firm, and her boss is selling some securities that call for five payments, $75 at the end of each of the next 4 years, plus a payment of $1,075 at the end of Year 5. Your friend says she can get you some of these securities at a cost of $960 each. Your money is now invested in a bank that pays an 8% nominal (quoted) interest rate, but with quarterly compounding. You regard the securities as being just as safe, and as liquid, as your bank deposit, so your required effective annual rate of return on the securities is the same as that on your bank deposit. You must calculate the value of the securities to decide whether they are a good investment. What is their present value to you?

a. $ 957.75
b. $ 888.66
c. $ 923.44
d. $1,015.25
e. $ 970.51

24. Your company is planning to borrow $500,000 on a 5-year, 7%, annual payment, fully-amortized term loan. What fraction of the payment made at the end of the *second* year will represent *repayment of principal*?

    a. 76.29%
    b. 42.82%
    c. 50.28%
    d. 49.72%
    e. 60.27%

25. Your firm can borrow from its bank for one month. The loan will have to be "rolled over" at the end of the month, but you are sure the rollover will be allowed. The nominal interest rate is 14%, but interest will have to be paid at the end of each month, so the bank interest rate is 14%, monthly compounding. Alternatively, your firm can borrow from an insurance company at a nominal rate that would involve quarterly compounding. What nominal rate with quarterly compounding would be equivalent to the rate charged by the bank?

    a. 12.44%
    b. 14.16%
    c. 14.93%
    d. 13.12%
    e. 14.55%

26. Assume that you have $15,000 in a bank account that pays 5% annual interest. You plan to go back to school for a combination MBA/law degree 5 years from today. It will take you an additional 5 years to complete your graduate studies. You figure you will need a fixed income of $25,000 in today's dollars; that is, you will need $25,000 of today's dollars during your first year and each subsequent year. *(Thus, your real income will decline while you are in school.)* You will withdraw funds for your annual expenses at the beginning of each year. Inflation is expected to occur at the rate of 3% per year. How much must you save during each of the next 5 years in order to achieve your goal? The first increment of savings will be deposited one year from today.

    a. $20,241.66
    b. $19,224.55
    c. $18,792.11
    d. $19,559.42
    e. $20,378.82

27. You plan to buy a new TV. The dealer offers to sell the set to you on credit. You will have 3 months in which to pay, but the dealer says you will be charged a 15% interest rate; that is, the nominal rate is 15%, quarterly compounding. As an alternative to buying on credit, you can borrow the funds from your bank, but the bank will make you pay interest each month. At what nominal bank interest rate should you be indifferent between the two types of credit?

    a. 13.7643%
    b. 14.2107%
    c. 14.8163%
    d. 15.5397%
    e. 15.3984%

79

28. Assume that your father is now 40 years old, that he plans to retire in 20 years, and that he expects to live for 25 years after he retires, that is, until he is 85. He wants a fixed retirement income that has the same purchasing power at the time he retires as $75,000 has today. (He realizes that the real value of his retirement income will decline year-by-year after he retires.) His retirement income will begin the day he retires, 20 years from today, and he will then receive 24 additional annual payments. Inflation is expected to be 4% per year from today forward; he currently has $200,000 saved; and he expects to earn a return on his savings of 7% per year, annual compounding. To the nearest dollar, how much must he save during each of the next 20 years (with deposits being made at the end of each year) to meet his retirement goal?

    a. $31,105.90
    b. $35,709.25
    c. $54,332.88
    d. $41,987.33
    e. $62,191.25

29. A rookie quarterback is in the process of negotiating his first contract. The team's general manager has offered him three possible contracts. Each of the contracts lasts for four years. All of the money is guaranteed and is paid at the end of each year. The payment terms of the contracts are listed below:

Year	Contract 1	Contract 2	Contract 3
1	$1.5 million	$1.0 million	$3.5 million
2	1.5 million	1.5 million	0.5 million
3	1.5 million	2.0 million	0.5 million
4	1.5 million	2.5 million	0.5 million

    The quarterback discounts all cash flows at 12%. Which of the three contracts offers the most value?

    a. Contract 1; its present value is $4.56 million.
    b. Contract 2; its present value is $5.10 million.
    c. Contract 3; its present value is $4.20 million.
    d. Either Contract 2 or Contract 3; each provides a present value of $5.10 million.
    e. Either Contract 1 or Contract 2; each provides a present value of $5.10 million.

30. The Wade family is interested in buying a home. The family is applying for a $200,000 30-year mortgage. Under the terms of the mortgage, they will receive $200,000 today to help purchase their home. The loan will be fully amortized over the next 30 years. Current mortgage rates are 7.5%. Interest is compounded monthly and all payments are due at the end of the month. What is the monthly mortgage payment?

    a. $ 989.66
    b. $1,047.50
    c. $1,111.25
    d. $1,398.43
    e. $1,563.97

31. Consider a $200,000 30-year mortgage with monthly payments. If the interest is 7.5% with monthly compounding, what portion of the mortgage payments during the *first* year will go toward *interest*?

    a.   89%
    b.   100%
    c.   75%
    d.   65%
    e.   95%

32. Consider a $200,000 30-year mortgage with monthly payments. If the interest is 7.5% with monthly compounding, what will be the remaining balance on the mortgage after five years?

    a. $ 73,141
    b. $166,752
    c. $189,235
    d. $195,750
    e. $190,433

33. Consider a $200,000 30-year mortgage with monthly payments. If the interest is 7.5% with monthly compounding, how much could you borrow today if you were willing to have an $1,800 monthly mortgage payment?

    a. $225,557
    b. $257,432
    c. $210,333
    d. $244,125
    e. $253,456

34. Janet and Denise have both been given $15,000 by their grandparents today on their 21st birthdays. They want to save for their future and have aspirations of one day being millionaires. Each woman plans to make annual contributions on her birthday, beginning next year. Janet and Denise have each opened investment accounts at the 1st National Bank and 2nd National Bank, respectively, and they expect to earn nominal returns of 6% and 7%, respectively. Janet has already decided to deposit $7,500 each year into her investment account, while Denise is unsure of the amount she will deposit annually. How many years will it take Janet before she reaches her investment goal of $1 million?

    a.   20.33
    b.   25.50
    c.   30.00
    d.   32.45
    e.   35.76

35. Refer to Problem 34. If Denise decides to make the same annual contributions as Janet, how much sooner (in years) would she reach the investment goal?

    a.   2.50
    b.   3.18
    c.   3.75
    d.   4.00
    e.   4.25

36. Refer to Problem 34. Suppose Denise was interested in reaching the investment goal at the same time as Janet. What is the minimum monthly contribution she could make in order to reach $1 million at the same time as Janet?

    a. $5,683.44
    b. $4,250.00
    c. $6,195.76
    d. $5,333.33
    e. $4,888.97

37. John has just won the state lottery and has three award options from which to choose. He can elect to receive a lump sum payment today of $46 million, 10 annual end-of-year payments of $7 million, or 30 annual end-of-year payments of $4 million. If he expects to earn a 7% annual return on his investments, which option should he choose?

    a. Lump sum
    b. 10 payments
    c. 30 payments
    d. It doesn't matter, the present value of each of the options is equal.

38. John has just won the state lottery and has three award options from which to choose. He can elect to receive a lump sum payment today of $46 million, 10 annual end-of-year payments of $7 million, or 30 annual end-of-year payments of $4 million. If he expects to earn an 8% annual return on his investments, which option should he choose?

    a. Lump sum
    b. 10 payments
    c. 30 payments
    d. It doesn't matter, the present value of each of the options is equal.

39. John has just won the state lottery and has three award options from which to choose. He can elect to receive a lump sum payment today of $46 million, 10 annual end-of-year payments of $7 million, or 30 annual end-of-year payments of $4 million. If he expects to earn a 9% annual return on his investments, which option should he choose?

    a. Lump sum
    b. 10 payments
    c. 30 payments
    d. It doesn't matter, the present value of each of the options is equal.

40. Henry has saved $5,000 and intends to use his savings as a down payment on a new car. After careful examination of his income and expenses, Henry has concluded that the most he can afford to spend every month on his car payment is $425. The car loan that Henry uses to buy the car will have an APR of 10%. What is the price of the most expensive car that Henry can afford if he finances his new car for 48 months?

    a. $16,756.97
    b. $17,500.00
    c. $19,125.25
    d. $21,756.97
    e. $22,450.50

41. Henry has saved $5,000 and intends to use his savings as a down payment on a new car. After careful examination of his income and expenses, Henry has concluded that the most he can afford to spend every month on his car payment is $425. The car loan that Henry uses to buy the car will have an APR of 10%. What is the price of the most expensive car that Henry can afford if he finances his new car for 60 months?

    a. $18,333.33
    b. $20,002.78
    c. $21,756.97
    d. $23,750.00
    e. $25,002.78

Web Appendix 5A

Note: Study the information given in Web Appendix 5A, Continuous Compounding and Discounting, before working the following problems.

1. If you receive $30,000 today and can invest it at a 4% annual rate compounded continuously, what will be its future value in 10 years?

    a. $31,224.32
    b. $38,327.77
    c. $40,765.66
    d. $44,754.74
    e. $42,121.00

2. What is the present value of $125,000 due in 15 years, if the appropriate continuous discount rate is 6%?

    a. $44,754.74
    b. $50,821.21
    c. $38,327.77
    d. $42,121.00
    e. $40,765.66

Web Appendix 5B

Note: Study the information given in Web Appendix 5B, Growing Annuities, before working the following problems.

1. If the nominal interest rate is 8% and the expected inflation rate is 2.8%, what is the expected real rate of return?

    a. 4.81%
    b. 5.06%
    c. 5.31%
    d. 5.58%
    e. 5.86%

2. You plan to make annual deposits into a bank account that pays a 4.50% nominal annual rate. You think inflation will amount to 3.20% per year. What is the expected annual real rate at which your money will grow?

   a. 1.26%
   b. 1.39%
   c. 1.52%
   d. 1.68%
   e. 1.84%

3. Your father now has $500,000 invested in an account that pays 7.00%. He expects inflation to average 2.50%, and he wants to make annual constant dollar (real) beginning-of-year withdrawals over each of the next 15 years and end up with a zero balance after the 15th year. How large will his initial withdrawal (and thus constant dollar (real) withdrawals) be?

   a. $36,053
   b. $37,950
   c. $39,947
   d. $42,050
   e. $44,263

4. Your father now has $500,000 invested in an account that pays 7.00%. He expects inflation to average 2.50%, and he wants to make annual constant dollar (real) end-of-year withdrawals over each of the next 15 years and end up with a zero balance after the 15th year. How large will his initial withdrawal (and thus constant dollar (real) withdrawals) be?

   a. $42,744
   b. $44,993
   c. $47,361
   d. $49,730
   e. $52,216

5. You anticipate that you will need $2,000,000 when you retire 25 years from now. You plan to make 25 deposits, beginning today, in a bank account that will pay 7% interest, compounded annually. You expect to receive annual raises of 2% to match expected inflation of 2%, so you will increase the amount you deposit each year by 2%. (That is, your 2nd deposit will be 2% greater than your first, the 3rd will be 2% greater than the 2nd, etc.) How much must your 1st deposit be if you are to meet your goal?

   a. $21,160
   b. $22,273
   c. $23,446
   d. $24,680
   e. $25,914

6. You want to accumulate $1,500,000 in your 401(k) plan by your retirement date, which is 30 years from now. You will make 30 deposits into your plan, with the first deposit occurring today. The plan's rate of return typically averages 8.5%. You expect to increase each deposit by 2.5% as your income grows with inflation. (That is, your 2nd deposit will be 2.5% greater than your first, the 3rd will be 2.5% greater than the 2nd, etc.) How much must your 1st deposit at t = 0 be to enable you to meet your goal?

    a. $7,913
    b. $8,329
    c. $8,768
    d. $9,206
    e. $9,666

Answers

Definitional Questions

1. present
2. interest
3. discounting; compounding
4. annuity; ordinary; due
5. sum
6. nominal; effective
7. line
8. perpetuity
9. Amortized
10. amortization

11. opportunity
12. PMT; CF
13. effective
14. annual
15. present
16. periodic; periods
17. annual
18. Fractional
19. growing annuity
20. real

Conceptual Questions

1. b. The EAR is always greater than or equal to the nominal rate.

2. a. Both these statements are correct.

3. d. The slower the cash flows come in and the higher the interest rate, the smaller the present value.

4. c. As the discount rate increases, the present value of a future sum decreases and eventually approaches zero.

5. d. Using a financial calculator, enter N = 2, I/YR = 2, PMT = 0, and FV = 1000 to find PV = -961.1688.

Solutions

Problems

1. d.

        0   8%   1   2   3   4   5   6
        |───────────────|───────────|───────────|───────────|───────────|───────────|
        -1,000   FV_6 = ?

    With a financial calculator, input N = 6, I/YR = 8, PV = -1000, PMT = 0, and solve for
    FV = $1,586.87.

2. a.

        0   1   2   3   4   5   6   Years
        0   4% 1   2   3   4   5   6   7   8   9   10 11 12 Periods
        |───────|───|───|───|───|───|───|───|───|───|───|───|
        -1,000   FV_12 = ?

    Semiannual compounding: Input N = 12, I/YR = 4, PV = -1000, and PMT = 0, and then solve for
    FV = $1,601.03.

    Annual compounding: Input N = 6, I/YR = 8, PV = -1000, and PMT = 0, and then solve for
    FV = $1,586.87.

    The difference, $1,601.03 – $1,586.87 = $14.16.

3. c.

        0   I = ?   1   2
        |───────────────|───────────|
        -500   600

    With a financial calculator, input N = 2, PV = -500, PMT = 0, FV = 600, and solve for I/YR
    = 9.54% ≈ 9.5%.

4. c.

        0   4%   N = ?
        |───────────────|
        -1.00   0.50

    With a financial calculator, input I/YR = 4, PV = -1.00, PMT = 0, and FV = 0.50. Solve for
    N = 17.67 ≈ 18 years.

5. e. Using your financial calculator, enter the following data: I/YR = 8; PV = -20000;
        PMT = -7500; FV = 375000; N = ? Solve for N = 18.4. It will take 18.4 years for Jane to
        accumulate $375,000.

6. c. Assume any value for the present value and double it:

        0   I = ?   1   2   3   4   5
        |───────────────|───────────|───────────|───────────|───────────|
        -1   2

    With a financial calculator, input N = 5, PV = -1, PMT = 0, FV = 2, and solve for I/YR = 14.87%.

7. b.

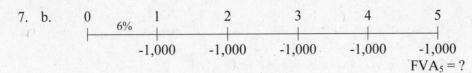

With a financial calculator, input N = 5, I/YR = 6, PV = 0, PMT = -1000, and solve for FV = $5,637.09.

8. d.

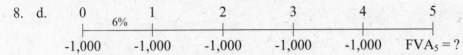

With a financial calculator, switch to "BEG" mode, then input N = 5, I/YR = 6, PV = 0, PMT = -1000, and solve for FV = $5,975.32. Be sure to switch back to "END" mode after working this problem.

9. e.

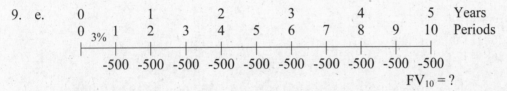

With a financial calculator, input N = 10, I/YR = 3, PV = 0, PMT = -500, and solve for FV = $5,731.94.

10. a.

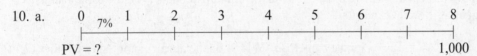

With a financial calculator, input N = 8, I/YR = 7, PMT = 0, FV = 1000, and solve for PV = -$582.01.

11. d.

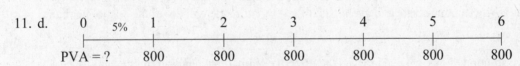

With a financial calculator, input N = 6, I/YR = 5, PMT = 800, FV = 0, and solve for PV = -$4,060.55.

12. c.

```
        0         1           2            3                20
        ├─── I = ? ┼───────────┼────────────┼──── • • • ────┤
    60,000    -7,047.55   -7,047.55    -7,047.55         -7,047.55
```

With a financial calculator, input N = 20, PV = 60000, PMT = -7047.55, FV = 0, and solve for I/YR = 10.00%.

13. c.

0		1		2		3		4		5	Years
0	1	2	3	4	5	6	7	8	9	10	Periods

3%

-PMT -PMT -PMT -PMT -PMT -PMT -PMT -PMT -PMT -PMT

7,500

With a financial calculator, input N = 10, I/YR = 3, PV = 0, FV = 7500, and solve for PMT = -$654.23.

14. e.　$PV = PMT/I = \$100/0.12 = \$833.33$

15. b.　With a financial calculator, using the cash flow register, CF_j, input 0; 2000; 2000; 2000; 3000; and -4000. Enter I/YR = 12 and solve for NPV = $4,440.51.

16. c.

$$\begin{aligned}
EAR &= (1 + I_{NOM}/M)^M - 1.0 \\
&= (1 + 0.12/12)^{12} - 1.0 \\
&= (1.01)^{12} - 1.0 \\
&= 1.1268 - 1.0 \\
&= 0.1268 = 12.68\%
\end{aligned}$$

With a financial calculator, enter P/YR = 12 and NOM% = 12, and then solve for EFF% = 12.68%. Don't forget to return P/YR = 1 after solving this problem.

17. d.　Here we want to have the same effective annual rate on the credit extended as on the bank loan that will be used to finance the credit extension.

First, we must find the EAR = EFF% on the bank loan. With a financial calculator, enter P/YR = 12, NOM% = 18, and press EFF% to get EAR = 19.56%.

Because 4 months of credit is being given there are 3 credit periods in a year, so enter P/YR = 3, EFF% = EAR = 19.56, and press NOM% to find the nominal rate of 18.41%. Therefore, if Martha charges an 18.41% nominal rate and gives credit for 4 months, she will cover the cost of her bank loan.

Alternative solution: First, we need to find the effective annual rate charged by the bank:

$$\begin{aligned}
EAR &= (1 + I_{NOM}/M)^M - 1 \\
&= (1 + 0.18/12)^{12} - 1 \\
&= (1.0150)^{12} - 1 = 19.56\%
\end{aligned}$$

Now, we can find the nominal rate Martha must quote her customers so that her financing costs are exactly covered:

$$\begin{aligned}
19.56\% &= (1 + I_{NOM}/3)^3 - 1 \\
1.1956 &= (1 + I_{NOM}/3)^3 \\
1.0614 &= 1 + I_{NOM}/3 \\
0.0614 &= I_{NOM}/3 \\
I_{NOM} &= 18.41\%
\end{aligned}$$

18. a. N = 20; I/YR = 10; PV = -60000; FV = 0; and solve for PMT = $7,047.58.

Year	Payment	Interest	Repayment on Principal	Remaining Principal Balance
1	$7,047.58	$6,000.00	$1,047.58	$58,952.42
2	7,047.58	5,895.24	1,152.34	57,800.08

19. d. Currently:

Find the future value of your current account:
With a financial calculator, input N = 2, I/YR = 16, PV = -1000, PMT = 0, and solve for FV = $1,345.60.

Find the future value of the new account:
With a financial calculator, input N = 8, I/YR = 4, PV = -1000, PMT = 0, and solve for FV = $1,368.57.

Thus, the new account will be worth $1,368.57 – $1,345.60 = $22.97 more after 2 years.

Determine how much you're willing to pay the agent today:
With a financial calculator, input N = 8, I/YR = 4, PMT = 0, FV = 22.97, and solve for PV = -$16.78.

Therefore, the most you should be willing to pay the agent for locating the new account is $16.78.

20. e. With a financial calculator, input cash flows into the cash flow register, using -11,958.20 as the cash flow for time 0 (CF$_0$), and using 0 as the value for the unknown cash flow, input I/YR = 12, and then press the NPV key to solve for the present value of the unknown cash flow, $4,783.29. This value should be compounded by $(1.12)^2$, so that $4,783.29(1.2544) = $6,000.16.

21. b. First, how much must you accumulate on your 18th birthday?

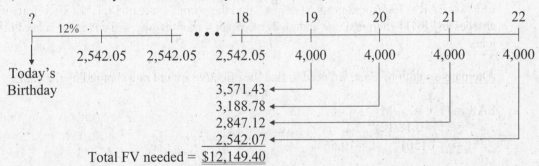

Using a financial calculator (with the calculator set for an ordinary annuity), enter N = 4, I/YR = 12, PMT = 4000, FV = 0, and solve for PV = -$12,149.40. This is the amount (or lump sum) that must be present in your bank account on your 18th birthday in order for you to be able to withdraw $4,000 at the end of each of the next 4 years.

89

Now, how many payments of $2,542.05 must you make to accumulate $12,149.40?

Using a financial calculator, enter I/YR = 12, PV = 0, PMT = -2542.05, FV = 12149.40, and solve for N = 4. Therefore, if you make payments at 18, 17, 16, and 15, you are now 14.

22. c.   This can be done with a calculator by specifying an interest rate of 4% per period for 40 periods.

$N = 20 \times 2 = 40$
$I = 8/2 = 4$
$PV = -50000$
$FV = 0$

PMT = $2,526.17

Set up an amortization table:

Period	Beginning Balance	Payment	Interest	Payment of Principal	Ending Balance
1	$50,000.00	$2,526.17	$2,000.00	$526.17	$49,473.83
2	49,473.83	2,526.17	1,978.95		
			$3,978.95		

You can really just work the problem with a financial calculator using the amortization function. Find the interest in each 6-month period, sum them, and you have the answer. Even simpler, with some calculators such as the HP-17BII, just input 2 for periods and press INT to get the interest during the first year, $3,978.95.

23. e.

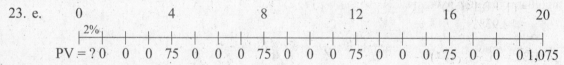

Input the cash flows in the cash flow register, input I/YR = 2, and solve for NPV = $970.51.

24. a.   Input N = 5, I/YR = 7, PV = -500000, and FV = 0 to solve for PMT = $121,945.35.

Year	Beginning Balance	Payment	Interest	Payment of Principal	Ending Balance
1	$500,000.00	$121,945.35	$35,000.00	$86,945.35	$413,054.65
2	413,054.65	121,945.35	28,913.83	93,031.52	320,023.13

The fraction that is principal is $93,031.52/$121,945.35 = 76.29%.

25. b. Start with a time line to picture the situation:

Bank: 14% nominal; EAR = 14.93%.

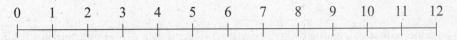

Insurance company: EAR = 14.93%; Nominal = 14.16%.

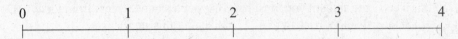

Here we must find the EAR on the bank loan and then find the nominal interest rate with quarterly compounding for that EAR. The bank loan rate is a nominal 14% with monthly compounding.

Using the interest conversion feature of the calculator, or the EAR formula, we must find the EAR on the bank loan. Enter P/YR = 12 and NOM% = 14, and then press the EFF% key to find EAR bank loan = 14.93%.

Now, we can find the nominal rate with quarterly compounding that also has an EAR of 14.93%. Enter P/YR = 4 and EFF% = 14.93, and then press the NOM% key to get 14.16%. If the insurance company quotes a nominal rate of 14.16%, with quarterly compounding, then the bank and insurance company loans would be equivalent in the sense that they both have the same effective annual rate, 14.93%.

Alternative solution:

$$\begin{aligned} EAR &= (1 + I_{NOM}/12)^{12} - 1 \\ &= (1 + 0.14/12)^{12} - 1 \\ &= 14.93\% \end{aligned}$$

$$\begin{aligned} 14.93\% &= (1 + I_{NOM}/4)^4 - 1 \\ 1.1493 &= (1 + I_{NOM}/4)^4 \\ 1.0354 &= 1 + I_{NOM}/4 \\ 0.0354 &= I_{NOM}/4 \\ I_{NOM} &= 14.16\% \end{aligned}$$

26. e. Inflation = 3%

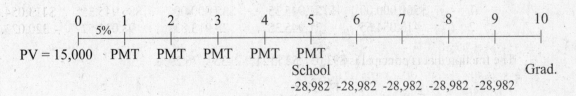

Fixed income = $25,000(1.03)^5 = $28,981.85$.

1. Find the FV of $25,000 compounded for 5 years at 3%; that FV, $28,981.85, is the amount you will need each year while you are in school. (Note: Your real income will decline.)

2. You must have enough in 5 years to make the $28,981.85 payments to yourself. These payments will begin as soon as you start school, so we are dealing with a 5-year, 5% interest rate *annuity due*. Set the calculator to "BEG" mode, because we are dealing with an annuity due, and then enter N = 5, I/YR = 5, PMT = -28981.85, and FV = 0. Then press the PV key to find the PV, $131,750.06. This is the amount you must have in your account 5 years from today. (Do not forget to switch the calculator back to "END" mode after this step.)

3. You now have $15,000. It will grow at 5% to $19,144.22 after 5 years. Enter N = 5, I/YR = 5, PV = -15000, and PMT = 0, to solve for FV = $19,144.22. You can subtract this amount to determine the FV of the amount you must save: $131,750.06 – $19,144.22 = $112,605.84.

4. Therefore, you must accumulate an additional $112,605.84 by saving PMT per year for 5 years, with the first PMT being deposited at the end of this year and earning a 5% interest rate. Now we have an ordinary annuity, so be sure you returned your calculator to "END" mode. Enter N = 5, I/YR = 5, PV = 0, FV = 112605.84, and then press PMT to find the required payments, -$20,378.82.

27. c. Find the EAR on the TV dealer's credit. Use the interest conversion feature of your calculator. First, though, note that if you are charged a 15% nominal rate, you will have to pay interest of 15%/4 = 3.75% after 3 months. The dealer then has the use of the interest, so he can earn 3.75% on it for the next three months, and so forth. Thus, we are dealing with quarterly compounding. The nominal rate is 15%, quarterly compounding.

Enter NOM% = 15, P/YR = 4, and then press EFF% to get EAR = 15.8650%.

You should be indifferent between the dealer credit and the bank loan if the bank loan has an EAR of 15.8650%. The bank is using monthly compounding, or 12 periods per year. To find the nominal rate at which you should be indifferent, enter P/YR = 12, EFF% = 15.8650, and then press NOM% to get NOM% = 14.8163%.

Conclusion: A loan that has a 14.8163% nominal rate with monthly compounding is equivalent to a 15% nominal rate loan with quarterly compounding. Both have an EAR of 15.8650%.

Alternative Solution

$$EAR = (1 + I_{NOM}/4)^4 - 1$$
$$= (1 + 0.15/4)^4 - 1$$
$$= (1.0375)^4 - 1$$
$$= 15.8650\%$$

$$15.8650\% = (1 + I_{NOM}/12)^{12} - 1$$
$$1.15865 = (1 + I_{NOM}/12)^{12}$$
$$1.012347 = 1 + I_{NOM}/12$$
$$I_{NOM} = 14.8163\%$$

28. a. Information given:

1. Will save for 20 years, then receive payments for 25 years.

2. Wants payments of $75,000 per year in today's dollars for first payment only. Real income will decline. Inflation will be 4%. Therefore, to find the inflated fixed payments, we have this time line:

Enter N = 20, I/YR = 4, PV = -75000, PMT = 0, and press FV to get FV = $164,334.24.

3. He now has $200,000 in an account that pays 7%, annual compounding. We need to find the FV of $200,000 after 20 years. Enter N = 20, I/YR = 7, PV = -200000, PMT = 0, and press FV to get FV = $773,936.89.

4. He wants to withdraw, or have payments of, $164,334.24 per year for 25 years, with the first payment made at the beginning of the first retirement year. So, we have a 25-year annuity due with PMT = $164,334.24, at an interest rate of 7%. (The interest rate is 7% annually, so no adjustment is required.) Set the calculator to "BEG" mode, then enter N = 25, I/YR = 7, PMT = -164334.24, FV = 0, and press PV to get PV = $2,049,138.53. This amount must be on hand to make the 25 payments.

5. Since the original $200,000, which grows to $773,936.89, will be available, he must save enough to accumulate $2,049,138.53 – $773,936.89 = $1,275,201.64.

6. The $1,275,201.64 is the FV of a 20-year ordinary annuity. The payments will be deposited in the bank and earn 7% interest. Therefore, set the calculator to "END" mode and enter N = 20, I/YR = 7, PV = 0, FV = 1275201.64, and press PMT to find PMT = $31,105.90.

29. b.   Contract 1:   Using your financial calculator, enter the following data: $CF_0 = 0$; CF_{1-4} = 1500000; I/YR = 12; NPV = ? Solve for NPV = \$4,556,024.02.

        Contract 2:   Using your financial calculator, enter the following data: $CF_0 = 0$; CF_1 = 1000000; CF_2 = 1500000; CF_3 = 2000000; CF_4 = 2500000; I/YR = 12; NPV = ? Solve for NPV = \$5,101,003.65.

        Contract 3:   Using your financial calculator, enter the following data: $CF_0 = 0$; $CF_1 = 3500000$; $CF_2 = 500000$; $CF_3 = 500000$; $CF_4 = 500000$; I/YR = 12; NPV = ? Solve for NPV = \$4,197,246.10.

        Contract 2 gives the quarterback the highest present value; therefore, he should accept Contract 2.

30. d.   Using your financial calculator, input the following data: N = 30 × 12 = 360; I/YR = 7.5/12 = 0.6250; PV = -200000; FV = 0; PMT = ? Solve for PMT = \$1,398.43.

31. a.   Use your financial calculator to find the monthly mortgage payment: N = 30 × 12 = 360; I/YR = 7.5/12 = 0.6250; PV = -200000; FV = 0; and solve for PMT = \$1,398.43.

        Then, use the amortization feature of your calculator to find interest and principal repayments during the year and the remaining mortgage balance as follows:

        1 INPUT 12 ■ AMORT
                = \$14,937.47 (Interest)
                = \$1,843.69 (Principal)
                = \$198,156.31 (Balance)

        Total mortgage payments made during the first year equals 12 × \$1,398.43 = \$16,781.16.

        Portion of first year mortgage payments that go towards interest equals \$14,937.47/\$16,781.16 = 89.01 ≈ 89%.

32. c.   Use your financial calculator to find the monthly mortgage payment: N = 30 × 12 = 360; I/YR = 7.5/12 = 0.6250; PV = -200000; FV = 0; and solve for PMT = \$1,398.43.

        Then, use the amortization feature of your calculator to find the remaining balance after 5 years:

        1 INPUT 60 ■ AMORT
                = \$73,140.61 (Interest)
                = \$10,765.19 (Principal)
                = \$189,234.81 (Balance)

33. b. Using your financial calculator, input the following data: N = 30 × 12 = 360; I/YR = 7.5/12 = 0.6250; PMT = -1800; FV = 0; PV = ? Solve for PV = $257,431.73 ≈ $257,432.

If you are willing to have a $1,800 monthly mortgage payment, you can borrow $257,432 today.

34. e. Using the information given in the problem, you can solve for the number of years required to reach $1 million. I/YR = 6; PV = 15000; PMT = 7500; FV = -1000000; and then solve for N = 35.76.

Therefore, it will take Janet 35.76 years to reach her investment goal.

35. b. Again, you can solve for the number of years required to reach $1 million. I/YR = 7; PV = 15000; PMT = 7500; FV = -1000000; and then solve for N = 32.58.

It will take Denise 32.58 years to reach her investment goal. The difference in time is 35.76 – 32.58 = 3.18 years.

36. a. Using the 35.76 year target, you can solve for the required payment. N = 35.76; I/YR = 7; PV = 15000; FV = -1000000; then solve for PMT = $5,683.44.

If Denise wishes to reach the investment goal at the same time as Janet, she can contribute as little as $5,683.44 every year.

37. c. If John expects a 7% annual return on his investments:

1 payment	10 payments	30 payments
	N = 10	N = 30
	I/YR = 7	I/YR = 7
	PMT = -7000000	PMT = -4000000
	FV = 0	FV = 0
PV = 46,000,000	PV = 49,165,071	PV = 49,636,165

John should accept the 30-year payment option as it carries the highest present value ($49,636,165).

38. b. If John expects an 8% annual return on his investments:

1 payment	10 payments	30 payments
	N = 10	N = 30
	I/YR = 8	I/YR = 8
	PMT = -7000000	PMT = -4000000
	FV = 0	FV = 0
PV = 46,000,000	PV = 46,970,570	PV = 45,031,133

John should accept the 10-year payment option as it carries the highest present value ($46,970,570).

39. a. If John expects a 9% annual return on his investments:

1 payment	10 payments	30 payments
	N = 10	N = 30
	I/YR = 9	I/YR = 9
	PMT = -7000000	PMT = -4000000
	FV = 0	FV = 0
PV = 46,000,000	PV = 44,923,604	PV = 41,094,616

John should accept the lump-sum payment option as it carries the highest present value ($46,000,000).

40. d. Using the information given in the problem, you can solve for the maximum attainable car price.

Financed for 48 months
N = 48
I/YR = 0.8333 (10/12 = 0.8333)
PMT = -425
FV = 0

PV = $16,756.97

You must add the value of the down payment to the present value of the car payments. If financed for 48 months, Henry can afford a car valued up to $21,756.97 ($16,756.97 + $5,000).

41. e. Using the information given in the problem, you can solve for the maximum attainable car price.

Financed for 60 months
N = 60
I/YR = 0.8333
PMT = -425
FV = 0

PV = $20,002.78

If financing for 60 months, Henry can afford a car valued up to $25,002.78 ($20,002.78 + $5,000).

Web Appendix 5A

1. d. $FV_N = PV\,e^{IN}$
$FV_{10} = \$30,000\,e^{0.04(10)}$
$= \$30,000\,e^{0.4}$
$= \$44,754.74$

2.　　b.　$PV = FV_N \, e^{-IN}$
　　　　　$= \$125,000 \, e^{-0.90}$
　　　　　$= \$50,821.21$

Web Appendix 5B

1.　b.　$r_{NOM} = 8.00\%$; Inflation $= 2.80\%$

　　　　$r_r = [(1 + r_{NOM})/(1 + \text{Inflation})] - 1$
　　　　$r_r = 5.06\%$

2.　a.　$r_{NOM} = 4.50\%$; Inflation $= 3.20\%$

　　　　$r_r = [(1 + r_{NOM})/(1 + \text{Inflation})] - 1$
　　　　$r_r = 1.26\%$

3.　e.　$r_{NOM} = 7.00\%$; Inflation $= 2.50\%$; Initial sum $= \$500,000$; Years $= 15$

　　　　$r_r = [(1 + r_{NOM})/(1 + \text{Inflation})] - 1$
　　　　$r_r = 4.390244\%$

　　　Begin Mode:
　　　N = 15
　　　I/YR = 4.390244%
　　　PV = -$500,000
　　　FV = 0

　　　PMT = $44,263.02

4.　c.　$r_{NOM} = 7.00\%$; Inflation $= 2.50\%$; Initial sum $= \$500,000$; Years $= 15$

　　　　$r_r = [(1 + r_{NOM})/(1 + \text{Inflation})] - 1$
　　　　$r_r = 4.390244\%$

　　　End Mode:
　　　N = 15
　　　I/YR = 4.390244%
　　　PV = -$500,000
　　　FV = 0

　　　PMT = $46,206.28

　　　Adj. PMT = PMT(1 + Inflation)
　　　Adj. PMT = ($46,206.28)(1.025)
　　　Adj. PMT = $47,361.43

5. d. Step 1: Calculate the purchasing power of $2,000,000 in 25 years at an inflation rate of 2%;

    N = 25
    I/YR = 2.0%
    PMT = 0
    FV = $2,000,000

    PV = $1,219,061.74

  Step 2: Calculate the real rate of return on the growing annuity:
    r_{NOM} = 7.0%; Inflation = 2.0%

    $r_r = [(1 + r_{NOM})/(1 + \text{Inflation})] - 1$
    $r_r = 4.90196\%$

  Step 3: Calculate the required initial payment of the growing annuity by using inputs converted to "real" terms:
    Begin Mode:
    N = 25
    I/YR = 4.90196%
    PV = 0
    FV = $1,219,061.74

    PMT = $24,679.75

6. c. Step 1: Calculate the purchasing power of $1,500,000 in 30 years at an inflation rate of 2.5%;

    N = 30
    I/YR = 2.5%
    PMT = 0
    FV = $1,500,000

    PV = $715,114.03

  Step 2: Calculate the real rate of return on the growing annuity:
    r_{NOM} = 8.5%; Inflation = 2.5%

    $r_r = [(1 + r_{NOM})/(1 + \text{Inflation})] - 1$
    $r_r = 5.85366\%$

  Step 3: Calculate the required initial payment of the growing annuity by using inputs converted to "real" terms:
    Begin Mode:
    N   30
    I/YR   5.85366%
    PV   0
    FV $715,114.03

    PMT $8,767.79

6

INTEREST RATES

Learning Objectives

1. List the various factors that influence the cost of money.

2. Discuss how market interest rates are affected by borrowers' need for capital, expected inflation, different securities' risks, and securities' liquidity.

3. Explain what the yield curve is, what determines its shape, and how you can use the yield curve to help forecast future interest rates.

Overview

In this chapter, we see how money costs are determined, and we explore the principal factors that determine both the general level of interest rates in the economy and the interest rate on a particular debt security. We look at what determines the shape of the yield curve and then we use the yield curve to estimate future interest rates. We also look at the impact of Federal Reserve policy, the federal budget deficit or surplus, international factors, and the level of business activity on interest rate levels. Finally, we discuss the impact of interest rates on business decisions.

Outline

I. **Capital in a free economy is allocated through the price system. The interest rate is the price paid to borrow debt capital. With equity capital, investors expect to receive dividends and capital gains, whose sum is the cost of equity.**

   A. There are four fundamental factors that affect the supply of, and demand for, investment capital, hence the cost of money.

      1. *Production opportunities,* the returns available within an economy from investments in productive (cash-generating) assets.

      2. Consumers' *time preferences for consumption:* current consumption as opposed to saving for future consumption.

      3. *Risk,* the chance that an investment will provide a low or negative return.

      4. *Inflation,* the amount by which prices increase over time.

B. If the entire population is living at the subsistence level, time preferences for current consumption would necessarily be high, aggregate savings would be low, interest rates would be high, and capital formation would be difficult.

C. The higher the perceived risk, the higher the required rate of return, and the higher expected inflation, the higher the required return.

D. Producers' expected returns on their business investments set an upper limit to how much they can pay for savings, while consumers' time preferences for consumption establish how much consumption they are willing to defer and, hence, how much they will save at different interest rates.

II. **Capital is allocated among borrowers by interest rates: Firms with the most profitable investment opportunities are willing and able to pay the most for capital, so they tend to attract it away from inefficient firms or from those whose products are not in demand.**

A. Supply and demand interact to determine interest rates in capital markets.

1. If the demand for funds declines, as it typically does during business recessions, the market-clearing, or equilibrium, interest rate declines.

2. If the Federal Reserve tightens credit, lowering the supply of funds, interest rates rise and the level of borrowing in the economy declines.

B. Capital markets are interdependent.

1. Investors are willing to accept higher risk in exchange for a risk premium.

C. There are many capital markets in the U.S.

1. U.S. firms also invest and raise capital throughout the world, and foreigners both borrow and lend in the U.S.

D. There is a price for each type of capital, and these prices change over time as shifts occur in supply and demand conditions.

1. Short-term interest rates are especially prone to rise during booms, as the demand for capital increases and inflationary pressures, which are strongest during booms, push up rates.

2. Conditions are reversed during recessions due to a drop in interest rates, as demand for credit is reduced and the inflation rate falls.

   a. The Federal Reserve increases the supply of funds to help stimulate the economy. The result is a decline in interest rates.

3. The current interest rate minus the current inflation rate is defined as the "current real rate of interest."

   a. It is called the "real rate" because it shows how much investors really earned after the effects of inflation are removed.

4. Tendencies in interest rate fluctuations do not hold exactly. The level of interest rates varies with changes in the current inflation rate and changes in expectations about future inflation.

III. **The quoted (or nominal) interest rate on a debt security, r, is composed of a real risk-free rate of interest, r*, plus several premiums that reflect inflation, the security's risk, its liquidity (or marketability), and the years to maturity:**

$$\text{Quoted interest rate} = r^* + IP + DRP + LP + MRP$$

$$r = \quad r_{RF} \quad + DRP + LP + MRP$$

A. The *real risk-free rate of interest (r*)* is the interest rate that would exist on a riskless security if no inflation were expected. It may be thought of as the rate of interest on short-term U.S. Treasury securities in an inflation-free world.

1. The real risk-free rate is not static—it changes over time depending on economic conditions, especially on (a) the rate of return corporations and other borrowers expect to earn on productive assets and (b) people's time preferences for current versus future consumption.

2. Borrowers' expected returns on real assets set an upper limit on how much they can afford to pay for borrowed funds, while savers' time preferences for consumption establish how much consumption they are willing to defer, hence the amount of money they will lend at different interest rates.

3. The best estimate of r* is the rate of return on indexed Treasury bonds.

B. The *quoted, or nominal, risk-free rate of interest (r_{RF})* on a security such as a U.S. Treasury bill is the real risk-free rate plus a premium for expected inflation: $r_{RF} = r^* + IP$.

1. An indexed U.S. Treasury security is free of most risks. These securities are free of default, maturity, and liquidity risks, and also of risk due to changes in the general level of interest rates. However, they are not free of changes in the real rate.

2. The term risk-free rate without a modifier generally means the nominal rate.

3. In general, we use the T-bill rate to approximate the short-term risk-free rate and the T-bond rate to approximate the long-term risk-free rate.

C. The *inflation premium (IP)*, which is the average *expected* inflation rate over the life of the security, compensates investors for the expected loss of purchasing power.

1. It is important to note that the inflation rate built into interest rates is the inflation rate expected in the future, not the rate experienced in the past.

2. Expectations for future inflation are closely, but not perfectly, correlated with rates experienced in the recent past.

D. The *default risk premium (DRP)* compensates investors for the risk that a borrower will default and hence not pay the interest or principal on a loan.

1. DRP is zero for U.S. Treasury securities, but it rises as the riskiness of issuers increases.

   a. Treasury securities carry the lowest interest rates on taxable securities in the United States.

2. The greater the default risk, the higher the interest rate.

3. For corporate bonds, the higher the bond's rating, the lower its default risk, and, consequently, the lower its interest rate.

4. The difference between the quoted interest rate on a T-bond and that on a corporate bond with similar maturity, liquidity, and other features is the default risk premium.

101

5. The average default risk premium varies over time, and it tends to get larger when the economy is weaker and borrowers are more likely to have a hard time paying off their debts.

E. A security that can be converted to cash quickly at a fair market value is said to be *liquid*. A *liquidity,* or *marketability, premium (LP)* is also added to the real rate for securities that are not liquid.

1. Different financial assets vary in their liquidity.

2. Assets with higher trading volume are generally easier to sell, and are therefore more liquid.

3. The average liquidity premium also varies over time.

F. Long-term securities are more price sensitive to interest rate changes than are short-term securities, so all long-term bonds have an element of risk called *interest rate risk*. Therefore, a *maturity risk premium (MRP)* is added to longer-term securities to compensate investors for interest rate risk.

1. The MRP is higher the longer the years to maturity.

2. This premium, like the others, is difficult to measure, but it varies somewhat over time, rising when interest rates are more volatile and uncertain, then falling when interest rates are more stable.

3. Although long-term bonds are heavily exposed to interest rate risk, short-term bills are heavily exposed to *reinvestment rate risk*.

   a. This is the risk that a decline in interest rates will lead to lower income when bonds mature and funds are reinvested.

   b. Although "investing short" preserves one's principal, the interest income provided by short-term T-bills is less stable than the interest income on long-term bonds.

IV. **The term structure of interest rates is the relationship between bond yields and maturities.**

A. When plotted, this relationship produces a *yield curve.*

B. Yield curves have different shapes depending on expected inflation rates and perceptions about the relative risk of securities with different maturities.

1. The *"normal" yield curve* is upward sloping because investors charge higher rates on longer-term bonds, even when inflation is expected to remain constant.

   a. An upward slope is the normal situation because short-term securities have less interest rate risk than longer-term securities, hence smaller MRPs. Therefore, short-term rates are normally lower than long-term rates.

2. An *inverted,* or *"abnormal,"* yield curve is downward sloping, and signifies that investors expect inflation to decrease.

3. A *"humped" yield curve* occurs when interest rates on medium-term maturities are higher than rates on both short- and long-term maturities.

V.   The shape of the yield curve depends primarily on two factors: (1) expectations about future inflation, and (2) effects of maturity on bonds' risk.

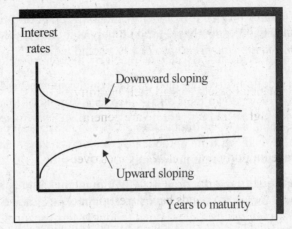

A. The *pure expectations theory,* sometimes referred to as the expectations theory, assumes that bond traders establish bond prices and interest rates strictly on the basis of expectations for future interest rates and that they are indifferent to maturity because they do not view long-term bonds as being riskier than short-term bonds.

1. The expectations theory holds that long-term interest rates are a geometric average of current and expected future short-term interest rates.

2. If the interest rate is expected to decline, the curve will be downward sloping, and if the interest rate is expected to increase, the curve will be upward sloping.

3. According to the pure expectations theory, the maturity risk premium is equal to zero because investors are indifferent with respect to maturity in the sense that they do not view long-term bonds as being riskier than short-term bonds.

B. Most evidence suggests that a positive maturity risk premium exists.

1. We can use the yield curve to estimate what the market expects the short-term rate to be next year.

2. The yield curve can be used to obtain insights into the direction of future interest rates.

3. We cannot back out expected interest rates with precision unless either the pure expectations theory holds exactly or else we know with certainty the exact maturity risk premium.

4. Forecasts of future interest rates are only approximations. Even if we could determine the market's consensus forecast for future rates, the market isn't always right.

VI.   There are macroeconomic factors that influence both the general level of interest rates and the shape of the yield curve. These primary factors are (1) Federal Reserve policy; (2) the federal budget deficit or surplus; (3) international factors, including the foreign trade balance and interest rates in other countries; and (4) the level of business activity.

A. Expansionary monetary policy (growth in monetary supply) by the Federal Reserve initially lowers the interest rate but inflationary pressures could cause a rise in the long-term interest rate. Contractionary monetary policy has the opposite effect.

1. During periods when the Fed is actively intervening in the markets, the yield curve may be temporarily distorted.

2. Short-term rates may be driven below the long-run equilibrium level if the Fed is easing credit and above the equilibrium rate if the Fed is tightening credit.

3. Long-term rates are not affected as much by Fed intervention.

B. Federal budget deficits drive up interest rates due to increased demand for loanable funds, while surpluses drive down rates due to increased supply of loanable funds.

C. Foreign trade deficits (when imports are greater than exports) push up interest rates because deficits must be financed from abroad and rates must be high enough relative to world interest rates to attract foreign investors.

1. A large trade deficit (and foreigners' holdings of U.S. debt that resulted from many years of deficits) hinders the Fed's ability to combat a recession by lowering interest rates.

D. In relation to the business cycle, there is a general tendency for interest rates to decline during a recession.

1. Short-term rates decline more sharply than long-term rates.

   a. The Fed operates mainly in the short-term sector, so its intervention has the strongest effect there.

   b. Long-term rates reflect the average expected inflation rate over the next 20 to 30 years, and this expectation doesn't change much.

2. Short-term rates are more volatile than long-term rates.

VII.   Interest rate movements have a significant impact on business decisions.

A. Wrong decisions, such as using short-term debt to finance long-term projects just before interest rates rise, can be very costly.

B. It is extremely difficult, if not impossible, to predict future interest rate levels. Interest rates will fluctuate—they always have, and they always will.

C. Sound financial policy calls for using a mix of long- and short-term debt as well as equity to position the firm, so that it can survive in almost any interest rate environment.

1. The optimal financial policy depends in an important way on the nature of the firm's assets.

   a. The easier it is to sell off assets to generate cash, the more feasible it is to use more short-term debt.

   b. This makes it logical for a firm to finance its current assets with short-term debt and to finance fixed assets with long-term debt.

D. Changes in interest rates also have implications for savers.

Self-Test

Definitional Questions

1. The risk that a borrower will not pay the interest or principal on a loan is _____ risk.

2. U. S. Treasury securities have _____ default risk.

3. A(n) _____ premium is added to the real risk-free rate to protect investors against loss of purchasing power.

4. The nominal rate of interest is determined by adding a(n) _____ premium plus a(n) _____ risk premium plus a(n) _____ premium plus a(n) _____ risk premium to the real risk-free rate of return.

5. The relationship between bond yields and maturities is called the _____ structure of interest rates, while the resulting plotted curve is the _____ curve.

6. The "normal" yield curve has a(n) _____ slope.

7. The _____ _____ theory holds that long-term interest rates are a geometric average of current and expected future short-term interest rates.

8. Because interest rates fluctuate, a sound financial policy calls for using a mix of _____ - and _____-_____ debt as well as _____.

9. The _____ rate is the price paid to borrow debt capital.

10. A(n) _____ risk premium is added to longer-term securities to compensate investors for interest rate risk.

11. There are four fundamental factors that affect the supply of, and demand for, investment capital: _____ opportunities, _____ preferences for consumption, _____, and _____.

12. Long-term securities are more price sensitive to interest rate changes than are short-term securities, so all long-term bonds have an element of risk called _____ rate risk.

13. Short-term bills are heavily exposed to _____ rate risk.

14. _____ is the chance an investment will provide a low or negative return.

15. _____ is the amount by which prices increase over time.

16. _____ opportunities are the returns available within an economy from investments in cash-generating assets.

17. _____ and _____ interact to determine interest rates in capital markets.

18. The current _____ rate minus the current _____ rate is defined as the current real rate of interest.

19. The real _____-_____ rate of interest is the interest rate that would exist on a riskless security if no inflation were expected.

20. The _____ risk-free rate of interest is the real risk-free rate plus an inflation premium.

21. The default risk premium is zero for U.S. Treasury securities, but it _____ as the riskiness of issuers increases.

22. A security that can be converted to cash quickly at a fair market value is said to be _____.

105

23. _____ securities carry the lowest interest rates on taxable securities in the United States.

24. Investing "short" preserves one's _____, but the interest income provided by short-term T-bills is less stable than the interest income on _____-_____ bonds.

25. A(n) _____, or _____, yield curve is downward sloping, and signifies that investors expect inflation to decrease.

26. A(n) _____ yield curve occurs when interest rates on medium-term maturities are higher than rates on both short- and long-term maturities.

27. The shape of the yield curve depends primarily on two factors: expectations about future _____ and effects of _____ on bonds' risk.

28. During periods when the Federal Reserve is actively intervening in the markets, the yield curve may be temporarily _____.

29. Federal budget _____ drive up interest rates due to increased demand for loanable funds, while _____ drive down rates due to increased supply of loanable funds.

30. Foreign trade _____ occur when imports are _____ than exports.

Conceptual Questions

1. If management is sure that the economy is at the peak of a boom and is about to enter a recession, a firm that needs to borrow money should probably use short-term rather than long-term debt.
   a. True
   b. False

2. Long-term interest rates reflect expectations about future inflation. Inflation has varied greatly from year to year over the last 10 years, and, as a result, long-term rates have fluctuated more than short-term rates.

   a. True
   b. False

3. Suppose the Fed takes actions that lower expectations for inflation this year by 1 percentage point, but these same actions raise expectations for inflation in Years 2 and thereafter by 2 percentage points. Other things held constant, the yield curve becomes steeper.

   a. True
   b. False

4. Assume interest rates on 30-year government and corporate bonds were as follows: T-bond = 7.72%; AAA = 8.72%; A = 9.64%; BBB = 10.18%. The differences in rates among these issues are caused primarily by:
   a. Tax effects.
   b. Default risk differences.
   c. Maturity risk differences.
   d. Inflation differences.
   e. Both default risk differences and inflation differences.

Problems

1. The real risk-free rate of interest is 2%. Inflation is expected to be 3% the next 2 years and 5% during the next 3 years after that. Assume that the maturity risk premium is zero. What is the yield on 3-year Treasury securities?

   a. 5.2%
   b. 5.7%
   c. 6.0%
   d. 6.2%
   e. 6.5%

2. The real risk-free rate of interest is 2%. Inflation is expected to be 3% the next 2 years and 5% during the next 3 years after that. Assume that the maturity risk premium is zero. What is the yield on 5-year Treasury securities?

   a. 5.2%
   b. 5.7%
   c. 6.0%
   d. 6.2%
   e. 6.5%

3. A Treasury bond that matures in 20 years has a yield of 8%. A 20-year corporate bond has a yield of 11%. Assume that the liquidity premium on the corporate bond is 1.0%. What is the default risk premium on the corporate bond?

   a. 0.50%
   b. 1.00%
   c. 1.50%
   d. 1.75%
   e. 2.00%

4. You have determined the following data for a given bond: Real risk-free rate (r^*) = 3%; inflation premium = 8%; default risk premium = 2%; liquidity premium = 2%; and maturity risk premium = 1%. What is the nominal risk-free rate, r_{RF}?

   a. 10%
   b. 11%
   c. 12%
   d. 13%
   e. 14%

5. You have determined the following data for a given bond: Real risk-free rate (r^*) = 3%; inflation premium = 8%; default risk premium = 2%; liquidity premium = 2%; and maturity risk premium = 1%. What is the interest rate on long-term Treasury securities, or T-bonds, of the relevant maturity?

   a. 10%
   b. 11%
   c. 12%
   d. 13%
   e. 14%

6. Assume that a 3-year Treasury note has no maturity risk or liquidity risk and that the real risk-free rate of interest falls to 2%. A 3-year T-note carries a yield to maturity of 12%. If the expected inflation rate is 12% for the coming year and 10% the year after, what is the implied expected inflation rate for the third year?

   a.   8%
   b.   9%
   c.   10%
   d.   11%
   e.   12%

7. Assume that the real risk-free rate is 2%, that the expected inflation rate during Year 2 is 3%, and that 2-year T-bonds yield 5.5%. If the maturity risk premium is zero, what is the inflation rate during Year 1?

   a.   3.0%
   b.   5.0%
   c.   3.5%
   d.   4.0%
   e.   2.5%

8. Assume that the real risk-free rate is 2%, that the expected inflation rate during Year 2 is 3%, and that 2-year T-bonds yield 5.5%. What is the rate of return on 1-year T-bonds?

   a.   5.5%
   b.   6.0%
   c.   5.0%
   d.   6.5%
   e.   4.5%

9. Assume that the real risk-free rate, r*, is 4% and that inflation is expected to be 7% in Year 1, 4% in Year 2, and 3% thereafter. Assume also that all Treasury bonds are highly liquid and free of default risk. If 2-year and 5-year Treasury bonds both yield 11%, what is the difference in the maturity risk premiums (MRPs) on the two bonds; that is, what is $MRP_5 - MRP_2$?

   a.   0.5%
   b.   1.0%
   c.   2.3%
   d.   1.5%
   e.   1.3%

10. Due to the recession, the rate of inflation expected for the coming year is only 3.5%. However, the rate of inflation in Year 2 and thereafter is expected to be constant at some level above 3.5%. Assume that the real risk-free rate is r* = 2% for all maturities and that the expectations theory fully explains the yield curve, so there are no maturity risk premiums. If 3-year Treasury bonds yield 3 percentage points (0.03) more than 1-year Treasury bonds, what rate of inflation is expected after Year 1?

   a.   4%
   b.   5%
   c.   7%
   d.   6%
   e.   8%

11. You read in *The Wall Street Journal* that 30-day T-bills are currently yielding 5%. Your brother-in-law, a broker at Fast Track Securities, has given you the following estimates of current interest rate premiums as indicated. On the basis of these data, what is the real risk-free rate of return?

- Inflation premium = 2.85%.
- Liquidity premium = 0.5%.
- Maturity risk premium = 1.5%.
- Default risk premium = 2.0%.

   a. 1.85%
   b. 2.00%
   c. 2.15%
   d. 2.25%
   e. 2.50%

12. The 5-year bonds of Englewood Enterprises are yielding 8.10% per year. Treasury bonds with the same maturity are yielding 5.65% per year. The real risk-free rate (r^*) has not changed in recent years and is 2.5%. The average inflation premium is 2.75% and the maturity risk premium takes the form: MRP = 0.1%(t – 1), where t = number of years to maturity. If the liquidity premium is 1.2%, what is the default risk premium on Englewood's corporate bonds?

   a. 0.50%
   b. 0.85%
   c. 1.00%
   d. 1.25%
   e. 1.60%

13. An investor in Treasury securities expects inflation to be 2.25% in Year 1, 2.75% in Year 2, and 3.30% each year thereafter. Assume that the real risk-free rate is 2.40%, and that this rate will remain constant over time. Three-year Treasury securities yield 5.60%, while 5-year Treasury securities yield 6.20%. What is the difference in the maturity risk premiums (MRPs) on the two securities, that is, what is $MRP_5 - MRP_3$?

   a. 0.39%
   b. 0.55%
   c. 0.75%
   d. 0.90%
   e. 1.20%

14. An analyst is evaluating securities in a developing nation where the inflation rate is very high. As a result, the analyst has been warned not to ignore the cross-product between the real rate and inflation. If the real risk-free rate is 5.5% and inflation is expected to be 20% each of the next 4 years, what is the yield on a 4-year security with no maturity, default, or liquidity risk? (Hint: You must consider the inflation cross-product in your answer.)

   a. 21.8%
   b. 24.3%
   c. 26.6%
   d. 28.2%
   e. 30.0%

15. Interest rates on 4-year Treasury securities are currently 6.5%, while 6-year Treasury securities yield 6.8%. If the pure expectations theory is correct, what does the market believe that 2-year securities will be yielding 4 years from now?

    a. 7.4%
    b. 7.2%
    c. 7.0%
    d. 6.8%
    e. 6.5%

Answers

Definitional Questions

1. default
2. zero
3. inflation
4. inflation; default; liquidity; maturity
5. term; yield
6. upward
7. pure expectations
8. short-; long-term; equity
9. interest
10. maturity
11. production; time; risk; inflation
12. interest
13. reinvestment
14. Risk
15. Inflation
16. Production
17. Supply; demand
18. interest; inflation
19. risk-free
20. nominal
21. rises
22. liquid
23. Treasury
24. principal; long-term
25. inverted; abnormal
26. humped
27. inflation; maturity
28. distorted
29. deficits; surpluses
30. deficits; greater

Conceptual Questions

1. a. The firm should borrow short-term until interest rates drop due to the recession, then go long-term. Predicting interest rates is extremely difficult because managers can rarely be sure about what is going to happen to the economy.

2. b. Fluctuations in long-term rates are smaller because the long-term inflation premium is an average of inflation expectations over many years, and hence the IP on long-term bonds is quite stable relative to the IP on short-term bonds. Also, short-term rates fluctuate as a result of Federal Reserve policy (the Fed intervenes in the short-term rather than the long-term market).

3. a. The yield curve becomes steeper. Although interest rates in Year 1 decrease by 1%, interest rates in the following years increase by 2%, making the yield curve steeper.

4. b. $r = r^* + IP + DRP + LP + MRP$. Since each of these bonds has a 30-year maturity, the MRP and IP would all be equal. Thus, the differences in the interest rates among these issues are the default risk and liquidity premiums.

Solutions

Problems

1. b. $r^* = 2\%$; $I_1 = 3\%$; $I_2 = 3\%$; $I_3 = 5\%$; $I_4 = 5\%$; $I_5 = 5\%$; MRP = 0; r_{T3} = ?
    Since these are Treasury securities, DRP = LP = 0.

    $r_{T3} = r^* + IP_3$
    $IP_3 = (3\% + 3\% + 5\%)/3 = 3.67\%$
    $r_{T3} = 2\% + 3.67\% = 5.67\% \approx 5.7\%$

2. d. $r^* = 2\%$, $I_1 = 3\%$; $I_2 = 3\%$; $I_3 = 5\%$; $I_4 = 5\%$; $I_5 = 5\%$; MRP = 0; r_{T5} = ?
    Since these are Treasury securities, DRP = LP = 0.

    $r_{T5} = r^* + IP_5$
    $IP_5 = (3\% + 3\% + 5\% + 5\% + 5\%)/5 = 4.2\%$
    $r_{T5} = 2\% + 4.2\% = 6.2\%$

3. e. $r_{T20} = 8\%$; $r_{C20} = 11\%$; LP = 1.0%; DRP = ?

    $r = r^* + IP + DRP + LP + MRP$
    $r_{T20} = 8\% = r^* + IP + MRP$; DRP = LP = 0
    $r_{C20} = 11\% = r^* + IP + DRP + 1.0\% + MRP$

    Because both bonds are 20-year bonds the inflation premium and maturity risk premium on both bonds are equal. The only differences between them are the liquidity and default risk premiums.

    $r_{C20} = 11\% = r^* + IP + MRP + 1.0\% + DRP$. But we know from above that $r^* + IP + MRP = 8\%$; therefore,

    $11\% = 8\% + 1.0\% + DRP$
    $2\% = DRP$

4. b. $r_{RF} = r^* + IP = 3\% + 8\% = 11\%$

5. c.   There is virtually no risk of default on a U.S. Treasury security, and they trade in active markets, which provide liquidity, so

    $r = r^* + IP + DRP + LP + MRP$
    $= 3\% + 8\% + 0\% + 0\% + 1\%$
    $= 12\%$

6. a. $r_{T3} = r^* + IP_3 + DRP_3 + LP_3 + MRP_3$. Since each of the
    $12\% = 2\% + IP_3 + 0\% + 0\% + 0\%$
    $IP_3 = 10\%$

Thus, the average expected inflation rate over the next three years (IP) is 10%. Given that the average expected inflation rate over the next three years is 10%, we can find the implied expected inflation rate for the third year by solving the equation that sets the two known plus the one unknown expected inflation rates equal to 10%:

$$\frac{12\% + 10\% + I_3}{3} = 10\%$$

$$I_3 = 8\%$$

7. d.

Year	r*	Inflation	Average Inflation	r_t
1	2%	?	$I_1/1 = ?$	?
2	2%	3	$(I_1 + 3\%)/2$	5.5%

$$2\% + (I_1 + 3\%)/2 = 5.5\%$$
$$(I_1 + 3\%)/2 = 3.5\%$$
$$I_1 + 3\% = 7\%$$
$$I_1 = 4\%$$

8. b.
$$2\% + (I_1 + 3\%)/2 = 5.5\%$$
$$(I_1 + 3\%)/2 = 3.5\%$$
$$I_1 + 3\% = 7\%$$
$$I_1 = 4\%$$

$$r_{T1} = r^* + IP = 2\% + 4\% = 6\%$$

9. d. First, note that we will use the equation $r_t = 4\% + IP_t + MRP_t$. We have the data needed to find the IPs:

$$IP_5 = (7\% + 4\% + 3\% + 3\% + 3\%)/5 = 20\%/5 = 4\%$$
$$IP_2 = (7\% + 4\%)/2 = 5.5\%$$

Now we can substitute into the equation:

$$r_{T2} = 4\% + 5.5\% + MRP_2 = 11\%$$
$$r_{T5} = 4\% + 4\% + MRP_5 = 11\%$$

Now we can solve for the MRPs, and find the difference:

$$MRP_5 = 11\% - 8\% = 3\%$$
$$MRP_2 = 11\% - 9.5\% = 1.5\%$$
$$\text{Difference} = 3\% - 1.5\% = 1.5\%$$

10. e. Basic relevant equations:

$$r_t = r^* + IP_t + DRP_t + MRP_t + LP_t$$

But $DRP_t = MRP_t = LP_t = 0$, so

$$r_t = r^* + IP_t$$

$$IP_t = \text{Average inflation} = \frac{I_1 + I_2 + I_t}{N}$$

We know that $I_1 = IP_1 = 3.5\%$ and $r^* = 2\%$. Therefore,
$r_{T1} = 2\% + 3.5\% = 5.5\%$
$r_{T3} = r_{T1} + 3\% = 5.5\% + 3\% = 8.5\%$

But $r_{T3} = r^* + IP_3 = 2\% + IP_3 = 8.5\%$, so
$IP_3 = 8.5\% - 2\% = 6.5\%$

We also know that $I_t = $ Constant after $t = 1$.

$(3.5\% + 2I)/3 = 6.5\%$
$\qquad 3.5\% + 2I = 19.5\%$
$\qquad\qquad 2I = 16\%$
$\qquad\qquad\quad I = 8\%$

We can set up this table:

Year	r^*	I_t	Avg. $I = IP_t$	$r = r^* + IP_t$
1	2%	3.5%	3.5%/1 = 3.5%	5.5%
2	2%	I	(3.5% + I)/2 = IP_2	
3	2%	I	(3.5 + I + I)/3 = IP_3	8.5%, so $IP_3 = 8.5\% - 2\% = 6.5\%$

11. c. T-bill rate $= r^* + IP$
$\qquad\qquad 5\% = r^* + 2.85\%$
$\qquad\qquad r^* = 2.15\%$

12. d. We're given all the components to determine the yield on the Englewood bonds except the default risk premium (DRP) and MRP. Calculate the MRP as $0.1\%(5 - 1) = 0.4\%$. Now, we can solve for the DRP as follows: $8.1\% = 2.5\% + 2.75\% + 0.4\% + 1.2\% + DRP$, or $DRP = 1.25\%$.

13. a. First, calculate the inflation premiums for the next three and five years, respectively. They are $IP_3 = (2.25\% + 2.75\% + 3.3\%)/3 = 2.77\%$ and $IP_5 = (2.25\% + 2.75\% + 3.3\% + 3.3\% + 3.3\%)/5 = 2.98\%$. The real risk-free rate is given as 2.40%. Since the default and liquidity premiums are zero on Treasury bonds, we can now solve for the maturity risk premium. Thus, $5.60\% = 2.40\% + 2.77\% + MRP_3$, or $MRP_3 = 0.43\%$. Similarly, $6.20\% = 2.40\% + 2.98\% + MRP_5$, or $MRP_5 = 0.82\%$. Thus, $MRP_5 - MRP_3 = 0.82\% - 0.43\% = 0.39\%$.

14. c. $r^* = 5.5\%$; $I_{1-4} = 20\%$, so $IP_4 = 20\%$; $MRP = DRP = LP = 0$; $r_4 = ?$
$r_4 = r_{RF}$

$r_{RF} = (1 + r^*)(1 + IP) - 1$
$\qquad = (1.055)(1.20) - 1$
$\qquad = 1.266 - 1 = 0.266 = 26.6\%$

15. a. Let $_4r_2$ equal the yield on 2-year securities 4 years from now:
$(1.065)^4(1 + {_4r_2})^2 = (1.068)^6$
$1.2865(1 + {_4r_2})^2 = 1.4840$
$\qquad 1 + {_4r_2} = (1.4840/1.2865)^{1/2}$
$\qquad\qquad {_4r_2} = 7.4\%$

113

7

BONDS AND THEIR VALUATION

Learning Objectives

1. Identify the different features of corporate and government bonds.

2. Discuss how bond prices are determined in the market, what the relationship is between interest rates and bond prices, and how a bond's price changes over time as it approaches maturity.

3. Calculate a bond's yield to maturity, its yield to call if it is callable, and determine the "true" yield.

4. Explain the different types of risk that bond investors and issuers face, and discuss how a bond's terms and collateral can be changed to affect its interest rate.

Overview

This chapter presents a discussion of the key characteristics of bonds, and then uses time value of money concepts to determine bond values. Bonds are one of the most important types of securities to investors and a major source of financing for corporations and governments.

The value of any financial asset is the present value of the cash flows expected from that asset. Therefore, once the cash flows have been estimated and a discount rate determined, the value of the financial asset can be calculated.

A bond is valued as the present value of the stream of interest payments (an annuity) plus the present value of the par value that is received by the investor on the bond's maturity date. Depending on the relationship between the current interest rate and the bond's coupon rate, a bond can sell at its par value, at a discount, or at a premium. The total rate of return on a bond is comprised of two components: an interest yield and a capital gains yield.

The bond valuation concepts developed earlier in the chapter are used to illustrate price and reinvestment risk. In addition, default risk, various types of corporate bonds, bond ratings, and bond markets are discussed.

Outline

I.   **A bond is a long-term contract under which a borrower agrees to make payments of interest and principal, on specific dates, to the bondholders. There are four main types of bonds: Treasury, corporate, municipal, and foreign. Each type differs with respect to expected return and degree of risk.**

   A. *Treasury bonds*, generally called Treasuries and sometimes referred to as government bonds, are issued by the Federal government.

      1. They are not exposed to default risk.

      2. Treasury bond prices decline when interest rates rise, so they are not completely riskless.

   B. *Corporate bonds* are issued by business firms and are exposed to default risk.

      1. Different corporate bonds have different levels of default risk, depending on the issuing company's characteristics and on the terms of the specific bond.

         a. Default risk is often referred to as "credit risk."

         b. The larger the default risk, the higher the interest rate investors demand.

   C. *Municipal bonds* are issued by state and local governments.

      1. The interest earned on most municipal bonds is exempt from federal taxes and from state taxes if the holder is a resident of the issuing state.

      2. Municipal bonds carry interest rates that are considerably lower than those on corporate bonds with equivalent risk because of the interest tax exemption.

   D. *Foreign bonds* are issued by foreign governments or foreign corporations.

      1. These bonds are not only exposed to default risk, but are also exposed to an additional risk if the bonds are denominated in a currency other than that of the investor's home currency.

II.   **Differences in contractual provisions, and in the underlying strength of the companies backing the bonds, lead to major differences in bonds' risks, prices, and expected returns. It is important to understand the key characteristics, which are common to all bonds, and how differences in these characteristics affect the values and risks of individual bonds.**

   A. The *par value* is the stated face value of a bond, usually $1,000.

      1. This is the amount of money that the firm borrows and promises to repay on the maturity date.

   B. The *coupon payment* is the specified dollar amount that is paid each period to a bondholder by the issuer for use of the loan.

      1. For a *fixed-rate bond*, this payment is a fixed amount, established at the time the bond is issued.

      2. The *coupon interest rate* is obtained by dividing the coupon payment (calculated as the coupon interest rate times par value) by the par value of the bond.

      3. *Floating-rate bonds* are bonds with a coupon payment that varies over time.

         a. Floating-rate debt is popular with investors because the market value of the debt is stabilized.

116

  b. It is advantageous to corporations because firms can issue long-term debt without committing themselves to paying a historically high interest rate for the entire life of the loan.

 4. *Zero coupon bonds* pay no coupons at all, but are offered at a substantial discount below their par values.

  a. They provide capital appreciation rather than interest income.

  b. Web Appendix 7A discusses zero coupon bonds and their valuation in more detail.

 5. In general, any bond originally offered at a price significantly below its par value is called an *original issue discount bond (OID)*.

C. The *maturity date* is the date on which the par value must be repaid.

 1. *Original maturity* is the number of years to maturity at the time a bond is issued.

 2. Most bonds have original maturities of from 10 to 40 years, but any maturity is legally permissible.

D. A *call provision* gives the issuing corporation the right to call the bonds for redemption under specified terms prior to the normal maturity date.

 1. The call provision generally states that if the bonds are called, the company must pay the bondholders an amount greater than the par value, a *call premium*.

  a. The call premium is often set equal to one year's interest if the bonds are called during the first year, and the premium declines at a constant rate of INT/N each year thereafter, where INT = annual interest and N = original maturity in years.

 2. A *deferred call* occurs when bonds are not callable until several years after they are issued. These bonds are said to have *call protection*.

 3. The call privilege is valuable to the firm but potentially detrimental to the investor, especially if the bonds were issued in a period when interest rates were cyclically high.

  a. The interest rate on a new issue of callable bonds will exceed that on a new issue of noncallable bonds.

 4. The process of using the proceeds of a new lower-interest-rate bond issue to retire a higher-interest-rate issue and reduce the firm's interest expense is called a *refunding operation*.

  a. The refunding operation is similar to a homeowner refinancing his or her home mortgage after a decline in rates.

E. A *sinking fund provision* facilitates the orderly retirement of a bond issue.

 1. The issuer can handle the sinking fund requirement in one of two ways, and the firm will choose the least-cost method.

  a. The company can call in for redemption (at par value) a certain percentage of bonds each year. If interest rates have fallen, a firm will call the bonds.

  b. The company may buy the required amount of bonds on the open market. If interest rates have risen, causing bond prices to fall, it will buy bonds in the open market at a discount.

117

2. Bonds that have a sinking fund are regarded as being safer than those without such a provision, so at the time they are issued sinking fund bonds have lower coupon rates than otherwise similar bonds without sinking funds.

3. A sinking fund call typically requires no call premium, but only a small percentage of the issue is normally callable in any one year.

4. A failure to meet the sinking fund requirement constitutes a default, which may throw the company into bankruptcy. Therefore, a sinking fund is a mandatory payment.

F. Several other types of bonds are also used.

1. *Convertible bonds* are securities that are exchangeable into shares of common stock, at a fixed price, at the option of the bondholder.

   a. Convertibles have a lower coupon rate than nonconvertible debt with similar credit risk, but they offer investors a chance for capital gains in exchange for the lower coupon rate.

2. Bonds issued with *warrants* are similar to convertibles.

   a. Warrants are options that permit the holder to buy stock for a stated price, thereby providing a capital gain if the stock's price rises.

   b. Bonds that are issued with warrants carry lower coupon rates than otherwise similar nonconvertible bonds.

3. *Putable bonds* contain provisions that allow the bonds' investors to sell the bonds back to the company prior to maturity at a specified price.

   a. If interest rates rise, then investors will put these bonds back to the company and reinvest in higher coupon bonds.

4. *Income bonds* pay interest only if the interest is earned.

   a. These securities cannot bankrupt a company, but from an investor's standpoint they are riskier than "regular" bonds.

5. The interest rate of an *indexed*, or *purchasing power, bond* is based on an inflation index such as the consumer price index (CPI), so the interest paid rises automatically when the inflation rate rises, thus protecting the bondholders against inflation.

   a. The U.S. Treasury is the main issuer of indexed bonds called Treasury Inflation Protected Securities (TIPS).

III. The value of any financial asset is simply the present value of the cash flows the asset is expected to produce. The cash flows from a specific bond depend on its contractual features.

A. A bond represents an annuity plus a lump sum, and its value is found as the present value of this payment stream:

$$\text{Bond value} = V_B = \sum_{t=1}^{N} \frac{\text{INT}}{(1+r_d)^t} + \frac{M}{(1+r_d)^N}$$

1. Here INT = dollars of interest paid each year, M = par, or maturity, value, which is typically $1,000, r_d = market interest rate on the bond, and N = number of years until the bond matures.

B. For example, consider a 15-year, $1,000 bond paying $100 annually, when the appropriate interest rate, r_d, is 10%. Using a financial calculator, enter N = 15, r_d = I/YR = 10, PMT = 100, and FV = 1000, and then press the PV key for an answer of $1,000.

   1. The value of the bond can be found using Excel's built-in function with the following format: PV(rate,nper,pmt,[fv],[type]).

   2. "Type" indicates whether cash flows occur at the end of periods or at the beginning of periods. A zero indicates end-of-period cash flows, while a 1 indicates beginning-of-period cash flows.

C. Bond prices and interest rates are inversely related; that is, they tend to move in the opposite direction from one another. Interest rates do change over time, but for a fixed-rate bond the coupon rate remains fixed after the bond has been issued.

   1. A fixed-rate bond will sell at par when its coupon interest rate is equal to the going rate of interest, r_d.

   2. A *discount bond* is a bond that sells below its par value, when the going rate of interest rises above the coupon rate.

   3. A *premium bond* is a bond that sells above its par value, when the going rate of interest falls below the coupon rate.

IV. **Unlike the coupon interest rate, which is fixed, a bond's yield varies from day to day depending on current market conditions. The expected interest rate on a bond, also called its "yield," can be calculated in a variety of different ways.**

A. To be most useful, the bond's yield should give us an estimate of the rate of return we would earn if we purchase the bond today and held it over its remaining life.

   1. A bond's yield can be calculated using Excel's built-in function with the following format: RATE(nper,pmt,pv,[fv],[type],[guess]).

B. The rate of return earned on a bond if it is held until maturity is known as the *yield to maturity (YTM)*.

   1. The yield to maturity is generally the same as the market rate of interest, r_d.

   2. The yield to maturity can also be viewed as the bond's promised rate of return.

   3. The yield to maturity equals the expected rate of return only if the probability of default is zero and the bond cannot be called.

   4. An investor who purchases a bond and holds it until it matures will receive the YTM that existed on the purchase date, but the bond's calculated YTM will change frequently between the purchase date and the maturity date.

C. If current interest rates are well below an outstanding bond's coupon rate, then a *callable bond* is likely to be called, and investors should estimate the expected rate of return on the bond as the *yield to call (YTC)* rather than as the yield to maturity. To calculate the YTC, solve this equation for r_d:

$$\text{Price of bond} = \sum_{t=1}^{N} \frac{\text{INT}}{(1+r_d)^t} + \frac{\text{Call price}}{(1+r_d)^N}$$

1. Here N is the number of years until the company can call the bond; call price is the price the company must pay in order to call the bond (which is often set equal to the par value plus one year's interest); and r_d is the YTC.

2. Whether a company calls its callable bonds depends on what the going interest rate is when they become callable and whether the benefit (interest savings) is greater than the cost of calling the bonds.

D. Brokerage houses occasionally report a bond's *current yield*.

1. The current yield is defined as the annual interest payment divided by the current price.

2. The current yield does not represent the actual return that investors should expect because it does not account for the capital gain or loss that will be realized if the bond is held until it matures or is called.

V. **When a coupon bond is issued, the coupon is generally set at a level that causes the bond's market price to equal its par value.**

A. A *new issue* is the term applied to a bond that has just been issued.

1. Once the bond has been on the market for a while, it is classified as an *outstanding bond*, or a *seasoned issue*.

B. The total rate of return on a bond consists of a current yield plus a capital gains yield.

1. A bond's current yield is calculated as the coupon interest divided by the bond's price.

2. A bond's capital gains yield is calculated as the bond's annual change in price divided by the beginning-of-year price.

3. In the absence of default risk and assuming market equilibrium, the total return is also equal to YTM and the market interest rate.

4. The market value of a bond will always approach its par value as its maturity date approaches, provided the firm does not go bankrupt.

VI. **The bond valuation model must be adjusted when interest is paid semiannually.**

A. Divide the annual coupon interest payment by 2 to determine the dollars of interest paid each six months; multiply the years to maturity by 2 to determine the number of semiannual periods; and divide the nominal interest rate by 2 to determine the periodic interest rate.

B. The value with semiannual interest payments is larger than the value when interest is paid annually.

1. This higher value occurs because interest payments are received somewhat faster under semiannual compounding.

VII. **Interest rates fluctuate over time, and an increase in interest rates leads to a decline in the value of outstanding bonds.**

A. People or firms who invest in bonds are exposed to risk from changing interest rates, or *price risk*.

1. For bonds with similar coupons, the longer the maturity of the bond, the greater the exposure to price risk.

2. Even if the risk of default on two bonds is exactly the same, the bond with the longer maturity is typically exposed to more risk from a rise in interest rates.

    a. This follows because the longer the maturity, the longer before the bond will be paid off and the bondholder can replace it with another bond having a higher coupon.

B. The risk of a decline in income due to a drop in interest rates is called *reinvestment risk*.

1. Reinvestment risk is high on callable bonds.

2. It is also high on short-term bonds, because the shorter the bond's maturity, the fewer the years before the relatively high old-coupon bonds will be replaced with new low-coupon bonds.

C. Price risk relates to the current market value of the bonds in a portfolio, while reinvestment risk relates to the income the portfolio produces. No fixed-rate bond can be considered totally riskless.

D. A bond's risk depends critically on how long the investor plans to hold the bond, which is referred to as the investor's *investment horizon*.

1. Even a small change in interest rates can have a large effect on the prices of long-term securities.

2. Investors with shorter investment horizons view long-term bonds as risky investments.

3. Short-term bonds tend to be riskier than long-term bonds for investors who have longer investment horizons.

E. To account for the effects related to both a bond's maturity and coupon, many analysts focus on a measure called *duration*. Web Appendix 7B discusses duration and its calculation in greater detail.

1. A bond's duration is the weighted average of the time it takes to receive each of the bond's cash flows.

2. A zero coupon bond whose only cash flow is paid at maturity has a duration equal to its maturity.

3. A bond's duration is calculated as follows:

$$\text{Duration} = \frac{\sum_{t=1}^{N} \frac{t(CF_t)}{(1 + r_d)^t}}{V_B}$$

Here r_d is the required return on the bond, N is the bond's years to maturity, t is the year each cash flow occurs, and CF_t is the cash flow in Year t. (CF_t = INT for t < N and CF_t = INT + M for t = N, where INT is the interest payment and M is the principal payment.)

4. Excel's DURATION function can be used to calculate a bond's duration.

F. One simple way to minimize price risk and reinvestment risk is to buy a zero-coupon Treasury security with a maturity that equals the investor's investment horizon.

1. The investor will receive a guaranteed payment equal to the bond's face value; hence, the investor faces no price risk.

2. As there are no coupons to reinvest, there is no reinvestment risk.

121

3. Investors in zeros have to pay taxes each year on their amortized gain in value, even though the bonds don't produce any cash until the bond matures or is sold.

4. Purchasing a zero-coupon bond with a maturity equal to the investor's investment horizon enables the investor to lock in a nominal cash flow, but the value of that cash flow will still depend on what happens to inflation during the investor's investment horizon.

G. A positive maturity risk premium would suggest that investors on average regard longer-term bonds as being riskier than shorter-term bonds.

VIII. Potential default is another important risk that bondholders face. If the issuer defaults, investors receive less than the promised return on the bond.

A. Default risk is influenced by both the financial strength of the issuer and the terms of the bond contract, especially whether collateral has been pledged to secure the bond.

B. The higher the probability of default, the higher the premium and thus the yield to maturity.

1. Default risk on Treasury securities is zero, but default risk can be substantial for lower-grade corporate and municipal bonds.

2. If a bond's default risk changes, this will affect the bond's price.

C. Corporations can influence the default risk of their bonds by changing the types of bonds they issue.

1. Under a *mortgage bond*, the corporation pledges certain assets as security for the bond.

   a. All mortgage bonds are written subject to an *indenture*, which is a legal document that spells out in detail the rights of both the bondholders and the corporation.

   b. These indentures are generally "open ended," meaning that new bonds can be issued from time to time under the same indenture.

   c. The amount of new bonds that can be issued is usually limited to a specific percentage of the firm's total "bondable" property.

2. A *debenture* is an unsecured bond, and as such, it provides no lien against specific property as security for the obligation.

   a. Debenture holders are general creditors whose claims are protected by property not otherwise pledged.

   b. In practice, the use of debentures depends both on the nature of the firm's assets and on its general credit strength.

3. *Subordinated debentures* have claims on assets, in the event of bankruptcy, only after senior debt as named in the subordinated debt's indenture has been paid.

   a. Subordinated debentures may be subordinated to designated notes payable or to all other debt.

   b. How subordination works, and how it strengthens the position of senior debtholders, is explained in detail in Web Appendix 7C.

D. Bond issues are normally assigned quality ratings by rating agencies. The three major rating agencies are Moody's Investors Service (Moody's), Standard & Poor's Corporation (S&P), and Fitch's Investor Service. These ratings reflect the probability that a bond will go into default.

1. Aaa (Moody's) and AAA (S&P) are the highest ratings. The triple- and double-A bonds are extremely safe.

2. Single-A and triple-B bonds are also strong enough to be called *investment-grade bonds* and they are the lowest-rated bonds that many banks and other institutional investors are permitted by law to hold.

3. Double-B and lower-rated bonds are speculative, or *junk, bonds,* which have a significant probability of going into default.

4. Bond rating assignments are based on both qualitative and quantitative factors including the firm's financial ratios and a firm's business risk, such as its competitiveness within its industry and the quality of its management.

    a. Companies with lower business risk, lower debt ratios, higher cash flow to debt, and lower debt to EBITDA typically have higher bond ratings.

5. Bond ratings are important both to firms and to investors.

    a. A bond's rating is an indicator of its default risk, so the rating has a direct, measurable influence on the bond's interest rate and the firm's cost of debt.

    b. Most bonds are purchased by institutional investors rather than individuals, and many institutions are restricted to investment-grade securities, securities with ratings of Baa/BBB or above.

6. Changes in a firm's bond rating affect both its ability to borrow capital and the cost of that capital.

7. Rating agencies review outstanding bonds on a periodic basis, occasionally upgrading or downgrading a bond as the issuer's circumstances change.

    a. If a company issues more bonds, this will trigger a review by the rating agencies.

    b. Over the long run, bond ratings have done a reasonably good job of measuring the average credit risk of bonds and of changing ratings whenever there is a significant change in credit quality.

    c. Bond ratings do not adjust immediately to changes in credit quality, and in some cases there can be a considerable lag between a change in credit quality and a change in rating.

E. In the event of *bankruptcy*, debtholders have a prior claim over the claims of both common and preferred stockholders to a firm's income and assets.

    1. When a business becomes *insolvent*, it does not have enough cash to meet scheduled interest and principal payments. Thus, it must decide whether to dissolve the firm through *liquidation* or to permit it to reorganize and thus stay alive. These issues are discussed in Chapters 7 and 11 of the federal bankruptcy statutes.

    2. In a *reorganization*, a plan may call for *restructuring* the firm's debt, in which case the interest rate may be reduced, the term to maturity lengthened, or some of the debt may be exchanged for equity.

        a. The point of the restructuring is to reduce the financial charges to a level that the firm's cash flows can support.

    3. Liquidation occurs if the company is deemed to be too far gone to be saved.

    a. Upon liquidation, assets are sold and the cash is distributed as specified in Chapter 7 of the Bankruptcy Act, beginning with highest priority to secured creditors and ending with lowest priority to common stockholders (assuming anything is left).

4. Stockholders generally receive little in reorganizations and nothing in liquidations because the assets are generally worth less than the amount of debt outstanding.

5. The major points of bankruptcy are:

    a. Federal bankruptcy statutes govern reorganization and liquidation.

    b. Bankruptcies occur frequently.

    c. A priority of the specified claims must be followed when the assets of a liquidated firm are distributed.

    d. Bondholders' treatment depends on the terms of the bond issue.

    e. Stockholders generally receive little in reorganizations and nothing in liquidations because the assets are usually worth less than the amount of debt outstanding.

6. Web Appendix 7C discusses bankruptcy and reorganization in more detail.

IX.   **Bonds are traded primarily in the over-the-counter market.**

A. Most bonds are owned by and traded among the large financial institutions, and it is relatively easy for the over-the-counter bond dealers to arrange the transfer of large blocks of bonds among the relatively few holders of the bonds.

B. *The Wall Street Journal* routinely reports key developments in the Treasury, corporate, and municipal bond markets.

1. The online edition also lists for each trading day the most actively traded investment-grade bonds, high-yield bonds, and convertible bonds.

Self-Test

Definitional Questions

1. A(n) _____ is a long-term contract under which a borrower agrees to make payments of interest and principal on specific dates.

2. _____ bonds are issued by state and local governments, and the _____ earned on these bonds is exempt from federal taxes.

3. The stated face value of a bond is referred to as its _____ value and is usually set at $_____.

4. The "coupon _____ rate" on a bond is determined by dividing the coupon _____ by the par value of the bond.

5. The date on which the par value of a bond is repaid to each bondholder is known as the _____ date.

6. A(n)_____-_____ bond is one whose interest rate fluctuates with shifts in the general level of interest rates.

7. A(n) _____ coupon bond is one that pays no annual interest but is sold at a discount below par, thus providing compensation to investors in the form of capital appreciation.

8. The legal document setting forth the terms and conditions of a bond issue is known as the _____.

9. In meeting its sinking fund requirements, a firm may _____ the bonds or purchase them on the open _____.

10. Except when the call is for sinking fund purposes, when a bond issue is called, the firm must pay a call _____, or an amount in excess of the _____ value of the bond.

11. A bond with annual coupon payments represents an annuity of INT dollars per year for N years, plus a lump sum of M dollars at the end of N years, and its value, V_B, is the _____ value of this payment stream.

12. At the time a bond is issued, the coupon interest rate is generally set at a level that will cause the market _____ and the par _____ of the bond to be approximately _____.

13. Market interest rates and bond prices move in _____ directions from one another.

14. The rate of return earned by purchasing a bond and holding it until maturity is known as the bond's _____ to _____.

15. To adjust the bond valuation formula for semiannual coupon payments, the _____ payment and _____ rate must be divided by 2, and the number of _____ must be multiplied by 2.

16. A bond secured by real estate is known as a(n) _____ bond.

17. _____ bonds are issued by the Federal government and are not exposed to default risk.

18. _____ bonds pay interest only if the interest is earned.

19. The interest rate of a(n) _____, or _____ power, bond is based on an inflation index, so the interest paid rises automatically when the inflation rate rises, thus protecting the bondholders against inflation.

20. Any bond originally offered at a price significantly _____ its par value is called an original issue _____ bond.

21. Once a bond has been on the market for a while, it is classified as an outstanding bond, or a(n) _____ issue.

22. The _____ yield is the annual coupon payment divided by the bond's current price.

23. _____ maturity is the number of years to maturity at the time a bond is issued.

24. A(n) _____ fund provision facilitates the orderly retirement of a bond issue.

25. The process of using the proceeds of a new lower-interest-rate bond issue to retire a higher-interest-rate issue and reduce the firm's interest expense is called a(n) _____ operation.

26. A(n) _____ provision gives the issuing corporation the right to redeem bonds at a premium under specified terms prior to the normal maturity date.

27. A(n) _____ issue is a bond that has just been issued.

28. A(n) _____ bond sells above its par value, when the going rate of interest falls below the coupon rate.

29. If current interest rates are well below an outstanding bond's coupon rate, then a callable bond is likely to be called, and investors should estimate the expected rate of return on the bond as the _____ to _____.

30. A(n) _____ is an unsecured bond, and as such, it provides no lien against specific property as security for the obligation.

31. A(n) _____ call occurs when bonds are not callable until several years after they are issued. These bonds are said to have call _____.

32. _____ bonds are securities that are exchangeable into shares of common stock, at a fixed price, at the option of the bondholder.

33. _____ bonds contain provisions that allow the bonds' investors to sell the bonds back to the company prior to maturity at a specified price.

34. For bonds with similar coupons, the longer the maturity of the bond, the greater the exposure to _____ risk.

35. The risk of a decline in income due to a drop in interest rates is called _____ risk.

36. The investment _____ is how long the investor plans to hold the bond.

37. In practice, the use of debentures depends both on the nature of the firm's _____ and on its general _____ strength.

38. Single-A and triple-B bonds are strong enough to be called _____-_____ bonds, and they are the lowest-rated bonds that many _____ and other institutional investors are permitted by law to hold.

39. In the event of _____, debtholders have a prior claim over the claims of both common and preferred stockholders to a firm's income and assets.

40. When a business becomes _____, it does not have enough cash to meet scheduled interest and principal payments.

41. _____ risk is often referred to as credit risk.

42. _____ bonds are exposed to an additional risk if the bonds are denominated in a currency other than that of the investor's home currency.

43. Bonds with _____ are similar to convertibles.

44. A(n) _____ bond is one that sells below its par value, when the going rate of interest rises above the coupon rate.

45. The total rate of return on a bond consists of a(n) _____ yield plus a capital _____ yield.

46. The market value of a bond will always approach its _____ value as its maturity date approaches, provided the firm does not go _____.

47. A(n) _____ maturity risk premium would suggest that investors on average regard longer-term bonds as being riskier than shorter-term bonds.

48. Double-B and lower-rated bonds are speculative, or _____, bonds, which have a significant probability of going into default.

49. A bond's _____ is an indicator of its default risk, and it has a direct measurable influence on the bond's interest rate and the firm's cost of debt.

50. Bonds are traded primarily in the _____-_____-_____ market.

Conceptual Questions

1. Changes in economic conditions cause interest rates and bond prices to vary over time.

    a. True
    b. False

2. If the appropriate rate of interest on a bond is greater than its coupon rate, the market value of that bond will be above par value.

    a. True
    b. False

3. A 20-year, annual coupon bond with one year left to maturity has the same price risk as a 10-year, annual coupon bond with one year left to maturity. Both bonds are of equal risk, have the same coupon rate, and the prices of the two bonds are equal.

    a. True
    b. False

4. There is a direct relationship between bond ratings and the required rate of return on bonds; that is, the higher the rating, the higher is the required rate of return.

    a. True
    b. False

5. The "penalty" for having a low bond rating is less severe when the Security Market Line is relatively steep than when it is not so steep.

    a. True
    b. False

6. Which of the following statements is *false*? In all of the statements, assume that "other things are held constant."

    a. Price sensitivity—that is, the change in price due to a given change in the required rate of return—increases as a bond's maturity increases.
    b. For a given bond of any maturity, a given percentage point increase in the going interest rate (r_d) causes a *larger* dollar capital loss than the capital gain stemming from an identical decrease in the interest rate.
    c. For any given maturity, a given percentage point increase in the interest rate causes a *smaller* dollar capital loss than the capital gain stemming from an identical decrease in the interest rate.
    d. From a borrower's point of view, interest paid on bonds is tax deductible.
    e. A 20-year zero-coupon bond has less reinvestment risk than a 20-year coupon bond.

7. Which of the following statements is correct?

   a. Ignoring interest accrued between payment dates, if the required rate of return on a bond is less than its coupon interest rate, and r_d remains below the coupon rate until maturity, then the market value of that bond will be below its par value until the bond matures, at which time its market value will equal its par value.

   b. Assuming equal coupon rates, a 20-year original maturity bond with one year left to maturity has more price risk than a 10-year original maturity bond with one year left to maturity.

   c. Regardless of the size of the coupon payment, the price of a bond moves in the same direction as interest rates; for example, if interest rates rise, bond prices also rise.

   d. For bonds, price sensitivity to a given change in interest rates generally increases as years remaining to maturity increases.

   e. Because short-term interest rates are much more volatile than long-term rates, you would, in the real world, be subject to more price risk if you purchased a 30-day bond than if you bought a 30-year bond.

8. Which of the following statements is correct?

   a. Bonds C and Z both have a $1,000 par value and 10 years to maturity. They have the same default risk, and they both have an effective annual rate (EAR) of 8%. If Bond C has a 15% annual coupon and Bond Z a zero coupon (paying just $1,000 at maturity), then Bond Z will be exposed to more *price risk*, which is defined as the *percentage* loss of value in response to a given increase in the going interest rate.

   b. If the words "price risk" were replaced by the words "reinvestment risk" in Statement a, then the statement would be true.

   c. The interest rate paid by the state of Florida on its debt would be lower, other things held constant, if interest on the debt were not exempt from federal income taxes.

   d. Given the conditions in Statement a, we can be sure that Bond Z would have the higher price.

   e. Statements a, b, c, and d are false.

9. If a company's bonds are selling at a *discount*, then:

   a. The YTM is the return investors probably expect to earn.
   b. The YTC is probably the expected return.
   c. Either a or b could be correct, depending on the yield curve.
   d. The current yield will exceed the expected rate of return.
   e. The after-tax cost of debt to the company will have to be less than the coupon rate on the bonds.

Problems

1. Delta Corporation has a bond issue outstanding with an annual coupon rate of 7% and 4 years remaining until maturity. The par value of the bond is $1,000. Determine the current value of the bond if present market conditions justify a 14% required rate of return.

   a. $1,126.42
   b. $1,000.00
   c. $ 796.04
   d. $ 791.00
   e. $ 536.38

2. Delta Corporation has a bond issue outstanding with a 7% coupon, semiannual payments, and 4 years remaining until maturity. The par value of the bond is $1,000. Determine the current value of the bond if present market conditions justify a 14% required rate of return.

    a. $1,126.42
    b. $1,000.00
    c. $ 796.04
    d. $ 791.00
    e. $ 536.38

3. Delta Corporation has a bond issue outstanding with an annual coupon rate of 7% and 20 years remaining until maturity. The par value of the bond is $1,000. Determine the current value of the bond if present market conditions justify a 14% required rate of return.

    a. $1,126.42
    b. $1,000.00
    c. $ 796.04
    d. $ 791.00
    e. $ 536.38

4. Delta Corporation has a bond issue outstanding with an annual coupon rate of 7% and 20 years remaining until maturity. The par value of the bond is $1,000 and present market conditions justify a 14% required rate of return. What is the bond's current yield?

    a. 12.20%
    b. 13.05%
    c. 13.75%
    d. 14.00%
    e. 14.50%

5. A bond that matures in 6 years sells for $950. The bond has a face value of $1,000 and a 5.5% annual coupon. What is the bond's current yield?

    a. 5.50%
    b. 6.00%
    c. 5.79%
    d. 6.25%
    e. 6.50%

6. A bond that matures in 6 years sells for $950. The bond has a face value of $1,000 and a 5.5% annual coupon. What is the bond's yield to maturity, r_d?

    a. 5.50%
    b. 5.79%
    c. 6.33%
    d. 6.53%
    e. 7.00%

7. Refer to Problem 6. Assume that the yield to maturity remains constant for the next two years. What will be the price of the bond two years from today?

    a. $ 964.61
    b. $ 975.25
    c. $ 988.89
    d. $1,000.00
    e. $1,250.00

8. Acme Products has a bond issue outstanding with 8 years remaining to maturity, a coupon rate of 10% with interest paid annually, and a par value of $1,000. If the current market price of the bond issue is $814.45, what is the yield to maturity, r_d?

    a. 12%
    b. 13%
    c. 14%
    d. 15%
    e. 16%

9. A bond that matures in 8 years has a 10% coupon rate, semiannual payments, a face value of $1,000, and an 8.5% current yield. What is the bond's nominal yield to maturity (YTM)?

    a. 6.9%
    b. 7.1%
    c. 7.7%
    d. 8.5%
    e. 10.0%

10. You have just been offered a bond for $863.73. The coupon rate is 8%, payable annually, and interest rates on new issues with the same degree of risk are 10%. You want to know how many more interest payments you will receive, but the party selling the bond cannot remember. If the par value is $1,000, how many interest payments remain?

    a. 10
    b. 11
    c. 12
    d. 13
    e. 14

11. The Graf Company needs to finance some new R&D programs, so it will sell new bonds for this purpose. Graf's currently outstanding bonds have a $1,000 par value, a 10% coupon rate, and pay interest semiannually. The outstanding bonds have 25 years remaining to maturity, are callable after 5 years at a price of $1,090, and currently sell at a price of $700. The yield curve is expected to remain flat. On the basis of these data, what is the best estimate of Graf's *nominal interest rate* on the new bonds it plans to sell?

    a. 21.10%
    b. 14.48%
    c. 15.67%
    d. 16.25%
    e. 18.29%

12. Bird Corporation's 12% coupon rate, semiannual payment, $1,000 par value bonds that mature in 20 years are callable at a price of $1,100 five years from now. The bonds sell at a price of $1,300, and the yield curve is flat. Assuming that interest rates in the economy are expected to remain at their current level, what is the best estimate of Bird's *nominal interest rate* on the new bonds?

    a. 8.46%
    b. 6.16%
    c. 9.28%
    d. 6.58%
    e. 8.76%

13. Hooper Printing, Inc. has a bond issue outstanding with 14 years left to maturity. The bond issue has a 7% annual coupon rate and a par value of $1,000, but due to changes in interest rates, each bond's value has fallen to $749.04. The capital gains yield earned by investors over the last year was -25.10%. What is the expected current yield for the next year on this bond issue?

    a. 8.24%
    b. 9.35%
    c. 10.00%
    d. 10.50%
    e. 8.75%

14. Refer to Problem 13. What is the yield to maturity on this bond issue?

    a. 8.24%
    b. 9.35%
    c. 10.00%
    d. 10.50%
    e. 8.75%

15. Refer to Problem 13. What is the expected capital gains yield for the next year on this bond issue?

    a. -1.00%
    b. 0.50%
    c. 1.15%
    d. 1.75%
    e. 2.00%

16. You have just purchased a 15-year, $1,000 par value bond. The coupon rate on this bond is 7.5% and interest is paid semiannually. If you require an "effective" annual interest rate of 6.09%, then how much should you have paid for this bond?

    a. $ 995.00
    b. $1,056.50
    c. $1,210.25
    d. $1,100.00
    e. $1,147.00

17. Suppose Hadden Inc. is negotiating with an insurance company to sell a bond issue. Each bond has a par value of $1,000, it would pay 10% per year in quarterly payments of $25 per quarter for 10 years, and then it would pay 12% per year ($30 per quarter) for the next 10 years (Years 11-20). The $1,000 principal would be returned at the end of 20 years. The insurance company's alternative investment is in a 20-year mortgage that has a nominal rate of 14% and provides monthly payments. If the mortgage and the bond issue are equally risky, how much should the insurance company be willing to pay Hadden for each bond?

    a. $750.78
    b. $781.50
    c. $804.65
    d. $710.49
    e. $840.97

Web Appendix 7A

Note: Study the information given in Web Appendix 7A, Zero Coupon Bonds, before working the following problems.

1. J.C. Nickel is planning a zero coupon bond issue. The bond has a par value of $1,000, matures in 10 years, and will be sold at an 80% discount, or for $200. The firm's marginal federal-plus-state tax rate is 40%. What is the annual after-tax cost of debt to Nickel on this issue?

    a. 10.48%
    b. 10.00%
    c. 11.62%
    d. 14.79%
    e. 17.46%

2. Assume that the city of Miami sold an issue of $1,000 maturity value, tax-exempt (muni), zero coupon bonds 10 years ago. The bonds had a 30-year maturity when they were issued, and the interest rate built into the issue was a nominal 12%, but with semiannual compounding. The bonds are now callable at a premium of 12% over the accrued value. What effective annual rate of return would an investor who bought the bonds when they were issued and who still owns them earn if they are called today?

    a. 13.33%
    b. 12.00%
    c. 12.37%
    d. 11.76%
    e. 13.64%

Web Appendix 7B

Note: Study the information given in Web Appendix 7B, Bond Risk and Duration, before working the following problems.

1. A bond that matures in 5 years has a 6% annual coupon and a face value of $1,000. The bond sells for $1,043.29 and has a yield to maturity of 5%. What is the bond's duration?

    a. 3.75 years
    b. 4.00 years
    c. 4.48 years
    d. 4.67 years
    e. 4.88 years

2. A bond that matures in 5 years has a 12% annual coupon and a face value of $1,000. The bond sells for $931.34 and has a yield to maturity of 14%. What is the bond's duration?

    a. 3.75 years
    b. 4.00 years
    c. 4.48 years
    d. 4.67 years
    e. 4.88 years

Web Appendix 7C

Note: Study the information given in Web Appendix 7C, Bankruptcy and Reorganization, before working the following problem.

1. The Stanton Marble Company has the following balance sheet:

Stanton Marble Company
Balance Sheet

Current assets	$15,120	Accounts payable	$ 3,240
		Notes payable (to bank)	1,620
		Accrued taxes	540
		Accrued wages	540
		Total current liabilities	$ 5,940
Fixed assets	8,100	First mortgage bonds	2,700
		Second mortgage bonds	2,700
		Total mortgage bonds	$ 5,400
		Subordinated debentures	3,240
		Total debt	$14,580
		Preferred stock	1,080
		Common stock	7,560
Total assets	$23,220	Total liabilities and equity	$23,220

The debentures are subordinated only to the notes payable. Suppose Stanton Marble goes bankrupt and is liquidated with $5,400 received from the sale of the fixed assets, which were pledged as security for the first and second mortgage bonds, and $8,640 received from the sale of current assets. The trustee's costs total $1,440. How much will the holders of subordinated debentures receive?

a. $2,052
b. $2,448
c. $3,240
d. $2,709
e. $3,056

Answers

Definitional Questions

1. bond
2. Municipal; interest
3. par; 1,000
4. interest; payment
5. maturity
6. floating-rate
7. zero
8. indenture
9. call; market
10. premium; par
11. present
12. price; value; equal
13. opposite
14. yield; maturity
15. coupon; interest; years
16. mortgage
17. Treasury
18. Income
19. indexed; purchasing
20. below; discount
21. seasoned
22. current
23. Original
24. sinking
25. refunding
26. call
27. new
28. premium
29. yield; call
30. debenture
31. deferred; protection
32. Convertible
33. Putable
34. price
35. reinvestment
36. horizon
37. assets; credit
38. investment-grade; banks
39. bankruptcy
40. insolvent
41. Default
42. Foreign
43. warrants
44. discount
45. current; gains
46. par; bankrupt
47. positive
48. junk
49. rating
50. over-the-counter

Conceptual Questions

1. a. For example, if inflation increases, the interest rate (or required return) will increase, resulting in a decline in bond price.

2. b. It will sell at a discount, so its market value will be less than its par value.

3. a. Both bonds are valued as 1-year bonds regardless of their original issue dates, and since they are of equal risk and have the same coupon rate, their prices must be equal.

4. b. The relationship is inverse. The higher the rating, the lower is the default risk and hence the lower is the required rate of return.

5. b. A steeper SML implies a higher risk premium on risky securities and thus a greater "penalty" on lower-rated bonds.

6. b. Statements a, d, and e are true. To determine which of the remaining statements is false, it is best to use an example. Assume you have a 10-year, 10% annual coupon bond that sold at par. If interest rates increase to 13%, the value of the bond decreases to $837.21, while if interest rates decrease to 7%, the value of the bond increases to $1,210.71. Thus, the capital gain is greater than the capital loss and statement b is false.

7. d. As years to maturity increase for a bond, the number of discount periods used in finding the current bond value also increases. Therefore, bonds with longer maturities will have more price sensitivity to a given change in interest rates.

8. a. Bond C has a high coupon (hence its name), so bondholders receive cash flows right away. Bond Z has a zero coupon, so its holders will receive no cash flows until the bond matures. Since all of the cash flows on Z come at the end, a given increase in the interest rate will cause this bond's value to fall sharply relative to the decline in value of the coupon bond.

   You could also use the data in the problem to find the value of the two bonds at two different interest rates, and then calculate the percentage change. For example, at $r_d = 15\%$, $V_C = \$1,000$ and $V_Z = \$247.18$. At $r_d = 20\%$, $V_C = \$790.38$ and $V_Z = \$161.51$. Therefore, Bond Z declines in value by 34.66%, while Bond C declines by only 20.96%. Note that Bond Z is exposed to *less* reinvestment risk than Bond C.

9. a. When bonds sell at a discount, the going interest rate (r_d) is above the coupon rate. If a company called the old discount bonds and replaced them with new bonds, the new coupon would be above the old coupon. This would increase a firm's interest cost; hence, the company would not call the discount bonds. Therefore, the YTM would be the expected rate of return.

Solutions

Problems

1. c. Calculator solution: Input N = 4, I/YR = 14, PMT = 70, FV = 1000, and solve for V_B = PV = $796.04.

2. d. Calculator solution: Input N = 8, I/YR = 7, PMT = 35, FV = 1000, and solve for V_B = PV = $791.00.

3. e. Calculator solution: Input N = 20, I/YR = 14, PMT = 70, FV = 1000, and solve for V_B = PV = $536.38.

4. b. Solve for the price of the bond: Input N = 20, I/YR = 14, PMT = 70, FV = 1000, and solve for V_B = PV = $536.38.

    Next, solve for the current yield:
    Current yield = Annual interest/Current price of bond
    $$= \$70/\$536.38$$
    $$= 13.05\%$$

5. c. V_B = $950; M = $1,000; INT = 0.055 × $1,000 = $55.

    Current yield = Annual interest/Current price of bond
    $$= \$55.00/\$950.00$$
    $$= 5.79\%$$

6. d. N = 6; PV = -950; PMT = 55; FV = 1000; YTM = ? Solve for I/YR = YTM = 6.5339% ≈ 6.53%.

7. a. N = 4; I/YR = 6.5339; PMT = 55; FV = 1000; PV = ? Solve for V_B = PV = $964.61.

8. c. Calculator solution: Input N = 8, PV = -814.45, PMT = 100, FV = 1000, and solve for I/YR = r_d = 14.00%.

9. b. N = 8 × 2 = 16; PMT = 0.10/2 × $1,000 = 50; FV = 1000; V_B = PV = ?; YTM = ?

    Solve for V_B = PV using the 8.5% current yield:
    Current yield = Annual interest payment/Current bond price
    $$8.5\% = \$100/V_B$$
    $$V_B = \$100/0.085$$
    $$V_B = \$1,176.47$$

Now, solve for YTM = r_d:

N = 16; PV = -1176.47; PMT = 50; FV = 1000; r_d = YTM = ?

Solve for I/YR = YTM = r_d/2 × 2 = 3.5368% × 2 = 7.0736% ≈ 7.1%.

When calculating the YTM, realize that the interest rate first obtained is a periodic rate. To arrive at the correct answer, the periodic interest rate must be put on an annual basis.

10. c. Using a financial calculator, input I/YR = 10, PV = -863.73, PMT = 80, FV = 1000, and solve for N = 12.

11. b. Investors would expect to earn either the YTM or the YTC, and the expected return on the old bonds is the cost Graf would have to pay in order to sell new bonds.

YTM: Enter N = 2(25) = 50; PV = -700; PMT = 100/2 = 50; and FV = 1000. Press I/YR to obtain r_d/2 = 7.24%. Multiply 7.24%(2) = 14.48% to get the YTM.

YTC: Enter N = 2(5) = 10, PV = -700, PMT = 50, FV = 1090, and then press I/YR to obtain r_d/2 = 10.55%. Multiply 10.55%(2) = 21.10% to calculate the YTC.

Would investors expect the company to call the bonds? Graf currently pays 10% on its debt (the coupon rate). New debt would cost at least 14.48%. Because r_d > 10% coupon rate, it would be stupid for the company to call the bonds, so investors would not expect a call. Therefore, they would expect to earn 14.48% on the bonds. This is r_d, so 14.48% is the rate Graf would probably have to pay on new bonds.

12. d. The bond is selling at a large premium, which means that its coupon rate is much higher than the going rate of interest. Therefore, the bond is likely to be called—it is more likely to be called than to remain outstanding until it matures. Thus, it will probably provide a return equal to the YTC rather than the YTM. So, there is no point in calculating the YTM; just calculate the YTC. Enter these values: N = 10, PV = -1300, PMT = 60, and FV = 1100. Solving for I/YR you obtain the periodic rate, which is 3.29%, so the nominal YTC = 2 × 3.29% = 6.58%. This would be close to the going rate, and it is about what Bird would have to pay on new bonds.

13. b. The current yield is defined as the annual coupon payment divided by the current price. CY = $70/$749.04 = 9.35%.

14. d. Solving for YTM:

N = 14, PV = -749.04, PMT = 70, FV = 1000; I/YR = YTM = ?

I/YR = YTM = 10.50%

15. c. Expected capital gains yield can be found as the difference between YTM and the current yield.

CGY = YTM − CY = 10.50% − 9.35% = 1.15%

Alternatively, you can solve for the capital gains yield by first finding the expected price next year.

N = 13, I/YR = 10.5, PMT = 70, FV = 1000; V_{B1} = PV = ?

V_{B1} = PV = $757.69

Hence, the capital gains yield is the percent price appreciation over the next year.
CGY = $(P_1 - P_0)/P_0$ = ($757.69 - $749.04)/$749.04 = 1.15%

16. e. Before you can solve for the price, we must find the appropriate semiannual rate at which to evaluate this bond.

$$EAR = (1 + I_{NOM}/2)^2 - 1$$
$$0.0609 = (1 + I_{NOM}/2)^2 - 1$$
$$1.0609 = (1 + I_{NOM}/2)^2$$
$$1.03 = 1 + I_{NOM}/2$$
$$0.03 = I_{NOM}/2$$
$$I_{NOM} = 0.06$$

Semiannual interest rate = 0.06/2 = 0.03 = 3%

Solving for price:
N = 30, I = 3, PMT = 37.50, FV = 1000; V_B = PV = ?
V_B = PV = -$1,147.00

17. a.
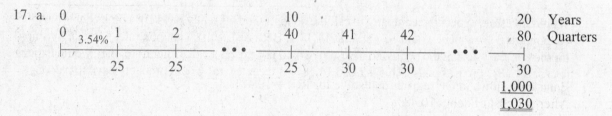

1. You could enter the time line values into the cash flow register, but one element is missing: the interest rate. Once we have the interest rate, we could press the NPV key to get the value of the bond.

2. We need a *periodic* interest rate, and it needs to be a quarterly rate, found as the annual nominal rate divided by 4: $I_{PER} = I_{NOM}/4$. So, we need to find I_{NOM} so that we can find I_{PER}.

3. The insurance company will insist on earning at least the same effective annual rate on the bond issue as it can earn on the mortgage. The mortgage pays 14% monthly, which is equivalent to an EAR = 14.93%. Using a financial calculator, enter NOM% = 14, P/YR = 12, and press EFF% to obtain 14.93%. So, the bond issue will have to have I_{NOM}, with quarterly payments, which translates into an EAR of 14.93%.

4. EAR = 14.93% is equivalent to a quarterly nominal rate of 14.16%; that is, a nominal rate of 14.16% with quarterly compounding is equivalent to an EAR of 14.93%. You can find this by entering EFF% = 14.93, P/YR = 4, and pressing the NOM% key to get NOM% = 14.16%. If this nominal rate is set on the bond issue, the insurance company will earn the same effective rate as it can get on the mortgage.

5. The periodic rate for a 14.16% nominal rate, with quarterly compounding, is 14.16%/4 = 3.54%. This 3.54% is the rate to use in the time line calculations.

With an HP-10BII calculator, enter the following data:
$CF_0 = 0$, CF_j = 25; N_j = 40; CF_j = 30; N_j = 39; CF_j = 1030; I/YR = 3.54.
Solve for V_B = NPV = $750.78.

With an HP-17BII calculator, enter the following data:
Flow(0) = 0 Input; Flow(1) = 25 Input; # Times = 40 Input; Flow(2) = 30 Input; # Times = 39 Input; Flow(3) = 1030 Input; # Times = 1 Input; Exit; Calc; I/YR = 3.54. Solve for V_B = NPV = $750.78.

If each bond is priced at $750.78, the insurance company will earn the same effective rate of return on the bond issue as on the mortgage.

Web Appendix 7A

1. a. Maturity = N = 10; Issue price = PV = 200; PMT = 0; Maturity value = FV = 1000; Corporate tax rate = 40%.

    Enter into a financial calculator: N = 10, PV = 200, PMT = 0, and FV = -1000, and then solve for r_d = I/YR = 17.46%. However, this is a before-tax cost of debt. $r_d(1 - T) = 17.46\%(1 - 0.4) = 10.48\%$.

    Alternatively, set the analysis up on a time line:

	0	1	2	3	4	5	6	7	8	9	10
Year-end accrued value[1]	200	234.92	275.94	324.12	380.71	447.18	525.25	616.96	724.69	851.22	1,000.00
Interest deduction[2]		34.92	41.02	48.18	56.59	66.47	78.07	91.71	107.73	126.53	148.78
Tax savings (40%)[3]		13.97	16.41	19.27	22.64	26.59	31.23	36.68	43.09	50.61	59.51
Cash flow[4]	200	13.97	16.41	19.27	22.64	26.59	31.23	36.68	43.09	50.61	-940.49

    Enter cash flows in CF register and solve for IRR = 10.48%.
    After-tax cost of debt: 10.48%

    Notes:
    [1]Year-end accrued value = Issue price $\times (1 + r_d)^N$
    [2]Interest in Year N = Accrued value$_N$ – Accrued value$_{N-1}$
    [3]Tax savings = (Interest deduction)(T)
    [4]Cash flow in Year 10 = Tax savings – Maturity value

2. e.

    -30.3143

    $\times (1.06)^{20} = $ 97.2222
    $\times$ 1.12
    108.8889

    -30.3143   IRR = 6.6024%

    Periodic rate = 6.6024%
    EAR = $(1.066024)^2 - 1 = 0.1364 = 13.64\%$

    The solution to this problem requires three steps:

    1. Solve for the PV of the original issue. Using a financial calculator, enter N = 60, I/YR = 6, PMT = 0, and FV = 1000, and then solve for PV = $30.3143.

2. Determine the accrued value at the end of 20 periods, and multiply by the call premium.

$$\$30.3143 \times (1.06)^{20} \times 1.12 = \$108.8889$$

3. Solve for the EAR to an investor if the bonds are called today. Using a financial calculator, enter N = 20, PV = -30.3143, PMT = 0, and FV = 108.8889, and then solve for $r_d/2$ = I/YR = 6.6024%.

$$EAR = (1.066024)^2 - 1 = 0.1364 = 13.64\%$$

Web Appendix 7B

1. c. $r_d = 5\%$

t	CF_t	$CF_t/(1 + r_d)^t$	$t(CF_t)/(1 + r_d)^t$
1	$ 60	$ 57.14	$ 57.15
2	60	54.42	108.84
3	60	51.83	155.49
4	60	49.36	197.44
5	1,060	830.54	4,152.70
	$V_B =$	$1,043.29	$4,671.61

Duration = $4,671.61/$1,043.29 = 4.48 years

2. b. $r_d = 14\%$

t	CF_t	$CF_t/(1 + r_d)^t$	$t(CF_t)/(1 + r_d)^t$
1	$ 120	$105.26	$ 105.26
2	120	92.34	184.68
3	120	81.00	243.00
4	120	71.05	284.20
5	1,120	581.69	2,908.45
	$V_B =$	$931.34	$3,725.59

Duration = $3,725.59/$931.34 = 4.00 years

Web Appendix 7C

1. a.

Claimant	Claim Amount (1)	Pro Rata Distribution (2)	Distribution after Subordinate Adjustment (3)	Percent of Claim (4)
Accounts payable	$ 3,240	$ 2,448	$ 2,448	75.56%
Notes payable	1,620	1,224	1,620	100.00
Accrued taxes	540	540	540	100.00
Accrued wages	540	540	540	100.00
1st mortgage bonds	2,700	2,700	2,700	100.00
2nd mortgage bonds	2,700	2,700	2,700	100.00
Subordinated debentures	3,240	2,448	2,052	63.33
Preferred stock	1,080	0	0	0.00
Common stock	7,560	0	0	0.00
Trustee	1,440	1,440	1,440	100.00
Total	$24,660	$14,040	$14,040	56.93%

Explanation of the columns:

(1) Values are taken from the balance sheet.

(2) Since the firm's total debt is $16,020 ($14,580 + $1,440) and only $14,040 ($5,400 + $8,640) is received from the sale of assets, the preferred and common stockholders are wiped out. These stockholders receive nothing.

The $5,400 from the sale of fixed assets is immediately allocated to the mortgage bonds. The holders of the first mortgage bonds are paid off first, so they receive $2,700. The remaining $2,700 from the sale of fixed assets is allocated to the second mortgage bonds, so these bondholders are also paid.

By law, trustee expenses have first claim on the remaining available funds, wages have second priority, and taxes have third priority. Thus, these claims are paid in full.

We now have $6,120 remaining and claims of $8,100, so the general creditors will receive 75.56 cents on the dollar:

$$\frac{\text{Funds available}}{\text{Unsatisfied debt}} = \frac{\$14,040 - \$5,400 - \$1,080 - \$1,440}{\$3,240 + \$1,620 + \$3,240} = 0.7556$$

General creditors are now initially allocated 75.56% of their original claims.

(3) This column reflects a transfer of funds from the subordinated debentures to the notes payable to the bank. Since subordinated debentures are subordinate to bank debt, notes payable to the bank must be paid in full before the debenture holders receive anything. The notes are paid in full by transferring the difference between their book value and initial allocation ($1,620 − $1,224 = $396) from subordinated debentures to notes payable. This reduces the allocation to subordinated debentures and increases the allocation to notes payable by $396.

8

RISK AND RATES OF RETURN

Learning Objectives

1. Explain the difference between stand-alone risk and risk in a portfolio context.

2. Explain how risk aversion affects a stock's required rate of return.

3. Discuss the difference between diversifiable risk and market risk, and explain how each type of risk affects well-diversified investors.

4. Describe what the CAPM is and illustrate how it can be used to estimate a stock's required rate of return.

5. Discuss how changes in the general stock and the bond markets could lead to changes in the required rate of return on a firm's stock.

6. Discuss how changes in a firm's operations might lead to changes in the required rate of return on the firm's stock.

Overview

Risk is an important concept in financial analysis, especially in terms of how it affects security prices and rates of return. Investment risk is associated with the probability of low or negative future returns.

The riskiness of an asset can be considered in two ways: (1) on a stand-alone basis, where the asset's cash flows are analyzed all by themselves, or (2) in a portfolio context, where the cash flows from a number of assets are combined, and then the consolidated cash flows are analyzed.

In a portfolio context, an asset's risk can be divided into two components: (1) a diversifiable risk component, which can be diversified away and hence is of little concern to diversified investors, and (2) a market risk component, which reflects the risk of a general stock market decline and cannot be eliminated by diversification, and therefore, is of concern to investors. Only market risk is relevant; diversifiable risk is irrelevant because it can be eliminated.

An attempt has been made to quantify market risk with a measure called beta. Beta is a measurement of how a particular firm's stock returns move relative to overall movements of stock market returns. The

Capital Asset Pricing Model (CAPM), using the concept of beta and investors' aversion to risk, specifies the relationship between market risk and the required rate of return. This relationship can be visualized graphically with the Security Market Line (SML). The slope of the SML can change, or the line can shift upward or downward, in response to changes in risk or required rates of return.

Outline

I. **Investors like returns and they dislike risk.**

    A. There is a fundamental trade-off between risk and return: to entice investors to take on more risk, you have to provide them with higher expected returns.

    B. Investors who are less comfortable bearing risk tend to gravitate towards lower-risk investments, while investors with a greater-risk appetite tend to put more of their money into higher-risk, higher-return investments.

        1. The average investor's willingness to take on risk also varies over time.

    C. At any point in time, an investor's goal should be to earn returns that are more than sufficient to compensate for the perceived risk of the investment.

    D. The trade-off between risk and return is also an important concept for companies trying to create value for their shareholders.

        1. If a company is investing in riskier projects, it must offer its investors (both bondholders and stockholders) higher expected returns.

        2. Riskier companies trying to increase their stock price must generate higher returns to compensate their stockholders for the additional risk.

        3. The returns that companies have to pay their investors represent the companies' costs of obtaining capital.

            a. From a company's perspective, the risk-return line represents its cost of obtaining capital, and the slope of the risk-return line reflects the average investor's current willingness to take on risk.

            b. Companies create value by investing in projects where the returns on the investments exceed their costs of capital. This translates into operating above the risk-return trade-off line.

II. **Risk refers to the chance that some unfavorable event will occur.**

    A. An asset's risk can be analyzed in two ways: (1) on a *stand-alone basis,* where the asset is considered in isolation, and (2) on a *portfolio basis,* where the asset is held as one of a number of assets in a portfolio.

    B. No investment will be undertaken unless the expected rate of return is high enough to compensate the investor for its perceived risk.

    C. Investment risk is related to the probability of actually earning a low or negative return; thus, the greater the chance of low or negative returns, the riskier the investment.

    D. The *probability distribution* for an event is the listing of all the possible outcomes for the event, with mathematical probabilities assigned to each outcome.

        1. An event's *probability* is defined as the chance that the event will occur.

        2. The sum of the probabilities for a particular event must equal 1.0.

E. The *expected rate of return* is the sum of the products of each possible outcome times its associated probability—it is a weighted average of the various possible outcomes, with the weights being their probabilities of occurrence:

$$\text{Expected rate of return} = \hat{r} = \sum_{i=1}^{N} P_i r_i$$

1. Where the number of possible outcomes is virtually unlimited, *continuous probability distributions* are used in determining the expected rate of return of the event.

2. The tighter, or more peaked, a distribution, the more likely it is that the actual outcome will be close to the expected value, and, consequently, the less likely it is that the actual return will end up far below the expected return.

3. The tighter the probability distribution of expected future returns, the smaller the risk of a given investment.

F. One measure for determining the tightness of a distribution is the *standard deviation*, σ:

$$\text{Standard deviation} = \sigma = \sqrt{\sum_{i=1}^{N} (r_i - \hat{r})^2 P_i}$$

1. The standard deviation is a probability-weighted average deviation from the expected value, and it provides an idea of how far above or below the expected value the actual value is likely to be.

   a. The smaller the standard deviation, the tighter the probability distribution, and, accordingly, the lower the risk of the stock.

2. The *variance, σ^2*, is the square of the standard deviation.

G. If only sample returns data over some past period are available, the standard deviation of returns should be estimated using this formula:

$$\text{Estimated } \sigma = S = \sqrt{\frac{\sum_{t=1}^{N} (\bar{r}_t - \bar{r}_{Avg})^2}{N-1}}$$

1. Because past variability is likely to be repeated, σ may be a good estimate of future risk. However, it is much less reasonable to expect that the average return during any particular past period is the best estimate of what investors think will happen in the future.

2. Calculators have no built-in formula for finding σ where probabilistic data are involved.

3. Both versions of the standard deviation (population versus sample data) are interpreted and used in the same manner—the only difference is in the way they are calculated.

H. Another useful measure of risk is the *coefficient of variation (CV)*, which is the standard deviation divided by the expected return.

1. It shows the risk per unit of return and provides a more meaningful basis for comparison when the expected returns on alternative investments are not the same:

$$\text{Coefficient of variation (CV)} = \frac{\sigma}{\hat{r}}$$

145

    2.   Because the coefficient of variation captures the effects of both risk and return, it is a better measure than the standard deviation for evaluating risk in situations in which investments have substantially different expected returns.

  I. Most investors are *risk averse.* This means that for two alternatives with the same expected rate of return, investors will choose the one with the lower risk. The average investor is risk averse with regard to his or her serious money.

    1.   Risk-averse investors require higher rates of return as an inducement to buy riskier securities.

    2.   The higher a security's risk, the lower its price and the higher its required return.

  J. *Risk premium, RP,* is the difference between the expected rate of return on a given risky asset and that on a less risky asset.

    1.   It represents the additional compensation investors require for assuming additional risk.

    2.   In a market dominated by risk-averse investors, riskier securities compared to less risky securities must have higher expected returns as estimated by the marginal investor. If this situation does not exist, buying and selling in the market will occur until it does exist.

III.   An asset held as part of a portfolio is less risky than the same asset held in isolation. This is important, because most financial assets are not held in isolation; rather, they are held as parts of portfolios. From the investor's standpoint, what is important is the return on his or her portfolio, and the portfolio's risk—not the fact that a particular stock's price rises or falls. Thus, the risk and return of an individual security should be analyzed in terms of how it affects the risk and return of the portfolio in which it is held.

  A. The expected return on a portfolio is the weighted average of the expected returns on the individual assets in the portfolio, with the weights the percentage of the total portfolio invested in each asset:

$$\hat{r}_p = \sum_{i=1}^{N} w_i \hat{r}_i$$

  B. The *realized rate of return* is the return that was actually earned during some past period. The actual return usually turns out to be different from the expected return except for riskless assets.

  C. The riskiness of a portfolio, σ_p, is generally *not* a weighted average of the standard deviations of the individual assets in the portfolio; the portfolio's risk will be smaller than the weighted average of the assets' σ's. The riskiness of a portfolio depends not only on the standard deviations of the individual stocks, but also on the *correlation between the stocks.*

    1.   The *correlation coefficient, ρ,* measures the tendency of two variables to move together. With stocks, these variables are the individual stock returns.

    2.   Diversification does nothing to reduce risk if the portfolio consists of *perfectly positively correlated* stocks.

    3.   As a rule, the risk of a portfolio will decline as the number of stocks in the portfolio increases.

    4.   However, in the typical case, where the correlation among the individual stocks is positive, but less than +1.0, some, but not all, risk can be eliminated.

5. In the real world, it is impossible to form completely riskless stock portfolios. Diversification can reduce risk, but cannot eliminate it.

D. A portfolio consisting of all stocks is called the *market portfolio*. While very large portfolios end up with a substantial amount of risk, it is not as much risk as if all the money were invested in only one stock.

1. Almost half of the risk inherent in an average individual stock can be eliminated if the stock is held in a reasonably well diversified portfolio, which is one containing 40 or more stocks. Some risk always remains, however, so it is virtually impossible to diversify away the effects of broad stock market movements that affect almost all stocks.

2. A portfolio's total risk can be divided into two parts: diversifiable risk and market risk.

3. *Diversifiable risk* is that part of the risk of a stock that can be eliminated by proper diversification. It is caused by random events that are unique to a particular firm. It is also known as company-specific, or unsystematic, risk.

4. *Market risk* is that part of the risk that cannot be eliminated, and it stems from factors that systematically affect most firms, such as war, inflation, recessions, high interest rates, and other macro factors. It is also known as nondiversifiable, systematic, or beta, risk.

    a. Market risk can be measured by the degree to which a given stock tends to move up or down with the market.

    b. Market risk is the *relevant risk*, which reflects a security's contribution to the portfolio's risk and thus is relevant to a rational investor.

    c. It is the risk that is inherent in the market.

5. Investors must be compensated for bearing risk. However, compensation is required only for risk that cannot be eliminated by diversification.

6. A *market portfolio* is a portfolio consisting of all stocks. There are several reasons why investors do not hold market portfolios.

    a. High administrative costs and commissions would more than offset the benefits for individual investors.

    b. *Index funds* can be used by investors for diversification, and many individuals can and do get broad diversification through these funds.

    c. Some people think that they can pick stocks that will beat the market so they buy them rather than the broad market.

    d. Some people can, through superior analysis, beat the market. They find and buy undervalued stocks and sell overvalued stocks and, in the process, cause most stocks to be properly valued—with their expected returns consistent with their risks.

E. The risk that remains once a stock is in a diversified portfolio is its contribution to the portfolio's market risk, and that risk can be measured by the extent to which the stock moves up or down with the market.

1. The tendency of a stock to move with the market is reflected in its *beta coefficient, b,* which is a measure of the stock's volatility relative to that of an average stock. Procedures for calculating betas are described in Web Appendix 8A.

    a. An average-risk stock is defined as one that tends to move up and down in step with the general market. By definition it has a beta of 1.0.

    b.   A stock that is twice as volatile as the market will have a beta of 2.0, while a stock that is half as volatile as the market will have a beta coefficient of 0.5.

  2. The beta coefficient of a portfolio of securities is the weighted average of the individual securities' betas:

$$b_p = \sum_{i=1}^{N} w_i \, b_i$$

  3. Because a stock's beta coefficient reflects its contribution to the riskiness of a portfolio, beta is the theoretically correct measure of a stock's riskiness.

  4. Because a stock's beta coefficient determines how the stock affects the riskiness of a diversified portfolio, beta is, in theory, the most *relevant* measure of a stock's risk.

IV.   The Capital Asset Pricing Model (CAPM) employs the concept of beta, which measures risk as the relationship between a particular stock's movements and the movements of the overall stock market. The CAPM uses a stock's beta, in conjunction with the average investor's degree of risk aversion, to calculate the return that investors require, r_s, on that particular stock.

  A. The *Capital Asset Pricing Model* is an important tool for analyzing the relationship between risk and rates of return.

    1. The model is based on the proposition that a stock's required rate of return is equal to the risk-free rate of return plus a risk premium, where risk reflects diversification.

    2. The model's primary conclusion is: The relevant riskiness of an individual stock is its contribution to the riskiness of a well-diversified portfolio.

  B. The Security Market Line (SML) shows the relationship between risk as measured by beta and the required rate of return for individual securities. The SML equation can be used to find the required rate of return on Stock i:

$$\text{SML: } r_i = r_{RF} + (r_M - r_{RF}) b_i$$

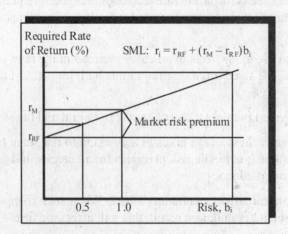

    1. Here r_{RF} is the interest rate on risk-free securities, b_i is the ith stock's beta, and r_M is the return on the market or, alternatively, on an average stock ($b_A = 1.0$).

    2. The term $r_M - r_{RF}$ is the *market risk premium, RP_M*. This is a measure of the additional return over the risk-free rate needed to compensate investors for assuming an average amount of risk.

    a. It is the slope of the SML and reflects the degree of risk aversion in the economy.

    b. The size of this premium depends on the perceived risk of the stock market and investors' degree of risk aversion.

    c. Historical data suggest that the market risk premium varies somewhat from year to year due to changes in investors' risk aversion, but that it has generally ranged from 4% to 8%.

3. In the CAPM, the market risk premium, $r_M - r_{RF}$, is multiplied by the stock's beta coefficient to determine the additional premium over the risk-free rate that is required to compensate investors for the risk inherent in a particular stock.

    a. This premium may be larger or smaller than the premium required on an average stock, depending on the riskiness of that particular stock relative to the overall market as measured by the stock's beta.

4. The risk premium calculated by $(r_M - r_{RF})b_i$ is added to the risk-free rate, r_{RF} (the rate on Treasury securities), to determine the total rate of return required by investors on a particular stock, r_s.

5. Both the Security Market Line and a company's position on it change over time due to changes in interest rates, investors' aversion to risk, and individual companies' betas.

    a. Riskless securities have $b = 0$; so the return on a riskless asset is r_{RF} and is shown as the vertical axis intercept when the SML is graphed.

    b. The slope of the SML reflects the degree of risk aversion in the economy.

C. The risk-free (also known as the nominal, or quoted) rate of interest consists of two elements: (1) a real inflation-free rate of return, r^*, and (2) an inflation premium, IP, equal to the anticipated inflation rate.

1. The real risk-free rate on long-term Treasury bonds has historically ranged from 2% to 4%, with a mean of about 3%.

2. As the expected inflation rate increases, a higher premium must be added to the real risk-free rate of return to compensate for the loss of purchasing power that results from inflation.

3. An increase in r_{RF} leads to an equal increase in the rates of return on all risky assets because the same inflation premium is built into required rates of return on both riskless and risky assets.

D. As risk aversion increases, so do the risk premium and the slope of the SML.

1. The greater the average investor's aversion to risk, then (a) the steeper the slope of the line, (b) the greater the risk premium for all stocks, and (c) the higher the required rates of return on all stocks.

E. Many factors can affect a company's beta. When such changes occur, the required rate of return also changes and, as a result, this will affect the firm's stock price.

1. A firm can influence its market risk, hence its beta, through changes in the composition of its assets and also through changes in the amount of debt it uses.

2. A company's beta can also change as a result of external factors such as increased competition in its industry and expiration of basic patents.

V.   A number of recent studies have raised concerns about the validity of the CAPM.

    A.   A study by Fama and French found no historical relationship between stocks' returns and their market betas.

    B.   As an alternative to the traditional CAPM, researchers and practitioners are developing more general multivariable models with more explanatory variables than just beta.

       1.   In these multivariable models, risk is assumed to be caused by a number of different factors, whereas the CAPM gauges risk only relative to returns on the market portfolio.

       2.   These models represent a potentially important step forward in finance theory; however, they still have some deficiencies when applied in practice, so CAPM is still the most widely used method for estimating required rates of return on stocks.

VI.   Because management's primary goal is stock price maximization, its overriding consideration is the riskiness of the firm's stock. The relevant risk of any physical asset must be measured in terms of its effect on the stock's risk as seen by investors.

    A.   A project that appears to be a risky investment when viewed on a stand-alone basis might not be very risky when viewed within the context of the company as a whole.

    B.   The real issue each time management makes an investment decision is how this investment will affect the risk of the stockholders.

    C.   Capital budgeting decisions impact a company's beta coefficient and its stockholders' risk.

    D.   Key ideas that all investors should consider:

       1.   There is a trade-off between risk and return.

       2.   Diversification is crucial.

       3.   Real returns are what matters.

       4.   The risk of an investment often depends on how long you plan to hold the investment.

       5.   While the past gives us insights into the risk and returns on various investments, there is no guarantee that the future will repeat the past.

VII. Web Appendix 8A contains a discussion of calculating beta coefficients.

    A.   The discussion concentrates on graphic and least squares regression techniques.

Self-Test

Definitional Questions

1. Investment risk is related to the _____ of actually earning low or negative returns; the greater the chance of low or negative returns, the riskier the investment.

2. A listing of all possible _____, with a probability assigned to each, is known as a probability _____.

3. Weighting each possible outcome of a distribution by its _____ of occurrence and summing the results give the expected _____ of the distribution.

4. One measure of the tightness of a probability distribution is the standard _____, a probability-weighted average deviation from the expected value.

5. Investors who prefer outcomes with a high degree of certainty to those that are less certain are described as being risk _____.

6. Owning a portfolio of securities enables investors to benefit from _____.

7. Diversification of a portfolio can result in lower _____ for the same level of return.

8. Diversification of a portfolio is achieved by selecting securities that are not perfectly _____ correlated with each other.

9. That part of a stock's risk that can be eliminated is known as _____ risk, while the portion that cannot be eliminated is called _____ risk.

10. The _____ coefficient measures a stock's volatility relative to that of an average stock.

11. A stock that is twice as volatile as the market would have a beta coefficient of _____, while a stock with a beta of 0.5 would be only _____ as volatile as the market.

12. The beta coefficient of a portfolio is the _____ average of the betas of the individual stocks.

13. The minimum expected return that will induce investors to buy a particular security is the _____ rate of return.

14. The security used to measure the _____-_____ rate is a U.S. Treasury security.

15. The risk premium for a particular stock may be calculated by multiplying the market risk premium times the stock's _____ coefficient.

16. A stock's required rate of return is equal to the _____-_____ rate plus the stock's _____ premium.

17. The risk-free rate of interest consists of two elements: the _____ risk-free rate of return plus a(n) _____ premium.

18. Changes in investors' risk aversion alter the _____ of the Security Market Line.

19. _____ refers to the chance that some unfavorable event will occur.

20. An asset's risk can be analyzed in two ways: (1) on a stand-alone basis and (2) on a(n) _____ basis.

21. Where the number of possible outcomes is virtually unlimited, _____ probability distributions are used in determining the expected rate of return of the event.

22. The _____ is the square of the standard deviation.

23. The _____ of _____ shows the risk per unit of return and provides a more meaningful basis for comparison when the expected returns on alternative investments are not the same.

24. The risk _____ is the difference between the expected rate of return on a given risky asset and that on a less risky asset.

25. The _____ coefficient measures the tendency of two variables to move together.

26. A portfolio consisting of all stocks is called the _____ portfolio.

27. Market risk is the _____ risk, which reflects a security's contribution to the portfolio's risk.

28. The Capital Asset Pricing Model is based on the proposition that a stock's _____ rate of return is equal to the risk-free rate of return plus a risk premium, where risk reflects _____.

29. The _____ risk premium is a measure of the additional return over the risk-free rate needed to compensate investors for assuming an average amount of risk.

30. The _____ rate of return is the return that was actually earned during some past period.

Conceptual Questions

1. The Y-axis intercept of the Security Market Line (SML) indicates the required rate of return on an individual stock with a beta of 1.0.

   a. True
   b. False

2. If a stock has a beta of zero, it will be riskless when held in isolation.

   a. True
   b. False

3. Each stock in a group of 200 stocks has a beta of 1.0. We can be certain that each of the stocks was positively correlated with the market.

   a. True
   b. False

4. Each stock in a group of 200 stocks has a beta of 1.0. If we combined these same 200 stocks into a portfolio, market risk would be reduced below the average market risk of the stocks in the portfolio.

   a. True
   b. False

5. Each stock in a group of 200 stocks has a beta of 1.0. If we combined these same 200 stocks into a portfolio, the standard deviation of the portfolio of these 200 stocks would be lower than the standard deviations of the individual stocks.

   a. True
   b. False

6. Suppose $r_{RF} = 7\%$ and $r_M = 12\%$. If investors became more risk averse, r_M would be likely to decrease.

   a. True
   b. False

7. Suppose $r_{RF} = 7\%$ and $r_M = 12\%$. The required rate of return for a stock with b = 0.5 would increase more than for a stock with b = 2.0.

   a. True
   b. False

8. Suppose $r_{RF} = 7\%$ and $r_M = 12\%$. If the expected inflation rate increased, the required rate of return on a b = 2.0 stock would rise by more than that of a b = 0.5 stock.

   a. True
   b. False

9. Which is the best measure of risk for an asset held in a well-diversified portfolio?

   a. Variance
   b. Standard deviation
   c. Beta
   d. Semi-variance
   e. Expected value

10. In a portfolio of three different stocks, which of the following could *not* be true?

   a. The riskiness of the portfolio is less than the riskiness of each stock held in isolation.
   b. The riskiness of the portfolio is greater than the riskiness of one or two of the stocks.
   c. The beta of the portfolio is less than the beta of each of the individual stocks.
   d. The beta of the portfolio is greater than the beta of one or two of the individual stocks.
   e. The beta of the portfolio is equal to the beta of one of the individual stocks.

11. If investors expected inflation to increase in the future, and they also became more risk averse, what could be said about the change in the Security Market Line (SML)?

   a. The SML would shift up and the slope would increase.
   b. The SML would shift up and the slope would decrease.
   c. The SML would shift down and the slope would increase.
   d. The SML would shift down and the slope would decrease.
   e. The SML would remain unchanged.

12. Which of the following statements is correct?

   a. The SML relates required returns to firms' market risk. The slope and intercept of this line can be controlled by the financial manager.
   b. The slope of the SML is determined by the value of beta.
   c. If you plotted the returns of a given stock against those of the market, and if you found that the slope of the regression line was negative, then the CAPM would indicate that the risk-free rate of return on the stock should be less than the required rate of return for a well-diversified investor, assuming that the observed relationship is expected to continue on into the future.
   d. If investors become less risk averse, the slope of the Security Market Line will increase.
   e. Both the SML and a company's position on it change over time due to changes in interest rates, investors' aversion to risk, and individual companies' betas.

13. Which of the following statements is correct?

   a. Normally, the Security Market Line has an upward slope. However, at one of those unusual times when the yield curve on bonds is downward sloping, the SML will also have a downward slope.
   b. The market risk premium, as it is used in the CAPM theory, is equal to the required rate of return on an average stock minus the required rate of return on an average company's bonds.
   c. If the marginal investor's aversion to risk decreases, then the slope of the yield curve would, other things held constant, tend to increase. If expectations for inflation also increased at the same time risk aversion was decreasing—say the expected inflation rate rose from 5% to 8%—the net effect could possibly result in a parallel upward shift in the SML.
   d. According to the text, it is theoretically possible to combine two stocks, each of which would be quite risky if held as your only asset, and to form a 2-stock portfolio that is riskless. However, the stocks would have to have a correlation coefficient of expected future returns of -1.0, and it is hard to find such stocks in the real world.
   e. A firm cannot influence its market risk.

153

14. Which of the following statements is correct?

   a. The expected future rate of return is always *above* the past realized rate of return except for highly risk-averse investors.

   b. The expected future rate of return is always *below* the past realized rate of return except for highly risk-averse investors.

   c. The expected future rate of return is always *below* the required rate of return except for highly risk-averse investors.

   d. There is no logical reason to think that any relationship exists between the expected future rate of return on a security and the security's required rate of return.

   e. The expected future return on a security should equal the required rate of return.

15. Which of the following statements is correct?

   a. Someone who is highly risk averse should invest in stocks with high betas (above +1.0), other things held constant.

   b. The returns on a stock might be highly uncertain in the sense that they could actually turn out to be much higher or much lower than the expected rate of return (that is, the stock has a high standard deviation of returns), yet the stock might still be regarded by most investors as being less risky than some other stock whose returns are less variable.

   c. The standard deviation is a better measure of risk when comparing securities than the coefficient of variation. This is true because the standard deviation "standardizes" risk by dividing each security's variance by its expected rate of return.

   d. Market risk can be reduced by holding a large portfolio of stocks, and if a portfolio consists of all traded stocks, market risk will be completely eliminated.

   e. The market risk in a portfolio declines as more stocks are added to the portfolio, and the risk decline is linear, that is, each additional stock reduces the portfolio's risk by the same amount.

Problems

1. Stock A has the following probability distribution of expected returns. What is Stock A's expected rate of return and standard deviation?

Probability	Rate of Return
0.1	-15%
0.2	0
0.4	5
0.2	10
0.1	25

   a. 8.0%; 9.5%
   b. 8.0%; 6.5%
   c. 5.0%; 3.5%
   d. 5.0%; 6.5%
   e. 5.0%; 9.5%

2. If $r_{RF} = 5\%$, $r_M = 11\%$, and $b = 1.3$ for Stock X, what is r_X, the required rate of return for Stock X?

   a. 18.7%
   b. 16.7%
   c. 14.8%
   d. 12.8%
   e. 11.9%

3. If r_{RF} = 5%, r_M = 11%, and b = 1.3 for Stock X, what would r_X be if investors expected the inflation rate to increase by 2 percentage points?

    a. 18.7%
    b. 16.7%
    c. 14.8%
    d. 12.8%
    e. 11.9%

4. If r_{RF} = 5%, r_M = 11%, and b = 1.3 for Stock X, what would r_X be if an increase in investors' risk aversion caused the market risk premium to increase by 3 percentage points? r_{RF} remains at 5%.

    a. 18.7%
    b. 16.7%
    c. 14.8%
    d. 12.8%
    e. 11.9%

5. If r_{RF} = 5%, r_M = 11%, and b = 1.3 for Stock X, what would r_X be if investors expected the inflation rate to increase by 2 percentage points and their risk aversion increased by 3 percentage points?

    a. 18.7%
    b. 16.7%
    c. 14.8%
    d. 12.8%
    e. 11.9%

6. A stock has a required return of 12%. The risk-free rate is 6% and the market risk premium is 5%. What is the stock's beta coefficient?

    a. 0.80
    b. 0.95
    c. 1.20
    d. 1.50
    e. 1.75

7. A stock has a required return of 12%. The risk-free rate is 6% and the market risk premium is 5%. If the market risk premium increases to 8%, what will happen to the stock's required rate of return? Assume the risk-free rate and the stock's beta remain unchanged.

    a. 11.75%
    b. 12.80%
    c. 13.10%
    d. 14.25%
    e. 15.60%

8. Jan Middleton owns a 3-stock portfolio with a total investment value equal to $300,000. What is the weighted average beta of Jan's 3-stock portfolio?

Stock	Investment	Beta
A	$100,000	0.5
B	100,000	1.0
C	100,000	1.5
Total	$300,000	

   a. 0.9
   b. 1.3
   c. 1.0
   d. 0.4
   e. 1.2

9. The Apple Investment Fund has a total investment of $450 million in five stocks. What is the fund's overall, or weighted average, beta?

Stock	Investment (Millions)	Beta
1	$130	0.4
2	110	1.5
3	70	3.0
4	90	2.0
5	50	1.0
Total	$450	

   a. 1.14
   b. 1.22
   c. 1.35
   d. 1.46
   e. 1.53

10. The Apple Investment Fund has a total investment of $450 million in five stocks. If the risk-free rate is 12% and the market risk premium is 6%, what is the required rate of return on the Apple Fund?

Stock	Investment (Millions)	Beta
1	$130	0.4
2	110	1.5
3	70	3.0
4	90	2.0
5	50	1.0
Total	$450	

   a. 20.76%
   b. 19.92%
   c. 18.81%
   d. 17.62%
   e. 15.77%

11. Stock A has a beta of 1.2, Stock B has a beta of 0.6, the expected rate of return on an average stock is 12%, and the risk-free rate of return is 7%. By how much does the required return on the riskier stock exceed the required return on the less risky stock?

    a. 4.00%
    b. 3.25%
    c. 3.00%
    d. 2.50%
    e. 3.75%

12. Stock A has an expected return of 8%, a beta coefficient of 0.72, and a standard deviation of expected returns of 28%. Stock B has an expected return of 10%, a beta coefficient of 0.96, and a standard deviation of expected returns of 20%. The risk-free rate is 5.5% and the market risk premium is 4%. What are the coefficients of variation for Stocks A and B?

    a. 3.5; 2.2
    b. 3.2; 2.0
    c. 3.5; 2.0
    d. 3.2; 2.2
    e. 3.5; 1.8

13. Stock A has an expected return of 8%, a beta coefficient of 0.72, and a standard deviation of expected returns of 28%. Stock B has an expected return of 10%, a beta coefficient of 0.96, and a standard deviation of expected returns of 20%. The risk-free rate is 5.5% and the market risk premium is 4%. What are the required rates of return for Stocks A and B?

    a. 7.75%; 9.34%
    b. 8.38%; 9.34%
    c. 8.38%; 10.25%
    d. 7.75%; 10.25%
    e. 6.50%; 9.34%

14. Stock A has an expected return of 8%, a beta coefficient of 0.72, and a standard deviation of expected returns of 28%. Stock B has an expected return of 10%, a beta coefficient of 0.96, and a standard deviation of expected returns of 20%. The risk-free rate is 5.5% and the market risk premium is 4%. What is the required return of a portfolio that has $60,000 invested in Stock A and $40,000 invested in Stock B?

    a. 9.00%
    b. 8.25%
    c. 8.55%
    d. 9.22%
    e. 8.76%

15. You are managing a portfolio of 10 stocks that are held in equal dollar amounts. The current beta of the portfolio is 1.8, and the beta of Stock A is 2.0. If Stock A is sold and the proceeds are used to purchase a replacement stock, what does the beta of the replacement stock have to be to lower the portfolio beta to 1.7?

    a. 1.4
    b. 1.3
    c. 1.2
    d. 1.1
    e. 1.0

16. Consider the following information for the Alachua Retirement Fund, with a total investment of $4 million. The market required rate of return is 12%, and the risk-free rate is 6%. What is its required rate of return?

Stock	Investment	Beta
A	$ 400,000	1.2
B	600,000	-0.4
C	1,000,000	1.5
D	2,000,000	0.8
Total	$4,000,000	

   a.   9.98%
   b. 10.45%
   c. 11.01%
   d. 11.50%
   e. 12.56%

17. What is the coefficient of variation of the expected dollar returns given the following distribution of returns?

Probability	Return
0.4	$30
0.5	25
0.1	-20

   a.   2.0625
   b.   0.6383
   c. 14.3614
   d.   0.7500
   e.   1.2500

18. If the risk-free rate is 8%, the expected return on the market is 13%, and the expected return on Security J is 15%, then what is the beta of Security J?

   a. 1.40
   b. 0.90
   c. 1.20
   d. 1.50
   e. 0.75

19. Consider the following information for three stocks: X, Y, and Z. The returns on each of the three stocks are positively correlated, but they are not perfectly correlated. (That is, all of the correlation coefficients are between 0 and 1.) Portfolio P has half of its funds invested in Stock X and half invested in Stock Y. Portfolio Q has one third of its funds invested in each of these three stocks. The risk-free rate is 5.2%, and the market is in equilibrium. (That is, required returns equal expected returns.) What is the market risk premium ($r_M - r_{RF}$)?

Stock	Expected Return	Standard Deviation	Beta
X	7.6%	15%	0.60
Y	10.2%	15	1.25
Z	12.0%	15	1.70

a. 5.25%
b. 3.30%
c. 6.00%
d. 4.00%
e. 4.75%

20. Hammond Industries (HI) has a beta of 1.75, while Longwood-Ocala Enterprises' (LOE) beta is 0.45. The risk-free rate is 5.5%, and the required rate of return on an average stock is 11.75%. Now the expected rate of inflation built into r_{RF} falls by 1.25 percentage points, the real risk-free rate remains constant, the required return on the market falls to 10.3%, and the betas remain constant. When all of these changes are made, what will be the difference in the required returns on HI's and LOE's stocks?

a. 7.865%
b. 6.355%
c. 5.765%
d. 7.333%
e. 5.250%

21. You have been managing a $3 million portfolio. The portfolio has a beta of 1.10 and a required rate of return of 10%. The current risk-free rate is 5.6%. Assume that you receive another $600,000. If you invest the money in a stock that has a beta of 0.60, what will be the required return on your $3.6 million portfolio?

a. 9.20%
b. 9.67%
c. 8.75%
d. 9.95%
e. 10.20%

Web Appendix 8A

Note: Study the information given in Web Appendix 8A, Calculating Beta Coefficients, before working the following problems.

1. Given the information below, calculate the betas for Stocks A and B. (Hint: Think rise over run.)

Year	Stock A	Stock B	Market
1	-5%	10%	-10%
2	10	20	10
3	25	30	30

a. 1.00; 0.50
b. 0.75; 0.50
c. 0.75; 1.00
d. 0.50; 0.50
e. 0.75; 0.25

2. Refer to the information shown below. The risk-free rate is equal to 7% and the market required return is equal to 10%. What is Stock N's beta coefficient?

Year	Stock N	Market
1	-5%	10%
2	-8	15
3	7	-10

159

  a. 1.00
  b. -0.50
  c. 0.60
  d. -0.75
  e. -0.60

3. Refer to the information shown below. The risk-free rate is equal to 7% and the market required return is equal to 10%. What is Stock N's required rate of return?

Year	Stock N	Market
1	-5%	10%
2	-8	15
3	7	-10

  a. 6.40%
  b. 5.20%
  c. 8.80%
  d. 5.90%
  e. 7.00%

4. Stock Y and the Market had the following rates of return during the last 4 years. What is Stock Y's beta? (Hint: You will need a financial calculator to determine the beta coefficient.)

Year	Y	Z	Market
2008	10.0%	10.0%	10.0%
2009	16.0	11.5	13.5
2010	-7.5	1.0	-4.0
2011	0.0	6.0	5.5

  a. 1.25
  b. 0.75
  c. 1.00
  d. 1.34
  e. 1.57

5. Stock Y, Stock Z, and the Market had the indicated rates of return during the last 4 years shown below.

Year	Y	Z	Market
2008	10.0%	10.0%	10.0%
2009	16.0	11.5	13.5
2010	-7.5	1.0	-4.0
2011	0.0	6.0	5.5

The expected future return on the market is 15%, the real risk-free rate is 3.75%, and the expected inflation rate is a constant 5%. If the market risk premium rises by 3 percentage points, what will be the change in the required rate of return of the riskier stock? (Hint: You will need a financial calculator to determine each stock's beta coefficient.)

  a. 4.01%
  b. 3.67%
  c. 4.88%
  d. 3.23%
  e. 4.66%

Answers

Definitional Questions

1. probability
2. outcomes; distribution
3. probability; return
4. deviation
5. averse
6. diversification
7. risk
8. positively
9. diversifiable; market
10. beta
11. 2.0; half
12. weighted
13. required
14. risk-free
15. beta

16. risk-free; risk
17. real; inflation
18. slope
19. Risk
20. portfolio
21. continuous
22. variance
23. coefficient; variation
24. premium
25. correlation
26. market
27. relevant
28. required; diversification
29. market
30. realized

Conceptual Questions

1. b. The Y-axis intercept of the SML is r_{RF}, which is the required rate of return of a security with a beta of zero.

2. b. A zero beta stock could be made riskless if it were combined with enough other zero beta stocks, but it would still have diversifiable risk and be risky when held in isolation.

3. a. By definition, if a stock has a beta of 1.0 it moves exactly with the market. In other words, if the market moves up by 7%, the stock will also move up by 7%, while if the market falls by 7%, the stock will fall by 7%.

4. b. Market risk is measured by the beta coefficient. The portfolio beta is a weighted average of the betas of the stocks, so b_p would also be 1.0. Thus, the market risk for the portfolio would be the same as the market risk of the stocks in the portfolio.

5. a. Note that with a 200-stock portfolio, the actual returns would all be on or close to the regression line. However, when the portfolio (and the market) returns are quite high, some individual stocks would have higher returns than the portfolio, and some would have much lower returns. Thus, the range of returns, and the standard deviation, would be higher for the individual stocks.

6. b. RP_M, which is equal to $r_M - r_{RF}$, would rise, leading to an increase in r_M.

7. b. The required rate of return for a stock with b = 0.5 would increase less than the return of a stock with b = 2.0.

8. b. If the expected inflation rate increased, the new SML would shift parallel to the old SML due to an increase in r_{RF}. Thus, the effect on the required rates of return for both the b = 0.5 and b = 2.0 stocks would be the same.

9. c. The best measure of risk is the beta coefficient, which is a measure of the extent to which the returns on a given stock move with the stock market.

10. c. The beta of the portfolio is a weighted average of the individual securities' betas, so it could not be less than the betas of all of the stocks.

11. a. The increase in inflation would cause the SML to shift up, and more risk-averse investors would cause the slope to increase.

12. e. Statement e is correct. The slope ($r_M - r_{RF}$) and intercept (r_{RF}) of the SML cannot be controlled by the financial manager. The slope of the SML is $r_M - r_{RF}$ not beta. A negative beta in the CAPM would indicate that the stock's required rate of return is less than the risk-free rate. Finally, if investors become less risk averse, the slope of the SML will decline not increase.

13. d. Statement d is correct. The yield curve determines the value of r_{RF}; however, SML = $r_{RF} + (r_M - r_{RF})$b. The average return on the market will always be greater than the risk-free rate; thus, the SML will always be upward sloping, so statement a is false. RP_M is equal to $r_M - r_{RF}$. r_{RF} is equal to the risk-free rate, not the rate on an average company's bonds, so statement b is false. A decrease in risk aversion and an increase in inflation would cause the SML slope to decrease and to shift upward simultaneously, so statement c is false. A firm can influence its market risk through the composition of its assets and the use of debt.

14. e. Statement e is correct; for equilibrium to exist, the expected return must equal the required return.

15. b. Statement b is correct. The stock with the higher standard deviation might not be highly correlated with most other stocks, hence have a relatively low beta, and thus not be very risky if held in a well-diversified portfolio. The other statements are simply false.

Solutions

Problems

1. e. $r_A = 0.1(-15\%) + 0.2(0\%) + 0.4(5\%) + 0.2(10\%) + 0.1(25\%) = 5.0\%$

   $$\text{Variance} = 0.1(-0.15 - 0.05)^2 + 0.2(0.0 - 0.05)^2 + 0.4(0.05 - 0.05)^2$$
   $$+ 0.2(0.10 - 0.05)^2 + 0.1(0.25 - 0.05)^2$$
   $$= 0.009$$

   Standard deviation = $\sqrt{0.009}$ = 0.0949 = 9.5%

2. d. $r_X = r_{RF} + (r_M - r_{RF})b_X = 5\% + (11\% - 5\%)1.3 = 12.8\%$

3. c. $r_X = r_{RF} + (r_M - r_{RF})b_X = 7\% + (13\% - 7\%)1.3 = 14.8\%$

   A change in the inflation premium does *not* change the market risk premium ($r_M - r_{RF}$) since both r_M and r_{RF} are affected.

4. b. $r_X = r_{RF} + (r_M - r_{RF})b_X = 5\% + (14\% - 5\%)1.3 = 16.7\%$

5. a. $r_X = r_{RF} + (r_M - r_{RF})b_X = 7\% + (16\% - 7\%)1.3 = 18.7\%$

6. c. $r = 12\%$; $r_{RF} = 6\%$; $RP_M = 5\%$; $b = ?$

$$r = r_{RF} + (r_M - r_{RF})b$$
$$12\% = 6\% + (5\%)b$$
$$6\% = 5\%b$$
$$b = 1.20$$

7. e. $r_{RF} = 6\%$; $RP_M = 5\%$; $r = 12\%$; $b = ?$

$$12\% = 6\% + (5\%)b$$
$$6\% = 5\%b$$
$$b = 1.20$$

RP_M now changes to 8%
$$r = r_{RF} + (r_M - r_{RF})b$$
$$= 6\% + (8\%)(1.2)$$
$$= 15.60\%$$

8. c. The calculation of the portfolio's beta is as follows:
$$b_p = (1/3)(0.5) + (1/3)(1.0) + (1/3)(1.5) = 1.0$$

9. d. $b_p = \sum_{i=1}^{5} w_i b_i$

$$= \frac{\$130}{\$450}(0.4) + \frac{\$110}{\$450}(1.5) + \frac{\$70}{\$450}(3.0) + \frac{\$90}{\$450}(2.0) + \frac{\$50}{\$450}(1.0) = 1.46$$

10. a. $b_p = \sum_{i=1}^{5} w_i b_i$

$$= \frac{\$130}{\$450}(0.4) + \frac{\$110}{\$450}(1.5) + \frac{\$70}{\$450}(3.0) + \frac{\$90}{\$450}(2.0) + \frac{\$50}{\$450}(1.0) = 1.46$$

$$r_p = r_{RF} + (r_M - r_{RF})b_p = 12\% + (6\%)1.46 = 20.76\%$$

11. c. We know $b_A = 1.20$, $b_B = 0.60$; $r_M = 12\%$, and $r_{RF} = 7\%$.

$r_i = r_{RF} + (r_M - r_{RF})b_i = 7\% + (12\% - 7\%)b_i$

$r_A = 7\% + 5\%(1.20) = 13.0\%$

$r_B = 7\% + 5\%(0.60) = 10.0\%$

$r_A - r_B = 13\% - 10\% = 3\%$

12. c. $CV_A = 28\%/8\% = 3.50$

$CV_B = 20\%/10\% = 2.00$

13. b. $r_A = r_{RF} + (r_M - r_{RF})b_A$
$= 5.5\% + (4\%)(0.72)$
$= 8.38\%$

$r_B = r_{RF} + (r_M - r_{RF})b_B$
$= 5.5\% + (4\%)(0.96)$
$= 9.34\%$

14. e. $b_p = 0.6(0.72) + 0.4(0.96)$
$= 0.432 + 0.384$
$= 0.816$

$r_p = r_{RF} + (r_M - r_{RF})b_p$
$= 5.5\% + (4\%)(0.816)$
$= 8.764\% \approx 8.76\%$

15. e. First find the beta of the remaining 9 stocks:

$1.8 = 0.9(b_R) + 0.1(b_A)$
$1.8 = 0.9(b_R) + 0.1(2.0)$
$1.8 = 0.9(b_R) + 0.2$
$1.6 = 0.9(b_R)$
$b_R = 1.7778$

Now find the beta of the new stock that produces $b_p = 1.7$:

$1.7 = 0.9(1.7778) + 0.1(b_N)$
$1.7 = 1.6 + 0.1(b_N)$
$0.1 = 0.1(b_N)$
$b_N = 1.0$

16. c.   Determine the weight each stock represents in the portfolio:

Stock	Investment	w_i	Beta	$w_i \times$ Beta
A	$ 400,000	0.10	1.2	0.1200
B	600,000	0.15	-0.4	-0.0600
C	1,000,000	0.25	1.5	0.3750
D	2,000,000	0.50	0.8	0.4000

$b_p = \underline{0.8350}$ = Portfolio beta

Write out the SML equation, and substitute known values including the portfolio beta. Solve for the required portfolio return.

$$r_p = r_{RF} + (r_M - r_{RF})b_p$$
$$= 6\% + (12\% - 6\%)0.8350$$
$$= 6\% + 5.01\% = 11.01\%$$

17. b.   Use the given probability distribution of returns to calculate the expected value, variance, standard deviation, and coefficient of variation.

P_i		r_i		$P_i r_i$	r_i		$\hat{r}$		$(r_i - \hat{r})$	$(r_i - \hat{r})^2$	$P(r_i - \hat{r})^2$
0.4	×	$30	=	$12.0	$30	–	$22.5	=	$ 7.5	$ 56.25	$ 22.500
0.5	×	25	=	12.5	25	–	22.5	=	2.5	6.25	3.125
0.1	×	-20	=	-2.0	-20	–	22.5	=	-42.5	1,806.25	180.625
		$\hat{r}$	=	$22.5						σ^2 = Variance =	$206.250

The standard deviation (σ) of $\hat{r}$ is $\sqrt{\$206.25}$ = \$14.3614.

Use the standard deviation and the expected return to calculate the coefficient of variation: $14.3614/$22.5 = 0.6383.

18. a.   Use the SML equation, substitute in the known values, and solve for beta.

$r_{RF} = 8\%$; $r_M = 13\%$; $\hat{r}_J = 15\%$.

$$\hat{r}_J = r_J = r_{RF} + (r_M - r_{RF})b_J$$
$$15\% = 8\% + (13\% - 8\%)b_J$$
$$7\% = (5\%)b_J$$
$$b_J = 1.4$$

19. d.   Using Stock X (or any stock):

$$7.6\% = r_{RF} + (r_M - r_{RF})b_X$$
$$7.6\% = 5.2\% + (r_M - r_{RF})0.6$$
$$(r_M - r_{RF}) = 4\%$$

165

20. a. $b_{HI} = 1.75$; $b_{LOE} = 0.45$. No changes occur.

$r_{RF} = 5.5\%$. Decreases by 1.25% to 4.25%.

$r_M = 11.75\%$. Falls to 10.3%.

Now SML: $r_i = r_{RF} + (r_M - r_{RF})b_i$.

$r_{HI} = 4.25\% + (10.3\% - 4.25\%)1.75 = 4.25\% + 6.05\%(1.75) = \quad 14.8375\%$
$r_{LOE} = 4.25\% + (10.3\% - 4.25\%)0.45 = 4.25\% + 6.05\%(0.45) = \quad \underline{6.9725\%}$
$$\text{Difference} = \quad \underline{7.8650\%}$$

21. b. Step 1: Determine the market risk premium from the CAPM:

$$0.10 = 0.056 + (r_M - r_{RF})1.10$$
$$(r_M - r_{RF}) = 0.04$$

Step 2: Calculate the beta of the new portfolio:

The beta of the new portfolio is
($600,000/$3,600,000)(0.60) + ($3,000,000/$3,600,000)(1.10) = 1.01667

Step 3: Calculate the required return on the new portfolio:

The required return on the new portfolio is
$5.6\% + (4\%)(1.01667) = 9.67\%$

Web Appendix 8A

1. b. Stock A: $b_A = \dfrac{\text{Rise}}{\text{Run}} = \dfrac{10 - (-5)}{10 - (-10)} = \dfrac{15}{20} = 0.75$

Stock B: $b_B = \dfrac{\text{Rise}}{\text{Run}} = \dfrac{20 - 10}{10 - (-10)} = \dfrac{10}{20} = 0.50$

This problem can also be worked using most financial calculators with statistical functions.

2. e. $b_N = \text{Rise/Run} = [-8 - (-5)]/(15 - 10) = -3/5 = -0.60$

Again, this problem can also be worked using most financial calculators with statistical functions.

3. b. $b_N = \text{Rise/Run} = [-8 - (-5)]/(15 - 10) = -3/5 = -0.60$

$r_N = 7\% + (10\% - 7\%)(-0.60) = 7\% + (-1.80\%) = 5.20\%$

4. d. Use the regression feature of the calculator. Enter data for the Market and Stock Y, and then find Beta$_Y$ = 1.3374 rounded to 1.34.

5. a. We know r_M = 15%; r^* = 3.75%; IP = 5%.

   Original RP$_M$ = $r_M - r_{RF}$ = 15% − (3.75% + 5%) = 6.25%

   RP$_M$ increases by 3% to 9.25%.

   Find the change in r = Δr for the riskier stock.

   First, find the betas for the two stocks. Enter data in the regression register, then find b$_Y$ = 1.3374 and b$_Z$ = 0.6161.

   Y is the riskier stock. Originally, its required return was r_Y = 8.75% + 6.25%(1.3374) = 17.11%. When RP$_M$ increases by 3%, r_Y = 8.75% + (6.25% + 3%)(1.3374) = 21.12%. Difference = 21.12% − 17.11% = 4.01%.

9

STOCKS AND THEIR VALUATION

Learning Objectives

1. Discuss the legal rights of stockholders.

2. Explain the distinction between a stock's price and its intrinsic value.

3. Identify the two models that can be used to estimate a stock's intrinsic value: the discounted dividend model and the corporate valuation model.

4. List the key characteristics of preferred stock, and describe how to estimate the value of preferred stock.

Overview

Common stock constitutes the ownership position in a firm, and is valued as the present value of its expected future dividend stream. As owners, common stockholders have certain rights and privileges, including the right to control the firm through election of directors and the right to the firm's residual earnings.

Common stock dividends are not specified by contract—they depend on the firm's earnings, which in turn depend on many random factors. This makes common stock valuation difficult. Two models are used to estimate a stock's intrinsic value: (1) the discounted dividend model and (2) the corporate valuation model.

The discounted dividend model values a common stock as the present value of its expected future cash flows at the firm's required rate of return. These cash flows consist of the dividends the investor receives each year while he or she holds the stock and the price received when the stock is sold. However, the price the investor receives when the stock is sold is simply the present value of the expected future dividend stream. Variations of the discounted dividend model are used to value constant growth stocks, zero growth stocks, and nonconstant growth stocks.

The corporate valuation model is used as an alternative to the discounted dividend model to determine the value of a firm, especially one that does not pay dividends or is privately held. This model first calculates the firm's free cash flows, then finds their present values at the firm's weighted average cost of capital to determine the firm's value.

169

The total rate of return on a stock is comprised of a dividend yield plus a capital gains yield. If a stock is in equilibrium, its total expected return must equal the average investor's required rate of return. A stock should be purchased if its price is less than its estimated intrinsic value, and it should be sold if its price exceeds its intrinsic value.

Preferred stock is a hybrid security—it is similar to bonds in some respects and to common stock in others. The value of a share of preferred stock that is expected to pay a constant dividend forever is found as the preferred dividend divided by the required rate of return.

Outline

I. **The corporation's common stockholders are the owners of the corporation, and as such, they have certain rights and privileges.**

   A. Common stockholders have control of the firm through their election of the firm's directors, who in turn elect officers who manage the business.

      1. In a large, publicly owned firm, the managers typically have some stock, but their personal holdings are generally insufficient to give them voting control.

      2. Managements of most publicly owned firms can be removed by the stockholders if the management team is not effective.

      3. Stockholders who are unable to attend annual meetings may still vote for directors by means of a *proxy*. Proxies can be solicited by any party seeking to control the firm.

      4. If earnings are poor and stockholders are dissatisfied, an outside group may solicit the proxies in an effort to overthrow management and take control of the business. This is known as a *proxy fight*.

      5. A *takeover* is an action whereby a person or group succeeds in ousting a firm's management and taking control of the company.

      6. A *poison pill* makes a possible acquisition unattractive and wards off hostile takeover attempts.

   B. The *preemptive right* gives current shareholders the right to purchase any new shares issued in proportion to their current holdings. The preemptive right may or may not be required by state law.

      1. The purpose of the preemptive right is twofold:

         a. It enables current stockholders to maintain their proportionate share of ownership and control of the business, which prevents management from seizing control of the corporation and frustrating the will of current stockholders.

         b. It also prevents the sale of shares at low prices to new stockholders, which would dilute the value of the previously issued shares.

II. **Special classes of common stock are sometimes created by a firm to meet special needs and circumstances. If two classes of stock were desired, one would normally be called "Class A" and the other "Class B."**

   A. Common stock that is given a special designation is called *classified stock*.

      1. Class A might be entitled to receive dividends before dividends can be paid on Class B stock.

2. Class B might have the exclusive right to vote.

    a. Note that Class A and Class B have no standard meanings.

B. *Founders' shares* are stock owned by the firm's founders that enables them to maintain control over the company without having to own a majority of stock.

III. **Market equilibrium occurs when the stock's price equals its intrinsic value. If the stock market is reasonably efficient, gaps between the stock price and intrinsic value should not be very large and they should not persist for very long.**

A. When investing in common stocks, one's goal is to purchase stocks that are undervalued (i.e., the price is below the stock's intrinsic value) and to avoid stocks that are overvalued.

B. Managers need to understand how intrinsic value is estimated.

    1. Managers need to know how alternative actions are likely to affect stock prices; and the models of intrinsic value covered in this chapter help demonstrate the connection between managerial decisions and firm value.

    2. Managers should consider whether their stock is significantly undervalued or overvalued before making certain decisions.

C. Two basic models are used to estimate intrinsic values.

    1. The *discounted dividend model* focuses on dividends.

    2. The *corporate valuation model* focuses on free cash flows.

IV. **Common stocks are valued by finding the present value of the expected future cash flow stream at the firm's required rate of return. The marginal investor is a representative investor whose actions reflect the beliefs of those people who are currently trading on a stock. It is the marginal investor who determines the equilibrium stock price.**

A. People typically buy common stock expecting to earn *dividends* plus a *capital gain* when they sell their shares at the end of some holding period. The capital gain may or may not be realized, but most people expect a gain or else they would not buy stocks.

B. The expected dividend yield on a stock during the coming year is equal to the expected dividend, D_1, divided by the current stock price, P_0.

C. The expected capital gains yield is:

$$(\hat{P}_1 - P_0)/P_0$$

D. The expected dividend yield plus the expected capital gains yield equals the expected total return.

E. The value of the stock today is calculated as the present value of an infinite stream of dividends. For any investor, cash flows consist of dividends plus the expected future sales price of the stock. This sales price, however, depends on dividends expected by future investors:

$$\text{Value of stock} = \hat{P}_0 = \text{PV of expected future dividends}$$

$$= \frac{D_1}{(1+r_s)^1} + \frac{D_2}{(1+r_s)^2} + \cdots + \frac{D_\infty}{(1+r_s)^\infty}$$

$$= \sum_{t=1}^{\infty} \frac{D_t}{(1+r_s)^t}$$

      1. Here r_s is the discount rate used to find the present value of the dividends.

    F. Dividends can be rising, falling, fluctuating randomly, or can even be zero for several years. The generalized equation above can be used to value the stock.

      1. With a computer spreadsheet this equation can easily be used to find a stock's intrinsic value for any dividend pattern. The hard part is obtaining an accurate forecast of the future dividends.

V.   For many companies, earnings and dividends are expected to grow at some normal, or constant, rate.

    A. Dividends in any future Year t may be forecasted as $D_t = D_0(1 + g)^t$, where D_0 is the last dividend paid and g is the expected growth rate.

      1. For a company that last paid a $2.00 dividend and has an expected 6% constant growth rate, the estimated dividend one year from now would be $D_1 = \$2.00(1.06) = \$2.12$; D_2 would be $\$2.00(1.06)^2 = \$2.25$, and the estimated dividend 4 years hence would be $D_t = D_0(1 + g)^t = \$2.00(1.06)^4 = \$2.525$.

      2. Using this method of estimating future dividends, the expected stock price today is determined as follows:

$$\hat{P}_0 = \frac{D_0(1+g)}{r_s - g} = \frac{D_1}{r_s - g}$$

    B. This equation for valuing a constant growth stock is often called the *constant growth model*, or the *Gordon Model*, after Myron J. Gordon, who developed it.

      1. If the stock is in equilibrium, the required rate of return must equal the expected rate of return.

      2. A necessary condition of this equation is that the required rate of return must be greater than the long-run growth rate, $r_s > g$. If the equation is used in situations when r_s is not greater than g, the results will be both wrong and meaningless.

        a. In the long run, growth in dividends depends primarily on the firm's payout ratio and its ROE.

        b. Growth rate = (1 − Payout ratio)(ROE).

      3. The company's growth rate is expected to remain constant in the future.

        a. The constant growth model is often appropriate for mature companies with a stable history of growth and stable future expectations.

        b. Expected growth rates vary somewhat among companies, but future dividend growth for most mature firms is generally expected to continue at about the same rate as nominal gross domestic product (real GDP plus inflation).

    C. For all stocks, the *total expected return* consists of an *expected dividend yield* plus an *expected capital gains yield*.

      1. For a *constant growth stock*, the formula for the total expected return can be written as:

$$\hat{r}_s = \frac{D_1}{P_0} + g$$

D. The constant growth model is sufficiently general to handle the case of a *zero growth stock*, where the dividend is expected to remain constant over time.

   1. If g = 0, then the stock can be valued as:

   $$\hat{P}_0 = D/r_s$$

   2. This is the same equation as the one used for valuing a perpetuity.

VI. **Firms typically go through periods of nonconstant growth, after which time their growth rate settles to a rate close to that of the economy as a whole. These firms can be valued by applying a variation of the general discounted dividend model and the constant growth model.**

A. The value of such a firm is equal to the present value of its expected future dividends. To find the value of such a stock, we proceed in three steps.

   1. Find the present value of the dividends during the period of nonconstant growth.

   2. Find the price of the stock at the end of the nonconstant growth period, at which point it has become a constant growth stock, and discount this price back to the present.

   3. Add these two components to find the intrinsic value of the stock.

B. *Supernormal (nonconstant) growth firms* are firms that are in that part of their life cycle in which they grow much faster than the economy as a whole.

C. The *terminal*, or *horizon*, *date* is the date when the growth rate becomes constant.

   1. At this date it is no longer necessary to forecast the individual dividends.

D. The *horizon*, or *continuing*, *value* is the value at the horizon date of all dividends expected thereafter.

VII. **The corporate valuation model is used as an alternative to the discounted dividend model to determine a firm's value, especially one with no history of dividends, or the value of a division of a larger firm.**

A. This model discounts a firm's free cash flows at the WACC to determine its value.

B. The value of a firm's stock is directly linked to a firm's total value.

C. The steps to the corporate valuation model approach are as follows:

   1. Find the firm's total value, which is the present value of its future FCFs.

   2. Subtract out the market value of the debt and preferred stock from the firm's total value. This calculated value is the market value of the firm's common equity.

   3. Divide the value of the common equity by the number of shares outstanding to obtain an estimate of the value per share.

      a. This estimate should, in theory, be identical to the share value found using the discounted dividend model.

D. The market value of any company can be expressed as follows:

$$V_{Company} = \text{PV of expected future free cash flows}$$

$$= \frac{FCF_1}{(1 + WACC)^1} + \frac{FCF_2}{(1 + WACC)^2} + \cdots + \frac{FCF_\infty}{(1 + WACC)^\infty}$$

173

1. Free cash flow represents the cash generated in a given year minus the cash needed to finance the capital expenditures and operating working capital needed to support future growth:

$$FCF = \left[EBIT(1 - T) + \begin{array}{c} \text{Depreciation and} \\ \text{amortization} \end{array} \right] - \left[\begin{array}{c} \text{Capital} \\ \text{expenditures} \end{array} + \begin{array}{c} \Delta \text{ Net operating} \\ \text{working capital} \end{array} \right]$$

   a. Free cash flow is the cash generated before making any payments to common or preferred stockholders, or to bondholders, so it is the cash flow that is available to all investors.

2. The FCF should be discounted at the company's weighted average cost of debt, preferred stock, and common stock, which is simply WACC.

E. To find the firm's total value, proceed as follows:

   1. Assume the firm will experience nonconstant growth for N years, after which it will grow at some constant rate.

   2. Calculate the expected FCF for each of the N nonconstant growth years, and find the PV of these cash flows.

   3. After Year N growth will be constant. Use the constant growth formula to find the firm's value at Year N. This horizon value is the sum of the PVs of the FCFs for N + 1 and all subsequent years, discounted back to Year N, calculated as:

   $$\frac{FCF_{N+1}}{WACC - g_{FCF}}$$

   The horizon value must be discounted back to the present to find its PV at Year 0.

   4. Sum all the PVs, those of the annual free cash flows during the nonconstant period plus the PV of the horizon value, to find the firm's value.

F. Estimates of intrinsic value will often deviate considerably from the actual stock price.

   1. Deviations occur because the forecaster's assumptions are different from those of the marginal investor in the marketplace.

G. Much can be learned from the corporate valuation model, so analysts today use it for all types of valuations.

   1. The process of projecting future financial statements can reveal a great deal about the company's operations and financing needs.

   2. This type of analysis can provide insights into actions that might be taken to increase the company's value, and for this reason it is integral to the planning and forecasting process.

VIII. **Preferred stock is a hybrid—it is similar to bonds in some respects and to common stock in others.**

   A. Preferred dividends are similar to interest payments on bonds—they are fixed in amount and generally must be paid before common stock dividends can be paid.

   B. If the preferred dividend is not earned, the directors can omit (or "pass") it without throwing the company into bankruptcy.

   1. Although preferred stock has a fixed payment like bonds, a failure to make this payment will not lead to bankruptcy.

C. Most preferred stocks entitle their owners to regular fixed dividend payments. If the payments last forever, the issue is a *perpetuity* whose value, V_p, is found as follows:

$$V_p = \frac{D_p}{r_p}.$$

1. Here D_p is the dividend to be received in each year and r_p is the required rate of return on the preferred stock.

IX. **Appendix 9A discusses stock market equilibrium.**

A. The appendix illustrates equilibrium with a graph of the SML equation.

B. The appendix then demonstrates how changes in the variables used in the CAPM and DCF equations impact equilibrium stock prices.

Self-Test

Definitional Questions

1. One of the fundamental rights of common stockholders is to elect a firm's _____, who in turn elect officers who manage the business.

2. If a stockholder cannot vote in person, participation in the annual meeting is still possible through a(n) _____.

3. The preemptive right protects stockholders against loss of _____ of the corporation as well as _____ of market value from the sale of new shares below market value.

4. Firms may find it desirable to separate the common stock into different _____ to meet special needs and circumstances.

5. Like other financial assets, the value of common stock is the _____ value of a future stream of cash flows.

6. The cash flow stream expected from a common stock consists of a(n) _____ yield and a capital gains yield.

7. If the future growth rate of dividends is expected to be _____, the rate of return is simply the _____ yield.

8. Investors always expect a(n) _____ return on stock investments, but in some years _____ returns may actually be earned.

9. Preferred stock is referred to as a hybrid because it is similar to _____ in some respects and to _____ stock in others.

10. If earnings are poor and stockholders are dissatisfied, an outside group may solicit the votes of stockholders, unable to attend the annual meeting, in an effort to overthrow management and take control of the business. This is known as a(n) _____ fight.

11. A(n) _____ is an action whereby a person or group succeeds in ousting a firm's management and gaining control of the company.

12. A(n) _____ pill makes a possible acquisition unattractive and wards off hostile takeover attempts.

13. A zero growth stock can be thought of as a(n) _____.

14. Only at the _____ price, where the expected and required rates of return are equal, will the stock's price be stable.

15. The _____ right gives the current shareholders the right to purchase any new shares issued in proportion to their current holdings.

16. Common stock that is given a special designation is called _____ stock.

17. The _____ investor is a representative investor whose actions reflect the beliefs of those people who are currently trading a stock and determines the equilibrium stock price.

18. _____ or _____ growth firms are those that are in that part of their life cycle in which they grow much faster than the economy as a whole.

19. The _____ or _____ date is the date when the growth rate becomes constant.

20. The _____ valuation model is used as an alternative to the discounted dividend model to determine a firm's value, especially one with no history of dividends, or the value of a division of a larger firm.

21. _____ cash _____ is the cash generated before making any payments to common and preferred stockholders, and bondholders, so it is available to all investors.

22. The _____ or _____ value is the value at the horizon date of all dividends expected thereafter.

23. _____ shares are stock owned by the firm's founders that enable them to maintain control over the company without having to own a majority of stock.

24. The constant growth model is often appropriate for _____ companies with a(n) _____ history of growth and stable future expectations.

25. The equation for valuing a constant growth stock is often called the constant growth model, or the _____ Model, after the individual who developed it.

26. The corporate valuation model discounts a firm's free cash flows at the _____ to determine the firm's value.

27. In the long run, growth in dividends depends primarily on the firm's _____ ratio and its _____.

28. The corporation's _____ stockholders are the _____ of the corporation, and as such, they have certain rights and privileges.

29. A necessary condition of the constant growth model is that r_s is _____ than g.

30. If the preferred dividend is not earned, the directors _____ omit it without throwing the company into _____.

Conceptual Questions

1. According to the valuation model developed in this chapter, the value that an investor assigns to a share of stock is independent of the length of time the investor plans to hold the stock.

   a. True
   b. False

2. Which of the following assumptions would cause the constant growth stock valuation model to be invalid? The constant growth model is given below:

$$\hat{P}_0 = \frac{D_0(1+g)}{r_s - g}$$

   a. The growth rate is negative.
   b. The growth rate is zero.
   c. The required rate of return is less than the growth rate.
   d. The required rate of return is above 30%.
   e. None of the above assumptions would invalidate the model.

3. Assume that a company's dividends are expected to grow at a rate of 25% per year for 5 years and then to slow down and to grow at a constant rate of 5% thereafter. The required (and expected) total return, r_s, is expected to remain constant at 12%. Which of the following statements is correct?

   a. The dividend yield will be higher in the early years and then will decline as the annual capital gains yield gets larger and larger, other things held constant.
   b. Right now, it would be easier (require fewer calculations) to find the dividend yield expected in Year 7 than the dividend yield expected in Year 3.
   c. The stock price will grow each year at the same rate as the dividends.
   d. The stock price will grow at a different rate each year during the first 5 years, but its average growth rate over this period will be the same as the average growth rate in dividends; that is, the average stock price growth rate will be (25% + 5%)/2.
   e. Because the growth rate is 25% in the first 5 years, the stock's realized return will always be greater than the stock's required return.

4. Which of the following statements is correct?

   a. According to the text, the constant growth stock valuation model is especially useful in situations where g is greater than 15% and r_s is 10% or less.
   b. According to the text, the constant growth model can be used as one part of the process of finding the value of a stock that is expected to experience a very rapid rate of growth for a few years and then to grow at a constant ("normal") rate.
   c. According to the text, the constant growth model cannot be used unless g is greater than zero.
   d. According to the text, the constant growth model cannot be used unless the constant g is greater than r.
   e. According to the text, the constant growth model is not appropriate for mature companies.

5. When stockholders assign their right to vote to another party, this is called

   a. A privilege.
   b. A preemptive right.
   c. An ex right.
   d. A proxy.
   e. A takeover.

177

Problems

1. Stability Inc. has maintained a dividend rate of $4 per share for many years. The same rate is expected to be paid in future years. If investors require a 12% rate of return on similar investments, determine the present value of the company's stock.

   a. $15.00
   b. $30.00
   c. $33.33
   d. $35.00
   e. $40.00

2. Your sister-in-law, a stockbroker at Invest Inc., is trying to sell you a stock with a current market price of $25. The stock's last dividend (D_0) was $2.00, and earnings and dividends are expected to increase at a constant growth rate of 10%. Your required return on this stock is 20%. From a strict valuation standpoint, you should:

   a. Buy the stock; it is fairly valued.
   b. Buy the stock; it is undervalued by $3.00.
   c. Buy the stock; it is undervalued by $2.00.
   d. Not buy the stock; it is overvalued by $2.00.
   e. Not buy the stock; it is overvalued by $3.00.

3. Lucas Laboratories' last dividend was $1.50. Its current equilibrium stock price is $15.75, and its expected growth rate is a constant 5%. If the stockholders' required rate of return is 15%, what is the expected dividend yield and expected capital gains yield for the coming year?

   a. 0%; 15%
   b. 5%; 10%
   c. 10%; 5%
   d. 15%; 0%
   e. 15%; 15%

4. The Canning Company has been hard hit by increased competition. Analysts predict that earnings (and dividends) will decline at a rate of 5% annually into the foreseeable future. If Canning's last dividend (D_0) was $2.00, and investors' required rate of return is 15%, what will be Canning's stock price in 3 years?

   a. $ 8.15
   b. $ 9.50
   c. $10.00
   d. $10.42
   e. $10.96

5. The Club Auto Parts Company has just recently been organized. It is expected to experience no growth for the next 2 years as it identifies its market and acquires its inventory. However, Club will grow at an annual rate of 5% in the third year and, beginning with the fourth year, should attain a 10% growth rate that it will sustain thereafter. The first dividend (D_1) to be paid at the end of the first year is expected to be $0.50 per share. Investors require a 15% rate of return on Club's stock. What is the current equilibrium stock price?

    a. $ 5.00
    b. $ 8.75
    c. $ 9.56
    d. $12.43
    e. $15.00

6. The Club Auto Parts Company has just recently been organized. It is expected to experience no growth for the next 2 years as it identifies its market and acquires its inventory. However, Club will grow at an annual rate of 5% in the third year and, beginning with the fourth year, should attain a 10% growth rate that it will sustain thereafter. The first dividend (D_1) to be paid at the end of the first year is expected to be $0.50 per share. Investors require a 15% rate of return on Club's stock. What will Club's stock price be at the end of the first year ($\hat{P}_1$) ?

    a. $ 5.00
    b. $ 8.75
    c. $ 9.57
    d. $12.43
    e. $15.00

7. The Club Auto Parts Company has just recently been organized. It is expected to experience no growth for the next 2 years as it identifies its market and acquires its inventory. However, Club will grow at an annual rate of 5% in the third year and, beginning with the fourth year, should attain a 10% growth rate that it will sustain thereafter. The first dividend (D_1) to be paid at the end of the first year is expected to be $0.50 per share. Investors require a 15% rate of return on Club's stock. What dividend yield and capital gains yield should an investor in Club expect for the first year?

    a. 7.5%; 7.5%
    b. 4.7%; 10.3%
    c. 5.7%; 9.3%
    d. 10.5%; 4.5%
    e. 11.5%; 3.5%

8. Johnson Corporation's stock is currently selling at $45.83 per share. The last dividend paid (D_0) was $2.50. Johnson is a constant growth firm. If investors require a return of 16% on Johnson's stock, what do they think Johnson's growth rate will be?

    a. 6%
    b. 7%
    c. 8%
    d. 9%
    e. 10%

9. Assume that the average firm in your company's industry is expected to grow at a constant rate of 7% and its dividend yield is 8%. Your company is about as risky as the average firm in the industry, but it has just successfully completed some R&D work that leads you to expect that its earnings and dividends will grow at a rate of 40% $[D_1 = D_0(1 + g) = D_0(1.40)]$ this year and 20% the following year, after which growth should match the 7% industry average rate. The last dividend paid (D_0) was $1. What is the current value per share of your firm's stock?

   a. $22.47
   b. $24.15
   c. $21.00
   d. $19.48
   e. $22.00

10. Chadmark Corporation is expanding rapidly, and it currently needs to retain all of its earnings, hence it does not pay any dividends. However, investors expect Chadmark to begin paying dividends, with the first dividend of $0.75 coming 2 years from today. The dividend should grow rapidly, at a rate of 40% per year, during Years 3 and 4. After Year 4, the company should grow at a constant rate of 10% per year. If the required return on the stock is 16%, what is the value of the stock today?

   a. $16.93
   b. $17.54
   c. $15.78
   d. $18.87
   e. $16.05

11. Some investors expect Endicott Industries to have an irregular dividend pattern for several years, and then to grow at a constant rate. Suppose Endicott has $D_0 = \$2.00$; no growth is expected for 2 years; then the expected growth rate is 8% for 2 years; and finally the growth rate is expected to be constant at 15% thereafter. If the required return is 20%, what will be the value of the stock?

   a. $28.53
   b. $25.14
   c. $31.31
   d. $21.24
   e. $23.84

12. Today is December 31, 2011. The following information applies to Harrison Corporation:

   • After-tax operating income [EBIT(1 – T)] for 2012 is expected to be $950 million.
   • The company's depreciation expense for 2012 is expected to be $190 million.
   • The company's capital expenditures for 2012 are expected to be $380 million.
   • No change is expected in the company's net operating working capital.
   • The company's free cash flow is expected to grow at a constant rate of 4% per year.
   • The company's cost of equity is 13%.
   • The company's WACC is 9%.
   • The market value of the company's debt is $5.2 billion.
   • The company has 250 million shares of stock outstanding.

Using the corporate valuation model, what should be the company's stock price today?

a. $35.00
b. $40.00
c. $37.50
d. $43.50
e. $52.50

13. Hidden Technologies Inc. (HTI) is expected to generate $75 million in free cash flow next year, and it is expected to grow at a constant rate of 6% per year. The firm has no debt or preferred stock and has a WACC of 9%. HTI has 50 million shares of stock outstanding. Using the corporate valuation model, what is the value of the company's stock per share?

a. $40.00
b. $43.33
c. $45.75
d. $50.00
e. $55.25

14. Hanebury Manufacturing Company (HMC) has preferred stock outstanding with a par value of $50. The stock pays a quarterly dividend of $1.25 and has a current price of $71.43. What is the nominal rate of return on the preferred stock?

a. 9.25%
b. 8.75%
c. 10.50%
d. 8.33%
e. 7.00%

15. Hanebury Manufacturing Company (HMC) has preferred stock outstanding with a par value of $50. The stock pays a quarterly dividend of $1.25 and has a current price of $71.43. What is the effective annual rate of return on the preferred stock?

a. 8.67%
b. 7.19%
c. 9.55%
d. 8.24%
e. 10.68%

16. Helen's Pottery Co.'s stock recently paid a $1.50 dividend ($D_0 = \$1.50$). This dividend is expected to grow by 15% for the next 3 years, and then grow forever at a constant rate, g. The current stock price is $40.92. If $r_s = 10\%$, at what constant rate is the stock expected to grow following Year 3?

a. 5.00%
b. 4.25%
c. 3.33%
d. 6.50%
e. 5.67%

181

17. A stock is expected to pay a dividend of $2.25 at the end of the year ($D_1 = \$2.25$). The dividend is expected to grow at a constant rate of 4% a year. The stock has a required return of 11%. What is the expected price of the stock five years from today?

    a. $32.14
    b. $36.67
    c. $39.11
    d. $40.25
    e. $42.00

Answers

Definitional Questions

1. directors	16. classified
2. proxy	17. marginal
3. control; dilution	18. Supernormal; nonconstant
4. classes	19. terminal; horizon
5. present	20. corporate
6. dividend	21. Free; flow
7. zero; dividend	22. horizon; continuing
8. positive; negative	23. Founders'
9. debt; common	24. mature; stable
10. proxy	25. Gordon
11. takeover	26. WACC
12. poison	27. payout; ROE
13. perpetuity	28. common; owners
14. equilibrium	29. greater
15. preemptive	30. can; bankruptcy

Conceptual Questions

1. a. The model considers all future dividends. This produces a current value that is appropriate for all investors independent of their expected holding period.

2. c. If this equation is used in situations when r_s is not greater than g, the results will be both wrong and meaningless.

3. b. Statement b is correct. We know that after Year 5, the stock will have a constant growth rate, and the capital gains yield will be equal to that growth rate. We also know that the total return is expected to be constant. Therefore, we could find the expected dividend yield in Year 7 simply by subtracting the growth rate from the total return: Yield = 12% – 5% = 7% in Year 7. The other statements are all false. This could be confirmed by thinking about how the dividend growth rate starts high, ends up at the constant growth rate, and must lie between these two rates and be declining between Years 1 and 5. The average growth rate in dividends during Years 1 through 5 will be (25 + 5)/2 = 15%, which is above r_s = 12%, so statements c and d must be false.

4. b.   Statement b is correct. In the case of a nonconstant growth stock that is expected to grow at a constant rate after Year N, we would find the value of D_{N+1} and use it in the constant growth model to find P_N. The other statements are all false. Note that the constant growth model can be used for $g = 0$, $g < 0$, and $g < r$. It is often appropriate to use the constant growth model for mature companies with a stable history of growth and stable future expectations.

5. d.   Recently, there has been a spate of proxy fights, whereby a dissident group of stockholders solicits proxies in competition with the firm's management. If the dissident group obtains a majority of the proxies, then it can gain control of the board of directors and oust existing management.

Solutions

Problems

1. c.   This is a zero-growth stock, or perpetuity:

$$\hat{P}_0 = D/r_s = \$4.00/0.12 = \$33.33$$

2. e. $\hat{P}_0 = \dfrac{D_0(1+g)}{r_s - g} = \dfrac{\$2.00(1.10)}{0.20 - 0.10} = \$22.00$

Since the stock is currently selling for \$25.00, the stock is not in equilibrium and is overvalued by \$3.00.

3. c.   Dividend yield $= \dfrac{D_1}{P_0} = \dfrac{D_0(1+g)}{P_0} = \dfrac{\$1.50(1.05)}{\$15.75} = 0.10 = 10\%$

Capital gains yield $= \dfrac{\hat{P}_1 - P_0}{P_0} = \dfrac{P_0(1+g) - P_0}{P_0} = \dfrac{\$16.5375 - \$15.75}{\$15.75} = g = 5\%$

4. a. $\hat{P}_0 = \dfrac{D_0(1+g)}{r_s - g} = \dfrac{\$2.00(0.95)}{0.15 - (-0.05)} = \dfrac{\$1.90}{0.20} = \$9.50$

$\hat{P}_3 = \hat{P}_0(1+g)^3 = \$9.50(0.95)^3 = \$9.50(0.8574) = \$8.15.$

The Gordon model can also be used:

$\hat{P}_3 = \dfrac{D_4}{r_s - g} = \dfrac{D_0(1+g)^4}{0.15 - (-0.05)} = \dfrac{\$2.00(0.95)^4}{0.20} = \dfrac{\$2.00(0.8145)}{0.20} = \$8.15$

183

5. b. To calculate the current value of a nonconstant growth stock, follow these steps:

   1. Determine the expected stream of dividends during the nonconstant growth period. Also, calculate the expected dividend at the end of the first year of constant growth that will be used later to calculate the stock price.

   $D_1 = \$0.50$
   $D_2 = D_1(1 + g) = \$0.50(1 + 0.0) = \$0.50$
   $D_3 = D_2(1 + g) = \$0.50(1.05) = \$0.525$
   $D_4 = D_3(1 + g) = \$0.525(1.10) = \$0.5775$

   2. Discount the expected dividends during the nonconstant growth period at the investor's required rate of return to find their present value.

   Year: 0   1   2   3
                $r_s = 15\%$
                        $D_1 = 0.50$ $D_2 = 0.50$ $D_3 = 0.525$
   Dividend:
        $0.43
         0.38
         0.35

   3. Calculate the expected stock price at the end of the final year of nonconstant growth. This occurs at the end of Year 3. Use the Gordon model for this calculation.

   $$\hat{P}_3 = \frac{D_4}{r_s - g} = \frac{\$0.5775}{0.15 - 0.10} = \$11.55$$

   Then discount this stock price back 3 periods at the investor's required rate of return to find its present value.

   $PV = \$11.55 \left[1/(1.15)^3\right] = \$11.55(0.6575) = \$7.59$

   4. Add the present value of the stock price expected at the end of Year 3 plus the dividends expected in Years 1, 2, and 3 to find the present value of the stock, P_0.

   Year: 0   1   2   3   4
                $r_s = 15\%$
   Dividend: 0.50   0.50   0.525 $D_4 = 0.5775$
        $0.43
         0.38
         0.35 $\$11.55 = \hat{P}_3 = D_4/(r_s - g)$
         7.59
        $8.75

   Alternatively, input 0, 0.5, 0.5, 12.075 (0.525 + 11.55) into the cash flow register, input I/YR = 15, and then solve for NPV = $8.75.

6. c. $D_1 = \$0.50$
$D_2 = D_1(1 + g) = \$0.50(1 + 0.0) = \$0.50$
$D_3 = D_2(1 + g) = \$0.50(1.05) = \$0.525$
$D_4 = D_3(1 + g) = \$0.525(1.10) = \$0.5775$

To calculate the expected stock price at the end of Year 1, $\hat{P}_1$, follow the same procedure you did to find the value of the nonconstant growth stock in Problem 5. However, discount values to Year 1 instead of Year 0. Also, remember that the dividend in Year 1, D_1, is not included in the valuation because it has already been paid and therefore adds nothing to the wealth of the investor buying the stock at the end of Year 1.

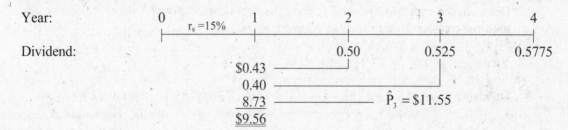

Alternatively, input 0, 0.5, 12.075 (0.525 + 11.55) into the cash flow register, input I/YR = 15, and then solve for NPV = $9.5652 ≈ $9.57.

7. c. Dividend yield $= \dfrac{D_1}{P_0} = \dfrac{\$0.50}{\$8.75} = 5.7\%$

Capital gains yield $= 15\% - 5.7\% = 9.3\%$

Alternatively,

Capital gains yield $= \dfrac{\hat{P}_1 - P_0}{P_0} = \dfrac{\$9.5652 - \$8.75}{\$8.75} = 9.3\%$

The Total yield = Dividend yield + Capital gains yield = 5.7% + 9.3% = 15%. The total yield must equal the required rate of return. Also, the capital gains yield is not equal to the growth rate during the nonconstant growth phase of a nonconstant growth stock. Finally, the dividend and capital gains yields are not constant until the constant growth state is reached.

8. e. $$P_0 = \dfrac{D_0(1+g)}{r_s - g}$$

$$\$45.83 = \dfrac{\$2.50(1+g)}{0.16 - g}$$

$$\$7.33 - \$45.83g = \$2.50 + \$2.50g$$

$$\$48.33g = \$4.83$$

$$g = 0.0999 \approx 10\%$$

9. d. $D_0 = \$1.00$; $r_s = 8\% + 7\% = 15\%$; $g_1 = 40\%$; $g_2 = 20\%$; $g_n = 7\%$, $P_0 = ?$

Year:

Dividend:

$$*\hat{P}_2 = \frac{\$1.7976}{0.15 - 0.07} = \$22.47$$

Alternatively, input 0, 1.40, 24.15 (1.68 + 22.47) into the cash flow register, input I/YR = 15, and then solve for NPV = $19.48.

10. a.   To calculate Chadmark's current stock price, follow the following steps: (1) Determine the expected stream of dividends during the nonconstant growth period. You will need to calculate the expected dividend at the end of Year 5, which is the first year of constant growth. This dividend will be used in the next step to calculate the stock price. (2) Calculate the expected stock price at the end of the final year of nonconstant growth. This occurs at the end of Year 4. Use the Gordon model for this calculation. (3) Add the value obtained in Step 2 to the dividend expected in Year 4. (4) Put the values obtained in the prior steps on a time line and discount them at the required rate of return to find the present value of Chadmark's stock. These steps are shown below.

$D_0 = \$0$; $D_1 = \$0$; $D_2 = \$0.75$; $D_3 = \$0.75(1.4) = \$1.05$; $D_4 = \$0.75(1.4)^2 = \$1.47$;
$D_5 = \$0.75(1.4)^2(1.10) = \$1.617$.

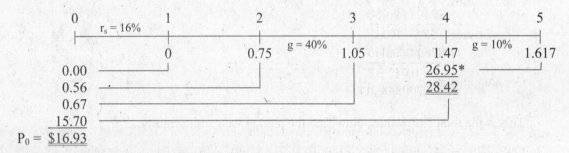

$$*\hat{P}_4 = \$1.617/(0.16 - 0.10) = \$26.95$$

$CF_0 = 0$; $CF_1 = 0$; $CF_2 = 0.75$; $CF_3 = 1.05$; $CF_4 = 28.42$

Alternatively, using a financial calculator you could input the cash flows as shown above into the cash flow register, input I/YR = 16, and press NPV to obtain the stock's value today of $16.93.

11. c.   First, set up the time line as follows. Note that D_5 is used to find $\hat{P}_4$, which is treated as part of the cash flow at t = 4:

$$
\begin{array}{ccccccc}
0 & & 1 & 2 & 3 & 4 & 5 \\
\end{array}
$$

$r_s = 20\%$

g = 0%   g = 8%   g = 15%

2.00   2.00   2.16   2.333   2.6827

1.667 ⎯⎯⎯⎯⎯   53.654* ⎯⎯⎯

1.389 ⎯⎯⎯⎯⎯⎯⎯⎯⎯ 55.987

1.250 ⎯⎯⎯⎯⎯⎯⎯⎯⎯⎯⎯⎯⎯

27.000 ⎯⎯⎯⎯⎯⎯⎯⎯⎯⎯⎯⎯⎯⎯⎯

$P_0 = \underline{\$31.306}$

$*\hat{P}_4 = \$2.6827/(0.20 - 0.15) = \$53.654$

Enter the time line values into the cash flow register, with I = 20, to find NPV = $31.31. Be sure to enter $CF_0 = 0$. Note that $\hat{P}_4$ is the PV, at t = 4, of dividends from t = 5 to infinity; that is, the PV of the dividends after the stock is expected to become a constant growth stock.

12. b.
$$
\text{FCF} = \left[\text{EBIT}(1-T) + \begin{array}{c}\text{Depreciation and}\\\text{amortization}\end{array} \right] - \left[\begin{array}{c}\text{Capital}\\\text{expenditures}\end{array} + \begin{array}{c}\Delta \text{ Net operating}\\\text{working capital}\end{array} \right]
$$

$$= [\$950{,}000{,}000 + \$190{,}000{,}000] - [\$380{,}000{,}000 + \$0]$$
$$= \$760{,}000{,}000$$

$$
\text{Firm value} = \frac{\text{FCF}_1}{\text{WACC} - g}
$$

$$
= \frac{\$760{,}000{,}000}{0.09 - 0.04}
$$

$$
= \frac{\$760{,}000{,}000}{0.05}
$$

$$
= \$15{,}200{,}000{,}000
$$

This is the total firm value. Now find the market value of its equity.

$$\text{MV}_{\text{Total}} = \text{MV}_{\text{Equity}} + \text{MV}_{\text{Debt}}$$
$$\$15{,}200{,}000{,}000 = \text{MV}_{\text{Equity}} + \$5{,}200{,}000{,}000$$
$$\text{MV}_{\text{Equity}} = \$10{,}000{,}000{,}000$$

This is the market value of all the equity. Divide by the number of shares to find the price per share:

$$\$10{,}000{,}000{,}000 / 250{,}000{,}000 = \$40.00$$

Each share of common stock is worth $40, according to the corporate valuation model.

13. d. The firm's free cash flow is expected to grow at a constant rate, hence we can apply a constant growth formula to the free cash flow to determine the total value of the firm.

$$\text{Firm value} = FCF_1/(WACC - g)$$
$$= \$75,000,000/(0.09 - 0.06)$$
$$= \$2,500,000,000$$

To find the value of an equity claim upon the company (share of stock), we must subtract out the market value of debt and preferred stock. This firm happens to be entirely equity funded, and this step is unnecessary. Hence, to find the value of a share of stock, we divide equity value (or in this case, firm value) by the number of shares outstanding.

$$\text{Equity value per share} = \text{Equity value/Shares outstanding}$$
$$= \$2,500,000,000/50,000,000$$
$$= \$50$$

Each share of common stock is worth $50, according to the corporate valuation model.

14. e. The preferred stock pays $5 annually in dividends. Therefore, its nominal rate of return would be:

Nominal rate of return = $5.00/$71.43 = 7%

Or alternatively, you could determine the security's periodic return and multiply by 4:

Periodic rate of return = $1.25/$71.43 = 1.75%

Nominal rate of return = $1.75\% \times 4 = 7\%$

15. b. Nominal rate of return = $(4 \times \$1.25)/\$71.43 = 7\%$

$$EAR = (1 + I_{NOM}/4)^4 - 1$$
$$= (1 + 0.07/4)^4 - 1$$
$$= (1.0175)^4 - 1$$
$$= 1.0719 - 1$$
$$= 0.0719 = 7.19\%$$

16. a. The value of any asset is the present value of all future cash flows expected to be generated from the asset. Hence, if we can find the present value of the dividends during the period preceding long-run constant growth and subtract that total from the current stock price, the remaining value would be the present value of the cash flows to be received during the period of long-run constant growth.

$D_1 = \$1.50 \times (1.15)^1 = \$1.7250$	$PV(D_1) = \$1.7250/(1.10)^1 = \$1.5682$
$D_2 = \$1.50 \times (1.15)^2 = \$1.98375$	$PV(D_2) = \$1.98375/(1.10)^2 = \$1.6395$
$D_3 = \$1.50 \times (1.15)^3 = \$2.2813125$	$PV(D_3) = \$2.2813125/(1.10)^3 = \$1.7140$
	$\Sigma\, PV(D_1 \text{ to } D_3) = \$4.9217$

Therefore, the PV of the remaining dividends is: $40.9200 − $4.9217 = $35.9983. Compounding this value forward to Year 3, we find that the value of all dividends received during constant growth is $47.9137. [$35.9983(1.10)^3 = $47.9137.] Applying the constant growth formula, we can solve for the constant growth rate:

$$\hat{P}_3 = D_3(1 + g)/(r_s − g)$$
$$\$47.9137 = \$2.2813125(1 + g)/(0.10 − g)$$
$$\$4.7914 − \$47.9137g = \$2.2813125 + \$2.2813125g$$
$$\$2.5101 = \$50.1950g$$
$$5.00\% = g$$

17. c. First, solve for the current price.

$$P_0 = D_1/(r_s − g)$$
$$= \$2.25/(0.11 − 0.04)$$
$$= \$32.1429 \approx \$32.14$$

If the stock is in a constant growth state, the constant dividend growth rate is also the capital gains yield for the stock and the stock price growth rate. Hence, to find the price of the stock five years from today:

$$\hat{P}_5 = P_0(1 + g)^5$$
$$= \$32.1429(1.04)^5$$
$$= \$39.1067 \approx \$39.11$$

10

THE COST OF CAPITAL

Learning Objectives

1. Explain why the weighted average cost of capital (WACC) is used in capital budgeting.

2. Estimate the costs of different capital components—debt, preferred stock, retained earnings, and common stock.

3. Combine the different component costs to determine the firm's WACC.

Overview

When companies issue stocks or bonds, they are raising capital that can be invested in various projects. Capital is a necessary factor of production, and like any other factor, it has a cost. This cost is equal to the marginal investor's required return on the security in question.

The firm's primary financial objective is to maximize shareholder value. Companies can increase shareholder value by investing in projects that earn more than the cost of capital. For this reason, the cost of capital is sometimes referred to as a hurdle rate: For a project to be accepted, it must earn more than its hurdle rate. The same factors that affect required rates of return on securities by investors also determine a firm's cost of capital, so investors and corporate treasurers often use exactly the same models.

Outline

I. **When calculating the WACC, the firm considers only the cost of capital provided by investors—interest-bearing debt, preferred stock, and common equity.**

   A. Accounts payable and accruals, which arise spontaneously when capital budgeting projects are taken on, are not included as part of investor-supplied capital because they do not come directly from investors.

   B. Investors are concerned with a firm's current market value of interest-bearing debt, preferred stock, and equity. So, market-value weights of investor-supplied capital are emphasized over accounting-based weights in calculating a firm's WACC.

   C. What ultimately matters to the firm are target weights of investor-supplied capital based on the firm's target capital structure.

      1. The *target capital structure* is the mix of debt, preferred stock, and common equity the firm plans to raise to fund its future projects.

2. A company's target capital structure reflects that there is an *optimal capital structure*—one where the percentages of debt, preferred stock, and common equity maximize the firm's value.

D. A firm's overall cost of capital is a weighted average of the costs of the various types of investor-supplied capital it uses, where the weights correspond to the company's target capital structure.

II. **Determining the firm's cost of capital, or the proper discount rate for use in calculating the present value of the cash inflows for the firm's projects, is an important element of the capital budgeting process.**

A. *Capital components* are the investor-supplied items on the right-hand side of the balance sheet used by firms to raise funds such as debt, preferred stock, and common equity. Increases in assets must be financed by increases in these capital components.

1. Each element of capital has a component cost that can be identified as follows:

a. r_d = interest rate on the firm's new debt, before taxes.

b. $r_d(1 - T)$ = after-tax component cost of new debt where T is the firm's marginal tax rate.

c. r_p = component cost of preferred stock.

d. r_s = component cost of retained earnings or *internal equity*.

e. r_e = component cost of *external equity*, or common equity raised by issuing new stock.

f. WACC = the weighted average, or overall, cost of capital; a weighted average of the component costs of debt, preferred stock, and common equity.

B. The *optimal capital structure* is the percentages of debt, preferred stock, and common equity that minimizes the firm's cost of capital and maximizes the firm's value.

III. **The after-tax cost of debt, $r_d(1 - T)$, is the interest rate on new debt, r_d, less the tax savings that result because interest is tax deductible. It is the relevant cost of new debt, taking into account the tax deductibility of interest, used in the firm's WACC calculation.**

A. The value of the firm's stock depends on after-tax cash flows. We are concerned with after-tax cash flows, and since cash flows and rates of return should be placed on a comparable basis, the interest rate should be adjusted downward for the preferential tax treatment of debt.

1. We are interested in maximizing the value of the firm's stock, and the stock price depends on after-tax cash flows.

B. If a firm has a tax rate of 40% and can borrow at a rate of 10%, then its after-tax cost of debt is $r_d = 10\%(1 - 0.40) = 10\%(0.60) = 6.0\%$.

C. In effect, the government pays part of the cost of debt because interest is tax deductible.

D. r_d is the interest rate on *new* debt, the marginal cost of debt, not on already outstanding debt.

1. The primary concern with the cost of capital is its use in capital budgeting decisions. The rate at which the firm has borrowed in the past is irrelevant because capital budgeting decisions must use the cost of new capital in the analysis.

2. The yield to maturity on outstanding debt (which reflects current market conditions) is a better measure of the cost of debt than the coupon rate.

3. The yield to maturity on the company's long-term debt is generally used to calculate the cost of debt because, more often than not, the capital is being raised to fund long-term projects.

IV. **The component cost of preferred stock, r_p, is the preferred dividend, D_p, divided by the current price of the preferred stock, P_p: $r_p = D_p/P_p$.**

   A. No tax adjustments are made when calculating r_p because preferred dividends, unlike interest on debt, are not deductible; so no tax savings are associated with preferred stock.

   B. If a firm's preferred stock pays a $10 dividend per share and sells for $97.50 per share, the firm's cost of preferred stock, r_p, is calculated as: $r_p = \$10.00/\$97.50 = 10.3\%$.

V. **The cost of retained earnings, r_s, is the rate of return stockholders require on the company's common stock.**

   A. New common equity is raised in two ways: (1) By retaining some of the firm's current year earnings and (2) by issuing new common stock.

      1. A corporation's management might be tempted to think that retained earnings are "free" because they represent money that is "left over" after paying dividends, but this capital still has a cost.

         a. Whereas debt and preferred stocks are contractual obligations whose costs are clearly stated on the contracts themselves, stocks have no comparable stated cost rate.

      2. The cost of retained earnings has a cost, an *opportunity cost*. The firm's after-tax earnings belong to its stockholders. These earnings serve to compensate stockholders for the use of their capital. Stockholders could have received the earnings as dividends and invested this money in other stocks, in bonds, in real estate, or in anything else.

         a. The firm should earn on its retained earnings at least as much as the stockholders themselves could earn on alternative investments of comparable risk.

         b. If the firm cannot invest retained earnings and earn at least r_s, it should pay those funds to its stockholders and let them invest directly in stocks or other assets that will provide that return.

      3. People experienced in estimating equity capital costs recognize that both careful analysis and sound judgment are required.

      4. The cost of new common stock, r_e, is the cost of external equity; it is based on the cost of retained earnings, but increased for flotation costs.

      5. The following equation can be used to produce reasonably good estimates of the cost of equity from retained earnings:

$$\text{Required rate of return} = \text{Expected rate of return}$$

$$r_s = r_{RF} + RP = \frac{D_1}{P_0} + g = \hat{r}_s$$

         a. We assume that a stock is in equilibrium.

         b. The left-hand side of the equation is based on the CAPM and the right-hand side of the equation is based on the discounted dividend model.

   B. There are three approaches used to estimate r_s:

      1. The Capital Asset Pricing Model (CAPM) works as follows:

a. Estimate the risk-free rate, r_{RF}, usually based on U.S. Treasury securities.

b. Estimate the stock's beta coefficient, b_i, as an index of the stock's risk.

c. Estimate the expected market risk premium, the difference between the return that investors require on an average stock and the risk-free rate.

d. Substitute the preceding values into the CAPM equation, $r_s = r_{RF} + (RP_M)b_i$, to estimate the required rate of return on the stock in question.

e. Thus, if $r_{RF} = 5.6\%$, $RP_M = 5\%$, and b_i is 1.48, then $r_s = 5.6\% + (5\%)1.48 = 13.0\%$.

f. Although the CAPM appears to yield an accurate, precise estimate of r_s, several potential problems exist.

  (1.) If a firm's stockholders are not well diversified, the firm's true investment risk would not be measured by its beta, and the CAPM estimate would understate the correct value of r_s.

  (2.) Even if the CAPM is valid, it is hard to obtain accurate estimates of the required inputs because there is controversy about whether to use long-term or short-term Treasury yields for r_{RF}, it is hard to estimate the beta that investors expect the company to have in the future, and it is difficult to estimate the proper market risk premium.

2. The *bond-yield-plus-risk-premium approach* is a subjective, ad hoc procedure to estimate a firm's cost of common equity. It estimates r_s by adding a risk premium of 3% to 5% to the firm's own long-term debt yield. Thus, $r_s = $ Bond yield + Risk premium.

a. It is logical to think that firms with risky, low-rated, and consequently high-interest-rate debt will also have risky, high-cost equity. This approach utilizes this logic.

b. If the firm uses a risk premium of 4%, and its bond rate is 10%, then using this approach $r_s = 10\% + 4\% = 14\%$.

c. Because the risk premium is a judgmental estimate, the estimated cost of equity is also judgmental; however, it does get us "into the right ballpark."

3. The required rate of return, r_s, may also be estimated by the *discounted cash flow (DCF) approach*. This approach is also called the *dividend-yield-plus-growth rate approach*, as it combines the expected dividend yield, D_1/P_0, with the expected future growth rate, g, of earnings and dividends, or

$$r_s = \hat{r}_s = \frac{D_1}{P_0} + \text{Expected g}$$

a. The DCF approach assumes that stocks are normally in equilibrium and that growth is expected to be at a constant rate. If growth is not constant, then a nonconstant growth model must be used.

b. The expected growth rate may be based on projections of past growth rates, if they have been relatively stable, or on expected future growth rates as estimated in some other manner.

c. Security analysts regularly forecast earnings and dividend growth rates, looking at such factors as projected sales, profit margins, and competition.

d. Intuitively, firms that are more profitable and retain a larger portion of their earnings for reinvestment in the firm will tend to have higher growth rates than firms that are less profitable and pay out a higher percentage of their earnings as dividends.

e. If the firm's next expected dividend is $1.25, its expected growth rate is 8.3% per year, and its stock is selling for $23.06 per share, then

$$r_s = \hat{r}_s = \frac{\$1.25}{\$23.06} + 8.3\%$$
$$= 5.4\% + 8.3\%$$
$$= 13.7\%$$

4. It is recommended that all three approaches be used in estimating the required rate of return on common stock. When the methods produce widely different results, judgment must be used in selecting the best estimate. In our example, estimates of r_s range from 13% to 14%, so a reasonable estimate might be the midpoint of this range, 13.5%.

CAPM:	13.0%
BY + RP:	14.0%
DCF:	13.7%

VI. Companies generally use an investment banker to assist them when they issue common stock, preferred stock, or bonds. In return for a fee, the investment banker helps the company structure the terms, sets a price for the issue, and then sells the issue to investors. The banker's fees are called flotation costs, and the total cost of capital raised reflects the investors' required return plus the flotation costs.

A. *Flotation costs* should be included in a complete analysis of the cost of capital. Two alternative approaches can be used to account for flotation costs.

1. The first approach simply adds the estimated dollar amount of flotation costs for each project to the project's up-front cost. Because of the now-higher investment cost, the project's expected rate of return and NPV are decreased.

2. The second approach involves adjusting the cost of capital rather than increasing the project's cost. If the firm plans to continue to use the capital in the future, as is generally true for equity, then this second approach is better. When calculating the cost of common equity, the DCF approach can be adapted to account for flotation costs. For a constant growth stock, the *cost of new common stock, r_e,* can be expressed as follows:

$$r_e = \frac{D_1}{P_0(1-F)} + g$$

a. Here F is the percentage flotation cost required to sell new stock, so $P_0(1-F)$ is the net price per share received by the company.

b. If the firm has a flotation cost of 10%, its cost of new outside equity is calculated as follows:

$$r_e = \frac{\$1.25}{\$23.06(1-0.10)} + 8.3\% = 14.3\%$$

c. If the firm can earn 14.3% on investments financed by new common stock, then earnings, dividends, and the growth rate will be maintained, and the price per share will not fall. If it earns more than 14.3%, the price will rise; while if it earns less, the price will fall.

  d. The *flotation cost adjustment* is the amount that must be added to r_s to account for flotation costs to find r_e.

$$\text{Flotation adjustment} = \text{Adjusted DCF cost} - \text{Pure DCF cost}$$

In our example, the flotation cost adjustment is calculated as $14.3\% - 13.7\% = 0.6\%$.

B. Because of flotation costs, dollars raised by selling new stock must "work harder" than dollars raised by retained earnings.

 1. Because no flotation costs are involved, retained earnings have a lower cost than new stock. Therefore, firms should utilize retained earnings to the greatest extent possible to avoid the cost of issuing new common stock.

 2. The *retained earnings breakpoint* represents the total amount of capital that can be raised before the firm is forced to sell new common stock, and is calculated as:

Retained earnings breakpoint = Addition to retained earnings for the year/Equity fraction

  a. It is important to recognize that this breakpoint is only suggestive—it is not written in stone. Rather than issuing new common stock, the company could use more debt (hence, less equity), or it could increase its additional retained earnings by reducing its dividend payout ratio. Both actions would increase the retained earnings breakpoint.

  b. Breakpoints could occur due to increases in the costs of debt and preferred.

  c. Firms that have a large number of good investment opportunities generally maximize their retained earnings by paying out a smaller percentage of income as dividends than firms with fewer good investment opportunities.

VII. **Each firm has an optimal capital structure, defined as that mix of debt, preferred, and common equity that causes its stock price to be maximized.**

A. The target proportions of debt, preferred stock, and common equity, along with the component costs of capital, are used to calculate the firm's *weighted average cost of capital (WACC)*.

B. The weighted average cost of capital calculation is shown below for a firm that finances 45% with debt, 2% with preferred stock, and 53% with retained earnings and that has the following after-tax component costs:

Component	Weight	$\times$	After-Tax Cost	$=$	Weighted Cost
Debt	0.45	$\times$	6.0%	$=$	2.700%
Preferred	0.02	$\times$	10.3	$=$	0.206
Common	0.53	$\times$	13.5	$=$	7.155
			WACC	$=$	$10.061\% \approx 10.1\%$

C. In more general terms, and in equation format,

$$\text{WACC} = w_d r_d (1 - T) + w_p r_p + w_c r_s$$

D. Web Appendix 10A discusses in more detail the connection between the WACC and the costs of issuing new common stock.

VIII. The cost of capital is affected by a variety of factors. Some of these factors the firm cannot control and others the firm can control.

    A. The three most important factors that the firm cannot directly control are interest rates in the economy, the general level of stock prices, and tax rates.

        1. If interest rates in the economy rise, the cost of debt increases because firms must pay bondholders more when it borrows.

        2. If stock prices in general decline, pulling the firm's stock price down, its cost of equity will rise.

        3. Tax rates are used in the calculation of the cost of debt, which is one of the components of WACC, so they have an important effect on the firm's cost of capital.

            a. There are other less apparent ways in which taxes can affect the cost of capital. When tax rates on dividends and capital gains were lowered relative to rates on interest income, stocks become relatively more attractive than debt; consequently, the cost of equity and WACC declined.

    B. A firm can affect its cost of capital by changing its capital structure, changing its dividend payout ratio, and by altering its capital budgeting decision rules to accept projects with more or less risk than projects previously undertaken.

        1. The firm can change its capital structure, and such a change can affect its cost of capital.

            a. If a firm decides to use more debt and less common equity, this change in the weights used in the WACC equation will tend to lower the WACC.

            b. However, an increase in the use of debt will increase the risk of both debt and equity, and these changes will tend to increase the WACC, and thus, offset the effects of the change in weights.

        2. Dividend policy affects the amount of retained earnings available to the firm and thus the need to sell new stock and incur flotation costs. The higher the dividend payout ratio, the smaller the addition to retained earnings, and thus the higher the cost of equity and therefore the WACC.

            a. Investors may prefer dividends to retained earnings, in which case reducing dividends might lead to an increase in both r_s and r_e.

            b. The optimal dividend policy is a complicated issue and this will be discussed in Chapter 14.

        3. Capital budgeting decisions can also affect its cost of capital. When we estimate the cost of capital, we use as the starting point the required rate of return on the firm's outstanding stock and bonds. These cost rates reflect the risk of the firm's existing assets.

            a. Therefore, we implicitly have been assuming that new capital will be invested in assets of the same type and with the same degree of risk as embedded in the existing assets. This assumption will be incorrect if the firm dramatically changes its investment policy.

            b. If the firm decides to invest in an entirely new and risky line of business, then its component costs of debt and equity, and thus its WACC, will increase.

197

IX. **The cost of capital is a key element in the capital budgeting process. A project should be accepted only if its estimated return exceeds its cost of capital. For this reason, the cost of capital is sometimes referred to as the "hurdle rate," because project returns must jump the "hurdle" to be accepted.**

    A. Investors require higher returns for riskier investments. Consequently, a company that is raising capital to take on risky projects will have a higher cost of capital than a company that is investing in safer projects.

    B. Ideally, the hurdle rate for each project should reflect the risk of the project itself, not necessarily the risks associated with the firm's average project as reflected in the firm's composite WACC.

    C. Applying a specific hurdle rate to each project insures that every project is evaluated properly.

    D. In general, failing to adjust for differences in risk would lead a firm to accept too many risky projects and reject too many safe ones. Over time, the firm will become more risky, its WACC will increase, and its shareholder value will suffer.

X. **A number of difficult issues relating to the cost of capital are listed below but they do not invalidate the usefulness of the procedures outlined in this chapter. These topics are covered in advanced finance courses.**

    A. Depreciation-generated funds are the largest single source of capital for many firms.

        1. The cost of depreciation-generated funds is approximately equal to the weighted average cost of capital that comes from retained earnings, preferred stock, and low-cost debt. Therefore, we can ignore it in our estimate of WACC.

    B. As a general rule, the same principles of cost of capital estimation apply to both privately held and publicly owned firms, but the problems of obtaining input data are somewhat difficult for each.

        1. Tax issues are also especially important in these cases.

    C. One cannot overemphasize the practical difficulties encountered when one actually attempts to estimate the cost of equity. As a result, we can never be sure of the accuracy of our estimated cost of capital.

    D. It is difficult to assign proper risk-adjusted discount rates to capital budgeting projects of differing degrees of riskiness because it is difficult to measure a project's risk.

    E. Establishing the target capital structure is a major task in itself.

Self-Test

Definitional Questions

1. The firm should calculate its cost of capital as a(n) _____ average of the after-tax costs of the various types of funds it uses.

2. Capital components are investor-supplied items on the right-hand side of the balance sheet such as the following: (1) _____, (2) _____ stock, and (3) _____ equity.

3. The cost of equity capital is defined as the _____ of _____ stockholders require on the firm's common stock.

4. There are _____ approaches that can be used to determine the cost of common equity.

5. Assigning a cost to retained earnings is based on a(n) _____ cost.

6. The cost of new outside equity capital is higher than the cost of internal equity (retained earnings) due to _____ costs.

7. Using the Capital Asset Pricing Model (CAPM), the required rate of return on common equity is found as a function of the _____-_____ rate, the firm's beta _____, and the market risk _____.

8. The cost of common equity may also be found by adding a(n) _____ premium to the interest rate on the firm's own _____ yield.

9. The required rate of return on common equity may also be estimated as the expected _____ yield on the common stock plus the expected future _____ rate of the dividends.

10. The proportions of _____, _____ stock, and _____ equity in the target capital structure should be used to calculate the weighted _____ cost of capital.

11. The component cost of preferred stock is calculated as the preferred _____ divided by the preferred stock's _____ price.

12. The capital structure that minimizes a firm's weighted average cost of capital also _____ its stock price.

13. The three most important factors that affect the cost of capital and that the firm cannot directly control are _____ rates, the general level of stock _____, and _____ rates.

14. A firm can affect its cost of capital by changing its capital _____, changing its _____ _____ _____, and altering its _____ _____ decisions.

15. Two approaches can be used to account for flotation costs: (1) Add the estimated dollar amount of flotation costs for each project to the project's ____-_____ cost and (2) _____ the cost of capital.

16. Firms that are more profitable and retain a larger portion of their earnings for reinvestment in the firm will tend to have _____ growth rates than firms who are less profitable and pay out a greater portion of their earnings as _____.

17. Flotation cost adjustments can also be made for _____ stock and _____, as well as for common stock.

18. The cost of capital is sometimes referred to as the _____ rate because projects must jump over it to be accepted.

19. Ideally, the hurdle rate for each project should reflect the _____ of the project itself, not necessarily those associated with the firm's _____ project as reflected in the firm's composite WACC.

20. In general, failing to adjust for differences in risk would lead a firm to accept too many risky projects and reject too many safe ones. Over time, it will become _____ risky, its WACC will _____, and its shareholder value will suffer.

21. The cost of depreciation-generated funds is approximately equal to the weighted average cost of capital in the interval in which capital comes from _____ earnings and low-cost.

22. In effect, the government pays part of the cost of debt because interest is _____ deductible.

199

23. New common equity is raised in two ways: (1) by _____ some of the firm's current year earnings and (2) by _____ new common stock.

24. The retained earnings _____ represents the total amount of capital that can be raised before the firm is forced to sell new common stock.

25. A value-maximizing firm will establish a(n) _____ capital _____ and then raise new capital in a manner designed to keep it on target over time.

26. The primary concern with the cost of capital is its use in capital _____ decisions.

27. It is important to recognize that the retained earnings breakpoint is not written in stone. Rather than issuing new common stock, the company could use more _____, or it could increase its additional retained earnings by reducing its dividend _____ ratio.

28. _____ _____ are investor-supplied items on the right-hand side of the balance sheet used by firms to raise funds.

29. The value of the firm's stock depends on after-tax _____ _____.

30. The rate at which the firm has borrowed in the past is _____.

Conceptual Questions

1. Funds acquired by the firm through preferred stock have a cost to the firm equal to the preferred dividend divided by the current price of the preferred stock. If significant flotation costs are involved the cost of the preferred should be adjusted upward.

   a. True
   b. False

2. Which of the following statements could be true concerning the costs of debt and equity?

   a. The cost of debt for Firm A is greater than the cost of equity for Firm A.
   b. The cost of debt for Firm A is greater than the cost of equity for Firm B.
   c. The cost of retained earnings for Firm A is less than its cost of new outside equity.
   d. The cost of retained earnings for Firm A is less than its cost of debt.
   e. Both statements b and c could be true.

3. Which of the following statements is correct?

   a. If Congress raised the corporate tax rate, this would lower the effective cost of debt but probably would also reduce the amount of retained earnings available to corporations, so the effect on the marginal cost of capital is uncertain.
   b. For corporate investors, 70% of the dividends received on both common and preferred stocks is exempt from taxes. However, neither preferred nor common dividends may be deducted by the issuing company. Therefore, the dividend exclusion has no effect on a company's cost of capital, so its WACC would probably not change at all if the dividend exclusion rule were rescinded by Congress.
   c. The calculation for a firm's WACC includes an adjustment to the cost of debt for taxes, since interest is deductible, and includes the cost of all current liabilities.
   d. Firms that have a large number of good investment opportunities generally minimize their retained earnings by paying out a larger percentage of income as dividends than firms with fewer good investment opportunities.
   e. In general, failing to adjust for differences in risk would lead a firm to accept too many safe projects and to reject too many higher-risk projects. Over time the firm's WACC would increase because shareholder value would be eroded.

Problems

1. Roland Corporation's next expected dividend (D_1) is $2.50. The firm has maintained a constant payout ratio of 50% during the past 7 years. Seven years ago its EPS was $1.50. The firm's beta coefficient is 1.2. The estimated market risk premium is 6%, and the risk-free rate is 7%. Roland's A-rated bonds are yielding 10%, and its current stock price is $30. Which of the following values is the most reasonable estimate of Roland's cost of retained earnings, r_s?

   a. 10%
   b. 12%
   c. 14%
   d. 20%
   e. 26%

2. The director of capital budgeting for See-Saw Inc., manufacturers of playground equipment, is considering a plan to expand production facilities in order to meet an increase in demand. He estimates that this expansion will produce a rate of return of 11%. The firm's target capital structure calls for a debt/equity ratio of 0.8. See-Saw currently has a bond issue outstanding that will mature in 25 years and has a 7% annual coupon rate. The bonds are currently selling for $804. The firm has maintained a constant growth rate of 6%. See-Saw's next expected dividend is $2 ($D_1$), its current stock price is $40, and its tax rate is 40%. Should it undertake the expansion? (Assume that there is no preferred stock outstanding and that any new debt will have a 25-year maturity.)

   a. No; the expected return is 2.5 percentage points lower than the cost of capital.
   b. No; the expected return is 1.0 percentage point lower than the cost of capital.
   c. Yes; the expected return is 0.5 percentage point higher than the cost of capital.
   d. Yes; the expected return is 1.0 percentage point higher than the cost of capital.
   e. Yes; the expected return is 2.5 percentage points higher than the cost of capital.

3. The management of Florida Phosphate Industries (FPI) is planning next year's capital budget. The company's earnings and dividends are growing at a constant rate of 5%. The last dividend, D_0, was $0.90; and the current equilibrium stock price is $7.73. FPI can raise new debt at a 14% before-tax cost. FPI is at its optimal capital structure, which is 40% debt and 60% equity, and the firm's marginal tax rate is 40%. FPI has the following independent, indivisible, and equally risky investment opportunities:

Project	Cost	Rate of Return
A	$15,000	17%
B	15,000	16
C	12,000	15
D	20,000	13

   What is FPI's optimal capital budget?

   a. $62,000
   b. $42,000
   c. $30,000
   d. $15,000
   e. $ 0

4. Gator Products Company (GPC) is at its optimal capital structure of 70% common equity and 30% debt. GPC's WACC is 14%. GPC has a marginal tax rate of 40%. Next year's dividend is expected to be $2.00 per share, and GPC has a constant growth in earnings and dividends of 6%. The after-tax cost of common stock used in the WACC is based on new outside equity with a flotation cost of 10%, while the before-tax cost of debt is 12%. What is GPC's current equilibrium stock price?

   a. $12.73
   b. $17.23
   c. $20.37
   d. $23.70
   e. $37.20

5. Sun Products Company (SPC) uses only debt and equity. It can borrow unlimited amounts at an interest rate of 12% so long as it finances at its target capital structure, which calls for 45% debt and 55% common equity. Its last dividend was $2.40, its expected constant growth rate is 5%, and its stock sells for $24. SPC's tax rate is 40%. Four projects are available: Project A has a cost of $240 million and a rate of return of 13%, Project B has a cost of $125 million and a rate of return of 12%, Project C has a cost of $200 million and a rate of return of 11%, and Project D has a cost of $150 million and a rate of return of 10%. All of the company's potential projects are independent and equally risky. What is SPC's cost of common equity?

   a. 15.50%
   b. 13.40%
   c. 7.20%
   d. 12.50%
   e. 16.00%

6. Sun Products Company (SPC) uses only debt and equity. It can borrow unlimited amounts at an interest rate of 12% so long as it finances at its target capital structure, which calls for 45% debt and 55% common equity. Its last dividend was $2.40, its expected constant growth rate is 5%, and its stock sells for $24. SPC's tax rate is 40%. Four projects are available: Project A has a cost of $240 million and a rate of return of 13%, Project B has a cost of $125 million and a rate of return of 12%, Project C has a cost of $200 million and a rate of return of 11%, and Project D has a cost of $150 million and a rate of return of 10%. All of the company's potential projects are independent and equally risky. What is SPC's WACC? In other words, what WACC should it use to evaluate capital budgeting projects (these four projects plus any others that might arise during the year, provided the WACC remains as it is currently)?

   a. 12.05%
   b. 13.40%
   c. 11.77%
   d. 12.50%
   e. 10.61%

7. Sun Products Company (SPC) uses only debt and equity. It can borrow unlimited amounts at an interest rate of 12% so long as it finances at its target capital structure, which calls for 45% debt and 55% common equity. Its last dividend was $2.40, its expected constant growth rate is 5%, and its stock sells for $24. SPC's tax rate is 40%. Four projects are available: Project A has a cost of $240 million and a rate of return of 13%, Project B has a cost of $125 million and a rate of return of 12%, Project C has a cost of $200 million and a rate of return of 11%, and Project D has a cost of $150 million and a rate of return of 10%. All of the company's potential projects are independent and equally risky. What is SPC's optimal capital budget (in millions)?

   a. $240
   b. $325
   c. $365
   d. $565
   e. $715

8. Sun Products Company (SPC) uses only debt and equity. It can borrow unlimited amounts at an interest rate of 12% so long as it finances at its target capital structure, which calls for 45% debt and 55% common equity. Its last dividend was $2.40, its expected constant growth rate is 5%, and its stock sells for $24. SPC's tax rate is 40%. Four projects are available: Project A has a cost of $240 million and a rate of return of 13%, Project B has a cost of $125 million and a rate of return of 12%, Project C has a cost of $200 million and a rate of return of 11%, and Project D has a cost of $150 million and a rate of return of 10%. All of the company's potential projects are independent and equally risky. Assume now that all four projects are independent; however, Project A has been judged a very risky project, while Projects C and D have been judged low-risk projects. Project B remains an average-risk project. If SPC adjusts its WACC by 2 percentage points up or down to account for risk, what is its optimal capital budget (in millions) now?

   a. $365
   b. $390
   c. $440
   d. $475
   e. $715

9. Hodor Manufacturing Co.'s (HMC) common stock currently sells for $50.00 per share. Assume the stock is in a state of constant growth, has an expected dividend yield of 4.5%, and an expected capital gains yield of 6.5%. The current dividend payout ratio is 30% and the firm's return on equity is 9.3%. The firm requires external funds for a new project and anticipates issuing additional shares of common stock at its current price of $50.00. However, the process of issuing this new equity is expected to result in a flotation expense equivalent to 10% of the stock price. If the firm goes ahead with its equity issue, what will be the firm's cost for this new common stock, r_e?

   a. 10.75%
   b. 11.50%
   c. 9.65%
   d. 12.00%
   e. 13.25%

10. Helena's Candies Co. (HCC) has a target capital structure of 55% equity and 45% debt to fund its $5 billion in assets. Furthermore, HCC has a WACC of 12.0%. Its before-tax cost of debt is 9%; and its tax rate is 40%. The company's retained earnings are adequate to fund the common equity portion of the capital budget. The firm's expected dividend next year (D_1) is $4 and the current stock price is $40. What is the company's expected growth rate?

   a. 4.50%
   b. 5.25%
   c. 5.75%
   d. 6.30%
   e. 7.40%

11. Helena's Candies Co. (HCC) has a target capital structure of 55% equity and 45% debt to fund its $5 billion in assets. Furthermore, HCC has a WACC of 12.0%. Its before-tax cost of debt is 9%; and its tax rate is 40%. The company's retained earnings are adequate to fund the common equity portion of the capital budget. The firm's expected dividend next year (D_1) is $4 and the current stock price is $40. If the firm's net income is expected to be $500 million, what portion of its net income is the firm expected to pay out as dividends?

   a. 33.33%
   b. 40.00%
   c. 59.30%
   d. 50.00%
   e. 45.00%

12. Sunrise Canoes Inc. has determined that its optimal capital structure consists of 55% equity and 45% debt. Sunrise must raise additional capital to fund its upcoming expansion. The firm has $0.5 million in retained earnings that has a cost of 11%. Its investment bankers have informed the company that it can issue an additional $3 million of new common equity at a cost of 14%. Furthermore, the firm can raise up to $1.5 million of debt at 10% and an additional $2 million at 12%. The firm has estimated that the proposed expansion will require an investment of $2.6 million. What is the WACC for the funds Sunrise will be raising?

   a. 10.40%
   b. 10.75%
   c. 11.20%
   d. 10.00%
   e. 11.50%

Answers

Definitional Questions

1. weighted
2. debt; preferred; common
3. rate; return
4. three
5. opportunity

6. flotation
7. risk-free; coefficient; premium
8. risk; bond
9. dividend; growth
10. debt; preferred; common; average

11. dividends; current
12. maximizes
13. interest; prices; tax
14. structure; dividend payout ratio; capital budgeting
15. up-front; adjust
16. higher; dividends
17. preferred; debt
18. hurdle
19. risk; average
20. more; increase

21. retained; debt
22. tax
23. retaining; issuing
24. breakpoint
25. optimal; structure
26. budgeting
27. debt; payout
28. Capital components
29. cash flows
30. irrelevant

Conceptual Questions

1. a. This statement is true.

2. e. If Firm A has more business risk than Firm B, Firm A's cost of debt could be greater than Firm B's cost of equity. Also, the cost of retained earnings is less than the cost of new outside equity due to flotation costs.

3. a. If Congress were to raise the tax rate, this would lower the cost of debt; however, a bigger chunk of the firm's earnings would go to Uncle Sam. The effect on the WACC would depend on which had the greater effect on the WACC.

Solutions

Problems

1. c. Use all three methods to estimate r_s.

CAPM: $r_s = r_{RF} + (RP_M)b = 7\% + (6\%)1.2 = 14.2\%$

Risk Premium: r_s = Bond yield + Risk premium = $10\% + 4\% = 14\%$

DCF: $r_s = D_1/P_0 + g = \$2.50/\$30 + g$,
where g can be estimated as follows using a financial calculator:

Enter N = 7, PV = -0.75, PMT = 0, FV = 2.50, and solve for I/YR = g = 18.77% ≈ 18.8%

Therefore, $r_s = 0.083 + 0.188 = 27.1\%$

Roland Corporation has apparently been experiencing supernormal growth during the past 7 years, and it is not reasonable to assume that this growth will continue. The first two methods yield r_s of about 14%, which appears reasonable.

2. e. Cost of equity = r_s = \$2/\$40 + 0.06 = 0.11 = 11%

Cost of debt = r_d = Yield to maturity on outstanding bonds based on current market price

Using a financial calculator: Input N = 25, PV = -804, PMT = 70, FV = 1000, and solve for I/YR = r_d = 9%.

In determining the capital structure weights, note that Debt/Equity = 0.8 or, for example, 4/5. Therefore, Debt/Assets is

$$\frac{D}{A} = \frac{Debt}{Debt + Equity} = \frac{4}{4+5} = \frac{4}{9},$$

and Equity/Assets = 5/9. Hence, the weighted average cost of capital is calculated as follows:

$$WACC = r_d(1 - T)(D/A) + r_s(1 - D/A)$$
$$= 0.09(1 - 0.4)(4/9) + 0.11(5/9)$$
$$= 0.024 + 0.061 = 0.085 = 8.5\%$$

The cost of capital is 8.5%, while the expansion project's rate of return is 11.0%. Since the expected return is 2.5 percentage points higher than the cost, the expansion should be undertaken.

3. b. The cost of common equity is as follows:

$$r_s = \frac{D_0(1+g)}{P_0} + g = \frac{\$0.90(1.05)}{\$7.73} + 0.05 = 0.1723 = 17.23\%$$

Now, determine the WACC:

$$WACC = w_d(r_d)(1 - T) + w_c(r_s)$$
$$= 0.4(14\%)(0.6) + 0.6(17.23\%) = 13.70\%$$

To determine FPI's optimal capital budget, we must determine those projects whose returns > WACC. (Note that all projects being considered are independent.) Since Projects A, B, and C all have returns > WACC, they should be accepted. Therefore, the optimal capital budget is \$42,000.

4. c. GPC's WACC = 14%. Therefore,

$$14\% = w_d(r_d)(1 - T) + w_c(r_e)$$
$$14\% = 0.3(12\%)(0.6) + 0.7(r_e)$$
$$11.84\% = 0.7(r_e)$$
$$r_e = 16.91\%$$

Now, at equilibrium:

$$\hat{r}_e = r_e = \frac{D_1}{P_0(1-F)} + g$$

$$0.1691 = \frac{\$2.00}{P_0(1-0.10)} + 0.06$$

$$0.1091 = \frac{\$2.222}{P_0}$$

$$P_0 = \$20.37$$

5. a. $r_s = [\$2.40(1.05)]/\$24 + 5\% = 0.1050 + 0.05 = 0.1550 = 15.50\%$

6. c. $r_d = 12\%; r_d(1 - T) = 12\%(0.6) = 7.2\%$

   $r_s = [\$2.40(1.05)]/\$24 + 5\% = 15.50\%$

   $WACC = 0.45(7.2\%) + 0.55(15.50\%) = 11.77\%$

7. c. $r_d = 12\%; r_d(1 - T) = 12\%(0.6) = 7.2\%$

   $r_s = [\$2.40(1.05)]/\$24 + 5\% = 15.50\%$

   $WACC = 0.45(7.2\%) + 0.55(15.50\%) = 11.77\%$

   Since all projects are equally risky and are independent, those projects whose returns > WACC should be chosen. Projects A and B have returns > 11.77%; therefore, the firm's optimal capital budget is $365 million.

8. d. $r_d = 12\%; r_d(1 - T) = 12\%(0.6) = 7.2\%$

   $r_s = [\$2.40(1.05)]/\$24 + 5\% = 15.50\%$

   $WACC = 0.45(7.2\%) + 0.55(15.50\%) = 11.77\%$

Project	Cost (Millions)	Return	Risk Level	Risk-Adjusted Cost of Capital
A	$240	13%	High	13.77%
B	125	12	Average	11.77
C	200	11	Low	9.77
D	150	10	Low	9.77

We adjust the firm's WACC up by 2% for high-risk projects and lower it by 2% for low-risk projects. Note that once the WACC is risk-adjusted, Projects B, C, and D are acceptable as their returns are greater than the risk-adjusted WACC. Therefore, the firm's optimal capital budget is $475 million.

9. b. If the firm's dividend yield is 4.5% and its stock price is $50.00, the next expected annual dividend can be calculated.

$$\text{Dividend yield} = D_1/P_0$$
$$4.5\% = D_1/\$50.00$$
$$D_1 = \$2.25$$

Next, the firm's cost of new common stock can be determined from the DCF approach for the cost of equity.

$$r_e = D_1/[P_0(1 - F)] + g$$
$$= \$2.25/[\$50.00(1 - 0.10)] + 0.065$$
$$= 11.50\%$$

10. e. Examining the DCF approach to the cost of retained earnings, the expected growth rate can be determined from the cost of common equity, price, and expected dividend. However, first, this problem requires that the formula for WACC be used to determine the cost of common equity.

$$\text{WACC} = w_d(r_d)(1 - T) + w_c(r_s)$$
$$12.0\% = 0.45(9\%)(1 - 0.4) + 0.55(r_s)$$
$$9.57\% = 0.55(r_s)$$
$$r_s = 0.1740 \text{ or } 17.40\%$$

From the cost of common equity, the expected growth rate can now be determined.

$$r_s = D_1/P_0 + g$$
$$0.1740 = \$4/\$40 + g$$
$$g = 0.0740 \text{ or } 7.40\%$$

11. c.
$$\text{WACC} = w_d(r_d)(1 - T) + w_c(r_s)$$
$$12.0\% = 0.45(9\%)(1 - 0.4) + 0.55(r_s)$$
$$9.57\% = 0.55(r_s)$$
$$r_s = 0.1740 \text{ or } 17.40\%$$

$$r_s = D_1/P_0 + g$$
$$0.1740 = \$4/\$40 + g$$
$$g = 0.0740 \text{ or } 7.40\%$$

From the formula for the long-run growth rate:

$$g = (1 - \text{Div. payout ratio}) \times \text{ROE}$$
$$g = (1 - \text{Div. payout ratio}) \times (\text{NI/Equity})$$
$$0.0740 = (1 - \text{Div. payout ratio}) \times [\$500 \text{ million}/(0.55 \times 5,000 \text{ million})]$$
$$0.0740 = (1 - \text{Div. payout ratio}) \times 0.181818$$
$$0.407 = (1 - \text{Div. payout ratio})$$
$$\text{Div. payout ratio} = 0.5930 \text{ or } 59.30\%$$

12. a. If the investment requires $2.6 million, that means that it requires $1.43 million (55%) of equity and $1.17 million (45%) of debt. In this scenario, the firm would exhaust its $0.5 million of retained earnings and be forced to raise new stock at a cost of 14%. Since the firm must raise $1.17 million in debt, it will have a 10% cost. (The problem states that the firm can raise up to $1.5 million in debt at a 10% cost.) Therefore, its WACC is calculated as follows:

WACC = 0.45(10%)(1 – 0.4) + 0.55(14%) = 10.4%

11

THE BASICS OF CAPITAL BUDGETING

Learning Objectives

1. Discuss capital budgeting.

2. Calculate and use the major capital budgeting decision criteria, which are NPV, IRR, MIRR, and payback.

3. Explain why NPV is the best criterion and how it overcomes problems inherent in the other methods.

Overview

Capital budgeting is similar in principle to security valuation in that future cash flows are estimated, risks are appraised and reflected in a cost of capital discount rate, and all cash flows are evaluated on a present value basis. Five primary methods can be used to determine which projects should be included in a firm's capital budget: (1) Net Present Value (NPV), (2) Internal Rate of Return (IRR), (3) payback, (4) discounted payback, and (5) Modified IRR (MIRR). Both payback methods have deficiencies, and thus should not be used as the sole criterion for making capital budgeting decisions. The NPV, IRR, and MIRR methods all lead to the same accept/reject decisions on independent projects. However, the methods may conflict when ranking mutually exclusive projects that differ in scale (project size) or timing of cash flows. Under these circumstances, the NPV method should be used to make the final decision.

Outline

I. **Capital budgeting is the process of planning expenditures on assets whose cash flows are expected to extend beyond one year.**

   A. A number of factors combine to make capital budgeting perhaps the most important function financial managers and their staffs must perform.

      1. Since the results of capital budgeting decisions continue for many years, the firm loses some of its flexibility.

      2. A firm's capital budgeting decisions define its strategic direction as outlined in its *strategic business plan*.

a. A firm's strategic business plan is a long-run plan that outlines in broad terms the firm's basic strategy for the next 5 to 10 years.

3. Timing is also important since capital assets must be available when they are needed.

B. The same general concepts that are used in security valuation are also involved in capital budgeting; however, there are two major differences.

1. Whereas a set of stocks and bonds exists in the securities market from which investors select, capital budgeting projects are created by the firm.

2. Most investors in the security markets have no influence on the cash flows produced by their investments, whereas corporations have a major influence on their projects' results.

C. A firm's growth, and even its ability to remain competitive and to survive, depends on a constant flow of ideas relating to new products, to improvements in existing products, and to ways of operating more efficiently.

D. Analyzing capital expenditure proposals has a cost, so firms classify projects into different categories to help differentiate the level of analysis required.

1. Replacement: needed to continue current operations.

2. Replacement: cost reduction.

3. Expansion of existing products or markets.

4. Expansion into new products or markets.

5. Safety and/or environmental projects.

6. Other miscellaneous projects.

7. Mergers.

E. Normally, a more detailed analysis is required for cost-reduction replacements, expansion, and new product decisions than for simple replacement and maintenance decisions.

1. Projects requiring larger investments will be analyzed more carefully than smaller projects.

II. **The net present value (NPV) method, which estimates how much a potential project will contribute to shareholder wealth, is the best selection criterion. The larger the NPV, the more value the project adds; and added value means a higher stock price.**

A. The *Net Present Value (NPV)* method of evaluating investment proposals is a discounted cash flow (DCF) technique that accounts for the time value of all cash flows from a project.

1. To implement the NPV, proceed as follows: (a) Find the present value of each cash flow, including both inflows and outflows, discounted at the project's risk-adjusted cost of capital, (b) sum these discounted cash flows to obtain the project's NPV, and (c) accept the project if the NPV is positive.

2. The NPV is defined as follows:

$$NPV = \sum_{t=0}^{N} \frac{CF_t}{(1+r)^t}$$

Here, CF_t is the expected net cash flow in Period t and r is the project's risk-adjusted cost of capital. Cash outflows are treated as negative cash flows.

3. If the NPV is positive, the project should be accepted; if negative, it should be rejected.

B. If two projects are *mutually exclusive* (that is, only one can be accepted), the one with the higher positive NPV should be chosen. If both projects have negative NPVs, neither should be chosen.

C. *Independent projects* are those whose cash flows are not affected by the acceptance or nonacceptance of other projects. Independent projects with NPV > 0 should be accepted.

D. Finding the NPV with a financial calculator is efficient and easy. Simply enter the different cash flows into the "cash flow register" along with the value of r = I/YR, and then press the NPV key for the solution.

E. Financial analysts generally use spreadsheets when dealing with capital budgeting projects. Once a spreadsheet has been set up, it is easy to change input values to see what would happen if inputs are changed.

   1. Excel's built-in function has the following format: =NPV(rate,CF_1 to CF_N). It's important to note that the negative CF_0 value must be "added" to this result.

III. **When deciding on a potential investment, it is useful to know the investment's most likely rate of return.**

A. The *Internal Rate of Return (IRR)* is defined as the discount rate that equates the present value of a project's expected cash inflows to the present value of its costs.

B. The equation for calculating the IRR is shown below:

$$\sum_{t=0}^{N} \frac{CF_t}{(1+IRR)^t} = 0$$

   1. This equation has one unknown, the IRR, and we can solve for the value of the IRR that will make the equation equal to zero.

   2. The solution value of IRR is defined as the internal rate of return.

   3. The IRR formula is simply the NPV formula solved for the particular discount rate that causes the NPV to equal zero.

C. To find the IRR with a financial calculator, simply enter the different cash flows into the cash flow register, making sure to input the t = 0 cash flow, and then press the IRR key for the solution.

   1. Excel's IRR function can be used to calculate a project's IRR.

D. The IRR is an estimate of the project's rate of return, and it is comparable to the YTM on a bond.

   1. If the internal rate of return exceeds the cost of the funds used to finance the project, then the excess goes to the firm's stockholders and causes the stock price to rise.

   2. If the IRR were less than the cost of capital, then stockholders would have to make up the shortfall, which would cause the stock price to decline.

   3. It is this "breakeven" characteristic that makes the IRR useful.

E. The same basic equation is used for both the NPV and the IRR methods, but with the NPV method the discount rate is given and we find the NPV, whereas with the IRR method the NPV is set equal to zero and the interest rate that produces this equality is calculated.

F. NPV and IRR can produce conflicting conclusions when a choice is being made between mutually exclusive projects; and when conflicts occur, the NPV is generally better.

IV. **Multiple IRRs can result when the IRR criterion is used with a project that has nonnormal cash flows.**

    A. Projects with *nonnormal* cash flows call for a large cash outflow sometime after cash inflows have commenced, meaning that the signs of the cash flows change more than once.

        1. In these cases, the NPV criterion can be easily applied, and this method leads to conceptually correct capital budgeting decisions.

        2. If a return is wanted, the *modified internal rate of return* can be used.

V. **The NPV calculation is based on the assumption that cash inflows can be reinvested at the project's risk-adjusted WACC, whereas the IRR calculation is based on the assumption that cash flows can be reinvested at the IRR.**

    A. For most firms, assuming reinvestment at the WACC is more reasonable for the following reasons.

        1. If a firm has reasonably good access to the capital markets, it can raise all the capital it needs at the going rate.

        2. If a firm has investment opportunities with positive NPVs, it should take them on and finance them at the cost of capital.

        3. If the firm uses internally generated cash flows from past projects rather than external capital, this will save it the firm's cost of capital. Thus, the cost of capital is the *opportunity cost* of the cash flows, and it is the effective return on reinvested funds.

    B. If the true reinvestment rate is less than the IRR, the true rate of return on the investment must be less than the calculated IRR; thus, the IRR is misleading as a measure of a project's profitability.

VI. **Business executives often prefer to work with percentage rates of return, such as IRR, rather than dollar amounts of NPV when analyzing investments. To overcome some of the IRR's limitations a Modified IRR, or MIRR, has been devised.**

    A. The MIRR is defined as the discount rate at which the present value of a project's cost is equal to the present value of its *terminal value (TV)*, where the terminal value is found as the sum of the future values of the cash inflows, compounded at the firm's cost of capital. Thus,

$$\text{PV costs} = \text{PV Terminal value}$$

$$\sum_{t=0}^{N} \frac{\text{COF}_t}{(1+r)^t} = \frac{\sum_{t=0}^{N} \text{CIF}_t (1+r)^{N-t}}{(1+\text{MIRR})^N}$$

$$\text{PV costs} = \frac{\text{TV}}{(1+\text{MIRR})^N}$$

    B. MIRR has two significant advantages over the regular IRR.

        1. The regular IRR assumes that the cash flows from each project are reinvested at the IRR itself, while MIRR assumes that cash flows are reinvested at the cost of capital.

            a. The MIRR is generally a better indicator than IRR of a project's true profitability.

        2. The MIRR eliminates the multiple IRR problem. There can never be more than one MIRR, and it can be compared with the cost of capital when deciding to accept or reject projects.

C. NPV, IRR, and MIRR will lead to the same project selection decision if projects are independent. So, the three criteria are equally good when evaluating independent projects.

    1. If projects are mutually exclusive and differ in size, conflicts can arise. In such cases, the NPV is best because it selects the project that maximizes value.

    2. MIRR is superior to IRR as an indicator of a project's "true" rate of return but NPV is better than IRR and MIRR when choosing among competing projects.

VII. A net present value profile is a graph that shows the relationship between a project's NPV and the firm's cost of capital.

A. The NPV profile crosses the Y-axis at the *undiscounted* NPV, while it crosses the X-axis at the IRR.

B. The *crossover rate* is the cost of capital at which the NPV profiles of two projects cross and, thus, at which the projects' NPVs are equal.

    1. The crossover rate can be found by calculating the IRR of the differences in the projects' cash flows.

C. A steeper NPV profile indicates that increases in the cost of capital lead to larger declines in its NPV.

    1. If a project has most of its cash flows coming in the later years, its NPV will decline sharply if the cost of capital increases; but a project whose cash flows come earlier will not be severely penalized by high capital costs.

D. If an *independent* project is being evaluated, then the NPV and IRR criteria always lead to the same accept/reject decision.

E. As long as the cost of capital is greater than the crossover rate, there is no conflict between the NPV and IRR methods.

F. If two *mutually exclusive* projects have NPV profiles that intersect in the upper right-hand quadrant, then there may be a conflict in rankings between NPV and IRR methods. Two basic conditions can lead to conflicts between NPV and IRR.

    1. *Timing differences* exist such that cash flows from one project come in the early years and most of the cash flows from the other project come in the later years.

    2. *Project size (or scale) differences* exist; that is, the cost of one project is larger than that of the other.

G. Given a conflict, the rate of return at which differential cash flows can be reinvested is a critical issue.

    1. Therefore, when conflicts exist between mutually exclusive projects, use the NPV method.

VIII. The earliest capital budgeting selection criterion was the payback period.

A. The *payback period* is the length of time required for an investment's cash flows to cover its cost. The payback period is calculated as follows:

$$\text{Number of years prior to full recovery} + \frac{\text{Unrecovered cost at start of year}}{\text{Cash flow during full recovery year}}$$

B. The shorter the payback, the better the project.

C. The payback has three main flaws:

1. Dollars received in different years are all given the same weight.

2. Cash flows beyond the payback year are given no consideration whatever, regardless of how large they might be.

3. Unlike the NPV, which tells us how much the project should increase shareholder wealth, and the IRR, which tells us how much a project yields over the cost of capital, the payback merely tells us when we recover the investment. There is no necessary relationship between a given payback and investor wealth maximization, so we do not know what an acceptable payback is.

D. The payback is a "break-even" calculation in the sense that if cash flows come in at the expected rate, the project will break even.

1. Since the regular payback doesn't consider the cost of capital, it doesn't specify the true break-even year.

E. A variant of the regular payback, the *discounted payback period* is defined as the length of time required for an investment's cash flows, discounted at the investment's cost of capital, to cover its cost.

F. Both payback methods do provide information about *liquidity* and *risk*.

1. The shorter the payback, other things held constant, the greater the project's liquidity.

   a. This factor is often important for smaller firms that don't have ready access to the capital markets.

2. Cash flows expected in the distant future are generally riskier than near-term cash flows, so the payback can be used as a risk indicator.

IX. **In making the accept/reject decision, each of the five capital budgeting decision methods provides decision makers with a somewhat different piece of relevant information. Since it is easy to calculate all of them, sophisticated firms generally calculate and consider all in the decision process. For most decisions, the greatest weight should be given to the NPV, but it would be foolish to ignore the information provided by the other criteria.**

A. NPV is the single best criterion because it provides a direct measure of value the project adds to shareholder wealth.

B. IRR measures profitability expressed as a percentage rate of return, which is interesting to decision makers.

1. IRR also contains information regarding a project's "safety margin."

C. The modified IRR has all the virtues of the IRR; however, it incorporates a better reinvestment rate assumption, and it also avoids the multiple rate of return problem.

D. Payback and discounted payback provide indications of a project's liquidity and risk.

1. A long payback means that investment dollars will be locked up for many years, hence the project is relatively illiquid, and also that cash flows must be forecasted far out into the future, hence the project is probably riskier than if it had a shorter payback.

Self-Test

Definitional Questions

1. A firm's _____ budget outlines its planned expenditures on fixed assets.

2. The number of years necessary to return the original investment in a project is known as the _____ period.

3. The shorter the payback period, other things held constant, the greater the project's _____.

4. One important weakness of payback analysis is the fact that cash _____ beyond the payback period are _____.

5. The Net Present Value (NPV) method of evaluating investment proposals is a(n) _____ cash flow technique.

6. A capital investment proposal should be accepted if its NPV is _____.

7. If two projects are mutually _____, the one with the _____ positive NPV should be selected.

8. In the IRR approach, a discount rate is sought that makes the NPV equal to _____.

9. A net present value _____ is a graph that shows the relationship between a project's _____ and the firm's cost of capital.

10. If two mutually exclusive projects are being evaluated and one project has a higher NPV while the other project has a higher IRR, the project with the higher _____ should be preferred.

11. The NPV method implicitly assumes reinvestment at the project's cost of _____, while the IRR method implicitly assumes reinvestment at the _____ rate of _____.

12. The MIRR method assumes reinvestment at the cost of _____, making it a better indicator of a project's profitability than IRR.

13. The internal rate of return (IRR) is the _____ rate that equates the present value of a project's expected cash inflows to the present value of its _____.

14. The MIRR is defined as the discount rate at which the present value of a project's cost is equal to the present value of its _____ value, which is found as the sum of the future values of the cash inflows, compounded at the firm's cost of capital.

15. Taking on a project whose IRR exceeds its cost of capital increases _____ wealth.

16. The NPV profile crosses the Y-axis at the _____ NPV, while it crosses the X-axis at the _____.

17. If a(n) _____ project is being evaluated, then the NPV and IRR criteria always lead to the same accept/reject decisions.

18. Two basic conditions can lead to conflicts between NPV and IRR: _____ and _____ differences.

19. _____ IRRs can result when the IRR criterion is used with a project that has nonnormal cash flows.

20. The _____ rate is the cost of capital at which the NPV profiles of two projects intersect and, thus, at which the projects' NPVs are equal.

21. _____ is superior to the regular IRR as an indicator of a project's "true" rate of return, or "expected long-term rate of return."

22. The discounted _____ period is the length of time required for an investment's cash flows, discounted at the investment's cost of capital, to cover its cost.

23. _____ projects are those whose cash flows are not affected by the acceptance or nonacceptance of other projects.

24. The _____ rate of return is an estimate of the project's rate of return.

25. A steeper NPV profile indicates that increases in the cost of capital lead to _____ declines in its NPV.

Conceptual Questions

1. The NPV of a project with cash flows that accrue relatively slowly is *more sensitive* to changes in the discount rate than is the NPV of a project with cash flows that come in more rapidly.

   a. True
   b. False

2. The NPV method is preferred over the IRR method because the NPV method's reinvestment rate assumption is better.

   a. True
   b. False

3. When you find the yield to maturity on a bond, you are finding the bond's net present value (NPV).

   a. True
   b. False

4. Other things held constant, a decrease in the cost of capital (discount rate) will cause an *increase* in a project's IRR.

   a. True
   b. False

5. The IRR method can be used in place of the NPV method for all independent projects.

   a. True
   b. False

6. The NPV and MIRR methods lead to the same decision for mutually exclusive projects regardless of the projects' relative sizes.

   a. True
   b. False

7. Projects with nonnormal cash flows sometimes have multiple MIRRs.

   a. True
   b. False

8. Projects A and B each have an initial cost of $5,000, followed by a series of positive cash inflows. Project A has total undiscounted cash inflows of $12,000, while B has total undiscounted inflows of $10,000. Further, at a discount rate of 10%, the two projects have identical NPVs. Which project's NPV will be *more sensitive* to changes in the discount rate? (Hint: Projects with steeper NPV profiles are more sensitive to discount rate changes.)

   a. Project A.
   b. Project B.
   c. Both projects are equally sensitive to changes in the discount rate since their NPVs are equal at all costs of capital.
   d. Neither project is sensitive to changes in the discount rate, since both have NPV profiles which are horizontal.
   e. The answer cannot be determined because not enough information is known.

9. Which of the following statements is correct?

   a. The IRR of a project whose cash flows accrue relatively rapidly is more sensitive to changes in the discount rate than is the IRR of a project whose cash flows come in more slowly.
   b. There are many conditions under which a project can have more than one IRR. One such condition is where an otherwise normal project has a negative cash flow at the end of its life.
   c. The phenomenon called "multiple internal rates of return" arises when two or more mutually exclusive projects that have different lives are being compared.
   d. The modified IRR (MIRR) method has wide appeal to professors, but most business executives prefer the NPV method to either the regular or modified IRR.
   e. Each of the above statements is false.

10. Which of the following statements is correct?

   a. If a project has an IRR greater than zero, then taking on the project will increase the value of the company's common stock because the project will make a positive contribution to net income.
   b. If a project has an NPV greater than zero, then taking on the project will increase the value of the firm's stock.
   c. Assume that you plot the NPV profiles of two mutually exclusive projects with normal cash flows and that the cost of capital is greater than the rate at which the profiles cross one another. In this case, the NPV and IRR methods will lead to contradictory rankings of the two projects.
   d. For independent (as opposed to mutually exclusive) normal projects, the NPV and IRR methods will generally lead to conflicting accept/reject decisions.
   e. Statements b, c, and d are true.

11. Which of the following statements is correct?

   a. Underlying the MIRR is the assumption that cash flows can be reinvested at the firm's cost of capital.
   b. Underlying the IRR is the assumption that cash flows can be reinvested at the firm's cost of capital.
   c. Underlying the NPV is the assumption that cash flows can be reinvested at the firm's cost of capital.
   d. The discounted payback method always leads to the same accept/reject decisions as the NPV method.
   e. Statements a and c are correct.

Problems

1. Your firm is considering a fast-food concession at the World's Fair. The cash flow pattern is somewhat unusual because you must build the stands, operate them for 2 years, and then tear the stands down and restore the site to its original condition. You estimate the cash flows to be as follows:

Time	Expected Cash Flows
0	($800,000)
1	700,000
2	700,000
3	(400,000)

What is the approximate IRR of this venture?

a. 5%
b. 15%
c. 25%
d. 35%
e. 45%

Exhibit 11-1

	Expected Cash Flows	
Year	Machine B	Machine O
0	($5,000)	($5,000)
1	2,085	0
2	2,085	0
3	2,085	0
4	2,085	9,677

2. Refer to Exhibit 11-1. What is the payback period for Machine B?

a. 1.0 year
b. 2.0 years
c. 2.4 years
d. 2.6 years
e. 3.0 years

3. Refer to Exhibit 11-1. If the cost of capital for both projects is 14%, which project would you choose?

a. Project B; it has the higher positive NPV.
b. Project O; it has the higher positive NPV.
c. Neither; both have negative NPVs.
d. Either; both have the same NPV.

Exhibit 11-2

	Expected Cash Flows	
Year	Project L	Project S
0	($100)	($100)
1	10	70
2	60	50
3	80	20

Both projects have a cost of capital of 10%.

4. Refer to Exhibit 11-2. What is the payback period for Project S?

   a. 1.6 years
   b. 1.8 years
   c. 2.1 years
   d. 2.5 years
   e. 2.8 years

5. Refer to Exhibit 11-2. What is Project L's NPV?

   a. $50.00
   b. $34.25
   c. $22.64
   d. $18.78
   e. $10.06

6. Refer to Exhibit 11-2. What is Project L's IRR?

   a. 18.1%
   b. 19.7%
   c. 21.4%
   d. 23.6%
   e. 24.2%

7. Refer to Exhibit 11-2. What is Project L's MIRR?

   a. 15.3%
   b. 16.5%
   c. 16.9%
   d. 17.1%
   e. 17.4%

8. Refer to Exhibit 11-2. What is Project S's MIRR?

   a. 15.3%
   b. 16.5%
   c. 16.9%
   d. 17.1%
   e. 17.4%

9. Your company is considering two mutually exclusive projects, X and Y, whose costs and cash flows are shown below:

Year	Project X	Project Y
0	($2,000)	($2,000)
1	200	2,000
2	600	200
3	800	100
4	1,400	100

   The projects are equally risky, and their cost of capital is 10%. You must make a recommendation, and you must base it on the modified IRR. What is the MIRR of the better project?

a. 11.50%
b. 12.00%
c. 11.70%
d. 12.50%
e. 13.10%

10. A company is analyzing two mutually exclusive projects, S and L, whose cash flows are shown below:

Year	Project S	Project L
0	($2,000)	($2,000)
1	1,800	0
2	500	500
3	20	800
4	20	1,600

The company's cost of capital is 9%, and it can get an unlimited amount of capital at that cost. What is the regular IRR (not MIRR) of the better project? (Hint: Note that the better project may or may not be the one with the higher IRR.)

a. 11.45%
b. 11.74%
c. 13.02%
d. 13.49%
e. 12.67%

11. The stock of Barkley Inc. and "the market" provided the following returns over the last 5 years:

Year	Barkley	Market
2007	-5%	-3%
2008	21	10
2009	9	4
2010	23	11
2011	31	15

Barkley finances only with retained earnings, and it uses the CAPM with a historical beta to determine its cost of equity. The risk-free rate is 7%, and the market risk premium is 5%. Barkley is considering a project that has a cost at t = 0 of $2,000 and is expected to provide cash inflows of $1,000 per year for 3 years. What is the project's MIRR?

a. 23.46%
b. 18.25%
c. 22.92%
d. 20.95%
e. 21.82%

12. CDH Worldwide's stock returns versus the market were as follows, and the same relative volatility is expected in the future:

Year	CDH	Market
2008	12%	15%
2009	-6	-3
2010	25	19
2011	18	12

The T-bond rate is 6%; the market risk premium is 7%; CDH finances only with equity from retained earnings; and it uses the CAPM to estimate its cost of equity. Now CDH is considering two alternative trucks. Truck S has a cost of $12,000 and is expected to produce cash flows of $4,500 per year for 4 years. Truck L has a cost of $20,000 and is expected to produce cash flows of $7,500 per year for 4 years. By how much would CDH's value rise if it buys the better truck, and what is the MIRR of the better truck?

a. $ 803.35; 17.05%
b. $1,338.91; 17.05%
c. $1,896.47; 16.06%
d. $1,338.91; 16.06%
e. $ 803.35; 14.41%

13. Assume that your company has a cost of capital of 14% and that it is analyzing the following project:

Project M:
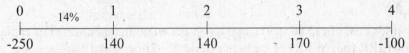

What are the project's IRR and MIRR?

a. 24.26%; 16.28%
b. 23.12%; 17.19%
c. 23.12%; 16.28%
d. 24.26%; 17.19%
e. None of the above.

14. You are evaluating a project that is expected to produce cash flows of $5,000 each year for the next 10 years and $7,000 each year for the following 10 years. The IRR of this 20-year project is 12%. If the firm's WACC is 8%, what is the project's NPV?

a. $10,989.95
b. $12,276.33
c. $14,321.21
d. $15,100.50
e. $16,000.00

15. A project has the following cash flows:

Year	Cash Flows
0	($250)
1	100
2	(X)
3	150
4	275
5	300

Notice this project requires two cash outflows at Years 0 and 2, and produces positive cash inflows in the remaining periods. The project's appropriate WACC is 10% and its modified internal rate of return (MIRR) is 13.50%. What is the value of the project's cash outflow in Year 2?

a. $295.20
b. $243.96
c. $375.00
d. $493.96
e. $288.75

Answers

Definitional Question

1. capital
2. payback
3. liquidity
4. flows; ignored
5. discounted
6. positive
7. exclusive; higher
8. zero
9. profile; NPV
10. NPV
11. capital; internal; return
12. capital
13. discount; costs
14. terminal
15. shareholders'
16. undiscounted; IRR
17. independent
18. scale; timing
19. Multiple
20. crossover
21. MIRR
22. payback
23. Independent
24. internal
25. large

Conceptual Questions

1. a. The more the cash flows are spread over time, the greater is the effect of a change in discount rate. This is because the compounding process has a greater effect as the number of years increases.

2. a. Project cash flows are substitutes for outside capital. Thus, the opportunity cost of these cash flows is the firm's cost of capital, adjusted for risk. The NPV method uses this cost as the reinvestment rate, while the IRR method assumes reinvestment at the IRR.

3. b. The yield to maturity on a bond is the bond's IRR.

4. b. The computation of IRR is independent of the project's cost of capital.

5. a. Both the NPV and IRR methods lead to the same accept/reject decisions for independent projects. Thus, the IRR method can be used as a proxy for the NPV method when choosing independent projects.

6. b. NPV and MIRR may not lead to the same decision when the projects differ in scale (project size) or timing of cash flows.

7. b. Multiple IRRs occur in projects with nonnormal cash flows, but there is only one MIRR for each project.

8. a. If we were to begin graphing the NPV profiles for each of these projects, we would know two of the points for each project. The Y-intercepts for Projects A and B would be $7,000 and $5,000, respectively, and the crossover rate would be 10%. Thus, from this information we can conclude that Project A's NPV profile would have the steeper slope and would be more sensitive to changes in the discount rate.

9. b.   Statement a is false because the IRR is independent of the discount rate. Statement b is true; the situation identified is that of a project with nonnormal cash flows, which has multiple IRRs. Statement c is false; multiple IRRs occur with projects with nonnormal cash flows, not with mutually exclusive projects with different lives. Statement d is false; business executives tend to prefer the IRR because it gives a measure of the project's safety margin.

10. b.   Statement b is true; the others are false. Note that IRR must be greater than the cost of capital; that conflicts arise if the cost of capital is less than the crossover rate; and that for independent normal projects NPV and IRR will lead to the same accept/reject decisions.

11. e.   Statement e is correct, because both statements a and c are true. The IRR assumes reinvestment at the IRR, and since the discounted payback ignores cash flows beyond the payback period, it could lead to rejections of projects with high late cash flows and hence NPV > 0.

Solutions

Problems

1. c.   Calculator solution: Input $CF_0 = -800000$, $CF_{1-2} = 700000$, $CF_3 = -400000$. Output: IRR = 25.48%. Note that this project actually has multiple IRRs, with a second IRR at about -53%.

2. c.   After Year 1, there is $5,000 – $2,085 = $2,915 remaining to pay back. After Year 2, only $2,915 – $2,085 = $830 is remaining. In Year 3, another $2,085 is collected. Assuming that the Year 3 cash flow occurs evenly over time, then payback occurs $830/$2,085 = 0.4 of the way through Year 3. Thus, the payback period is 2.4 years.

3. a.   Calculate NPVs:
    Machine B: $CF_0 = -5000$; $CF_{1-4} = 2085$; I/YR = 14; solve for $NPV_B = \$1,075.09$.
    Machine O: $CF_0 = -5000$; $CF_{1-3} = 0$; $CF_4 = 9677$; I/YR = 14; solve for $NPV_O = \$729.56$.

4. a.   After the first year, there is only $30 remaining to be repaid, and $50 is received in Year 2. Assuming an even cash flow throughout the year, the payback period is 1 + $30/$50 = 1.6 years.

5. d. $NPV_L = -\$100 + \$10/1.10 + \$60/(1.10)^2 + \$80/(1.10)^3 = -\$100 + \$9.09 + \$49.59 + \$60.11 = \$18.79$. Financial calculator solution: Input the cash flows into the cash flow register, I/YR = r = 10, and solve for NPV = $18.78.

6. a.   Input the cash flows into the cash flow register and solve for IRR = 18.1%.

7. b. $\displaystyle\sum_{t=0}^{N} \frac{COF_t}{(1+r)^t} = \frac{\displaystyle\sum_{t=0}^{N} CIF_t(1+r)^{N-t}}{(1+MIRR)^N}$

$PV\ cost = \dfrac{TV}{(1+MIRR_L)^N}$

$\$100 = \dfrac{\$10(1.10)^2 + \$60(1.10)^1 + \$80(1.10)^0}{(1+MIRR_L)^3}$

$\$100 = \dfrac{\$12.10 + \$66.00 + \$80.00}{(1+MIRR_L)^3}$

$\$100 = \dfrac{\$158.10}{(1+MIRR_L)^3}$

$MIRR_L = 16.50\%$

Input N = 3, PV = -100, PMT = 0, FV = 158.10, and solve for I/YR = $MIRR_L$ = 16.50%.

8. c. $\$100 = \dfrac{\$70(1.10)^2 + \$50(1.10)^1 + \$20(1.10)^0}{(1+MIRR_S)^3}$

$\$100 = \dfrac{\$84.70 + \$55.00 + \$20.00}{(1+MIRR_S)^3}$

$\$100 = \dfrac{\$159.70}{(1+MIRR_S)^3}$

$MIRR_S = 16.89\% \approx 16.9\%$

Input N = 3, PV = -100, PMT = 0, FV = 159.70, and solve for I/YR = $MIRR_S$ = 16.89% ≈ 16.9%.

9. e. Project X:

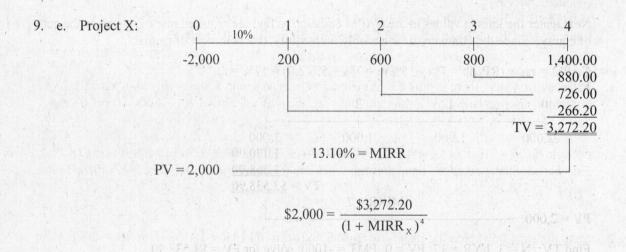

$\$2,000 = \dfrac{\$3,272.20}{(1+MIRR_X)^4}$

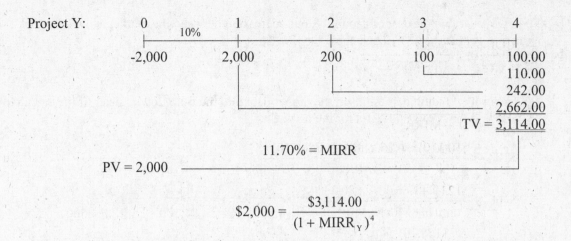

Project Y:

$$\$2,000 = \frac{\$3,114.00}{(1 + MIRR_Y)^4}$$

Project X has the higher MIRR; $MIRR_X = 13.10\%$.

Alternate step: You could calculate NPVs, see that X has the higher NPV, and just calculate $MIRR_X$. $NPV_X = \$234.96$ and $NPV_Y = \$126.90$.

10. b. Put the cash flows into the cash flow register, and then calculate NPV at 9% and IRR:

Project S: $NPV_s = \$101.83$; $IRR_s = 13.49\%$.

Project L: $NPV_L = \$172.07$; $IRR_L = 11.74\%$.

Because $NPV_L > NPV_S$, it is the better project. $IRR_L = 11.74\%$.

11. d. First, calculate the beta coefficient. Barkley's stock has been exactly twice as volatile as the market; thus, beta = 2.0. This can be calculated as $[21 - (-5)]/[10 - (-3)] = 26/13 = 2.0$. (Alternatively, you could use a calculator with statistical functions to determine the beta.)

Next, enter the known values in the CAPM equation to find the required rate of return, or the cost of equity. Since the company finances only with equity, this is its cost of capital:

$$CAPM = r_{RF} + (RP_M)b = 7\% + (5\%)b = 7\% + 5\%(2.0) = 17\% = r_s$$

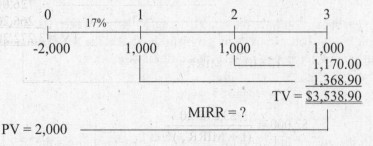

Find TV: N = 3; I/YR = 17; PV = 0; PMT = -1000; solve for FV = $3,538.90.

Find MIRR: N = 3; PV = -2000; PMT = 0; FV = 3538.90; I/YR = MIRR = 20.95%.

227

12. b.   First, we must find the cost of capital. Run a regression between the market and CDH stock returns to get beta = 1.31. Then apply the SML:

$r_{CDH} = 6\% + (7\%)1.31 = 15.17\%$

   (1) Now set up the time lines, insert the proper data into the cash flow register of the calculator, and find the NPVs and IRRs for the trucks.

   Truck S: NPV = $803.35; IRR = 18.45%

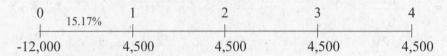

   Truck L: NPV = $1,338.91; IRR = 18.45%

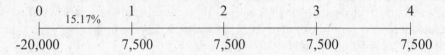

   $NPV_L > NPV_S$, thus Truck L is the better truck.

   (2) To find Truck L's MIRR, compound its cash inflows at 15.17% to find the TV, then find the MIRR = I/YR that causes PV of TV = $20,000:

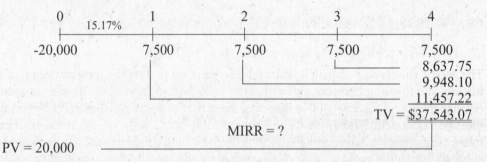

   Find TV: Enter N = 4; I/YR = 15.17; PV = 0; PMT = -7500; and solve for FV = $37,543.07.

   Find MIRR: Enter N = 4; PV = -20000; PMT = 0; FV = 37543.07; and solve for I/YR = MIRR = 17.05%.

   It is interesting to note that both trucks have the same IRR and MIRR; however, the NPV rule should be used so Truck L is the better truck. This problem shows that the NPV method is superior when choosing among competing projects that differ in size.

13. d.   IRR = 24.26%; MIRR = 17.19%.

   To calculate the IRR, enter the given values into the cash flow register and press the IRR key to get IRR = 24.26%.

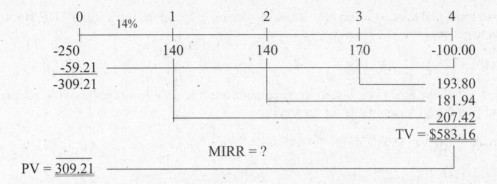

Enter N = 4; PV = -309.21; PMT = 0; FV = 583.16; and solve for MIRR = I/YR = 17.19%.

14. c. Since the IRR is the cost of capital at which the NPV of a project equals zero, the project's inflows can be evaluated at the IRR and the present value of these inflows must equal the initial investment.

Using a financial calculator, enter the following:
$CF_0 = 0$; $CF_1 = 5000$; $N_j = 10$; $CF_1 = 7000$; $N_j = 10$; I/YR = 12; solve for NPV = $40,985.66.

Therefore, the initial investment for this project is $40,985.66. Using a calculator, the project's NPV can now be solved at a WACC of 8%.

$CF_0 = -40985.66$; $CF_1 = 5000$; $N_j = 10$; $CF_1 = 7000$; $N_j = 10$; I/YR = 8; solve for NPV = $14,321.21.

15. a. The MIRR can be solved with a financial calculator by finding the terminal value of the cash inflows and the initial present value of cash outflows, and solving for the discount rate that equates these two values. In this instance, the MIRR is given, but a cash outflow is missing and must be calculated. Therefore, if the terminal value of the cash inflows is found, it can be entered into a financial calculator, along with the number of years the project lasts and the MIRR, to solve for the initial present value of the cash outflows. One of these cash outflows occurs in Year 0 and the remaining value must be the present value of the missing cash outflow in Year 2.

Cash inflows	Compounding Rate	FV in Year 5 @ 10%
$CF_1 = 100$	$\times (1.10)^4$	146.41
$CF_3 = 150$	$\times (1.10)^2$	181.50
$CF_4 = 275$	$\times 1.10$	302.50
$CF_5 = 300$	$\times 1.00$	300.00
		930.41

Using the financial calculator to solve for the present value of cash outflows:
N = 5; I/YR = 13.50; PV = ?; PMT = 0; FV = 930.41

The total present value of cash outflows is $493.96, and since the outflow for Year 0 is $250, the present value of the Year 2 cash outflow is $243.96. Therefore, the missing cash outflow for Year 2 is $243.96 \times (1.10)^2 = 295.20.

12

CASH FLOW ESTIMATION AND RISK ANALYSIS

Learning Objectives

1. Identify "relevant" cash flows that should and should not be included in a capital budgeting analysis.

2. Estimate a project's relevant cash flows and put them into a time line format that can be used to calculate a project's NPV, IRR, and other capital budgeting metrics.

3. Explain how risk is measured and use this measure to adjust the firm's WACC to account for differential project riskiness.

4. Discuss how some projects can be altered after they have been accepted, and how these alterations can change a project's cash flows and thus its realized NPV.

5. Describe the post-audit, which is an important part of the capital budgeting process, and discuss its relevance in capital budgeting decisions.

Overview

One of the most critical steps in capital budgeting analysis is cash flow estimation. The key to correct cash flow estimation is to consider only incremental cash flows. However, the process is complicated by such factors as sunk costs, opportunity costs, externalities, net operating working capital changes, and salvage values. Cash flow estimation for replacement projects is similar to that for expansion projects, except that there are more cash flows to consider when analyzing replacement projects. Adjustments to the analysis must be made for the effects of inflation.

Project risk analysis focuses on three issues: (1) the effect of a project on the firm's beta coefficient (market risk), (2) the project's effect on the probability of bankruptcy (corporate risk), and (3) the risk of the project independent of both the firm's other projects and investors' diversification (stand-alone risk). Market risk directly affects the value of the firm's stock. Corporate risk affects the financial strength of the firm, and this, in turn, influences its ability to use debt, and to maintain smooth operations over time. Stand-alone risk is measured by the variability of a project's expected returns. Techniques for measuring stand-alone risk include sensitivity analysis, scenario analysis, and Monte Carlo simulation.

Real options offer the right but not the obligation to take some future action. Several types of real options are discussed, an example of an abandonment option is illustrated, and the calculation of an option's value

231

is demonstrated. How managers forecast the total capital budget in practice is discussed. The optimal capital budget and capital rationing are defined, and finally, the post-audit, which is used to improve forecasts and operations, is discussed.

Outline

I.   **The most important, and also the most difficult, step in the analysis of a capital project is estimating its cash flows—the investment outlays and the annual net cash inflows after a project goes into operation. Two key issues to recognize are: (1) capital decisions must be based on cash flows, not accounting income, and (2) only incremental cash flows are relevant.**

    A. A firm's free cash flow is defined as:

$$FCF = \left[EBIT(1-T) + \begin{array}{c} \text{Depreciation} \\ \text{and amortization} \end{array} \right] - \left[\begin{array}{c} \text{Capital} \\ \text{expenditures} \end{array} + \Delta NOWC \right]$$

        1. EBIT(1 − T) + Depreciation and amortization represents the project's operating cash flows.

        2. At the end of a project the firm receives the salvage value, after taxes, for fixed assets sold and recovers its NOWC outlay made at t = 0.

    B. In most capital budgeting project analyses, we simply assume that all cash flows occur at the end of the year.

        1. However, for some projects it might be useful to assume that cash flows occur at mid-year, or even quarterly or monthly.

    C. A project's *incremental cash flow* is defined as one that will occur if and only if the firm takes on the project.

    D. A *sunk cost* is a cash outlay that has already been incurred and that cannot be recovered regardless of whether the project is accepted or rejected.

        1. In capital budgeting, we are concerned with future incremental cash flows—we want to know if the new investment will generate enough incremental cash flow to justify the incremental investment.

        2. Including sunk costs in the analysis could lead to an incorrect decision.

        3. Sunk costs are not relevant to the analysis so they are not included.

    E. *Opportunity costs* are cash flows that could be generated from an asset the firm already owns, provided the asset is not used for the project in question.

        1. They represent the return on the best alternative use of an asset, or the highest return that will not be earned if funds are invested in a particular project.

        2. They should be included in the analysis.

    F. *Externalities* are the effects a project has on other parts of the firm or the environment, and they must be included in the analysis. There are negative within-firm externalities, positive within-firm externalities, and environmental externalities.

        1. A type of negative within-firm externality is *cannibalization*.

    a.   This is the situation when a new project reduces cash flows that the firm would otherwise have had.

   2.   A positive within-firm externality results when a new project is complementary to an old one, in which case cash flows in the old operation will be increased when the new one is introduced.

   3.   The most common type of negative externality is a project's impact on the environment.

       a.   Government rules and regulations constrain what companies can do, but firms have some flexibility in dealing with the environment.

II.   **A firm's capital budgeting process involves analyzing new projects or expansion projects. All of an expansion project's cash flows are incremental.**

   A. The project's cash flows are separated into three categories:

      1.   Initial investments that include capital expenditures and changes in net operating working capital (ΔNOWC).

      2.   Operating cash flows the company receives over the life of the project.

      3.   Terminal cash flows realized when the project is completed include the after-tax salvage value of the equipment and the recovery of NOWC.

   B. The use of accelerated depreciation rather than straight-line depreciation increases a project's NPV.

   C. Spreadsheet models are used in analyzing capital budgeting projects in the real world.

   D. The discount rate used to evaluate the project's cash flows is WACC.

III.   **A firm's replacement projects are analyzed differently from its expansion projects.**

   A. When replacement projects are analyzed, cash flow differentials between the new and old projects are calculated, and these differentials are the incremental cash flows used in the analysis.

IV.   **Three separate and distinct types of risk can be identified in capital budgeting: (1) stand-alone risk, (2) corporate (within-firm) risk, and (3) market (beta) risk.**

   A. *Stand-alone risk* is the risk an asset would have if it were a firm's only asset and if investors owned only one stock.

      1.   It is measured by the variability of the asset's expected returns.

   B. *Corporate*, or *within-firm*, *risk* is the risk considering the firm's diversification but not stockholder diversification.

      1.   It is the project's risk to the corporation, given consideration to the fact that it represents only one project in the firm's portfolio of assets, hence that some of its risk will be eliminated by diversification within the firm.

      2.   It is measured by a project's effect on uncertainty about the firm's future earnings.

   C. *Market*, or *beta*, *risk* is the riskiness of the project as seen by well-diversified stockholders who recognize that the project is only one of the firm's assets and that the firm's stock is but one part of their portfolios.

      1.   Market risk is measured by the project's effect on the firm's beta coefficient.

2. Taking on a project with a high degree of either stand-alone or corporate risk will not necessarily affect the firm's beta.

3. Market risk is theoretically the most relevant because it is the one reflected in stock prices. It is also the most difficult to estimate.

D. If the project has highly uncertain returns, and if these returns are highly correlated with returns on the firm's other assets and with most other firms in the economy, the project will have a high degree of all types of risk.

E. Most decision makers do a quantitative analysis of stand-alone risk and then consider the other two risk measures in a qualitative manner.

    1. Projects are generally classified into several categories.

    2. *Risk-adjusted costs of capital* are developed for each category.

    3. A firm might establish three risk classes, then assign the corporate WACC to average-risk projects, use a somewhat higher cost rate for higher-risk projects, and a somewhat lower rate for lower-risk projects.

V. **A project's stand-alone risk reflects the uncertainty about its cash flows. Three techniques for assessing a project's stand-alone risk are: (1) sensitivity analysis, (2) scenario analysis, and (3) Monte Carlo simulation.**

A. *Sensitivity analysis* is a technique that indicates how much a project's NPV will change in response to a given change in an input variable, other things held constant.

    1. The analysis begins with expected values for unit sales, sales price, fixed costs, and variable costs to give an expected, or base-case, NPV. A series of "what if" questions may then be asked to find the change in NPV, given a change in one of the input variables.

        a. The *base-case NPV* is the NPV when sales and other input variables are set equal to their most likely (or base-case) values.

    2. Each variable is changed by several percentage points above and below the expected value, holding all other variables constant.

        a. The resulting set of NPVs is plotted against the variable that was changed to show how sensitive NPV is to changes in each variable.

    3. The steeper the slope, the more sensitive the NPV is to a change in the variable.

    4. When comparing two projects, the one with the steeper sensitivity lines would be riskier, because relatively small changes in an input variable would produce large changes in the project's expected NPV.

        a. Sensitivity analysis provides useful insights into a project's risk.

B. *Scenario analysis* provides a more complete analysis, because in addition to the sensitivity of NPV to changes in key variables, it considers the range of likely values of these variables (the probability distributions of the inputs). It allows for changes in more than one variable at a time.

    1. It is a risk analysis technique in which bad and good sets of financial circumstances are compared with a most likely, or base-case situation.

    2. Worst-case and best-case scenarios are estimated and the input values from these scenarios are used to find the worst-case NPV and the best-case NPV.

    a. A *base-case scenario* is an analysis in which all of the input variables are set at their most likely values.

    b. A *worst-case scenario* is an analysis in which all of the input variables are set at their worst reasonably forecasted values.

    c. A *best-case scenario* is an analysis in which all of the input variables are set at their best reasonably forecasted values.

3. Probabilities can be assigned to the best-, worst-, and base-case NPVs to obtain the expected NPV.

4. The project's coefficient of variation can be compared to the coefficient of variation of the firm's "average" project to determine the project's relative stand-alone risk.

5. Scenario analysis provides useful information about a project's stand-alone risk.

    a. It is limited in that it only considers a few discrete outcomes, even though there are an infinite number of possibilities.

C. *Monte Carlo simulation,* which ties together sensitivities and input variable probability distributions, requires a computer along with an efficient financial planning software package.

1. It is a risk analysis technique in which probable future events are simulated on a computer, generating estimated rates of return and risk indexes.

2. The computer repeatedly selects a random value for each uncertain variable based on its specified probability distribution, along with values for fixed factors.

    a. The end result is a continuous NPV probability distribution.

3. The mean and standard deviation of the set of NPVs is determined.

    a. The mean, or average value, is used as a measure of the project's expected profitability.

    b. The standard deviation (or coefficient of variation) is used as a measure of the project's risk.

4. A simulation is more comprehensive than scenario analysis because it considers an infinite number of possible outcomes.

VI. Experienced managers generally have a "feel" for how a project's returns will relate to returns on the firm's other assets. Generally, positive correlation is expected; and if the correlation is high, stand-alone risk will be a good proxy for within-firm risk.

A. Projects occasionally involve an entirely new product line. In such cases, the firm may be able to obtain betas for *pure-play* companies in the new area.

1. Use the average beta of comparable companies in the single related business to calculate a WACC.

B. Here are our conclusions regarding risk analysis:

1. It is very difficult, if not impossible to quantitatively measure projects' within-firm and beta risks.

2. Most projects' returns are positively correlated with returns on the firm's other assets and with returns on the stock market.

   a. This being the case, stand-alone risk is correlated with within-firm and market risk.

   3. Experienced managers make many judgmental assessments, including those related to risk; and they work them into the capital budgeting process.

   4. Good managers understand and use the theory of finance, but they apply it with judgment.

VII. **DCF techniques, originally developed to value passive investments, do not always lead to proper capital budgeting decisions, which involve real assets and are not passive investments.**

   A. *Real options* are opportunities involving real assets that permit you to take some future action that can increase cash flows.

   1. Real options are valuable, and as this value is not captured by conventional NPV analysis, it must be considered separately.

   2. There are several types of real options.

      a. An *abandonment option* is a situation where the project can be shut down if its cash flows turn out to be lower than expected.

      b. A *timing option* is a situation where a project can be delayed until more information about demand and/or costs can be obtained.

      c. An *expansion option* is a situation where the project can be expanded if demand turns out to be stronger than expected.

      d. An *output flexibility option* is a situation where the output can be changed if market conditions change.

      e. An *input flexibility option* is a situation where the inputs used in the production process can be changed if input prices and/or availability change.

   3. Real options can both raise expected profitability and lower project risk.

   4. A *decision tree* is a diagram that lays out different branches that are the result of different decisions made or the result of different economic situations.

   5. The *option value* is the difference between the expected NPVs with and without the relevant option.

      a. It is the value that is not accounted for in a traditional NPV analysis.

      b. A positive option value expands the firm's opportunities.

VIII. **For planning purposes, managers must also forecast the total capital budget, because the amount of capital raised affects the WACC and thus influences projects' NPVs.**

   A. In practice, the steps in this process include:

   1. The treasurer obtains an estimate of the firm's overall composite WACC.

   2. The corporate WACC is scaled up or down for each of the firm's divisions to reflect the division's capital structure and risk characteristics.

   3. Financial managers within each of the firm's divisions estimate relevant cash flows and risks of each of their potential projects.

      a. The estimated cash flows should explicitly consider any embedded real options, which include opportunities to repeat the projects at a later date.

4. Each project's NPV is then determined, using its risk-adjusted cost of capital.

    a. The optimal capital budget consists of all independent projects with positive NPVs plus those mutually exclusive projects with the highest positive NPVs.

B. The *optimal capital budget* is the annual investment in long-term assets that maximizes the firm's value.

    1. For large, mature firms with good track records it is reasonable to assume that they can obtain financing for all of their profitable projects.

C. *Capital rationing* is the situation where a firm can raise only a specified, limited amount of capital regardless of how many good projects it has.

    1. Smaller firms, new firms, and firms with dubious track records may have difficulties raising capital, even for projects that the firm concludes would have highly positive NPVs.

        a. In these circumstances, the size of the firm's capital budget may be constrained.

        b. In this situation, procedures have been developed for allocating capital so as to maximize the aggregate NPV subject to the constraint that the capital rationing ceiling is not exceeded.

IX. **An important aspect of the capital budgeting process is the post-audit, which involves comparing actual results with those predicted by the project's sponsors and explaining why any differences occurred.**

A. The results of the post-audit help to improve forecasts and to increase efficiency of the firm's operations.

B. The *post-audit* is not a simple process—a number of factors can cause complications.

    1. Each element of the cash flow forecast is subject to uncertainty, so a percentage of all projects undertaken by any reasonably aggressive firm will necessarily go awry.

    2. Projects sometime fail to meet expectations for reasons beyond the control of the operating executives and for reasons that no one could realistically be expected to anticipate.

    3. It is often difficult to separate the operating results of one investment from those of a larger system.

    4. It is often hard to hand out blame or praise, because the executives who were responsible for launching a given long-term investment may have moved on by the time the results are known.

C. Observations of both businesses and governmental units suggest that the best-run and most successful organizations are the ones that put the greatest emphasis on post-audits.

    1. Post-audits are an important element in a good capital budgeting system.

X. **Appendix 12A covers tax depreciation including lists of major classes and recovery allowance percentages.**

XI. **There are numerous Web Appendices for this chapter. Web Appendix 12B discusses refunding operations. Web Appendix 12C discusses using the CAPM to estimate the risk-adjusted cost of capital. Web Appendix 12D covers techniques for measuring beta risk. Web Appendix 12E discusses comparing mutually exclusive projects with unequal lives. Finally, Web Appendix 12F covers real options in more detail, specifically investment timing, growth, and flexibility options.**

237

Self-Test

Definitional Questions

1. An increase in net operating working capital would show up as a cash _____ at Time 0 and then again as a cash _____ at the _____ of the project's life.

2. A(n) _____ cost is a cash outlay that has already been incurred and that cannot be recovered regardless of whether the project is accepted or rejected.

3. A(n) _____ cash flow is defined as one that will occur if and only if the firm takes on the project.

4. One of the most critical steps in capital budgeting analysis is cash flow _____.

5. _____ costs are cash flows that could be generated from assets the firm already owns provided they are not used for the project in question, and they must be included in capital budgeting analysis.

6. _____ are the effects a project has on other parts of the firm or the environment, and their effects need to be considered in the capital budgeting analysis.

7. When a new project reduces cash flows that the firm would otherwise have had, this is called _____.

8. Three separate and distinct types of risk have been identified in capital budgeting decisions: _____-_____ risk, _____ or within-firm risk, and _____ risk.

9. A commonly used method of risk analysis based on constructing optimistic, pessimistic, and expected value estimates for key variables is called _____ analysis.

10. In project analysis, changing one key variable at a time and determining the effect on its NPV is known as _____ analysis.

11. One purpose of sensitivity analysis is to determine which one of the _____ variables has the greatest influence on the project's NPV.

12. Monte Carlo _____ ties together _____ and input variable probability distributions, and requires a computer along with an efficient financial planning software package.

13. A(n) _____ project is defined as one where old and less efficient equipment is replaced by newer and more efficient equipment.

14. The _____-_____ NPV is the NPV when sales and other input variables are set equal to their most likely values.

15. A(n) _____-_____ scenario is an analysis in which all of the input variables are set at their worst reasonably forecasted values.

16. A(n) _____-_____ scenario is an analysis in which all of the input variables are set at their most likely values.

17. A(n) _____-_____ scenario is an analysis in which all of the input variables are set at their best reasonably forecasted values.

18. The _____ the slope, the more sensitive NPV is to changes in each of the input variables.

19. Capital decisions must be based on cash _____, not accounting income.

20. _____-_____ risk is the risk an asset would have if it were a firm's only asset and if investors owned only one stock.

21. _____, or _____-_____, risk is the project's risk to the corporation, given consideration to the fact that it represents only one project in the firm's portfolio of assets, hence that some of its risk will be eliminated by diversification within the firm.

22. _____, or _____, risk is the riskiness of the project as seen by well-diversified stockholders who recognize that the project is only one of the firm's assets and that the firm's stock is but one small part of their total portfolios.

23. Market risk is measured by the project's effect on the firm's _____ coefficient.

24. Stand-alone risk is measured by the variability of the asset's _____ returns.

25. _____-_____ costs of capital are developed for projects that have been classified into subjective risk categories.

26. _____ options are opportunities involving real assets that permit you to take some future action that can increase cash flows.

27. A(n) _____ option is a situation where the project can be shut down if its cash flows turn out to be lower than expected.

28. A(n) _____ option is a situation where a project can be delayed until more information about demand and/or costs can be obtained.

29. A(n) _____ option is a situation where the project can be expanded if demand turns out to be stronger than expected.

30. A(n) _____ flexibility option is a situation where the inputs used in the production process can be changed if input prices and/or availability change.

31. Real options can both raise expected _____ and lower project _____.

32. The _____ _____ is the difference between the expected NPVs with and without the relevant option.

33. The _____ capital _____ is the annual investment in long-term assets that maximizes the firm's value.

34. Capital _____ is the situation where a firm can raise only a specified, limited amount of capital regardless of how many good projects it has.

35. The _____-_____ involves comparing actual results of the capital budgeting decision with those predicted and explaining why any differences occurred.

Conceptual Questions

1. In general, the value of land currently owned by a firm is irrelevant to a capital budgeting decision because the cost of that property is a sunk cost.

    a. True
    b. False

2. McDonald's is planning to open a new store across from the student union. Annual revenues are expected to be $5 million. However, opening the new location will cause annual revenues to drop by $3 million at McDonald's existing stadium location. The relevant sales revenues for the capital budgeting analysis are $2 million per year.

    a. True
    b. False

3. In capital budgeting decisions, corporate risk will be of least interest to:

    a. Employees.
    b. Stockholders with few shares.
    c. Institutional investors.
    d. Creditors.
    e. The local community.

4. Two corporations are formed. They are identical in all respects except for their methods of depreciation. Firm A uses MACRS depreciation, while Firm B uses the straight-line method. The applicable MACRS depreciation rates are 20%, 32%, 19%, 12%, 11%, and 6%. Both plan to depreciate their assets for tax purposes over a 5-year life (6 calendar years), which is equal to the useful life, and both pay a 35% tax rate. (Note: The half-year convention will apply, so the firm using the straight-line method will take 10% depreciation in Year 1 and 10% in Year 6.) Which of the following statements is *false*?

    a. Firm A will generate higher cash flows from operations in the first year than Firm B.
    b. Firm A will pay more Federal corporate income taxes in the first year than Firm B.
    c. If there is no change in tax rates over the 6-year period, and if we disregard the time value of money, the total amount of funds generated from operations by these projects for each corporation will be the same over the 6 years.
    d. Firm B will pay the same amount of federal corporate income taxes over the 6-year period as Firm A.
    e. Firm A could, if it chose to, use straight-line depreciation for stockholder reporting even if it used MACRS for tax purposes.

Problems

1. Franklin Corporation is considering an expansion project. The necessary equipment could be purchased for $15 million and shipping and installation costs are another $500,000. The project will also require an initial $2 million investment in net operating working capital. If the company's tax rate is 40%, what is the project's initial investment outlay (in millions)?

   a. $15.0
   b. $15.5
   c. $16.5
   d. $17.0
   e. $17.5

2. Hobart Industries is trying to estimate its first-year operating cash flow (at $t = 1$) for a proposed project. The financial staff has collected the following information:

Projected sales	$3,000,000
Operating costs	1,200,000
Depreciation	450,000
Interest expense	330,000

   The company faces a 40% tax rate. What is the project's operating cash flow for the first year ($t = 1$)?

   a. $1,260,000
   b. $ 810,000
   c. $1,080,000
   d. $1,500,000
   e. $1,800,000

3. The capital budgeting director of National Products Inc. is evaluating a new 3-year project that would decrease operating costs by $30,000 per year without affecting revenues. The project's cost is $50,000. The project will be depreciated using the MACRS method over its 3-year class life. The applicable MACRS depreciation rates are 33%, 45%, 15%, and 7%. It will have a *zero salvage value* after 3 years. The marginal tax rate of National Products is 35%, and the project's cost of capital is 12%. What is the project's NPV?

   a. $ 7,068
   b. $ 8,324
   c. $10,214
   d. $11,010
   e. $12,387

4. Your firm has a marginal tax rate of 40% and a cost of capital of 14%. You are performing a capital budgeting analysis on a new project that will cost $500,000. The project is expected to have a useful life of 10 years, although its MACRS class life is only 5 years. The applicable MACRS depreciation rates are 20%, 32%, 19%, 12%, 11%, and 6%. The project is expected to increase the firm's net income by $61,257 per year and to have a salvage value of $35,000 at the end of 10 years. What is the project's NPV?

   a. $ 95,356
   b. $108,359
   c. $135,256
   d. $162,185
   e. $177,902

5. The Board of Directors of National Brewing Inc. is considering the acquisition of a new still. The still is priced at $600,000 but would require $60,000 in transportation costs and $40,000 for installation. The still has a useful life of 10 years but will be depreciated over its 5-year MACRS life. The applicable MACRS depreciation rates are 20%, 32%, 19%, 12%, 11%, and 6%. It is expected to have a salvage value of $10,000 at the end of 10 years. The still would increase revenues by $120,000 per year and increase annual operating costs by $20,000 per year. Additionally, the still would require a $30,000 increase in net operating working capital. The firm's marginal tax rate is 40%, and the project's cost of capital is 10%. What is the NPV of the still?

   a. $ 18,430
   b. -$ 12,352
   c. -$ 65,204
   d. -$130,961
   e. -$203,450

6. Consolidated Inc. uses a weighted average cost of capital of 12% to evaluate average-risk projects and adds/subtracts two percentage points to evaluate projects of greater/lesser risk. Currently, two mutually exclusive projects are under consideration. Both have a cost of $200,000 and last four years. Project A, which is riskier than average, will produce annual after-tax cash flows of $71,000. Project B, which has less-than-average risk, will produce after-tax cash flows of $146,000 in Years 3 and 4 only. What should Consolidated do?

   a. Accept Project B with an NPV of $9,412.
   b. Accept both projects since both NPVs are greater than zero.
   c. Accept Project A with an NPV of $6,874.
   d. Accept neither project since both NPVs are less than zero.
   e. Accept Project A with an NPV of $15,652.

7. Conglomerated Industries' overall cost of capital (WACC) is 10%. Division HR is riskier than average, Division AR has average risk, and Division LR is less risky than average. Conglomerated adjusts for risk by adding or subtracting 2 percentage points. What is the risk-adjusted project cost of capital for a low-risk project in the HR division?

   a. 6%
   b. 8%
   c. 10%
   d. 12%
   e. 14%

Exhibit 12-1

The Carlisle Corporation is considering a proposed project for its capital budget. The company estimates that the project's NPV is $5 million. This estimate assumes that the economy and market conditions will be average over the next few years. The company's CFO, however, forecasts that there is only a 40% chance that the economy will be average. Recognizing this uncertainty, she has also performed the following scenario analysis:

Economic Scenario	Probability of Outcome	NPV
Recession	0.05	($28 million)
Below Average	0.25	(10 million)
Average	0.40	5 million
Above Average	0.25	8 million
Boom	0.05	15 million

8. Refer to Exhibit 12-1. What is the project's expected NPV (in millions)?

    a. $0.25
    b. $0.85
    c. $1.20
    d. $1.50
    e. $2.00

9. Refer to Exhibit 12-1. What is the project's standard deviation?

    a. $10.04
    b. $12.78
    c. $15.65
    d. $21.37
    e. $29.43

10. Refer to Exhibit 12-1. What is the project's coefficient of variation?

    a. 5.02
    b. 2.75
    c. 6.39
    d. 1.25
    e. 11.81

11. You are evaluating a capital budgeting project for your company that is expected to last for six years. The project begins with the purchase of a $1,200,000 investment in equipment. You are unsure what method of depreciation to use in your analysis, straight-line depreciation or the 5-year MACRS accelerated method. Straight-line depreciation results in the cost of the equipment depreciated evenly over its life. The 5-year MACRS depreciation rates are 20%, 32%, 19%, 12%, 11%, and 6%. Your company's WACC is 10.5% and it has a tax rate of 35%. For purposes of this question, we are ignoring the half-year convention for the straight-line depreciation method. Under the straight-line and MACRS depreciation methods, what would the depreciation expense be for the *second* year?

    a. $200,000; $132,000
    b. $200,000; $228,000
    c. $200,000; $384,000
    d. $200,000; $144,000
    e. $200,000; $240,000

243

12. You are evaluating a capital budgeting project for your company that is expected to last for six years. The project begins with the purchase of a $1,200,000 investment in equipment. You are unsure what method of depreciation to use in your analysis, straight-line depreciation or the 5-year MACRS accelerated method. Straight-line depreciation results in the cost of the equipment depreciated evenly over its life. The 5-year MACRS depreciation rates are 20%, 32%, 19%, 12%, 11%, and 6%. Your company's WACC is 10.5% and it has a tax rate of 35%. For purposes of this question, we are ignoring the half-year convention for the straight-line depreciation method. What is the NPV of the project given by the better depreciation method, i.e., the method that gives the higher NPV?

   a. $16,333.33
   b. $17,500.00
   c. $18,182.88
   d. $20,473.06
   e. $21,250.75

Exhibit 12-2

The Braxton Corp. has the following investment opportunities in the coming planning period:

Project	Net Investment	IRR
F	$300,000	18%
G	100,000	15
H	200,000	13
H*	200,000	12
I	100,000	10

Projects H and H* are mutually exclusive. The firm's WACC is 11%.

13. Refer to Exhibit 12-2. Assume that all projects have average risk. What is the dollar total of the firm's optimal capital budget?

   a. $300,000
   b. $400,000
   c. $500,000
   d. $600,000
   e. $700,000

14. Refer to Exhibit 12-2. Now assume that Project F is riskier than average and that Project I is less risky than average. The remaining projects have average risk. Braxton's policy is to adjust the WACC up or down by 2 percentage points to account for risk. What is the effect of differential risk on Braxton's optimal capital budget?

   a. The capital budget is not changed.
   b. Project F is now unacceptable and the capital budget is now $300,000.
   c. The capital budget is now $700,000 and Project I is acceptable.
   d. Project F is now unacceptable and the capital budget is now $400,000.
   e. Projects H and H* are now both acceptable and the capital budget is now $900,000.

15. The Alaska Oil Company is deciding whether to drill for oil on a tract of land that the company owns. The company estimates that the project would cost $5.6 million today. The firm estimates that once drilled, the oil will generate positive new cash flows of $2.8 million a year at the end of each of the next four years. While the company is fairly confident about its cash flow forecast, it recognizes that if it waits two years, they would have more information about the local geology as well as the price of oil. Alaska Oil estimates that if it waits two years, the project would cost $6.3 million. Moreover, if it waits two years, there is a 90% chance that the net cash flows would be $2.94 million a year for four years, and there is a 10% chance that the cash flows will be $1.54 million a year for four years. Assume that all cash flows are discounted at a 10% WACC. If the company chooses to drill today, what is the project's net present value (in millions)?

    a. $2.3134
    b. $2.9875
    c. $3.2756
    d. $3.9181
    e. $4.6795

16. The Alaska Oil Company is deciding whether to drill for oil on a tract of land that the company owns. The company estimates that the project would cost $5.6 million today. The firm estimates that once drilled, the oil will generate positive new cash flows of $2.8 million a year at the end of each of the next four years. While the company is fairly confident about its cash flow forecast, it recognizes that if it waits two years, they would have more information about the local geology as well as the price of oil. Alaska Oil estimates that if it waits two years, the project would cost $6.3 million. Moreover, if it waits two years, there is a 90% chance that the net cash flows would be $2.94 million a year for four years, and there is a 10% chance that the cash flows will be $1.54 million a year for four years. Assume that all cash flows are discounted at a 10% WACC. What is the project's net present value (in millions) in today's dollars, if the firm waits two years before deciding whether to drill?

    a. $2.2458
    b. $2.7175
    c. $3.0194
    d. $3.2756
    e. $3.9181

17. The Alaska Oil Company is deciding whether to drill for oil on a tract of land that the company owns. The company estimates that the project would cost $5.6 million today. The firm estimates that once drilled, the oil will generate positive new cash flows of $2.8 million a year at the end of each of the next four years. While the company is fairly confident about its cash flow forecast, it recognizes that if it waits two years, they would have more information about the local geology as well as the price of oil. Alaska Oil estimates that if it waits two years, the project would cost $6.3 million. Moreover, if it waits two years, there is a 90% chance that the net cash flows would be $2.94 million a year for four years, and there is a 10% chance that the cash flows will be $1.54 million a year for four years. Assume that all cash flows are discounted at a 10% WACC. Should Alaska Oil wait two years before taking on this project?

    a. Yes, since the NPV of waiting two years is greater than the NPV of doing the project today.
    b. No, since the NPV of waiting two years is less than the NPV of doing the project today.
    c. It makes no difference. The NPVs of the two decisions are identical.
    d. Don't have enough information to make the decision.

Answers

Definitional Questions

1. outflow; inflow; end
2. sunk
3. incremental
4. estimation
5. Opportunity
6. Externalities
7. cannibalization
8. stand-alone; corporate; market
9. scenario
10. sensitivity
11. input
12. simulation; sensitivities
13. replacement
14. base-case
15. worst-case
16. base-case
17. best-case
18. steeper
19. flows
20. Stand-alone
21. Corporate; within-firm
22. Market; beta
23. beta
24. expected
25. Risk-adjusted
26. Real
27. abandonment
28. timing
29. expansion
30. input
31. profitability; risk
32. option value
33. optimal; budget
34. rationing
35. post-audit

Conceptual Questions

1. b. The net market value of land currently owned is an opportunity cost of the project. If the project is not undertaken, the land could be sold to realize its current market value less any taxes and expenses. Thus, project acceptance means forgoing this cash inflow.

2. a. Incremental revenues, which are relevant in a capital budgeting decision, must consider the effects on other parts of the firm.

3. c. Institutional investors are well diversified and, therefore, more concerned with beta risk.

4. b. Statement a is true; MACRS is an accelerated depreciation method, so Firm A will have a higher depreciation expense than Firm B. We are also given that both firms are identical except for depreciation methods used. In Year 1, Firm A's depreciation expense is twice as great as Firm B's; however, Firm A's lower net income is more than compensated for by the addition of depreciation (which is twice as high as Firm B's). Thus, in Year 1, Firm A's net cash flow is greater than Firm B's. Statement b is false; because Firm A's depreciation expense is larger, its earnings before taxes will be lower, and thus it will pay less income taxes than Firm B. Statements c, d, and e are all true.

Solutions

Problems

1. e. Initial investment outlay:

Purchase price	$15,000,000
Shipping/Installation	500,000
Net operating working capital	2,000,000
Total investment outlay	$17,500,000

2. a. Operating cash flow:

Sales	$3,000,000
Operating costs	1,200,000
Depreciation	450,000
EBIT	$1,350,000
Taxes (40%)	540,000
EBIT(1 − T)	$ 810,000
Add: Depreciation	450,000
EBIT(1 − T) + DEP = OCF	$1,260,000

3. d. The first step is to determine the project's cash flows for Years 1 through 3. (Note that a reduction in operating costs increases revenues.)

	1	2	3
Revenues	$30,000	$30,000	$30,000
Depreciation[a]	16,500	22,500	7,500
EBIT	$13,500	$ 7,500	$22,500
Taxes (35%)	4,725	2,625	7,875
EBIT(1 − T)	$ 8,775	$ 4,875	$14,625
+ Depreciation	16,500	22,500	7,500
EBIT(1 − T) + DEP	$25,275	$27,375	$22,125
SV tax savings[b]			1,225
Project CFs	$25,275	$27,375	$23,350

[a]Depreciation schedule: Cost basis = $50,000.

Year	Allowance Percentage	Depreciation	Ending Book Value
1	0.33	$16,500	$33,500
2	0.45	22,500	11,000
3	0.15	7,500	3,500
4	0.07	3,500	0
		$50,000	

[b]At the end of Year 3, the project will not be fully depreciated. Its book value is $3,500; however, its salvage value is zero. Thus, National can reduce its taxable income by $3,500, producing a 0.35($3,500) = $1,225 tax savings.

The project's cash flows are then placed on a time line as follows and discounted at the project's cost of capital:

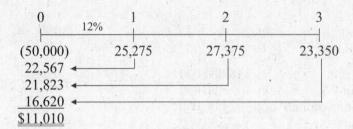

```
        0           1          2          3
           12%
     (50,000)    25,275     27,375     23,350
      22,567  ←
      21,823  ←
      16,620  ←
      $11,010
```

Alternatively, input the cash flows into the cash flow register, input I/YR = 12, and then solve for NPV = $11,010.

4. e. In this case, the *net income* of the project is $61,257. Net cash flow = Net income + Depreciation = $61,257 + Depreciation. The depreciation allowed in each year is calculated as follows:

$Dep_1 = \$500,000(0.20) = \$100,000$
$Dep_2 = \$500,000(0.32) = \$160,000$
$Dep_3 = \$500,000(0.19) = \$95,000$
$Dep_4 = \$500,000(0.12) = \$60,000$
$Dep_5 = \$500,000(0.11) = \$55,000$
$Dep_6 = \$500,000(0.06) = \$30,000$
$Dep_{7-10} = \$0$

In the final year (Year 10), the firm receives $35,000 from the sale of the machine. However, the book value of the machine is $0. Thus, the firm would have to pay 0.4($35,000) = $14,000 in taxes; and the net salvage value is $35,000 − $14,000 = $21,000. The time line is as follows:

0	1	2	3	4	5	6	7	8	9	10
14%										
(500,000)	61,257	61,257	61,257	61,257	61,257	61,257	61,257	61,257	61,257	61,257
(_____)	100,000	160,000	95,000	60,000	55,000	30,000				21,000
(500,000)	161,257	221,257	156,257	121,257	116,257	91,257	61,257	61,257	61,257	82,257

The project's NPV can be found by discounting each of the cash flows at the firm's 14% cost of capital. The project's NPV, found by using a financial calculator, is $177,902.

5. d. The first step to this problem is to determine the project's cash flows for Years 1 through 10.

	1	2	3	4	5	6	7 – 9	10
Revenues	120,000	120,000	120,000	120,000	120,000	120,000	120,000	120,000
Operating costs	20,000	20,000	20,000	20,000	20,000	20,000	20,000	20,000
Depreciation[a]	140,000	224,000	133,000	84,000	77,000	42,000		
EBIT	(40,000)	(124,000)	(33,000)	16,000	23,000	58,000	100,000	100,000
Taxes (40%)	(16,000)	(49,600)	(13,200)	6,400	9,200	23,200	40,000	40,000
EBIT(1 – T)	(24,000)	(74,400)	(19,800)	9,600	13,800	34,800	60,000	60,000
+ Depreciation	140,000	224,000	133,000	84,000	77,000	42,000		
EBIT(1 – T) + DEP	116,000	149,600	113,200	93,600	90,800	76,800	60,000	60,000
SV (AT)[b]								6,000
Recovery of NOWC								30,000
Project CFs	116,000	149,600	113,200	93,600	90,800	76,800	60,000	96,000

[a]Depreciation schedule: Cost basis = Price + Transportation + Installation
= $600,000 + $60,000 + $40,000 = $700,000

Year	Percentage	Allowance Depreciation	Ending Book Value
1	0.20	$140,000	$560,000
2	0.32	224,000	336,000
3	0.19	133,000	203,000
4	0.12	84,000	119,000
5	0.11	77,000	42,000
6	0.06	42,000	0
		$700,000	

[b]At the end of Year 10 the still has a salvage value of $10,000; however, it has been fully depreciated so the firm must pay taxes of 0.4($10,000) = $4,000. Therefore, the still's after-tax salvage value is $10,000 – $4,000 = $6,000. The still's cash flows are then placed on a time line as follows and discounted at the project's cost of capital:

```
 0        1        2        3        4        5        6        7        8        9       10
   10%
(700,000) 116,000 149,600 113,200  93,600  90,800  76,800  60,000  60,000  60,000  96,000
( 30,000)*
(730,000)
```

*An increase in net operating working capital is required in Year 0, and this must be added back to the cash flow at the end of the project's life. This amount is included in the Year 10 cash flow shown.

With a financial calculator enter the cash flows into the cash flow register and enter I/YR = 10 and then solve for NPV = -$130,961.

6. a. Project A:

```
 0        1        2        3        4
   14%
(200,000)  71,000   71,000   71,000   71,000
 206,874 ◄
$  6,874 = NPVA
```

Alternatively, input the cash flows in the cash flow register, enter I/YR = 14, and then solve for $NPV_A = \$6,873.57$.

Project B:

```
 0        1           2           3           4
   10%
(200,000)  0           0        146,000     146,000
 109,692 ◄
  99,720 ◄
$  9,412 = NPVB
```

Alternatively, input the cash flows in the cash flow register, enter I/YR = 10, and then solve for $NPV_B = \$9,411.93$.

Note that both discount rates are adjusted for risk. Since the projects are mutually exclusive, the project with the higher NPV is chosen.

7. c. $r_{HR} = 10\% + 2\% = 12\%$; $r_{Project} = 12\% - 2\% = 10\%$

8. b. $E(NPV) = 0.05(-\$28) + 0.25(-\$10) + 0.40(\$5) + 0.25(\$8) + 0.05(\$15)$
          $= -\$1.40 + -\$2.50 + \$2.00 + \$2.00 + \$0.75$
          $= \$0.85$ million

9. a. $\sigma = [0.05(-\$28 - \$0.85)^2 + 0.25(-\$10 - \$0.85)^2 + 0.40(\$5 - \$0.85)^2 + 0.25(\$8 - \$0.85)^2$
          $+ 0.05(\$15 - \$0.85)^2]^{1/2}$
          $= [\$41.62 + \$29.43 + \$6.89 + \$12.78 + \$10.01]^{1/2}$
          $= [\$100.73]^{1/2}$
          $= \$10.04$

10. e. $CV = \dfrac{\$10.04}{\$0.85} = 11.81$

11. c.   The applicable depreciation values are as follows for the two scenarios:

Year	Scenario 1 (Straight-Line)	Scenario 2 (MACRS)
1	$200,000	$240,000
2	200,000	384,000
3	200,000	228,000
4	200,000	144,000
5	200,000	132,000
6	200,000	72,000

12. d.   To find the difference in net present values under these two methods, we must determine the difference in incremental cash flows each method provides. The depreciation expenses cannot simply be subtracted from each other, as there are tax ramifications due to depreciation expense. The full depreciation expense is subtracted from revenues to get operating income, and then taxes due are computed. Then, depreciation is added to after-tax operating income to get the project's operating cash flow. Therefore, if the tax rate is 35%, only 65% of the depreciation expense is actually subtracted out during the after-tax operating income calculation and the full depreciation expense is added back to get operating income. So, there is a tax benefit associated with the depreciation expense that amounts to 35% of the depreciation expense. Therefore, the differences between depreciation expenses under each scenario should be computed and multiplied by 0.35 to determine the benefit provided by the depreciation expense.

Year	Depr. Exp. Difference (2 – 1)	Depr. Exp. Diff. × 0.35
1	$ 40,000	$14,000
2	184,000	64,400
3	28,000	9,800
4	-56,000	-19,600
5	-68,000	-23,800
6	-128,000	-44,800

Now to find the difference in NPV to be generated under these scenarios, just enter the cash flows that represent the benefit from depreciation expense and solve for net present value based upon a WACC of 10.5%.

$CF_0 = 0$; $CF_1 = 14000$; $CF_2 = 64400$; $CF_3 = 9800$; $CF_4 = -19600$; $CF_5 = -23800$; $CF_6 = -44800$; $I/YR = 10.5$; solve for NPV = $20,473.06.

So, all else equal the use of the accelerated depreciation method will result in a higher NPV by $20,473.06 than would the use of the straight-line depreciation method.

13. d.   Since all projects have average risk, they are all evaluated at a project cost of capital of 11%. Clearly, Projects F and G are acceptable since their IRRs exceed 11%. (Since they are independent projects, it is permissible to use the IRR method as a proxy for the NPV method.) The decision between Projects H and H* must be made according to the NPV rule. Since we do not know the project cash flows, we cannot calculate their NPVs. However, one of the two would be chosen since both will have positive NPVs. Thus, the optimal capital budget consists of Projects F and G, and either Project H or H*, and totals $600,000.

14. c.   Since Project F is riskier than average, its cost of capital must be adjusted upward to 11% + 2% = 13%. However, its IRR is 18% so Project F remains acceptable. On the other hand, Project I's cost of capital is adjusted downward to 9%, and hence it becomes acceptable. Thus, the optimal capital budget increases to $700,000. Since Projects H and H* are mutually exclusive, only one of those projects can be selected.

15. c.

0	1	2	3	4
10%				
-5.6	2.8	2.8	2.8	2.8

NPV = $3.2756 million

16. a.

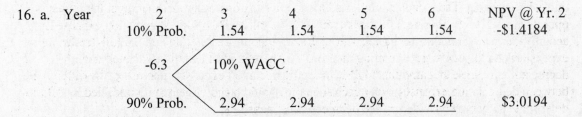

Year	2	3	4	5	6	NPV @ Yr. 2
10% Prob.		1.54	1.54	1.54	1.54	-$1.4184
	-6.3	10% WACC				
90% Prob.		2.94	2.94	2.94	2.94	$3.0194

If the cash flows are only $1.54 million, the NPV of the project is negative and, thus, would not be undertaken. The value of the option of waiting two years is evaluated as 0.10($0) + 0.90($3.0194) = $2.7175. However, we need to discount this back two years at 10% to evaluate it in today's dollars: $NPV_0 = \$2.7175/(1.10)^2 = \$2.2458$ million.

17. b.   No. Since the NPV of waiting two years is less than going ahead and proceeding with the project today, it makes sense to drill today.

13

CAPITAL STRUCTURE AND LEVERAGE

Learning Objectives

1. Explain why there may be differences in a firm's capital structure when measured on a book value basis, a market value basis, or a target basis.

2. Distinguish between business risk and financial risk, and explain the effects that debt financing has on the firm's expected return and risk.

3. Discuss the analytical framework used when determining the optimal capital structure.

4. Discuss capital structure theory, and use it to explain why firms in different industries tend to have different capital structures.

Overview

Capital structure theory suggests that some optimal capital structure exists that simultaneously maximizes a firm's stock price and minimizes its cost of capital. The use of debt tends to increase earnings per share, which will lead to a higher stock price; but, at the same time, the use of debt also increases the risk borne by stockholders, which lowers the stock price. The optimal capital structure strikes a balance between these risk and return effects. While it is difficult to determine the optimal capital structure with precision, it is possible to identify the factors that influence it. A firm's target capital structure is generally set equal to the estimated optimal capital structure. The target may change over time as conditions vary, but, at any given moment, a well-managed firm's management has a specific structure in mind; and financing decisions are made so as to be consistent with this target capital structure.

Outline

I. **Capital refers to investor-supplied funds—debt, preferred stock, common stock, and retained earnings. A firm's capital structure is defined as the percentage of each type of investor-supplied capital that is used to finance the firm's assets, and the optimal capital structure maximizes the stock's intrinsic value. The capital structure that maximizes the stock's intrinsic value also minimizes the firm's WACC.**

    A. Most financial theorists agree that market values should be used to measure capital structure.

253

    1. However, financial analysts report data on a book value basis and bond rating agencies give book values as much weight as market values.

    2. Stock prices are volatile, so market value weights will also be volatile. For this reason, some analysts argue for using book values to measure capital structure.

  B. In a perfect world, a firm would identify its optimal capital structure based on market values, raise capital so as to maintain that structure, and use the optimal percentages to calculate its WACC.

    1. However, most firms focus on a *target capital structure* range.

  C. Firms' actual capital structures change over time, and for two quite different reasons.

    1. Deliberate actions.

    2. Market actions.

  D. At any given moment, most firms have a specific target range in mind.

    1. If the actual debt ratio has surpassed the target, a firm can sell a large stock issue and use the proceeds to retire debt.

    2. If the stock price has increased and pushed the debt ratio below the target, it can issue bonds and use the proceeds to repurchase stock.

    3. A firm can also gradually move toward its target through its annual financings to support its capital budget.

II.   In this chapter we look at two new dimensions of risk: business risk and financial risk.

  A. Business risk is the single most important determinant of capital structure. It represents the amount of risk that is inherent in the firm's operations even if it uses no debt financing.

    1. A commonly used measure of business risk is the standard deviation of the firm's return on invested capital (ROIC).

      a. Since ROIC doesn't vary with changes in capital structure, the standard deviation of ROIC measures the underlying risk of the firm before considering the effects of debt financing.

    2. Business risk varies from one industry to another and also among firms in a given industry.

      a. It can also change over time.

    3. Business risk depends on a number of factors, the more important of which are: (1) competition, (2) demand variability, (3) sales price variability, (4) input cost variability, (5) product obsolescence, (6) foreign risk exposure, (7) regulatory risk and legal exposure, and (8) operating leverage (the extent to which costs are fixed).

      a. Each of these factors is determined partly by the firm's industry characteristics and partly by managerial decisions.

  B. *Operating leverage* is the extent to which a firm uses fixed costs in its operations.

    1. Higher fixed costs are generally associated with more highly automated, *capital intensive* firms and industries.

    2. A high degree of operating leverage, other factors held constant, implies that a relatively small change in sales will result in a large change in ROIC.

3. The higher a firm's degree of operating leverage, the higher its operating break-even point tends to be.

    a. The *operating break-even point* is defined as the output quantity at which EBIT = 0.

    b. The break-even point is calculated as fixed costs divided by the difference in sales price and variable cost per unit: $Q_{BE} = F/(P - V)$.

4. In general, holding other factors constant, the higher the degree of operating leverage, the greater the firm's business risk.

5. To a large extent, operating leverage is determined by technology.

    a. Although industry factors do exert a major influence, all firms have some control over their operating leverage.

    b. So, by its capital budgeting decisions, a firm can influence its operating leverage and hence its business risk.

    c. Once a corporation's operating leverage has been established, this factor exerts a major influence on its capital structure decision.

C. Financial leverage refers to the firm's use of fixed-income securities such as debt and preferred stock in the firm's capital structure, and financial risk is an increase in stockholders' risk, over and above the firm's basic business risk, resulting from the use of financial leverage.

1. The use of debt concentrates the firm's business risk on the stockholders.

2. Typically, using debt increases the expected rate of return for an investment. However, debt also increases risk to the common stockholders.

3. The degree to which a firm employs financial leverage will affect its expected earnings per share (EPS) and the riskiness of these earnings—both would affect the firm's stock price.

    a. Using leverage has both positive and negative effects.

    b. Financial leverage will cause EPS to rise; however, the degree of risk associated with the firm will also increase as leverage increases.

    c. Firms need to balance the positive and negative effects of leverage.

III.   **The optimal capital structure is the one that maximizes the price of the firm's stock, and this generally calls for a debt/capital ratio that is lower than the one that maximizes expected EPS.**

A. Stock prices are positively related to expected earnings but negatively related to higher risk.

B. At first, EPS will rise as the use of debt increases.

1. Interest charges rise, but the number of outstanding shares will decrease as equity is replaced by debt.

2. At some point EPS will peak.

3. Beyond this point interest rates will rise so fast that EPS is depressed in spite of the fact that the number of shares outstanding is decreasing.

C. Risk, as measured by the coefficient of variation of EPS, rises continuously as the use of debt increases.

D. Managers should set as the target capital structure the capital component mix that maximizes the firm's stock price.

    1. The capital structure that maximizes the stock price is also the one that minimizes the WACC.

E. An increase in the debt/capital ratio raises the costs of both debt and equity.

    1. Bondholders recognize that if a firm has a higher debt/capital ratio, this increases the risk of financial distress, which leads to higher interest rates.

    2. Sophisticated financial managers use their forecasted ratios to predict how bankers and other lenders will judge their firms' risks and thus their costs of debt.

F. An increase in the debt/capital ratio increases the risk faced by shareholders, which raises the the cost of equity, r_s. It is harder to quantify leverage's effects on the cost of equity than on debt, but a theoretical formula can help measure the effect.

    1. It has been demonstrated, both theoretically and empirically, that beta increases with financial leverage.

G. The *Hamada equation* specifies the effect of financial leverage on beta:

$$b_L = b_U[1 + (1 - T)(D/E)]$$

    1. The Hamada equation shows how increases in the debt/equity ratio increase beta.

    2. b_L is the firm's actual, current beta, which presumably is based on the existence of some financial leverage.

    3. D/E is the measure of financial leverage used in the Hamada equation.

    4. b_U is the firm's unlevered beta coefficient, the beta the firm would have if it has no debt.

        a. When the firm has no debt, beta would depend entirely upon business risk and thus be a measure of the firm's "basic business risk."

H. Beta is the only variable under management's control in the CAPM cost of equity equation.

    1. Both the risk-free rate and the market risk premium are determined by market forces that are beyond the firm's control.

    2. Beta is determined by the firm's operating decisions, which affect its basic business risk, and by its capital structure decisions, as reflected in its debt/capital (or debt/equity) ratio.

I. Once b_U is determined, the Hamada equation can be used to estimate how changes in the debt/equity ratio would affect the levered beta and the cost of equity. A firm's cost of equity consists of the following components:

$$r_s = r_{RF} + \text{Premium for business risk} + \text{Premium for financial risk}$$

    1. The premium for financial risk rises at an increasing rate as the firm's debt ratio increases.

J. Although the component cost of equity is generally higher than that of debt, using only lower-cost debt would not maximize value because of the feedback effects of debt on the costs of debt and equity.

K. The expected stock price will at first increase with financial leverage, will then reach a peak, and finally will decline as financial leverage becomes excessive due to the importance of potential bankruptcy costs.

IV. **Modern capital structure theory began in 1958, when Professors Franco Modigliani and Merton Miller (MM) published what has been called the most influential finance article ever written.**

    A. MM proved, under a very restrictive set of assumptions, that a firm's value is unaffected by its capital structure.

        1. MM's results suggest that it doesn't matter how a firm finances its operations, hence capital structure is irrelevant.

        2. Their theory produces what is often referred to as the "irrelevance result."

    B. By indicating the conditions under which capital structure is irrelevant, MM provided us with some clues about what is required to make capital structure relevant and, therefore, to affect a firm's value. Consequently, MM's work was only the beginning of capital structure research.

        1. Subsequent research has focused on relaxing the MM assumptions in order to develop a more robust and realistic theory of capital structure.

    C. MM published a follow-up paper in 1963 in which they relaxed the assumption that there are no corporate taxes.

        1. MM demonstrated that if all of their other assumptions hold, the asymmetry of the tax deductibility of interest versus the non-deductibility of dividend payments leads to an optimal capital structure that calls for 100% debt financing.

    D. Merton Miller then analyzed the effects of personal taxes. While an increase in the corporate tax rate makes debt look better to corporations, an increase in the personal tax rate encourages additional equity financing.

        1. All income from bonds is generally interest, which is taxed as personal income at rates going up to 35%.

        2. Income from stocks generally comes partly from dividends and partly from capital gains.

            a. Long-term capital gains are generally taxed at a maximum rate of 15%.

            b. Capital gains tax is deferred until the stock is sold and the gain realized.

            c. If stock is held until the owner dies, no capital gains tax whatever must be paid.

        3. On balance, returns on common stocks are taxed at lower effective rates than returns on debt.

    E. The deductibility of interest favors the use of debt financing, but the more favorable tax treatment of income from stocks lowers the required rates of return on stocks and thus favors the use of equity.

        1. It is difficult to say what the net effect of these two factors is. Most observers believe that interest deductibility has a stronger effect, hence that our tax system still favors the corporate use of debt.

            a. However, that effect is certainly reduced by the lower taxes on stock income.

            b. John Graham has estimated the overall tax benefits of debt financing represents about 7% of the average firm's value.

            c. His study indicates that if a leverage-free firm decided to use an average amount of debt, its value would rise by 7%.

F. Bankruptcy-related problems are more likely to arise when a firm includes more debt in its capital structure. The threat of bankruptcy, not just bankruptcy per se, brings about problems. Therefore, bankruptcy costs discourage firms from pushing their use of debt to excessive levels.

   1. Bankruptcy-related costs have two components: the probability of their occurrence and the costs that will be incurred if financial distress arises.

   2. Firms whose earnings are more volatile, all else equal, face a greater chance of bankruptcy and, therefore, should use less debt than more stable firms.

   3. Firms with high operating leverage, and thus greater business risk, should limit their use of financial leverage.

   4. Firms whose assets are illiquid and thus would have to be sold at "fire sale" prices should limit their use of debt financing.

G. The *trade-off theory of leverage* recognizes that firms trade off the *benefits* of debt financing (favorable corporate tax treatment) against the *costs* of debt financing (higher interest rates and bankruptcy costs).

   1. In effect, the government pays part of the cost of debt; debt provides *tax shelter benefits*.

   2. Many large, successful firms use far less debt than the trade-off theory suggests. This led to the development of signaling theory.

H. *Signaling theory* recognizes the fact that investors and managers do *not* have the same information regarding a firm's prospects, as was assumed by the trade-off theory. This is called *asymmetric information*, and it has an important effect on the optimal capital structure.

   1. *Symmetric information* is the situation in which investors and managers have identical information about firms' prospects.

   2. Because of asymmetric information one would expect a firm with very favorable prospects to try to avoid selling stock and to attempt to raise any required new capital by other means, including using debt beyond the normal target capital structure level.

      a. A firm with unfavorable prospects would want to finance with stock, which would mean bringing in new investors to share the losses.

   3. The announcement of a stock offering by a mature firm that seems to have financing alternatives is taken as a *signal* that the firm's prospects as seen by its management are not bright.

      a. This, in turn, suggests that when a firm announces a new stock offering, more often than not, the price of its stock will decline.

      b. Empirical studies have shown that this situation does indeed exist.

   4. The implication of the signaling theory for capital structure decisions is that firms should, in normal times, maintain a *reserve borrowing capacity* that can be used in the event that some especially good investment opportunity comes along.

      a. This means that firms should, in normal times, use more equity and less debt than is suggested by the tax benefit/bankruptcy cost trade-off model.

I. Conflicts of interest are particularly likely when the firm's managers have too much cash at their disposal. Managers with limited *free cash flow* are less able to make wasteful expenditures. Firms can reduce excess cash flow in a variety of ways:

    1. Funnel cash back to shareholders through higher dividends or stock repurchases.

    2. Shift the capital structure toward more debt in the hope that higher debt service requirements will force managers to become more disciplined.

    3. A leveraged buyout (LBO) is one way to reduce excess cash flow.

        a. In an LBO, debt is used to finance the purchase of a high percentage of the company's shares.

        b. High debt payments after the LBO force managers to conserve cash by eliminating unnecessary expenditures.

J. Increasing debt and reducing free cash flow has its downside: It increases the risk of bankruptcy, which can be costly.

    1. Adding debt to a firm's capital structure is like putting a dagger into the steering wheel of a car.

    2. The dagger motivates you to drive more carefully, but you may get stabbed if someone runs into you, even if you're being careful.

    3. Higher debt forces managers to be more careful with shareholders' money, but even well-run firms could face bankruptcy (get stabbed) if some event beyond their control occurs.

    4. The capital structure decision comes down to deciding how big a dagger stockholders should use to keep managers in line.

K. In practice, capital structure decisions must be made using a combination of judgment and numerical analysis.

    1. An understanding of the theoretical issues about capital structure can help managers make better judgments about capital structure issues.

L. Another factor that may influence capital structure is the idea that managers have a preferred *pecking order* when it comes to raising capital and that this pecking order affects capital structure decisions.

    1. Pecking order is the sequence in which firms prefer to raise capital; first spontaneous credit, then retained earnings, then other debt, and finally new common stock.

    2. This "pecking order" makes sense because no flotation costs are incurred to raise capital as spontaneous credit or retained earnings, and costs are relatively low when issuing new debt.

        a. Flotation costs for new stock issues are quite high, and the existence of asymmetric information/signaling effects makes it even more undesirable to finance with new common stock.

M. *Windows of opportunity* are those occasions when a company's managers adjust its firm's capital structure to take advantage of certain market situations.

V. **Firms generally consider the following factors when making capital structure decisions. The goal is to maintain financial flexibility, which, from an operational viewpoint, means maintaining adequate reserve borrowing capacity. Determining the adequate reserve is judgmental, but it clearly depends on the firm's forecasted need for funds, predicted capital market conditions, management's confidence in its forecasts, and the consequences of a capital shortage.**

A. *Sales stability*. If sales are stable, a firm can safely take on increased debt and incur higher fixed charges than a company with unstable sales.

B. *Asset structure*. Firms whose assets can readily be pledged as collateral for loans will tend to operate with a higher degree of financial leverage.

C. *Operating leverage*. Less operating leverage generally permits a firm to employ more debt.

D. *Growth rate*. Firms that are growing rapidly generally need large amounts of external capital. The flotation costs associated with debt are generally less than those for common stock, so rapidly growing firms tend to use more debt. At the same time, however, rapidly growing firms often face greater uncertainty, which tends to reduce their willingness to use debt.

E. *Profitability*. A high degree of profitability would indicate an ability to carry a high level of debt. However, many profitable firms are able to meet most of their financing needs with retained earnings, and do so.

F. *Taxes*. Interest charges are tax deductible, while dividend payments are not. This factor favors the use of debt over equity for firms in high tax brackets.

G. *Control*. Management control issues such as voting, job security, and fear of takeover, all influence a firm's capital structure.

H. *Management attitudes*. Managements vary in their attitudes toward risk. More conservative managers will use stock rather than debt financing, while less conservative managers will use more debt.

I. *Lender and rating agency attitudes*. This factor will penalize firms that go beyond the industry average in the use of financial leverage.

J. *Market conditions*. At any point in time, securities markets may favor either debt or equity. Conditions in the stock and bond markets undergo long- and short-run changes that can have an important bearing on a firm's optimal capital structure.

K. *Firm's internal conditions*. Expected future earnings patterns and internal factors will influence management's choices of debt versus equity.

L. *Financial flexibility*. Most treasurers have as a goal to always be in a position to raise the capital needed to support operations, even under adverse conditions. Therefore, they want to always maintain adequate reserve borrowing capacity.

VI. **There are wide variations in the use of financial leverage both among industries and among individual firms within each industry.**

A. The times-interest-earned ratio gives an indication of how vulnerable the company is to financial distress.

1. TIE ratios depend on three factors: (a) the percentage of debt, (b) the interest rate on debt, and (c) the company's profitability.

2. Generally, low-leveraged industries have high coverage ratios, while those industries that finance heavily with debt have low coverage ratios.

3. Wide variations also exist among firms within given industries.

a. Factors unique to individual firms, including managerial attitudes, play an important role in setting target capital structures.

VII. **Web Appendix 13A discusses the degree of leverage concepts. The degree of leverage concept is useful primarily for the insights it provides regarding the joint effects of operating and financial leverage on EPS.**

    A. *Degree of operating leverage* is defined as the percentage change in operating income that results from a given percentage change in sales.

    B. *Degree of financial leverage* is defined as the percentage change in earnings per share that results from a given percentage change in earnings before interest and taxes.

    C. The *degree of total leverage* shows how a given change in sales will affect earnings per share.

Self-Test

Definitional Questions

1. The _____ capital structure is the one that maximizes the firm's _____ price.

2. A firm's _____ capital structure is generally set equal to the estimated optimal structure.

3. _____ risk is the amount of risk that is inherent in the firm's operations even if it uses no debt financing.

4. Some of the factors that influence a firm's business risk include: (1) _____ variability, (2) sales price variability, and (3) _____ leverage.

5. A commonly used measure of business risk is the _____ deviation of the firm's return on invested capital (ROIC).

6. _____ risk represents the increase in stockholders' risk as a result of using debt.

7. Expected EPS generally _____ as the debt/capital ratio increases.

8. As financial leverage increases, the stock price will first begin to rise, but it will then decline as financial leverage becomes excessive because potential _____ costs become increasingly important.

9. _____ leverage refers to the use of debt financing.

10. Debt has a(n) _____ advantage over equity in that _____ is a deductible expense while _____ are not.

11. Management may prefer additional _____ as opposed to common stock in order to help maintain _____ of the company.

12. _____ flexibility is the ability to raise capital on reasonable terms under adverse conditions.

13. The _____ break-even _____ is defined as the output quantity at which EBIT = 0.

14. The _____-_____ theory of leverage recognizes that firms balance the benefits of debt financing against the costs of debt financing.

15. _____ theory recognizes the fact that investors and managers do not have the same information regarding a firm's prospects.

16. The fact that investors and managers do not have the same information regarding a firm's prospects is called _____ information.

17. The implication of the signaling theory for capital structure decisions is that firms should, in normal times, maintain a(n) _____ borrowing capacity that can be used in the event that some especially good investment opportunity comes along.

18. The _____ a firm's tax rate, the more advantageous debt is to the firm.

19. The _____-_____-_____ ratio gives an indication of how vulnerable the company is to financial distress.

20. TIE ratios depend on three factors: (1) the _____ of debt, (2) the _____ rate on debt, and (3) the company's _____.

21. _____ leverage is the extent to which a firm uses fixed costs in its operations.

22. The higher the degree of operating leverage, the _____ the firm's business risk.

23. The higher a firm's degree of operating leverage, the higher its operating _____-_____ point tends to be.

24. The optimal capital structure is the one that maximizes the price of the firm's stock, and this generally calls for a debt ratio that is _____ than the one that maximizes expected EPS.

25. _____, as measured by the coefficient of EPS, rises continuously as the use of debt increases.

26. The capital structure that maximizes the stock price is also the one that _____ the WACC.

27. The _____ equation specifies the effect of financial leverage on beta.

28. Beta is determined by the firm's _____ decisions, which affect its basic business risk, and by its capital _____ decisions, as reflected in its debt/capital (or debt/equity) ratio.

29. MM's results suggest that it doesn't matter how a firm finances its operations, hence capital structure is _____.

30. _____ information is the situation in which investors and managers have identical information about firms' prospects.

31. The tax deductibility of interest _____ the effective cost of debt.

32. The greater the probability that capital will be needed, and the worse the consequences of not being able to obtain it, the _____ the balance sheet should be.

33. Higher fixed costs are generally associated with more highly automated, capital _____ firms and industries.

34. Bondholders recognize that if a firm has a higher debt ratio, this increases the risk of financial distress, and more risk leads to higher _____ rates.

35. To a large extent, operating leverage is determined by _____.

Conceptual Questions

1. Firm A has a higher degree of business risk than Firm B. Firm A can offset this by increasing its operating leverage.

    a. True
    b. False

2. Two firms operate in different industries, but they have the same expected EPS and the same standard deviation of expected EPS. Thus, the two firms must have the same financial risk.

    a. True
    b. False

3. Two firms could have identical financial and operating leverage yet have different degrees of business risk.

    a. True
    b. False

4. As a general rule, the capital structure that maximizes stock price also

    a. Maximizes the weighted average cost of capital.
    b. Maximizes EPS.
    c. Maximizes bankruptcy costs.
    d. Minimizes the weighted average cost of capital.
    e. Minimizes the required rate of return on equity.

5. A decrease in the debt ratio will normally have no effect on

    a. Financial risk.
    b. Total risk.
    c. Business risk.
    d. Systematic risk.
    e. Firm-unique risk.

6. Which of the following statements is correct?

    a. If a firm is exposed to a high degree of business risk as a result of its high operating leverage, then it probably should offset this risk by using a larger-than-average amount of financial leverage. This follows because debt has a lower after-tax cost than equity.
    b. Financial risk can be reduced by replacing common equity with preferred stock.
    c. The Hamada equation specifies the effect of financial leverage on beta. It shows how increases in the debt/equity ratio lowers beta.
    d. In the text it was stated that the capital structure that minimizes the WACC also maximizes the firm's stock price and its total value, but generally not its expected EPS. One reason given for why debt is beneficial is that it shelters operating income from taxes, while it was stated that a disadvantage of excessive debt has to do with costs associated with bankruptcy and financial distress generally.
    e. A firm's unlevered beta depends entirely upon its financial risk, and thus is a measure of the firm's "basic financial risk."

263

Problems

1. The Fisher Company will produce 50,000 10-gallon aquariums next year. Variable costs will equal 40% of dollar sales, while fixed costs total $100,000. At what price must each aquarium be sold for the firm's EBIT to be $90,000?

   a. $5.00
   b. $5.33
   c. $5.50
   d. $6.00
   e. $6.33

2. Hairston Industries has $25 million in assets (assets also equal capital), which is financed with $5 million of debt and $20 million in equity. If Hairston's beta is currently 1.75 and its tax rate is 40%, what is its unlevered beta, b_U?

   a. 0.7564
   b. 1.0000
   c. 1.2525
   d. 1.5217
   e. 2.0125

3. The Hampton Hardware Company is trying to estimate its optimal capital structure. Hampton's current capital structure consists of 20% debt and 80% equity; however, management believes the firm should use more debt. The risk-free rate, r_{RF}, is 7%, the market risk premium is 5%, and the firm's tax rate is 35%. Currently, Hampton's cost of equity is 16%, which is determined on the basis of the CAPM. What would be Hampton's estimated cost of equity if it were to change its capital structure from its present capital structure to 40% debt and 60% equity?

   a. 14.93%
   b. 15.45%
   c. 18.10%
   d. 19.25%
   e. 20.33%

4. Brown Products is a new firm just starting operations. The firm will produce backpacks that will sell for $22.00 each. Fixed costs are $500,000 per year, and variable costs are $2.00 per unit of production. The company expects to sell 50,000 backpacks per year, and its effective federal-plus-state tax rate is 40%. Brown needs $2 million to build facilities, obtain working capital, and start operations. If Brown borrows part of the money, the interest charges will depend on the amount borrowed as follows:

Amount Borrowed	Percentage of Debt in Capital Structure	Interest Rate on Total Amount Borrowed
$ 200,000	10%	9.00%
400,000	20	9.50
600,000	30	10.00
800,000	40	15.00
1,000,000	50	19.00
1,200,000	60	26.00

Assume that stock can be sold at a price of $20 per share on the initial offering, regardless of how much debt the company uses. Then after the company begins operating, its price will be determined as a multiple of its earnings per share. The multiple (or the P/E ratio) will depend upon the capital structure as follows:

Debt/Capital	P/E	Debt/Capital	P/E
0.0%	12.5×	40.0%	8.0×
10.0	12.0	50.0	6.0
20.0	11.5	60.0	5.0
30.0	10.0		

What is Brown's optimal capital structure, which maximizes stock price, as measured by the debt/capital ratio? The firm will use only debt and common equity in its capital structure.

a. 10%
b. 20%
c. 30%
d. 40%
e. 50%

5. Tapley Dental Supplies Inc. is in a stable, no-growth situation. Its $1,000,000 of debt consists of perpetuities that have a 10% coupon and sell at par. Tapley's EBIT is $500,000, its cost of equity is 15%, it has 100,000 shares outstanding, all earnings are paid out as dividends, and its federal-plus-state tax rate is 40%. Tapley could borrow an additional $500,000 at an interest rate of 13% without having to retire the original debt, and it would use the proceeds to repurchase stock *at the current price*, not at the new equilibrium price. The increased risk from the additional leverage will raise the cost of equity to 17%. If Tapley does recapitalize, what will be the new stock price?

a. $17.20
b. $16.00
c. $16.50
d. $17.00
e. $16.75

6. Backroads Sporting Goods is trying to determine its optimal capital structure, which now consists of only debt and common equity. The firm does not currently use preferred stock in its capital structure, and it does not plan to do so in the future. To estimate how much its debt would cost at different debt levels, the company's treasury staff has consulted with investment bankers and, on the basis of those discussions, has created the following table:

Debt-to-Capital Ratio (w_d)	Equity-to-Capital Ratio (w_c)	Debt-to-Equity Ratio (D/E)	Bond Rating	Before-Tax Cost of Debt (r_d)
0.0	1.0	0.00	A	6.5%
0.2	0.8	0.25	BBB	7.5
0.4	0.6	0.67	BB	9.5
0.6	0.4	1.50	C	11.5
0.8	0.2	4.00	D	14.5

Backroads uses the CAPM to estimate its cost of common equity, r_s. The company estimates that the risk-free rate is 6%, the market risk premium is 5%, and its tax rate is 40%. Backroads estimates that if it had no debt, its "unlevered" beta, b_U, would be 1.25. On the basis of this information, what would be the WACC at the optimal capital structure?

a.   9.56%
b.   10.48%
c.   11.13%
d.   11.45%
e.   12.25%

7. Currently, Pam's Petals Inc. (PPI) has a capital structure consisting of 30% debt and 70% equity. PPI's debt currently has a 7% yield to maturity. The risk-free rate (r_{RF}) is 5.5% and the market risk premium (RP_M) is 5%. Using the CAPM, PPI estimates that its cost of equity is currently 11.75%. The company has a 35% tax rate. What is PPI's current WACC?

a.   8.33%
b.   8.67%
c.   9.00%
d.   9.59%
e.   10.25%

8. Currently, Pam's Petals Inc. (PPI) has a capital structure consisting of 30% debt and 70% equity. PPI's debt currently has a 7% yield to maturity. The risk-free rate (r_{RF}) is 5.5% and the market risk premium (RP_M) is 5%. Using the CAPM, PPI estimates that its cost of equity is currently 11.75%. The company has a 35% tax rate. What is the current beta on PPI's common stock?

a.   1.3350
b.   1.2500
c.   1.0000
d.   1.1000
e.   0.9777

9. Currently, Pam's Petals Inc. (PPI) has a capital structure consisting of 30% debt and 70% equity. PPI's debt currently has a 7% yield to maturity. The risk-free rate (r_{RF}) is 5.5% and the market risk premium (RP_M) is 5%. Using the CAPM, PPI estimates that its cost of equity is currently 11.75%. The company has a 35% tax rate. What would PPI's beta be if the company had no debt in its capital structure? (That is, what is PPI's unlevered beta, b_U?)

a.   1.3350
b.   1.2500
c.   1.0000
d.   1.1000
e.   0.9777

10. Currently, Pam's Petals Inc. (PPI) has a capital structure consisting of 30% debt and 70% equity. PPI's debt currently has a 7% yield to maturity. The risk-free rate (r_{RF}) is 5.5% and the market risk premium (RP_M) is 5%. Using the CAPM, PPI estimates that its cost of equity is currently 11.75%. The company has a 35% tax rate.

    PPI's financial staff is considering changing its capital structure to 45% debt and 55% equity. If the company went ahead with the proposed change, the yield to maturity on the company's bonds would now be 8.75%. The proposed change will have no effect on the company's tax rate. What would be the company's new cost of equity if it adopted the proposed change in capital structure?

    a. 12.99%
    b. 12.25%
    c. 11.75%
    d. 13.35%
    e. 14.00%

11. Currently, Pam's Petals Inc. (PPI) has a capital structure consisting of 30% debt and 70% equity. PPI's debt currently has a 7% yield to maturity. The risk-free rate (r_{RF}) is 5.5% and the market risk premium (RP_M) is 5%. Using the CAPM, PPI estimates that its cost of equity is currently 11.75%. The company has a 35% tax rate.

    PPI's financial staff is considering changing its capital structure to 45% debt and 55% equity. If the company went ahead with the proposed change, the yield to maturity on the company's bonds would rise to 8.75%. The proposed change will have no effect on the company's tax rate. What would be the company's new WACC if it adopted the proposed change in capital structure?

    a. 8.76%
    b. 11.20%
    c. 9.70%
    d. 10.10%
    e. 9.33%

12. On the basis of your answers to Problems 7 and 11, would you advise PPI to adopt the proposed change in capital structure?

    a. Yes, the firm's new WACC after the proposed capital structure change is made declines from 9.59% to 9.33%.
    b. No, the firm's new WACC after the proposed capital structure change is made increases from 9.59% to 9.70%.
    c. A decision cannot be made because there is insufficient information.
    d. Yes, the firm's new WACC after the proposed capital structure change is made declines from 9.00% to 8.76%.
    e. No, the firm's new WACC after the proposed capital structure change is made increases from 10.25% to 11.20%.

Answers

Definitional Questions

1. optimal; stock
2. target
3. Business
4. demand; operating
5. standard
6. Financial
7. increases
8. bankruptcy
9. Financial
10. tax; interest; dividends
11. debt; control
12. Financial
13. operating; point
14. trade-off
15. Signaling
16. asymmetric
17. reserve
18. higher
19. times-interest-earned
20. percentage; interest; profitability
21. Operating
22. greater
23. break-even
24. lower
25. Risk
26. minimizes
27. Hamada
28. operating; structure
29. irrelevant
30. Symmetric
31. lowers
32. stronger
33. intensive
34. interest
35. technology

Conceptual Questions

1. b. Increasing operating leverage will increase Firm A's business risk; therefore, Firm A should use less operating leverage.

2. b. The two firms would have the same total risk. However, they could have different combinations of business and financial risk.

3. a. Business risk consists of several elements in addition to operating leverage, for example, sales variability, and it does not depend on financial risk at all.

4. d. The optimal capital structure balances risk and return to maximize the stock price. The capital structure that maximizes stock price also minimizes the firm's weighted average cost of capital.

5. c. Business risk measures the riskiness of a firm's operations assuming no debt is used.

6. d. Statement d is the correct choice. Statement a is false; if a firm is exposed to a high degree of business risk this implies that it should offset this risk by using a lower amount of financial leverage. Statement b is false; preferred stock is a fixed-income security, and as such, would increase financial risk. Statement c is false; an increase in the debt/equity ratio increases beta. A firm's unlevered beta depends entirely on its business risk and is a measure of its basic business risk; so statement e is false.

Solutions

Problems

1. e. $EBIT = PQ - VQP - F$
$\$90,000 = P(50,000) - 0.4(50,000)P - \$100,000$
$30,000P = \$190,000$
$P = \$6.33$

2. d.   From the Hamada Equation, $b = b_U[1 + (1 - T)(D/E)]$, we can calculate b_U as

$b_U = b/[1 + (1 - T)(D/E)]$
$= 1.75/[1 + (1 - 0.4)(\$5,000,000/\$20,000,000)]$
$= 1.75/1.15$
$= 1.5217$

3. c.   Facts as given: Current capital structure: 20%D, 80%E; $r_{RF} = 7\%$; $RP_M = 5\%$; $T = 35\%$; $r_s = 16\%$

Step 1: Determine the firm's current beta.

$r_s = r_{RF} + (RP_M)b$
$16\% = 7\% + (5\%)b$
$9\% = 5\%b$
$1.8 = b$

Step 2: Determine the firm's unlevered beta, b_U.

$b_U = b/[1 + (1 - T)(D/E)]$
$= 1.8/[1 + (1 - 0.35)(0.20/0.80)]$
$= 1.8/1.1625$
$= 1.5484$

Step 3: Determine the firm's beta under the new capital structure.

$b_L = b_U[1 + (1 - T)(D/E)]$
$= 1.5484[1 + (1 - 0.35)(0.4/0.6)]$
$= 1.5484(1.4333)$
$= 2.2194$

Step 4: Determine the firm's new cost of equity under the changed capital structure.

$r_s = r_{RF} + (RP_M)b$
$= 7\% + (5\%)2.2194$
$= 18.1\%$

4. b. The first step is to calculate EBIT:

Sales in dollars [50,000($22)]	$1,100,000
Less: Fixed costs	500,000
Variable costs [50,000($2)]	100,000
EBIT	$ 500,000

The second step is to calculate the EPS at each debt/capital ratio using the formula:

$$EPS = \frac{(EBIT - I)(1 - T)}{Shares\ outstanding}$$

Recognize (1) that I = Interest charges = (Dollars of debt)(Interest rate at each Debt/Capital ratio), and (2) that shares outstanding = (Capital – Debt)/Initial price per share = ($2,000,000 – Debt)/$20.00.

Debt/Capital	EPS	Debt/Capital	EPS
0%	$3.00	40%	$3.80
10	3.21	50	3.72
20	3.47	60	2.82
30	3.77		

Finally, the third step is to calculate the stock price at each debt/capital ratio using the following formula: Price = (P/E)(EPS).

Debt/Capital	Price	Debt/Capital	Price
0%	$37.50	40%	$30.40
10	38.52	50	22.32
20	39.91	60	14.10
30	37.70		

Thus, a debt/capital ratio of 20% maximizes stock price. This is the optimal capital structure.

5. a. Value of stock = [$500,000 – 0.1($1,000,000)](0.6)/0.15 = $1,600,000
   P_0 = $1,600,000/100,000 = $16

   After the recapitalization, value of stock is equal to
   [$500,000 – 0.1($1,000,000) – 0.13($500,000)](0.6)/0.17 = $1,182,353

   P_0 = $1,182,353/[100,000 – ($500,000/$16)] = $17.20

6. c. Tax rate = 40%; r_{RF} = 6.0%; b_U = 1.25; RP_M = 5.0%

From data given in the problem and table we can develop the following table:

Debt/ Capital	Equity/ Capital	D/E	r_d	$r_d(1-T)$	Leveraged beta[a]	r_s[b]	WACC[c]
0.00	1.00	0.0000	6.5%	3.90%	1.2500	12.2500%	12.25%
0.20	0.80	0.2500	7.5	4.50	1.4375	13.1875	11.45
0.40	0.60	0.6667	9.5	5.70	1.7500	14.7500	11.13
0.60	0.40	1.5000	11.5	6.90	2.3750	17.8750	11.29
0.80	0.20	4.0000	14.5	8.70	4.2500	27.2500	12.41

Notes:
[a] These beta estimates were calculated using the Hamada equation: $b = b_U[1 + (1 - T)(D/E)]$.
[b] These r_s estimates were calculated using the CAPM: $r_s = r_{RF} + (RP_M)b$.
[c] These WACC estimates were calculated with the following equation: $WACC = w_d(r_d)(1 - T) + (w_c)(r_s)$.

The firm's optimal capital structure is that capital structure which minimizes the firm's WACC. Backroads' WACC is minimized at a capital structure consisting of 40% debt and 60% equity. At that capital structure, the firm's WACC is 11.13%.

7. d. Using the standard formula for the WACC, we find:

$$WACC = w_d r_d(1 - T) + w_c r_s$$
$$= (0.3)(7\%)(1 - 0.35) + (0.7)(11.75\%)$$
$$= 1.365\% + 8.225\%$$
$$= 9.59\%$$

8. b. Find the firm's current levered beta at 30% debt using the CAPM formula.

$$r_s = r_{RF} + (RP_M)b$$
$$11.75\% = 5.5\% + (5\%)b$$
$$6.25\% = (5\%)b$$
$$b = 1.25$$

9. e. Find the firm's current levered beta at 30% debt using the CAPM formula.

$$r_s = r_{RF} + (RP_M)b$$
$$11.75\% = 5.5\% + (5\%)b$$
$$6.25\% = (5\%)b$$
$$b = 1.25$$

Next, "unlever" the firm's beta, using the Hamada Equation, to calculate b_U.

$$b_L = b_U[1 + (1 - T)(D/E)]$$
$$1.25 = b_U[1 + (1 - 0.35)(0.3/0.7)]$$
$$1.25 = b_U(1.278571)$$
$$b_U = 0.9777$$

10. a. Find the firm's current levered beta at 30% debt using the CAPM formula.

$$r_s = r_{RF} + (RP_M)b$$
$$11.75\% = 5.5\% + (5\%)b$$
$$6.25\% = (5\%)b$$
$$b = 1.25$$

Next, "unlever" the firm's beta, using the Hamada Equation, to calculate b_U.

$$b_L = b_U[1 + (1 - T)(D/E)]$$
$$1.25 = b_U[1 + (1 - 0.35)(0.3/0.7)]$$
$$1.25 = b_U(1.278571)$$
$$b_U = 0.9777$$

To determine the firm's new cost of common equity, one must find the firm's new beta under its new capital structure. Consequently, you must "relever" the firm's beta at the new capital structure using the Hamada Equation:

$$b_{L,45\%} = b_U[1 + (1 - T)(D/E)]$$
$$= 0.9777 [1 + (1 - 0.35)(0.45/0.55)]$$
$$= 0.9777 (1.5318)$$
$$= 1.4977$$

The firm's new cost of equity is now calculated using the CAPM and the new levered beta.

$$r_s = r_{RF} + (RP_M)b$$
$$= 5.5\% + (5\%)1.4977$$
$$= 12.99\%$$

11. c. Find the firm's current levered beta at 30% debt using the CAPM formula.

$$r_s = r_{RF} + (RP_M)b$$
$$11.75\% = 5.5\% + (5\%)b$$
$$6.25\% = (5\%)b$$
$$b = 1.25$$

Next, "unlever" the firm's beta, using the Hamada Equation, to calculate b_U.

$$b_L = b_U[1 + (1 - T)(D/E)]$$
$$1.25 = b_U[1 + (1 - 0.35)(0.3/0.7)]$$
$$1.25 = b_U(1.278571)$$
$$b_U = 0.9777$$

To determine the firm's new cost of common equity, one must find the firm's new beta under its new capital structure. Consequently, you must "relever" the firm's beta at the new capital structure using the Hamada Equation:

$$b_{L,45\%} = b_U[1 + (1 - T)(D/E)]$$
$$= 0.9777 \, [1 + (1 - 0.35)(0.45/0.55)]$$
$$= 0.9777 \, (1.5318)$$
$$= 1.4977$$

The firm's new cost of equity is now calculated using the CAPM and the new levered beta.

$$r_s = r_{RF} + (RP_M)b$$
$$= 5.5\% + (5\%)1.4977$$
$$= 12.99\%$$

Again, the standard formula for the WACC is used. Remember, the WACC is a marginal, after-tax cost of capital and hence the relevant before-tax cost of debt is now 8.75% and the new cost of equity is 12.99%.

$$WACC = w_d r_d(1 - T) + w_c r_s$$
$$= (0.45)(8.75\%)(1 - 0.35) + (0.55)(12.99\%)$$
$$= 9.70\%$$

12. b. The firm should be advised not to proceed with the recapitalization because it causes its WACC to increase from 9.59% to 9.70%. If the recapitalization were made, it would lead to a decrease in firm value. The optimal capital structure that maximizes the firm's stock price minimizes its WACC.

14

DISTRIBUTIONS TO SHAREHOLDERS: DIVIDENDS AND SHARE REPURCHASES

Learning Objectives

1. Explain why some investors like the firm to pay more dividends while other investors prefer reinvestment and the resulting capital gains.

2. Discuss the various trade-offs that companies face when trying to establish their optimal dividend policy.

3. Differentiate between stock splits and stock dividends.

4. List the advantages and disadvantages of stock repurchases vis-à-vis dividends from both investors' and companies' perspectives.

Overview

Dividend policy involves the decision to pay out earnings as dividends or to retain and reinvest them in the firm. If the decision is made to distribute income to stockholders, three key issues arise: (1) How much should be distributed? (2) Should the distribution be in the form of dividends or should the cash be passed on to shareholders by buying back stock? (3) How stable should the distribution be?

Any change in dividend policy has both favorable and unfavorable effects on the firm's stock price: higher dividends mean higher immediate cash flows to investors, which is good, but lower future growth, which is bad. The optimal dividend policy balances these opposing forces and maximizes stock price.

Theories regarding the relationship between dividend payout and stock price have been proposed: (1) dividend irrelevance, which states that dividend policy has no effect on the firm's stock price, and (2) the "bird-in-the-hand" theory, which states that investors prefer dividends because they are less risky than potential capital gains. In addition, the Tax Code encourages many individual investors to prefer capital gains to dividends. Since 2003, the maximum tax rate on dividends and long-term capital gains has been set at 15%. This change lowered the tax disadvantage of dividends, but reinvestment and the accompanying capital gains still have tax advantages over dividends.

Dividend policy is further complicated due to signaling and clientele effects. It is simply not possible to state that any one dividend policy is correct, and hence it is impossible to develop a precise model for use in establishing dividend policy. Thus, financial managers must consider a number of factors when setting their firms' dividend policies.

Outline

I. **Dividend policy involves the decision to pay out earnings or to retain them for reinvestment in the firm.**

   A. The *target payout ratio* is defined as the percentage of net income paid out as cash dividends as desired by the firm, and it should be based in large part on investors' preferences for dividends versus capital gains.

      1. The constant growth stock model, $P_0 = D_1/(r_s - g)$, shows that paying out more dividends will increase stock price.

      2. However, if D_1 is raised then less money will be available for reinvestment, that will cause the expected growth rate to decline, and that would tend to lower the stock's price.

      3. The *optimal dividend policy* strikes a balance between current dividends and future growth and maximizes the firm's stock price.

   B. A number of theories have been proposed to explain how factors interact to determine a firm's optimal dividend policy. These theories include: (1) the dividend irrelevance theory and (2) the "bird-in-the-hand" theory.

      1. Modigliani and Miller (MM), the principal proponents of the *dividend irrelevance theory*, argue that the value of the firm depends only on the income produced by its assets, not on how this income is split between dividends and retained earnings.

         a. MM prove their proposition, but only under a set of restrictive assumptions including the absence of taxes and brokerage costs.

         b. Obviously, taxes and brokerage costs do exist, so the MM conclusions on dividend irrelevance may not be valid under real-world conditions.

         c. In defense of their theory, MM noted that many stocks are owned by institutional investors who pay no taxes and who can buy and sell stocks with very low transactions costs. For such investors, dividend policy might well be irrelevant. If these investors dominate the market and represent the "marginal investor," MM's theory could be valid in spite of its unrealistic assumptions.

      2. The principal conclusion of MM's dividend irrelevance theory is that dividend policy does not affect stock prices and thus the required rate of return on equity, r_s. Relaxing this assumption provides the basis for the "bird-in-the-hand" theory.

         a. Myron Gordon and John Lintner argue that r_s decreases as the dividend payout is increased because investors are less certain of receiving the capital gains that are supposed to result from retaining earnings than they are of receiving dividend payments.

b. MM call the Gordon-Lintner argument the *"bird-in-the-hand" fallacy* because Gordon and Lintner believe that investors view dividends in the hand as being less risky than capital gains in the bush.

c. In MM's view, however, most investors plan to reinvest their dividends in the stock of the same or similar firms, and the riskiness of the firm's cash flows to investors in the long run is determined by the riskiness of operating cash flows, not by dividend payout policy.

d. In reality, many investors face transactions costs when they sell stock; so investors who are looking for a steady stream of income would logically prefer that companies pay regular dividends.

C. The Tax Code encourages many individual investors to prefer capital gains to dividends.

1. Since 2003, the maximum tax rate on dividends and long-term capital gains has been set at 15%.

2. The new tax treatment of dividends lowered the tax disadvantage of dividends, but reinvestment and the accompanying capital gains still have two tax advantages over dividends.

a. Taxes must be paid on dividends the year they are received, whereas taxes on capital gains are not paid until the stock is sold. Due to time value effects, a dollar of taxes paid in the future has a lower effective cost than a dollar of taxes paid today.

b. If a stock is held by someone until he or she dies, there is no capital gains tax at all—the beneficiaries who receive the stock can use the stock's value on the death date as their cost basis, which permits them to completely escape the capital gains tax.

3. Because of these tax advantages, some investors prefer to have companies retain most of their earnings, and those investors might be willing to pay more for low-payout companies than for otherwise similar high-payout companies.

II. **There are two other issues that have a bearing on optimal dividend policy: (1) the information content, or signaling, hypothesis and (2) the clientele effect.**

A. It has been observed that a dividend increase announcement is often accompanied by an increase in the stock price, while a dividend cut generally leads to a stock price decline.

1. This might be interpreted by some to mean that investors prefer dividends over capital gains, thus supporting the Gordon-Lintner hypothesis.

a. A *signal* is an action taken by a firm's management that provides clues to investors about how management views the firm's prospects.

2. However, MM argue that a dividend increase is a signal to investors that the firm's management forecasts good future earnings.

a. Thus, MM argue that investors' reactions to dividend announcements do not necessarily show that investors prefer dividends to retained earnings.

b. Rather, the fact that the stock price changes merely indicates that there is important information content in dividend announcements. This is referred to as the *information content, or signaling, hypothesis.*

      c.   Signaling effects should definitely be considered when a firm is contemplating a change in dividend policy. Managers should consider signaling effects when they set dividend policy.

  B. MM also suggest that a *clientele effect* might exist.

    1. *Clienteles* are different groups of stockholders who prefer different dividend payout policies.

    2. A clientele effect is the tendency of a firm to attract a set of investors who like its dividend policy.

    3. Some stockholders (for example, retirees) prefer current income; therefore, they would want the firm to pay out a high percentage of its earnings as dividends.

    4. Other stockholders have no need for current income (for example, doctors in their peak earning years) and they would simply reinvest any dividends received, after first paying income taxes on the dividend income. Therefore, they would want the firm to retain most of its earnings.

    5. All of this suggests that a clientele effect exists, which means that firms have different clienteles and that the clienteles have different preferences—hence, that a change in dividend policy might upset the majority clientele and have a negative effect on the stock's price.

    6. This suggests that a company should follow a stable, dependable dividend policy so as to avoid upsetting its clientele.

  C. Borrowing from the ideas of behavioral finance, some recent research suggests that investors' preference for dividends varies over time.

    1. *Catering theory* suggests that investors' preference for dividends varies over time and that corporations adapt their dividend policy to cater to the current desires of investors.

III. When deciding how much cash should be distributed to stockholders, two points should be kept in mind: (1) The overriding objective is to maximize shareholder value, and (2) the firm's cash flows really belong to its shareholders, so management should not retain income unless they can reinvest those earnings at higher rates of return than shareholders can earn themselves. On the other hand, internal equity is cheaper than external equity, so if good investments are available, it is better to finance them with retained earnings than with new stock.

  A. When establishing a dividend policy, one size does not fit all.

    1. Over the past few decades, there has been an increasing number of young, high-growth firms trading on the stock exchanges.

      a. A study by Fama and French shows that the proportion of firms paying dividends has fallen sharply over time.

      b. As a result of the 2003 tax changes, which lowered the tax rate on dividends, many companies initiated dividends or increased their payouts.

    2. Dividend payouts and dividend yields for large corporations vary considerably.

  B. Firms in stable, cash-producing industries pay relatively high dividends, whereas companies in rapidly growing industries tend to pay lower dividends.

    1. Average dividends also differ significantly across countries.

C. The optimal payout ratio is a function of four factors: (1) management's opinion about its investors' preferences for dividends versus capital gains, (2) the firm's investment opportunities, (3) the firm's target capital structure, and (4) the availability and cost of external capital.

   1. These factors are combined in the residual dividend model.

D. The *residual dividend model* is based on the premise that investors are indifferent between dividends and capital gains.

   1. A firm using the residual model would follow these four steps:

      a. Determine the optimal capital budget.

      b. Determine the amount of equity required to finance the optimal capital budget given its target capital structure.

      c. To the extent possible, use retained earnings to meet equity requirements.

      d. Pay dividends only if more earnings are available than are needed to support the optimal capital budget.

   2. The word residual implies "leftover," and the residual policy implies that dividends are paid out of "leftover" earnings.

E. If a firm rigidly follows the residual dividend policy, then dividends paid in any given year can be expressed as follows:

$$\text{Dividends} = \text{Net income} - [(\text{Target equity ratio})(\text{Total capital budget})]$$

F. Since investment opportunities and earnings will surely vary from year to year, strict adherence to the residual dividend policy would result in fluctuating, unstable dividends.

   1. Firms should use the residual policy to help set their *long-run target payout ratios*, but not as a guide to the payout in any one year.

G. Companies use the residual dividend model in a conceptual sense, then implement it with a computerized financial forecasting model.

   1. Most companies use the computer model to find a dividend pattern over the forecast period that will provide sufficient equity to support the capital budget without having to sell new common stock or move the capital structure ratio outside the optimal range.

H. Some companies, especially those in cyclical industries, have difficulty maintaining a dividend in bad times that would be too low in good times.

   1. These companies set a very low "regular" dividend and then supplement it with an "extra" dividend when times are good. This is called a *low-regular-dividend-plus-extras* policy.

      a. Investors recognize that the extras might not be maintained in the future, so they do not interpret them as a signal that the companies' earnings are increasing permanently, nor do they take the elimination of the extra as a negative signal.

I. Dividends clearly depend more on cash flows, which reflect the company's ability to pay cash dividends, than on current earnings, which are heavily influenced by accounting practices and which do not necessarily reflect the firm's cash position.

J. Firms usually pay dividends on a quarterly basis in accordance with the following payment procedures.

279

1. *Declaration date.* This is the day on which the board of directors declares the dividend.

   a. At this time they set the amount of the dividend to be paid, the holder-of-record date, and the payment date.

   b. For accounting purposes, the declared dividend becomes an actual liability on the declaration date.

2. *Holder-of-record date.* This is the date the stock transfer books of the corporation are closed.

   a. Those shareholders who are listed on the company's books on this date are the holders of record and they receive the announced dividend.

3. *Ex-dividend date.* The date on which the right to the current dividend no longer accompanies a stock.

   a. This date is two business days prior to the holder-of-record date.

   b. This practice is a convention of the brokerage business that allows sufficient time for stock transfers to be made on the books of the corporation.

4. *Payment date.* This is the day when dividend checks are actually mailed to the holders of record.

IV. **Many firms have instituted dividend reinvestment plans (DRIPs) whereby stockholders can automatically reinvest dividends received in the stock of the paying corporation. Income taxes on the amount of the dividends must be paid even though stock rather than cash is received.**

   A. There are two types of DRIPs.

      1. Plans that involve only "old stock" that is already outstanding.

      2. Plans that involve newly issued stock. Hence, this type of plan raises new capital for the firm.

   B. Stockholders choose between continuing to receive dividend checks and having the company use the dividends to buy more stock in the corporation.

   C. One interesting aspect of DRIPs is that they are forcing corporations to reexamine their basic dividend policies.

      1. A high participation rate in a DRIP suggests that stockholders might be better off if the firm simply reduced cash dividends, which would save stockholders some personal income taxes.

   D. Companies switch from old stock to new stock DRIPs depending on their need for equity.

   E. Some companies have expanded their DRIPs by moving to *open enrollment* whereby anyone can purchase the firm's stock directly and bypass brokers' commissions.

V. **Dividend policy decisions are based more on informed judgment than on quantitative analysis. Regardless of the debate on the relevancy of dividend policy, it is possible to identify several factors that influence dividend policy. These factors are grouped into four broad categories.**

   A. Constraints on dividend payments: (1) Bond indentures, (2) preferred stock restrictions, (3) impairment of capital rule, (4) availability of cash, and (5) penalty tax on improperly accumulated earnings.

B. Investment opportunities: (1) Number of profitable investment opportunities and (2) possibility of accelerating or delaying projects.

C. Availability and cost of alternative sources of capital: (1) Cost of selling new stock, (2) ability to substitute debt for equity, and (3) control.

D. Effects of dividend policy on r_s: (1) Stockholders' desire for current versus future income, (2) perceived riskiness of dividends versus capital gains, (3) the tax advantage of capital gains, and (4) the information content of dividends (signaling).

VI. **Stock dividends and stock splits are often used to lower a firm's stock price and, at the same time, to conserve its cash resources.**

A. The effect of a *stock split* is an increase in the number of shares outstanding and a reduction in the par, or stated, value of the shares. For example, if a firm had 1,000 shares of stock outstanding with a par value of $100 per share, a 2-for-1 split would reduce the par value to $50 and increase the number of shares to 2,000.

1. The total net worth of the firm remains unchanged.

2. The stock split does not involve any cash payment, only additional certificates representing new shares.

3. Stock splits often occur due to the widespread belief that there is an *optimal price range* for each stock.

   a. "Optimal" means that if the price is within this range, the price/earnings ratio, hence the firm's value, will be maximized.

4. Stock splits are generally used after a sharp price run-up to produce a large price reduction.

5. By creating more shares and lowering the stock price, stock splits may also increase the stock's liquidity. This tends to increase the firm's value.

6. There is also evidence that stock splits change the mix of shareholders.

   a. The proportion of trades made by individual investors tends to increase after a stock split, whereas the proportion of trades made by institutional investors tends to fall.

B. A *stock dividend* requires an accounting entry transfer from retained earnings to common stock.

1. Again, no cash is involved with this "dividend." Net worth remains unchanged, and the number of shares is increased.

2. Stock dividends used on a regular annual basis will keep the stock price more or less constrained.

C. Unless the total amount of dividends paid on shares is increased, any upward movement in the stock price following a stock split or dividend is likely to be temporary.

1. The price will normally fall in proportion to the dilution in earnings and dividends unless earnings and dividends rise.

D. Stock dividends and splits provide management with a relatively low-cost way of signaling that the firm's prospects look good. Because small stock dividends create bookkeeping problems and unnecessary expenses, firms use stock splits far more often than stock dividends.

VII. **Stock repurchases are an alternative to dividends for transmitting cash to stockholders.**

A. There are three principal types of repurchases: (1) Situations in which the firm has cash available for distribution to its stockholders, and it distributes this cash by repurchasing shares rather than by paying cash dividends; (2) situations where the firm concludes that its capital structure is too heavily weighted with equity, and it sells debt and uses the proceeds to buy back its stock; and (3) situations where the firm has issued options to employees and it uses open market repurchases to obtain stock for use when the options are exercised.

B. Stock repurchased by the issuing firm is called *treasury stock*.

C. Assuming that the repurchase does not adversely affect the firm's future earnings, the earnings per share on the remaining shares will increase, resulting in a higher market price per share. As a result, capital gains will have been substituted for dividends.

D. Advantages of repurchases include:

1. The repurchase is often motivated by management's belief that the firm's shares are undervalued.

2. The stockholder is given a choice of whether or not to sell his stock to the firm.

3. The repurchase can remove a large block of stock overhanging the market.

4. If an increase in cash flow is temporary, the cash can be distributed to stockholders as a repurchase rather than as a dividend, which could not be maintained in the future.

5. The company has more flexibility in adjusting the total distribution than it would if the entire distribution were in the form of cash dividends, because repurchases can be varied from year to year without giving off adverse signals.

6. Repurchases can be used to produce large-scale changes in capital structures.

7. Companies that use stock options as an important component of employee compensation can repurchase shares and then use those shares when employees exercise their options.

E. Disadvantages of repurchases include:

1. Repurchases are not as dependable as cash dividends; therefore, the stock price may benefit more from cash dividends.

2. Selling stockholders may not be fully aware of all the implications of a repurchase; therefore, repurchases are usually announced in advance.

3. If a firm pays too high a price for the repurchased stock, it is to the disadvantage of the remaining stockholders.

F. Conclusions on repurchases may be summarized as follows:

1. Because of the deferred tax on capital gains, repurchases have a tax advantage over dividends as a way to distribute income to stockholders.

2. Because of signaling effects, companies should not pay fluctuating dividends—that would lower investors' confidence in the company and adversely affect its cost of equity and its stock price.

3. Repurchases are also useful when a firm wants to make a large, rapid shift in its capital structure, wants to distribute cash from a one-time event such as the sale of a division, or wants to obtain shares for use in an employee stock option plan.

G. Increases in the size and frequency of repurchases in recent years suggest that companies are doing more repurchases and paying out less cash as dividends.

VIII. **Web Appendix 14A illustrates a computerized financial forecasting model that uses the residual dividend model to help set long-run target payout ratios.**

Self-Test

Definitional Questions

1. MM argue that a firm's _____ policy has no effect on a stock's price.

2. Gordon and Lintner hypothesize that investors value a dollar of _____ more highly than a dollar of expected _____ gains.

3. Some stockholders prefer dividends to _____ gains because of a need for current _____.

4. If a firm's stock _____ increases with the announcement of an increase in dividends, it may be due to the _____ content in the dividend announcement rather than to a preference for dividends over capital gains.

5. A firm with _____ or _____ earnings is most appropriate for using the policy of "extra" dividends.

6. The stock transfer books of a corporation are closed on the _____-____-_____ date.

7. The ____-_____ date occurs two business days prior to the _____-____-_____ date and provides time for stock transfers to be recorded on the firm's books.

8. Actual payment of a dividend is made on the _____ date as announced by the board of directors.

9. Many firms have instituted dividend _____ plans whereby stockholders can use their dividends to purchase additional shares of the company's stock.

10. A stock split involves a reduction in the _____ value of the common stock, but no accounting transfers are made between accounts.

11. The assumption that some investors prefer a high dividend payout while others prefer a low payout is called the _____ effect.

12. Stock repurchased by the firm that issued it is called _____ stock.

13. _____ policy involves the decision to pay out earnings or to retain them for reinvestment in the firm.

14. The target _____ ratio is defined as the percentage of net income to be paid out as cash dividends as desired by the firm, and it should be based in large part on investors' preferences for _____ versus capital gains.

15. The _____ dividend model is based on the premise that investors are indifferent between dividends and capital gains, and it implies that dividends are paid out of "leftover" earnings.

16. Some companies have expanded their DRIPs by moving to open _____ whereby anyone can purchase the firm's stock directly and bypass brokers' commissions.

17. Stock _____ are an alternative to dividends for transmitting cash to stockholders.

18. The _____-_____-_____-_____ fallacy states that investors prefer dividends because they are less risky than potential capital gains.

19. The _____ dividend _____ strikes a balance between current dividends and future growth that maximizes the firm's stock price.

20. Modigliani and Miller, the principal proponents of the dividend _____ theory, argue that the value of the firm depends only on the income produced by its assets, not on how income is split between dividends and retained earnings.

21. A stock _____ requires an accounting entry transfer from retained earnings to common stock.

22. The optimal payout ratio is a function of four factors: (1) management's opinion about its investors' preferences for dividends versus capital gains, (2) the firm's _____ opportunities, (3) the firm's target capital _____, and (4) the _____ and _____ of external capital.

23. The Tax Code encourages many individual investors to prefer _____ _____ to dividends.

24. A(n) _____ is an action taken by a firm's management that provides clues to investors about how management views the firm's prospects.

25. A company should follow a(n) _____ dividend policy so as to avoid upsetting its clientele.

Conceptual Questions

1. An increase in cash dividends will always result in an increase in the price of the common stock because D_1 will increase in the stock valuation model.

    a. True
    b. False

2. A stock split will affect the amounts shown in which of the following balance sheet accounts?

    a. Common stock
    b. Paid-in capital
    c. Retained earnings
    d. Cash
    e. None of the above accounts.

3. If investors prefer dividends to capital gains, then

    a. The required rate of return on equity, r_s, will not be affected by a change in dividend policy.
    b. The cost of capital will not be affected by a change in dividend policy.
    c. r_s will increase as the payout ratio is reduced.
    d. r_s will decrease as the retention rate increases.
    e. A policy conforming to the residual dividend model will maximize stock price.

4. Which of the following statements is correct?

   a. Modigliani and Miller's theory of the effect of dividend policy on the value of a firm has been called the "bird-in-the-hand" fallacy, because MM argued that a dividend in the hand is less risky than a potential capital gain in the bush. After extensive empirical tests, this theory is now accepted by most financial experts.

   b. According to proponents of the "dividend irrelevance theory," if a company's stock price rises after the firm announces a greater-than-expected dividend increase, the price increase occurs because of signaling effects, not because of investors' preferences for dividends over capital gains.

   c. The tax preference theory states that the value of the firm depends only on the income produced by its assets, not on how this income is split between dividends and retained earnings.

   d. Neither the clientele effect nor the signaling hypothesis is relevant to dividend policy.

   e. Because of recent tax law changes, companies have lowered their dividend payouts because the maximum tax rate on dividends is the same as the capital gains tax rate.

5. Which of the following statements is correct?

   a. The residual dividend model calls for the establishment of a fixed, stable dividend (or dividend growth rate) and then for the level of investment each year to be determined as a residual equal to net income minus the established dividends.

   b. According to the residual dividend model, if a firm has a large number of profitable investment opportunities this will tend to produce a lower optimal dividend payout ratio.

   c. According to the text, a firm would probably maximize its stock price if it established a specific dividend payout ratio, say 40%, and then paid that percentage of earnings out each year because stockholders would then know exactly how much dividend income to count on when they planned their spending for the coming year. Because strict adherence to the residual dividend policy results in unstable dividends, the residual policy should be used to help firms set up long-run target payout ratios.

   d. If you buy a stock after the ex-dividend date but before the dividend has been paid, then you, and not the seller, will receive the next dividend check the company mails.

   e. Because strict adherence to the residual dividend policy would result in stable dividends, firms should use the residual policy to set their target payout ratio for one year at a time.

6. Which of the following statements is correct?

   a. The Tax Code encourages many individual investors to prefer dividends to capital gains because recent tax changes have lowered the tax rate on dividends to the same tax rate as on capital gains.

   b. According to the "bird-in-the-hand" theory, investors prefer cash to paper (stock), so if a company announces that it plans to repurchase some of its stock, this causes the price of the stock to increase.

   c. According to the dividend irrelevance theory developed by Modigliani and Miller, stock dividends (but not cash dividends) are irrelevant because they "merely divide the pie into thinner slices."

   d. According to the information content, or signaling, hypothesis, the fact that stock prices generally increase when an increase in the dividend is announced demonstrates that investors prefer higher to lower payout ratios.

   e. According to the text, the residual dividend model is more appropriate for setting a company's long-run target payout ratio than for determining the payout ratio on a year-to-year basis.

7. Which of the following statements is correct?

   a. Stock prices generally rise on the ex-dividend date, and that increase is especially great if the company increases the dividend.

   b. Dividend reinvestment plans are popular with investors because investors who do not need cash income can have their dividends reinvested in the company's stock and thereby avoid having to pay income taxes on the dividend income until they sell the stock.

   c. In the past, stock dividends and stock splits were frequently used by corporations that wanted to lower the prices of their stocks to an "optimal trading range." However, recent empirical studies have demonstrated that stock dividends and stock splits generally cause stock prices to decline, so companies today rarely split their stock or pay stock dividends.

   d. Some companies, especially those in cyclical industries, have difficulty maintaining in bad times a dividend that is really too low in good times. In this situation, a low-regular-dividend-plus-extras policy is often used.

   e. Stock splits, due to the result of lowering a stock's price, have been shown to lower a stock's liquidity and to keep the mix of a firm's shareholders constant.

Problems

1. Express Industries' expected net income for next year is $1 million. The company's target and current capital structure is 40% debt and 60% common equity. The optimal capital budget for next year is $1.2 million. If Express uses the residual theory of dividends to determine next year's dividend payout, what is the expected payout ratio?

   a. 0%
   b. 10%
   c. 28%
   d. 42%
   e. 56%

2. Amalgamated Shippers has a current and target capital structure of 30% debt and 70% equity. This past year Amalgamated, which uses the residual dividend model, had a dividend payout ratio of 47.5% and net income of $800,000. What was Amalgamated's capital budget?

   a. $400,000
   b. $500,000
   c. $600,000
   d. $700,000
   e. $800,000

3. Hiers Automotive Supply Inc.'s stock trades at $100 a share. The company is contemplating a 4-for-3 stock split. Assuming that the stock split will have no effect on the market value of its equity, what will be the company's stock price following the stock split?

   a. $50.00
   b. $62.50
   c. $70.00
   d. $75.00
   e. $80.00

4. The Aikman Company's optimal capital structure calls for 40% debt and 60% common equity. The interest rate on its debt is a constant 12%; its cost of common equity is 18%; and its federal-plus-state tax rate is 40%. Aikman has the following investment opportunities:

    Project A: Cost = $5 million; IRR = 22%
    Project B: Cost = $5 million; IRR = 14%
    Project C: Cost = $5 million; IRR = 11%

    Aikman expects to have net income of $7 million. If Aikman bases its dividends on the residual policy, what will be its payout ratio?

    a. 22.62%
    b. 14.29%
    c. 31.29%
    d. 25.62%
    e. 18.75%

5. Ridgdill Corporation has net income of $8,000,000 and it has 1,000,000 shares of common stock outstanding. The company's stock currently trades at $30 a share. Ridgdill is considering a plan in which it will use available cash to repurchase 15% of its shares in the open market. The repurchase is expected to have no effect on either net income or the company's P/E ratio. What will be its stock price following the stock repurchase?

    a. $35.29
    b. $32.00
    c. $36.89
    d. $35.15
    e. $31.43

6. Hammond Industries is expecting to pay an annual dividend per share of $1.50 out of annual earnings per share of $4.50. Currently, Hammond's stock is selling for $40 per share. Adhering to the company's target capital structure, the firm has $20 million in assets, of which 45% is funded by debt. Assume that the firm's book value of equity equals its market value. In past years, the firm has earned a return on equity (ROE) of 15%, which is expected to continue this year and into the foreseeable future. On the basis of the above information, what long-run growth rate can the firm be expected to maintain? [Hint: g = Retention rate × ROE.]

    a. 5.0%
    b. 6.5%
    c. 7.3%
    d. 8.2%
    e. 10.0%

7. Hammond Industries is expecting to pay an annual dividend per share of $1.50 out of annual earnings per share of $4.50. Currently, Hammond's stock is selling for $40 per share. Adhering to the company's target capital structure, the firm has $20 million in assets, of which 45% is funded by debt. Assume that the firm's book value of equity equals its market value. In past years, the firm has earned a return on equity (ROE) of 15%, which is expected to continue this year and into the foreseeable future. What is the stock's required return?

    a. 10.00%
    b. 11.50%
    c. 12.60%
    d. 13.75%
    e. 14.00%

8. Hammond Industries is expecting to pay an annual dividend per share of $1.50 out of annual earnings per share of $4.50. Currently, Hammond's stock is selling for $40 per share. Adhering to the company's target capital structure, the firm has $20 million in assets, of which 45% is funded by debt. Assume that the firm's book value of equity equals its market value. In past years, the firm has earned a return on equity (ROE) of 15%, which is expected to continue this year and into the foreseeable future.

    If the firm were to change its dividend policy and pay an annual dividend of $3.00 per share, financial analysts predict that the change in policy will have no effect upon the firm's stock price or ROE. Therefore, what must be the firm's new expected long-run growth rate and required return?

    a. 4%; 10.7%
    b. 5%; 12.5%
    c. 5%; 13.0%
    d. 9%; 14.2%
    e. 5%; 14.8%

9. Hammond Industries is expecting to pay an annual dividend per share of $1.50 out of annual earnings per share of $4.50. Currently, Hammond's stock is selling for $40 per share. Adhering to the company's target capital structure, the firm has $20 million in assets, of which 45% is funded by debt. Assume that the firm's book value of equity equals its market value. In past years, the firm has earned a return on equity (ROE) of 15%, which is expected to continue this year and into the foreseeable future.

    Suppose the firm has decided to proceed with its plan of disbursing $1.50 per share to shareholders, but the firm intends to do so in the form of a stock dividend rather than a cash dividend. The firm will allot new shares based on the current stock price of $40. In other words, for every $40 in dividends due to shareholders, a share of stock will be issued. How large will the stock dividend be relative to the firm's current market capitalization? [Hint: Remember market capitalization = $P_0 \times$ number of shares outstanding.]

    a. 3.75%
    b. 4.00%
    c. 2.50%
    d. 4.50%
    e. 5.00%

10. Hammond Industries is expecting to pay an annual dividend per share of $1.50 out of annual earnings per share of $4.50. Currently, Hammond's stock is selling for $40 per share. Adhering to the company's target capital structure, the firm has $20 million in assets, of which 45% is funded by debt. Assume that the firm's book value of equity equals its market value. In past years, the firm has earned a return on equity (ROE) of 15%, which is expected to continue this year and into the foreseeable future.

Suppose the firm has decided to proceed with its plan of disbursing $1.50 per share to shareholders, but the firm intends to do so in the form of a stock dividend rather than a cash dividend. The firm will allot new shares based on the current stock price of $40. In other words, for every $40 in dividends due to shareholders, a share of stock will be issued.

If this plan is implemented, how many new shares of stock will be issued, and by how much will the company's earnings per share be diluted?

   a. 13,750; $0.10
   b. 15,000; $0.12
   c. 13,750; $0.16
   d. 15,000; $0.16
   e. 17,500; $0.25

Answers

Definitional Questions

1. dividend
2. dividends; capital
3. capital; income
4. price; information
5. volatile; fluctuating
6. holder-of-record
7. ex-dividend; holder-of-record
8. payment
9. reinvestment
10. par
11. clientele
12. treasury
13. Dividend
14. payout; dividends
15. residual
16. enrollment
17. repurchases
18. bird-in-the-hand
19. optimal; policy
20. irrelevance
21. dividend
22. investment; structure; availability; cost
23. capital gains
24. signal
25. stable (dependable)

Conceptual Questions

1. b. A dividend increase could be perceived by investors as signifying poor investment opportunities and hence lower growth in future earnings, thus reducing g in the DCF model. The net effect on stock price is uncertain.

2. e. A stock split will affect the par value and number of shares outstanding. However, no dollar values will be affected.

3. c. This is the Gordon-Lintner hypothesis. If investors view dividends as being less risky than potential capital gains, then the cost of equity is inversely related to the payout ratio.

4. b. The proponents of the "bird-in-the-hand" theory were Gordon and Lintner and empirical tests have not proven any of the dividend theories. The dividend irrelevance theory states that the value of the firm depends only on the income produced by its assets. Both the clientele effect and the signaling hypothesis have a bearing on the optimal dividend policy. Recent tax law changes, which lowered the tax rate on dividends to that on capital gains, have resulted in many companies increasing their dividend payments.

5. b. The residual dividend model calls for the determination of the optimal capital budget and then the dividend is established as a residual of net income minus the amount of retained earnings necessary for the capital budget. A constant payout policy would lead to uncertainty of dividends due to fluctuating earnings. If a stock is bought after the ex-dividend date the dividend remains with the seller of the stock.

6. e. The residual dividend model is more appropriate for setting a firm's long-run target payout ratio than its annual payout ratio; the other statements are simply false.

7. d. Statement d is correct; the other statements are simply false.

Solutions

Problems

1. c. The $1,200,000 capital budget will be financed using 40% debt and 60% equity. Therefore, the equity requirement will be $0.6(\$1,200,000) = \$720,000$. Since the expected net income is $1,000,000, $280,000 will be available for dividends. Thus, the payout ratio is expected to be $280,000/\$1,000,000 = 0.28 = 28\%$.

2. c. Of the $800,000 in net income, $0.475(\$800,000) = \$380,000$ was paid out as dividends. Thus, $420,000 was retained in the firm for investment. This is the equity portion of the total capital budget, or 70% of the total capital budget. Therefore, the total capital budget was $420,000/0.7 = \$600,000$.

3. d. $P_0 = \$100$; Split = 4 for 3; New $P_0 = ?$

$$P_{0\ New} = \frac{\$100}{4/3} = \$75.00$$

4. b. WACC = 0.4(12%)(0.6) + 0.6(18%) = 13.68%

   We see that the capital budget should be $10 million, since only Projects A and B have IRRs > WACC. We know that 60% of the $10 million should be equity. Therefore, the company should pay dividends of:

   Dividends = NI – Needed equity = $7,000,000 – $6,000,000 = $1,000,000

   Payout ratio = $1,000,000/$7,000,000 = 0.1429 = 14.29%

5. a. NI = $8,000,000; Shares = 1,000,000; P_0 = $30; Repurchase = 15%; New P_0 = ?

   Repurchase = 0.15 × 1,000,000 = 150,000 shares

   Repurchase amount = 150,000 × $30.00 = $4,500,000

   $$EPS_{Old} = \frac{NI}{Shares} = \frac{\$8,000,000}{1,000,000} = \$8.00$$

   $$P/E = \frac{\$30}{\$8} = 3.75\times$$

   $$EPS_{New} = \frac{\$8,000,000}{1,000,000 - 150,000} = \frac{\$8,000,000}{850,000} = \$9.41$$

   $Price_{New} = EPS_{New} \times P/E = \$9.41 \times 3.75 = \$35.29$

6. e. Before finding the long-run growth rate, the dividend payout ratio must be determined.

   Dividend payout ratio = DPS/EPS = $1.50/$4.50 = 0.3333

   The firm's long-run growth rate can be found by multiplying the portion of a firm's earnings that are retained times the firm's return on equity.

   g = ROE × Retention ratio
     = (Net income/Equity capital) × (1 – Dividend payout ratio)
     = 15% × (1 – 0.3333) = 10%

7. d. Before finding the long-run growth rate, the dividend payout ratio must be determined.

   Dividend payout ratio = DPS/EPS = $1.50/$4.50 = 0.3333

   The firm's long-run growth rate can be found by multiplying the portion of a firm's earnings that are retained times the firm's return on equity.

g = ROE × Retention ratio
 = (Net income/Equity capital) × (1 − Dividend payout ratio)
 = 15% × (1 − 0.3333) = 10%

The required return can be calculated using the DCF approach.

r_s = D_1/P_0 + g
 = $1.50/$40.00 + 0.10
 = 0.1375 or 13.75%

8. b. The new payout ratio can be calculated as:

$3.00/$4.50 = 0.6667

The new long-run growth rate can now be calculated as:

g = ROE × (1 − Dividend payout ratio)
 = 15% × (1 − 0.6667) = 5%

The firm's required return would be:

r_s = D_1/P_0 + g
 = $3.00/$40.00 + 0.05
 = 0.125 or 12.5%

9. a. The firm's original plan was to issue a dividend equal to $1.50 per share, which equates to a total dividend of $1.50 times the number of shares outstanding. So, first the number of shares outstanding must be determined from the EPS.

Amount of equity capital = Total assets × Equity ratio
 = $20 million × 0.55 = $11 million

Net income = Equity × ROE = $11 million × 0.15 = $1.65 million

EPS = Net income/Number of shares
$4.50 = $1.65 million/Number of shares
Number of shares = 366,667

With 366,667 shares outstanding, the total dividend that would be paid would be $1.50 × 366,667 shares = $550,000. The firm's current market capitalization is $14,666,680, determined by 366,667 shares at $40 per share. If the stock dividend is implemented, it shall account for 3.75% of the firm's current market capitalization ($550,000/$14,666,680 = 0.0375).

10. c.   The firm's original plan was to issue a dividend equal to $1.50 per share, which equates to a total dividend of $1.50 times the number of shares outstanding. So, first the number of shares outstanding must be determined from the EPS.

Amount of equity capital = Total assets × Equity ratio
= $20 million × 0.55 = $11 million

Net income = Equity × ROE = $11 million × 0.15 = $1.65 million .

EPS = Net income/Number of shares
$4.50 = $1.65 million/Number of shares
Number of shares = 366,667

With 366,667 shares outstanding, the total dividend that would be paid would be $1.50 × 366,667 shares = $550,000. The firm's current market capitalization is $14,666,680, determined by 366,667 shares at $40 per share. If the stock dividend is implemented, it shall account for 3.75% of the firm's current market capitalization ($550,000/$14,666,680 = 0.0375).

If the total amount of value to be distributed to shareholders is 366,667 × $1.50 = $550,000, at a price of $40 per share, then the number of new shares issued is calculated as:

Number of new shares = Dividend value/Price per share
= $550,000/$40
= 13,750 shares

The stock dividend will leave the firm's net income unchanged, therefore the firm's new EPS is its net income divided by the new total number of shares outstanding.

New EPS = Net income/(Old shares outstanding + New shares outstanding)
= $1,650,000/(366,667 + 13,750)
= $4.3373 ≈ $4.34

The dilution of earnings per share is the difference between old EPS and new EPS.

Dilution of EPS = Old EPS − New EPS
= $4.50 − $4.34
= $0.16 per share

15

WORKING CAPITAL MANAGEMENT

Learning Objectives

1. Explain how different amounts of current assets and current liabilities affect firms' profitability and thus their stock prices.

2. Discuss how the cash conversion cycle is determined, how the cash budget is constructed, and how each is used in working capital management.

3. Explain how companies decide on the proper amount of each current asset—cash, marketable securities, accounts receivable, and inventory.

4. Discuss how companies set their credit policies and explain the effect of credit policy on sales and profits.

5. Describe how the costs of trade credit, bank loans, and commercial paper are determined, and how that information impacts decisions for financing working capital.

6. Explain how companies use security to lower their costs of short-term credit.

Overview

A large amount of a typical financial manager's time is devoted to working capital management, and many students' first jobs will involve working capital. This is particularly true of smaller businesses, where most new jobs are being created.

Working capital policy involves two basic questions: (1) What is the optimal amount of each type of current asset for the firm to carry and (2) how should current asset holdings be financed?

Sound working capital management goes beyond finance. Indeed, most of the ideas for improving working capital management often stem from other disciplines.

Outline

I. **It is useful to begin by reviewing some basic definitions and concepts.**

    A. *Working capital* is defined as current assets.

    B. *Net working capital* is defined as current assets minus current liabilities.

    C. *Net operating working capital* is defined as current assets minus the difference between current liabilities and notes payable.

II. **A firm's current asset levels rise and fall with business cycles and seasonal trends. At the peak of such cycles, businesses carry their maximum amounts of current assets.**

    A. There are three alternative policies regarding the total amount of current assets carried. Each policy differs with regard to the amount of current assets carried to support any given level of sales, hence in the turnover of those assets.

        1. A *relaxed current asset policy* is one in which relatively large amounts of cash, marketable securities, and inventories are carried, and a liberal credit policy results in a high level of receivables.

        2. A *restricted current asset policy* is one in which holdings of cash, marketable securities, inventories, and receivables are constrained. Current assets are turned over more frequently, so each dollar of current assets is forced to "work harder."

        3. A moderate current asset policy lies between the relaxed and restricted policies.

        4. Generally, the decision on the current assets level involves a risk/return tradeoff.

            a. The relaxed policy minimizes risk, but it also has the lowest expected return (a low total assets turnover ratio).

            b. The restricted policy offers the highest expected return (a high total assets turnover ratio) coupled with the highest risk.

            c. The moderate policy falls in between the two extremes in terms of expected risk and return.

            d. The optimal strategy is the one that maximizes the firm's long-run earnings and the stock's intrinsic value.

        5. Changing technologies can lead to changes in the optimal current asset policy.

III. **Investments in current assets must be financed. The primary sources of funds include bank loans, credit from suppliers, accrued liabilities, long-term debt, preferred stock, and common equity.**

    A. Current assets rarely drop to zero, and this fact has led to the development of the idea of *permanent current assets*.

        1. These are the current assets needed at the low point of the business cycle.

    B. *Temporary current assets* are those that fluctuate with seasonal or cyclical variations in sales.

    C. The manner in which current assets are financed is called the firm's *current asset financing policy*.

        1. The *maturity matching, or "self-liquidating," approach* matches asset and liability maturities.

a. Defined as a moderate current asset financing policy, this would use permanent financing for permanent assets (permanent current assets and fixed assets), and use short-term financing to cover seasonal and/or cyclical temporary assets (fluctuating current assets).

b. This strategy minimizes the risk that the firm will be unable to pay off its maturing obligations.

c. Two factors prevent exact maturity matching: (1) there is uncertainty about the lives of assets, and (2) some common equity must be used, and common equity has no maturity.

2. The *aggressive approach* is used by a firm that finances all of its fixed assets with long-term capital but part of its permanent current assets with short-term, nonspontaneous credit.

a. There can be different degrees of aggressiveness.

b. The reason for adopting the aggressive policy is to take advantage of the fact that the yield curve is generally upward sloping, hence short-term rates are generally lower than long-term rates.

c. A strategy of financing long-term assets with short-term debt is really quite risky due to potential problems with loan renewals.

3. A *conservative approach* would be to use permanent capital to meet some of the cyclical demand, and then hold the temporary surpluses as marketable securities at the trough of the cycle (storing liquidity).

a. Here, the amount of permanent financing exceeds permanent assets.

b. The firm uses a small amount of short-term, nonspontaneous credit to meet its peak requirements, but it also meets a part of its seasonal needs by storing liquidity in the form of marketable securities.

D. The three possible financing policies are distinguished by the relative amounts of short-term debt used under each policy.

E. The cost of short-term debt is generally lower than that of long-term debt; however, short-term debt has disadvantages compared to long-term debt.

1. Short-term debt is riskier to the borrowing firm.

a. If a firm borrows on a long-term basis, its interest costs will be relatively stable over time, but if it uses short-term credit, its interest expense can fluctuate widely.

b. If a firm borrows heavily on a short-term basis, a temporary recession may adversely affect its financial ratios and render it unable to repay this debt. If the borrower's financial position is weak, the lender may not renew the loan, which could force the borrower into bankruptcy.

F. Short-term debt does have some advantages when compared to long-term debt.

1. Short-term loans can generally be negotiated much faster than long-term loans.

2. Short-term debt may offer greater flexibility than long-term debt.

3. Short-term credit agreements generally have fewer restrictions than long-term loans.

G. All things considered, it is not possible to state that either long-term or short-term financing is better than the other.

1. The firm's specific conditions will affect the choice, as will the preferences of managers.

2. Optimistic and/or aggressive managers will probably lean more toward short-term credit to gain an interest cost advantage, while more conservative managers will lean toward long-term financing to avoid potential loan renewal problems.

IV. **Firms typically follow a cycle in which they purchase inventory, sell goods on credit, and then collect accounts receivable. This cycle is referred to as the cash conversion cycle, and it highlights the strengths and weaknesses of the company's working capital policy. It focuses on the length of time between when the company makes payments and when it receives cash inflows.**

A. Sound working capital policy is designed to minimize the time between cash expenditures on materials and the collection of cash on sales.

B. The following terms and definitions are used:

1. *Inventory conversion period* is the average time required to convert raw materials into finished goods and then to sell these goods.

$$\text{Inventory conversion period} = \frac{\text{Inventory}}{\text{Cost of goods sold per day}}$$

2. *Average collection period (ACP)* is the average length of time required to convert the firm's receivables into cash, that is, to collect cash following a sale. It is also called the days sales outstanding (DSO).

$$\text{Average collection period} = \text{DSO} = \frac{\text{Receivables}}{\text{Sales/365}}$$

3. *Payables deferral period* is the average length of time between the purchase of materials and labor and the payment of cash for them.

$$\text{Payables deferral period} = \frac{\text{Payables}}{\text{Cost of goods sold/365}}$$

4. The *cash conversion cycle* is the average length of time a dollar is tied up in current assets.

$$\begin{array}{c} \text{Inventory} \\ \text{conversion} \\ \text{period} \end{array} + \begin{array}{c} \text{Average} \\ \text{collection} \\ \text{period} \end{array} - \begin{array}{c} \text{Payables} \\ \text{deferral} \\ \text{period} \end{array} = \begin{array}{c} \text{Cash} \\ \text{conversion} \\ \text{cycle} \end{array}$$

C. The firm's goal should be to shorten its cash conversion cycle as much as possible without hurting operations because this will lower interest charges, increase profits, and increase stock price performance.

1. The cash conversion cycle can be shortened (1) by reducing the inventory conversion period by processing and selling goods more quickly, (2) by reducing the receivables collection period by speeding up collections, or (3) by lengthening the payables deferral period by slowing down the firm's own payments.

2. Some firms are able to operate with negative working capital, which means that working capital provides cash, not uses it.

D. Results of a recent study of over 2,900 companies during a recent 20-year period found that shortening the cash conversion cycle results in higher profits and better stock price performance. This study demonstrates that good working capital management is important.

V.   Firms need to forecast their cash flows, and the primary forecasting tool is the cash budget. A cash budget projects cash inflows and outflows over some specified period of time.

A. The basis for a cash budget is the sales forecast and a projection when actual collections will occur. A forecast of disbursements for materials purchases, labor, taxes, and other expenses is made.

B. Cash budgets can be created for any interval, but firms typically use a monthly cash budget for the coming year, a weekly budget for the coming month, and a daily budget for the coming week, or something similar.

   1. The monthly cash budgets are used for planning purposes, and the daily or weekly budgets for actual cash control.

C. A typical cash budget consists of several sections.

   1. The *collections section* summarizes the firm's cash collections based on its collection history.

   2. The *payments section* summarizes the firm's payments for materials, wages, taxes, and the like.

   3. The *net cash flow (NCF) section* lays out the cash inflows and outflows, and the cumulative NCF which adds the prior month's NCF to the current month's NCF.

   4. The *cash surplus or loan requirement section* summarizes the firm's cumulative need for loans and cumulative surplus cash based on its target cash balance.

      a. The *target cash balance* is the desired cash balance that a firm plans to maintain in order to conduct business.

D. If the firm's inflows and outflows are not uniform over the budget interval, say monthly, the cash budget will overstate or understate the firm's cash needs.

E. Spreadsheet programs are particularly well suited for constructing and analyzing cash budgets, especially with respect to the sensitivity of cash flows to changes in sales, the target cash balance, customers' payments, and so forth.

   1. The effects of changes in credit policy and inventory management could be examined through the cash budget.

VI.   Cash as reported on balance sheets generally includes currency, bank demand deposits, and short-term securities (which are also called cash equivalents).

A. A firm's marketable security holdings can be divided into two categories.

   1. *Operating short-term securities* are held primarily to provide liquidity and are bought and sold as needed to provide funds for operations.

   2. *Other short-term securities* are holdings in excess of the amount needed to support normal operations.

B. The importance of currency has decreased over time due to the rise of credit cards, debit cards, and other payments mechanisms.

      1.   Each firm decides its own optimal level, but currency generally represents a small part of total cash holdings.

   C. Demand (checking) deposits are used for transactions and are far more important than currency for most businesses. Commercial demand deposits typically earn no interest, so firms try to minimize their holdings while still ensuring they are able to pay suppliers promptly, take trade discounts, and take advantage of bargain purchases.

      1.   The following techniques are used to optimize demand deposit holdings:

         a.   Hold marketable securities rather than demand deposits to provide liquidity.

         b.   Borrow on short notice.

         c.   Forecast payments and receipts better.

         d.   Speed up payments through the use of lockboxes.

         e.   Use credit cards, debit cards, wire transfers, and direct deposits.

         f.   Synchronize cash flows so as to reduce the firm's need for cash balances.

   D. Given the size and importance of marketable security holdings, how they are managed can have a significant effect on profits. There must also be coordination between the management of demand deposits and marketable securities.

      1.   There is a trade-off between risk and return.

         a.   The firm wants to earn high returns, but since marketable securities are held primarily to provide liquidity, treasurers want to hold securities that can be sold very quickly and at a known price.

         b.   This means high-quality, short-term instruments. Treasury bills, most commercial paper, bank certificates of deposit, and money market funds are suitable holdings.

      2.   A firm's relationship with its bank, especially its ability to borrow on short notice, has a significant effect on its need for demand deposits and marketable securities.

         a.   If a company has a firmly committed line of credit under which it can obtain funds with a simple phone call, it won't need much in the way of liquid reserves.

      3.   Larger corporations shop for securities all around the world, buying wherever risk-adjusted rates are highest.

         a.   This "shopping" tends to equalize worldwide rates.

VII.   Inventories, which may be classified as supplies, raw materials, work-in-process, and finished goods, is an essential part of virtually all business operations.

   A. Optimal inventory levels depend upon sales, so sales must be forecasted before target inventory levels can be established.

   B. Errors in the establishment of inventory levels quickly lead either to lost sales or to excessive carrying costs, so inventory management is quite important.

   C. Inventory management is under the operational control of production managers and marketing people rather than financial managers. However, it is discussed in Web Appendix 15A.

      1.   Financial managers are still involved in many ways.

     a. Capital budgeting analysis is involved in selecting computers used to manage inventories.

     b. The financial manager must raise the capital needed to acquire the additional inventory.

     c. The financial manager is responsible for identifying any area of weakness that affects the firm's overall profitability, using ratios and other procedures for comparing the firm to its benchmark companies. Therefore, the CFO will compare the firm's inventory-to-sales ratio with those of its benchmarks to see if things look reasonable.

VIII. Carrying receivables has both direct and indirect costs, but it also has an important benefit—granting credit will increase sales.

A. *Accounts receivable* are created when a firm sells goods or performs services on credit rather than on a cash basis. When cash is received, accounts receivable are reduced by the same amount.

B. The firm's credit policy is the primary determinant of accounts receivable. The firm's credit policy consists of four variables.

    1. The *credit period* is the length of time buyers are given to pay for their purchases.

     a. Increasing the credit period often stimulates sales, but there is a cost involved in carrying the increased receivables.

     b. A firm's regular *credit terms* include the credit period and any discount offered.

    2. Discounts attract customers and encourage early payment but reduce the dollar amount received on each discount sale.

     a. Discounts amount to a price reduction, and lower prices stimulate sales.

     b. Offering discounts should cause a reduction in the days sales outstanding, because some existing customers will pay more promptly in order to receive the discount.

    3. *Credit standards* refer to the financial strength and creditworthiness a customer must exhibit to qualify for credit.

     a. Setting credit standards requires a measurement of *credit quality*, which is defined in terms of the probability of a customer's default.

     b. Credit evaluation is a well-established practice, and a good credit manager can make reasonably accurate judgments of the probability of default by different classes of customers.

     c. Computerized information systems can assist in making better credit decisions, but in the final analysis, most credit decisions are really exercises in informed judgment.

    4. *Collection policy* refers to the procedures the firm follows to collect past-due accounts.

     a. The collection process can be expensive in terms of both out-of-pocket expenditures and lost goodwill, but at least some firmness is needed to prevent an undue lengthening of the collection period and to minimize outright losses.

     b. A balance must be struck between the costs and benefits of different collection policies.

C. Credit policy is important for three main reasons.

    1. It has a major effect on sales.

2. It influences the amount of funds tied up in receivables.

3. It affects bad debt losses.

D. *Credit scores,* numerical scores that are based on a statistical analysis, indicate the likelihood that a person or business will pay on time.

E. The total amount of accounts receivable outstanding at any given time is determined by the volume of credit sales and the average length of time between sales and collections. Receivables must be actively managed to ensure that the firm's receivables policy is effective.

1. The *days sales outstanding (DSO),* sometimes called the average collection period (ACP), measures the average length of time it takes a firm's customers to pay off their credit purchases.

   a. The DSO is calculated by dividing the receivables balance by average daily credit sales.

   b. The DSO can be compared with the industry average and the firm's own credit terms to get an indication of how well customers are adhering to the terms prescribed and how customers' payments, on average, compare with the industry average.

IX. **Accounts payable, or trade credit, is the largest single category of short-term debt. Trade credit is a "spontaneous" source of funds because it arises from ordinary business transactions. Most firms make purchases on credit, recording the debt as an account payable.**

A. Lengthening the credit period, as well as expanding sales and purchases, generates additional financing.

B. The cost of trade credit is made up of discounts lost by not paying invoices within the discount period.

1. For example, if credit terms are 2/10, net 30, the cost of 20 additional days' credit is 2% of the dollar value of the purchases made.

2. The following equation may be used to calculate the nominal percentage cost, on an annual basis, of not taking discounts:

$$\frac{\text{Nominal annual}}{\text{percentage cost}} = \frac{\text{Discount \%}}{100 - \text{Discount \%}} \times \frac{365 \text{ days}}{\text{Days credit is outstanding} - \text{Discount period}}$$

3. The nominal annual cost formula does not consider compounding so, in effective annual interest terms, the rate is even higher. Note that the first term on the right-hand side of the nominal cost equation is the periodic cost, and the second term is the number of periods per year.

C. Trade credit can be divided into two components: *Free trade credit* is that credit received during the discount period. *Costly trade credit* is obtained by foregoing discounts. This costly component should be used only when it is less expensive than funds obtained from other sources.

1. Financial managers should always use the free component, but they should use the costly component only after analyzing the cost of this capital to make sure that it is less than the cost of funds that could be obtained from other sources.

2. The cost of not taking discounts is relatively expensive, so stronger firms will avoid using it.

3. Competitive conditions may permit firms to do better than the stated credit terms by taking discounts beyond the discount period or by deliberately paying late.

    a. Such practices, called *stretching accounts payable*, reduce the cost of trade credit, but they also result in poor relationships with suppliers.

X.   **Bank loans appear on a firm's balance sheet as notes payable and represent another important source of short-term financing.**

A. Bank loans are not generated spontaneously but must be negotiated and renewed on a regular basis.

1. When a firm obtains a bank loan, a *promissory note* is signed. It is a document specifying the terms and conditions of a loan including the amount borrowed, the interest rate, the repayment schedule, any collateral offered as security, loan guarantees, and other terms and conditions to which the bank and the borrower have agreed.

2. When the note is signed, the bank credits the borrower's checking account with the funds, so on the borrower's balance sheet both cash and notes payable increase.

B. A *line of credit* is an informal agreement between a bank and a borrower indicating the maximum credit the bank will extend to the borrower during a designated period.

1. Such a line of credit is informal and nonbinding.

C. A *revolving credit agreement* is a formal line of credit often used by large firms.

1. Normally, the borrower will pay the bank a *commitment fee* to compensate the bank for guaranteeing that the funds will be available.

    a. This fee is paid in addition to the regular interest charge on funds actually borrowed.

2. As a general rule, the interest rate on "revolvers" is pegged to the prime rate, the T-bill rate, or some other market rate, so the cost of the loan varies over time as interest rates change.

3. Note that a revolving credit agreement is very similar to an informal line of credit, but with an important difference: The bank has a *legal obligation* to honor a revolving credit agreement, and for this it receives a commitment fee.

    a. Neither the legal obligation nor the fee exists under the informal line of credit.

D. The interest cost of loans will vary for different types of borrowers and for all borrowers over time. Rates charged will vary depending on economic conditions, the risk of the borrower, and the size of the loan. If a firm can qualify as a "prime credit" because of its size and financial strength, it can borrow at the *prime rate*, a published interest rate charged by commercial banks to large, strong borrowers. Interest charges on bank loans can be calculated in one of several ways listed below.

1. *Regular, or simple, interest.* The nominal interest rate is divided by the number of days in the year to calculate the rate per day. This rate is then multiplied by the actual number of days during the specific payment period, and then this product is multiplied by the amount of the loan.

$$\text{Simple interest rate per day} = \frac{\text{Nominal rate}}{\text{Days in year}}$$

$$\text{Interest charge for period} = (\text{Days in period})(\text{Rate per day})(\text{Amount of loan})$$

   a. The effective rate on the loan depends on how frequently interest must be paid—the more frequently, the higher the effective rate. If interest is paid once a year, the nominal rate also will be the effective rate.

2. *Installment loans: add-on interest.* Interest charges are calculated and then added on to the amount received to determine the loan's face value, which is paid off in equal installments.

   a. The borrower has use of the full amount of the funds received only until the first installment is paid.

   b. The approximate annual rate is double the stated rate, because the average amount of the loan outstanding is only about half the face amount borrowed.

$$\text{Approximate annual rate}_{\text{Add-on}} = \frac{\text{Interest paid}}{(\text{Amount received})/2}$$

   c. To determine the effective rate of an add-on loan, lay out all the cash flows on a time line and solve for the interest rate.

   d. The payments are calculated as the total amount to be repaid, which consists of principal plus the total interest divided by the number of periods for which the loan is outstanding.

3. *Annual percentage rate (APR)* is a rate reported by banks and other lenders on loans when the effective rate exceeds the nominal rate of interest.

$$\text{APR rate} = (\text{Periods per year})(\text{Rate per period})$$

4. Other features of bank financing such as discount interest and compensating balances are discussed in Web Appendix 15B.

XI. **Commercial paper, another source of short-term credit, is an unsecured promissory note.**

A. It is generally sold to other business firms, to insurance companies, to banks, and to money market mutual funds.

B. Only large, financially strong firms are able to tap the commercial paper market.

C. It is usually issued in denominations of $100,000 or more and has an interest rate somewhat below the prime rate.

D. A large majority of the commercial paper outstanding has been issued by financial institutions.

XII. **One source of short-term funds is accrued wages and taxes, which increase and decrease spontaneously as a firm's operations expand and contract.**

A. This type of debt is "free" in the sense that no interest is paid on funds raised through accrued liabilities.

B. A firm cannot ordinarily control its accrued liabilities.

1. The timing of wage payments is set by economic forces and industry custom, while tax payment dates are established by law.

2. Firms use all the accruals they can, but they have little control over their levels.

XIII. **For a strong firm, borrowing on an unsecured basis is generally cheaper and simpler than on a secured loan basis because of the administrative costs associated with the use of security.**

    A. However, firms often find that they can borrow only if they put up some type of collateral to protect the lender, or that by using security they can borrow at a lower rate.

        1. Most secured short-term business borrowing involves the use of accounts receivable and inventories as collateral.

Self-Test

Definitional Questions

1. Current assets are also referred to as _____ capital.

2. _____ working capital is defined as _____ assets minus current liabilities.

3. Inventory is usually classified as _____, raw _____, _____-____-_____, and _____ goods.

4. Accounts _____ are created when goods are sold or services are performed on credit.

5. A firm's outstanding accounts receivable will be determined by the _____ of credit sales and the length of time between _____ and _____.

6. Sales volume and the collection period will be affected by a firm's _____ policy.

7. Credit terms generally specify the _____ for which credit is granted and any cash _____ that is offered for early payment.

8. _____ policy refers to the manner in which a firm tries to obtain payment from past-due accounts.

9. The most comprehensive picture of a firm's liquidity is obtained by examining its _____ budget, which forecasts a firm's cash inflows and outflows.

10. A(n) _____ current asset policy is one in which relatively large amounts of cash, marketable securities, and inventories are carried, and sales are stimulated by the use of a credit policy that provides liberal financing to customers and a corresponding high level of receivables.

11. A(n) _____ current asset policy is one in which holdings of cash, securities, inventories, and receivables are minimized.

12. The _____ cash balance is the desired cash balance that a firm plans to maintain in order to conduct business.

13. Credit _____ is defined in terms of the probability of a customer's default.

14. In the maturity matching approach to working capital financing, permanent assets should be financed with _____ or _____-_____ capital, while _____ assets should be financed with short-term credit.

15. Some firms use short-term financing to finance permanent assets. This approach maximizes _____ return, but also has the _____ risk.

16. Short-term borrowing provides more _____ for firms that are uncertain about their _____ borrowing needs.

17. Short-term borrowing will be less expensive than borrowing long-term if the yield curve is _____ sloping.

18. Short-term interest rates fluctuate _____ than long-term rates.

19. _____ wages and taxes are a common source of short-term credit. However, most firms have little control over the _____ of these accounts.

20. Accounts payable, or _____ credit, is the largest single source of short-term credit for most businesses.

21. Trade credit is a(n) _____ source of funds in the sense that it automatically increases when sales increase.

22. Trade credit can be divided into two components: _____ trade credit and _____ trade credit.

23. Free trade credit is that credit received during the _____ period.

24. _____ trade credit should only be used when the cost of the trade credit is less than the cost of alternative sources.

25. The instrument signed when bank credit is obtained is called a(n) _____ note.

26. A(n) _____ loan is one in which collateral such as _____ or _____ have been pledged in support of the loan.

27. A(n) _____ of credit is an informal agreement between a bank and a borrower as to the maximum loan that will be permitted during a designated period.

28. The fee paid to a bank to secure a revolving credit agreement is known as a(n) _____ fee.

29. With a(n) _____ loan, the average amount of the usable funds during the loan period is equal to approximately _____-_____ of the face amount of the loan.

30. Commercial paper can only be issued by _____, financially strong firms.

31. _____ current assets are those current assets on hand at the low point of a business cycle.

32. Seasonal current assets are defined as _____ current assets.

33. Competitive conditions may permit firms to do better than the stated credit terms by taking discounts beyond the discount period or by simply paying late; such practices are called _____ accounts _____.

34. A(n) _____ credit _____ is a formal line of credit often used by large firms.

35. _____ percentage rate is a rate reported by banks and other lenders on loans when the effective rate exceeds the nominal rate of interest, and it is calculated as the number of periods per year times the rate per period.

36. A(n) _____ approach to financing is used by a firm that finances all of its fixed assets with long-term capital but part of its permanent current assets with short-term, nonspontaneous credit.

37. A(n) _____ approach to financing would be to use permanent capital to meet some of the cyclical demand, and then hold the temporary surpluses as marketable securities at the trough of the cycle.

38. Bank _____ appear on a firm's balance sheet as notes payable and represent another important source of short-term financing.

39. The _____ _____ period is the average time required to convert raw materials into finished goods and then to sell those goods.

40. The _____ _____ _____ is the average length of time a dollar is tied up in current assets. It is the sum of the inventory conversion period and the average collection period less the payables deferral period.

Conceptual Questions

1. A firm changes its credit policy from 2/10, net 30, to 3/10, net 30. The change is to meet competition, so no increase in sales is expected. The firm's average investment in accounts receivable will probably increase as a result of the change.

    a. True
    b. False

2. If a credit policy change increases the firm's accounts receivable, the entire increase must be financed by some source of funds.

    a. True
    b. False

3. The matching of asset and liability maturities is considered desirable because this strategy minimizes interest rate (price) risk.

    a. True
    b. False

4. Accrued liabilities are "free" in the sense that no interest must be paid on these funds.

    a. True
    b. False

5. Which of the following statements is correct?

    a. If you had just been hired as Working Capital Manager for a firm with but one stockholder, and that stockholder told you that she had all the money she could possibly use, hence that her primary operating goal was to avoid even the remotest possibility of bankruptcy, then you should set the firm's working capital financing policy on the basis of the "Maturity Matching, or Self-Liquidating, Approach."
    b. Due to the existence of positive maturity risk premiums, at most times short-term debt carries lower interest rates than long-term debt. Therefore, if a company finances primarily with short-term as opposed to long-term debt, its expected TIE ratio, hence its overall riskiness, will be lower than if it finances with long-term debt. Therefore, the more conservative the firm, the greater its reliance on short-term debt.
    c. If a firm buys on terms of 2/10, net 30, and pays on the 30th day, then its accounts payable may be thought of as consisting of some "free" and some "costly" trade credit. Since the percentage cost of the costly trade credit is lowered if the payment period is reduced, the firm should try to pay earlier than on Day 30, say on Day 25.
    d. Suppose a firm buys on terms of 2/10, net 30, but it normally pays on Day 60. Disregarding any "image" effects, it should, if it can borrow from the bank at an effective rate of 14%, take out a bank loan and start taking discounts.
    e. Each of the above statements is false.

Problems

1. Simmons Brick Company sells on terms of 3/10, net 30. Gross sales for the year are $1,216,667 and the collections department estimates that 30% of the customers pay on the tenth day and take discounts; 40% pay on the thirtieth day; and the remaining 30% pay, on average, 40 days after the purchase. What is the days sales outstanding?

   a. 10 days
   b. 13 days
   c. 20 days
   d. 27 days
   e. 40 days

2. Simmons Brick Company sells on terms of 3/10, net 30. Gross sales for the year are $1,216,667 and the collections department estimates that 30% of the customers pay on the tenth day and take discounts; 40% pay on the thirtieth day; and the remaining 30% pay, on average, 40 days after the purchase. What is the current receivables balance?

   a. $60,000
   b. $70,000
   c. $75,000
   d. $80,000
   e. $90,000

3. Simmons Brick Company sells on terms of 3/10, net 30. Gross sales for the year are $1,216,667 and the collections department estimates that 30% of the customers pay on the tenth day and take discounts; 40% pay on the thirtieth day; and the remaining 30% pay, on average, 40 days after the purchase. What would be the new receivables balance if Simmons toughened up on its collection policy, with the result that all nondiscount customers paid on the thirtieth day?

   a. $60,000
   b. $70,000
   c. $75,000
   d. $80,000
   e. $90,000

4. Haberdash Inc. last year reported sales of $12 million and an inventory turnover ratio of 3. The company is now adopting a just-in-time inventory system. If the new system is able to reduce the firm's inventory level and increase the firm's inventory turnover ratio to 7.5, while maintaining the same level of sales, how much cash will be freed up?

   a. $2,400,000
   b. $1,600,000
   c. $4,000,000
   d. $3,000,000
   e. $5,250,000

5. Tauscher Textiles Corporation has an inventory conversion period of 45 days, a receivables collection period of 36 days, and a payables deferral period of 35 days. What is the length of the firm's cash conversion cycle?

    a.   35 days
    b.   46 days
    c.   52 days
    d.   81 days
    e.   117 days

6. Tauscher Textiles Corporation has an inventory conversion period of 45 days, a receivables collection period of 36 days, and a payables deferral period of 35 days. Tauscher's sales are $4,309,028 and all sales are on credit. In addition, its cost of goods sold is 75% of sales. What is the firm's investment in accounts receivable?

    a. $325,000
    b. $375,000
    c. $425,000
    d. $500,000
    e. $575,000

7. Tauscher Textiles Corporation has an inventory conversion period of 45 days, a receivables collection period of 36 days, and a payables deferral period of 35 days. Tauscher's sales are $4,309,028 and all sales are on credit. In addition, its cost of goods sold is 75% of sales. How much inventory is on the firm's balance sheet?

    a. $398,438
    b. $402,175
    c. $458,679
    d. $500,301
    e. $525,089

8. Tauscher Textiles Corporation has an inventory conversion period of 45 days, a receivables collection period of 36 days, and a payables deferral period of 35 days. Tauscher's sales are $4,309,028 and all sales are on credit. In addition, its cost of goods sold is 75% of sales. How many times per year does Tauscher turn over its inventory?

    a.   3.14
    b.   5.35
    c.   7.50
    d.   10.81
    e.   11.25

9. Ridgdill Industries currently has $51,500 in cash, $60,000 in accounts receivable, $63,750 in inventories, $12,500 in accrued liabilities, and $90,000 in accounts payable on its balance sheet. The firm's production manager has determined that cost of goods sold accounts for 75% of the sales revenue produced. Furthermore, the firm has determined that the length of the firm's cash conversion cycle is 20 days. What is Ridgdill's annual sales?

    a. $400,000
    b. $428,333
    c. $456,250
    d. $478,125
    e. $500,000

10. Ridgdill Industries currently has $51,500 in cash, $60,000 in accounts receivable, $63,750 in inventories, $12,500 in accrued liabilities, and $90,000 in accounts payable on its balance sheet. The firm's production manager has determined that cost of goods sold account for 75% of the sales revenue produced. Furthermore, the firm has determined that the length of the firm's cash conversion cycle is 20 days.

The firm's production manager has determined that through negotiation with its suppliers, the firm could reduce the ratio of the cost of goods sold to sales down to 65%, and thus reduce its cash conversion cycle time. However, the firm would then take this opportunity to use cash to reduce its accounts payable. The firm realizes that reducing accounts payable increases the cash conversion cycle time, but it is more concerned with pleasing its creditors, who are unhappy with the firm's liquidity position. None of these changes is expected to have any impact upon sales. If the firm reduces accounts payable enough to improve the current ratio to 2.25, what would be the length of the firm's cash conversion cycle?

    a. 35.52
    b. 45.98
    c. 30.00
    d. 28.66
    e. 24.33

11. A firm buys on terms of 2/10, net 30, but generally does not pay until 40 days after the invoice date. Its purchases total $1,095,000 per year. How much "non-free" trade credit does the firm use on average each year?

    a. $120,000
    b. $ 90,000
    c. $ 60,000
    d. $ 30,000
    e. $ 20,000

12. A firm buys on terms of 2/10, net 30, but generally does not pay until 40 days after the invoice date. Its purchases total $1,095,000 per year. What is the nominal cost of the "non-free" trade credit?

    a. 16.2%
    b. 19.4%
    c. 21.9%
    d. 24.8%
    e. 27.9%

13. A firm buys on terms of 2/10, net 30, but generally does not pay until 40 days after the invoice date. Its purchases total $1,095,000 per year. What is the effective cost rate of the costly credit?

    a. 16.2%
    b. 19.4%
    c. 21.9%
    d. 24.8%
    e. 27.9%

14. Lawton Pipelines Inc. has developed plans for a new pump that will allow more economical operation of the company's oil pipelines. Management estimates that $2,400,000 will be required to put this new pump into operation. Funds can be obtained from a bank at 12% simple interest, or the company can finance the expansion by delaying payment to its suppliers. Presently, Lawton purchases under terms of 2/10, net 40, but management believes payment could be delayed 30 additional days without penalty; that is, payment could be made in 70 days. Which means of financing should Lawton use? (Use the nominal cost of trade credit.)

    a. Trade credit, since the cost is about 1 percentage point less than the bank loan.
    b. Trade credit, since the cost is about 0.41 percentage points less than the bank loan.
    c. Bank loan, since the cost is about 0.41 percentage points less than trade credit.
    d. Bank loan, since the cost is about 1 percentage point less than trade credit.
    e. The firm could use either since the costs are identical.

15. You plan to borrow $10,000 from your bank, which offers to lend you the money at a 10% nominal, or stated, rate on a 1-year loan. What is the approximate interest rate if the loan is an add-on interest loan with 12 monthly payments?

    a. 11.1%
    b. 13.3%
    c. 15.0%
    d. 17.5%
    e. 20.0%

16. You plan to borrow $10,000 from your bank, which offers to lend you the money at a 10% nominal, or stated, rate on a 1-year loan. What is the annual percentage rate if the loan is an add-on interest loan with 12 monthly payments?

    a. 10.00%
    b. 13.25%
    c. 15.33%
    d. 17.97%
    e. 19.53%

17. You plan to borrow $10,000 from your bank, which offers to lend you the money at a 10% nominal, or stated, rate on a 1-year loan. What is the effective interest rate if the loan is an add-on interest loan with 12 monthly payments?

    a. 10.00%
    b. 13.25%
    c. 15.33%
    d. 17.97%
    e. 19.53%

18. Gibbs Corporation needs to raise $1,000,000 for one year to supply working capital to a new store. Gibbs buys from its suppliers on terms of 4/10, net 90, and it currently pays on the 10th day and takes discounts, but it could forego discounts, pay on the 90th day, and receive the needed $1,000,000 in the form of costly trade credit. Alternatively, Gibbs could borrow from its bank on a 9% add-on interest loan with 12 monthly payments. What is the effective annual cost rate of the lower cost source?

   a. 20.47%
   b. 18.75%
   c. 17.48%
   d. 18.00%
   e. 19.01%

Answers

Definitional Questions

1. working
2. Net; current
3. supplies; materials; work-in-process; finished
4. receivable
5. volume; sales; collections
6. credit
7. period; discount
8. Collection
9. cash
10. relaxed
11. restricted
12. target
13. quality
14. permanent; long-term; temporary
15. expected; greatest
16. flexibility; future
17. upward
18. more
19. Accrued; size
20. trade
21. spontaneous
22. free; costly
23. discount
24. Costly
25. promissory
26. secured; receivables; inventory
27. line
28. commitment
29. installment; one-half
30. large
31. Permanent
32. temporary
33. stretching; payable
34. revolving; agreement
35. Annual
36. aggressive
37. conservative
38. loans
39. inventory conversion
40. cash conversion cycle

Conceptual Questions

1. b. No new customers are being generated. The current customers pay either on Day 10 or Day 30. The increase in trade discount will induce some customers who are now paying on Day 30 to pay on Day 10. Thus, the days sales outstanding is shortened which, in turn, will cause a decline in accounts receivable.

2. b. Receivables are based on sales price, which presumably includes some profit. Only the actual cash outlays associated with receivables must be financed. The remainder, or profit, appears on the balance sheet as an increase in retained earnings.

3. b. The matching of maturities minimizes default risk, or the risk that the firm will be unable to pay off its maturing obligations, and reinvestment rate risk, or the risk that the firm will have to roll over the debt at a higher rate.

4. a. Neither workers nor the IRS require interest payments on wages and taxes that are not paid as soon as they are earned.

5. d. Statement a is false; the conservative approach would be the safest current asset financing policy. Statement b is false; short-term debt fluctuates more than long-term debt, thus, the greater the firm's reliance on short-term debt, the riskier the firm. Statement c is false; it makes no difference in the cost if the firm pays on Day 25 versus Day 30 in this instance. Statement d is true; if the firm can "stretch" its payables the nominal cost is 14.90% (the effective cost is 15.89%). Thus, the firm should obtain the 14% bank loan to take discounts as this is the lowest cost to the firm.

Solutions

Problems

1. d. 0.3(10 days) + 0.4(30 days) + 0.3(40 days) = 27 days

2. e. 0.3(10 days) + 0.4(30 days) + 0.3(40 days) = 27 days
   Receivables = (DSO)(Sales/365) = 27($1,216,667/365) = $90,000

3. d. New days sales outstanding = 0.3(10) + 0.7(30) = 24 days
   Sales per day = $1,216,667/365 = $3,333.33
   Receivables = $3,333.33(24 days) = $80,000.00

4. a. Inventory turnover ratio$_{Old}$ = Sales/Inventory
   $$3 = \$12,000,000/I$$
   $$3I = \$12,000,000$$
   $$I = \$4,000,000$$

   Inventory turnover ratio$_{New}$ = Sales/Inventory
   $$7.5 = \$12,000,000/I$$
   $$I = \$12,000,000/7.5$$
   $$I = \$1,600,000$$

   Cash freed up = $4,000,000 − $1,600,000 = $2,400,000

5. b. Cash conversion cycle $= 45 + 36 - 35 = 46$ days

6. c. $\text{DSO} = \dfrac{\text{AR}}{\text{Sales}/365}$

$\quad\quad 36 = \dfrac{\text{AR}}{\$4,309,028/365}$

$\quad\quad \text{AR} = \$425,000$

7. a. $\dfrac{\text{Inventory}}{\text{COGS}/365} = 45$

$\quad \dfrac{\text{Inventory}}{(0.75)(\$4,309,028)/365} = 45$

$\quad\quad \dfrac{\text{Inventory}}{\$8,854.17} = 45$

$\quad\quad\quad \text{Inventory} = \$398,437.52 \approx \$398,438$

8. d. Need to calculate inventory first:

$\dfrac{\text{Inventory}}{\text{COGS}/365} = 45$

$\dfrac{\text{Inventory}}{(0.75)(\$4,309,028)/365} = 45$

$\quad \dfrac{\text{Inventory}}{\$8,854.17} = 45$

$\quad\quad \text{Inventory} = \$398,437.52$

$\text{Inventory turnover} = \dfrac{\text{Sales}}{\text{Inventory}}$

$\quad\quad\quad\quad = \dfrac{\$4,309,028}{\$398,437.52}$

$\quad\quad\quad\quad = 10.81\times$

9. c. Setting up the formula for the cash conversion cycle, sales can be calculated as follows:

$$\text{CCC} = \frac{\text{Acccounts receivable}}{\text{Avg. daily sales}} + \frac{\text{Inventory}}{\text{Avg. daily COGS}} - \frac{\text{Accounts payable}}{\text{Avg. daily COGS}}$$

$\quad\quad 20 = (\$60,000/\text{ADS}) + (\$63,750/0.75\text{ADS}) - (\$90,000/0.75\text{ADS})$

$\quad\quad 20 = (\$60,000/\text{ADS}) + (\$85,000/\text{ADS}) - (\$120,000/\text{ADS})$

$\quad\quad 20 = \$25,000/\text{ADS}$

$20(\text{ADS}) = \$25,000$

$\quad\quad \text{ADS} = \$1,250.00$

Therefore, annual sales equal \$456,250 (\$1,250 × 365 = \$456,250)

10. b. Setting up the formula for the cash conversion cycle, sales can be calculated as follows:

$$CCC = \frac{\text{Acccounts receivable}}{\text{Avg. daily sales}} + \frac{\text{Inventory}}{\text{Avg. daily COGS}} - \frac{\text{Accounts payable}}{\text{Avg. daily COGS}}$$

$$20 = (\$60,000/ADS) + (\$63,750/0.75ADS) - (\$90,000/0.75ADS)$$
$$20 = (\$60,000/ADS) + (\$85,000/ADS) - (\$120,000/ADS)$$
$$20 = \$25,000/ADS$$
$$20(ADS) = \$25,000$$
$$ADS = \$1,250.00$$

On the basis of the information given, the firm's current assets equal $175,250 ($51,500 + $60,000 + $63,750). Therefore, for its current ratio to increase to 2.25, it must reduce accounts payable to a level such that current liabilities total $77,889 ($175,250/2.25). If accrued liabilities on the balance sheet equal $12,500, accounts payable must be reduced to $65,389 ($77,889 − $12,500). The firm's new average daily cost of goods sold would equal $1,250 × 0.65 = $812.50. Combined with the original information, the new CCC can be determined as follows:

$$CCC = \frac{\text{Acccounts receivable}}{\text{Avg. daily sales}} + \frac{\text{Inventory}}{\text{Avg. daily COGS}} - \frac{\text{Accounts payable}}{\text{Avg. daily COGS}}$$

$$= (\$60,000/\$1,250) + (\$63,750/\$812.50) - (\$65,389/\$812.50)$$
$$= 48.00 + 78.46 - 80.48$$
$$= 45.98 \text{ days}$$

11. b. $1,095,000/365 = $3,000 in purchases per day. Typically, there will be $3,000(40) = $120,000 of accounts payable on the books at any given time. Of this, $3,000(10) = $30,000 is "free" credit, while $3,000(30) = $90,000 is "non-free" credit.

12. d. $$\text{Nominal cost} = \frac{\text{Discount \%}}{100 - \text{Discount \%}} \times \frac{365}{\text{Days credit is outstanding} - \text{Discount period}}$$

$$= \frac{2}{100 - 2} \times \frac{365}{40 - 10} = \frac{2}{98} \times \frac{365}{30} = 24.8\%$$

13. e. The periodic rate is 2/98 = 2.04%, and there are 365/30 = 12.1667 periods per year. Thus, the effective annual rate is 27.9%:

$$\left(1 + \frac{r_{NOM}}{M}\right)^N - 1.0 = (1.0204)^{12.1667} - 1.0$$

$$= 1.2785 - 1.0 = 0.2785 = 27.9\%$$

14. c. Credit terms are 2/10, net 40, but delaying payments 30 additional days is the equivalent of 2/10, net 70. Assuming no penalty, the nominal cost is as follows:

$$\text{Nominal cost} = \frac{\text{Discount \%}}{100 - \text{Discount \%}} \times \frac{365}{\text{Days credit is outstanding} - \text{Discount period}}$$

$$= \frac{2}{100 - 2} \times \frac{365}{70 - 10} = \frac{2}{98} \times \frac{365}{60} = 0.0204(6.0833) = 12.41\%$$

Therefore, the loan cost is 0.41 percentage points less than trade credit.

15. e. Approximate annual rate = (0.10)($10,000)/($10,000/2) = $1,000/$5,000 = 20.0\%

16. d. The total amount to be repaid = $10,000 + (0.10 \times $10,000) = $11,000
Monthly payments = $11,000/12 = $916.67

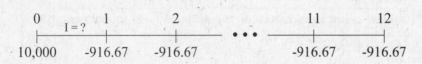

Using a financial calculator, enter $CF_0 = 10000$; $CF_{1-12} = -916.67$; and then solve for IRR/YR = 1.4977\%; however, this is a monthly periodic rate.

$APR_{\text{Add-on}} = 12(0.014977) = 17.97\%$

17. e. The total amount to be repaid = $10,000 + (0.10 \times $10,000) = $11,000
Monthly payments = $11,000/12 = $916.67

Using a financial calculator, enter $CF_0 = 10000$; $CF_{1-12} = -916.67$; and then solve for IRR/YR = 1.4977\%; however, this is a monthly periodic rate.

$EFF\%_{\text{Add-on}} = (1.014977)^{12} - 1 = 19.53\%$

18. c. Accounts payable:
Nominal cost = (4/96)(365/80) = 0.04167(4.5625) = 19.01\%
EAR cost = $(1.04167)^{4.5625} - 1.0 = 20.47\%$

Cost of notes payable:
The total amount to be repaid = $1,000,000 + (0.09)($1,000,000) = $1,090,000

Monthly payments = $1,090,000/12 = $90,833.33

```
    0        I = ?      1                    12
    ├─────────┼─────────┼──── • • • ────────┤
1,000,000        -90,833.33            -90,833.33
```

Using a financial calculator, enter $CF_0 = 1000000$; $CF_{1\text{-}12} = -90833.33$; and then solve for IRR/YR $= 1.3514\%$; however, this is a monthly periodic rate.

$$EFF\%_{\text{Add-on}} = (1.013514)^{12} - 1 = 17.48\%$$

16

FINANCIAL PLANNING AND FORECASTING

Learning Objectives

1. Discuss the importance of strategic planning and the central role that financial forecasting plays in the overall planning process.

2. Explain how firms forecast sales.

3. Use the Additional Funds Needed (or AFN) equation and discuss the relationship between asset growth and the need for funds.

4. Explain how spreadsheets are used in the forecasting process, starting with historical statements, ending with projected statements, and including a set of financial ratios based on those projected statements.

5. Discuss how planning is an iterative process.

Overview

Managers and investors need to understand how to forecast future results. Managers use projected financial statements in four ways. First, by looking at projected statements, managers can assess whether the firm's anticipated performance is in line with the firm's own internal targets and with investors' expectations. Second, these statements can be used to estimate the impact of proposed operating changes. Third, managers use them to anticipate the firm's future financing needs, and to arrange the necessary financing. Finally, projected financial statements are used to estimate free cash flows, which determine the company's overall value. Managers forecast free cash flows under different operating plans, forecast their capital requirements, and then choose the plan that maximizes shareholder value. Security analysts make the same types of projections as managers, and influence investors, who determine the future of managers.

In this chapter we explain how to create and use projected financial statements, beginning with the strategic plan, the foundation for these statements. We focus on three key elements of the financial plan: (1) the sales forecast, (2) the projected financial statements, and (3) the external financing plan. In addition, we discuss the AFN equation, which provides a "preliminary" forecast of additional funds needed. Finally, the chapter discusses using regression analysis to improve financial forecasts and using individual ratios in the forecasting process.

Outline

I.   **Financial planning should be done within the context of a well-articulated strategic plan that contains a number of elements.**

   A.   The plan should begin with a *mission statement*.

   1.   The mission statement is a condensed version of a firm's strategic plan.

   2.   The corporate focus on creating wealth for stockholders is common in the United States and in developed countries around the world.

   B.   The *corporate scope* defines a firm's lines of business and geographic areas of operation.

   1.   Some firms deliberately limit their scope, on the theory that it is better for top managers to focus sharply on a narrow range of functions as opposed to spreading the company over many different types of businesses.

   2.   Several recent studies have found that investors generally value focused firms more highly than diversified firms.

   3.   The stated corporate scope should be logical and consistent with the firm's capabilities.

   C.   *Corporate objectives* set forth the specific goals that operating managers are expected to meet.

   1.   Most companies have both qualitative and quantitative objectives.

   D.   *Corporate strategies* are broad approaches developed for achieving a firm's goals.

   E.   A detailed *operating plan* provides management with detailed implementation guidance, based on the corporate strategy, to help meet the corporate objectives.

   1.   Operating plans can be developed for any time horizon, but most companies use a five-year horizon.

   2.   The plan explains in considerable detail those people responsible for each particular function, deadlines for specific tasks, sales and profit targets, and the like.

   F.   The *financial plan* is the final element of the overall corporate plan.

   1.   It is the document that includes assumptions, projected financial statements, and projected ratios and ties the entire planning process together.

   2.   Financial planning is often called "value-based management," meaning that the effects of various decisions on the firm's financial position and value are studied by simulating their effects within the firm's financial model.

II.   **The sales forecast generally begins with a review of sales during the past five to ten years.**

   A.   The *sales forecast* is a forecast of a firm's unit and dollar sales for some future period, and it is generally based on recent sales trends plus forecasts of the economic prospects for the nation, region, industry, and so forth.

   B.   If the sales forecast is off, the consequences can be serious. An accurate sales forecast is critical to the firm's well being.

   C.   The sales forecast is the most important input in the firm's forecast of financial statements, including the projected EPS.

III. **Increasing sales require additional assets, these assets must be financed, and it may or may not be possible to obtain all the funds needed for the firm's business plan. A key element in the financial forecasting process is to determine the external financing requirements. The AFN equation can be used to approximate the funds needed assuming that ratios remain constant.**

A. The equation is as follows:

$$\begin{matrix} \text{Additional} \\ \text{funds needed} \\ \text{or AFN} \end{matrix} = \begin{matrix} \text{Projected} \\ \text{increase in assets} \end{matrix} - \begin{matrix} \text{Spontaneous} \\ \text{increase in liabilities} \end{matrix} - \begin{matrix} \text{Increase in} \\ \text{retained earnings} \end{matrix}$$

$$= (A_0^*/S_0)\Delta S - (L_0^*/S_0)\Delta S - MS_1(1 - \text{Payout})$$

1. A_0^*/S_0 = assets that must increase if sales are to increase, assets that are tied directly to sales.

2. L_0^*/S_0 = liabilities that increase spontaneously as a percentage of sales, or spontaneously generated financing per \$1 increase in sales.

   a. These are called *spontaneously generated funds*.

   b. These are funds that arise out of the normal business operations from its suppliers, employees, and the government (such as accounts payable and accrued wages and taxes) that reduce the firm's need for external financing.

3. S_1 = total expected sales for the year in question. S_0 = last year's sales.

4. ΔS = change in sales = $S_1 - S_0$.

5. M = profit margin, or profit per \$1 of sales.

6. The term $(1 - \text{Payout})$ is known as the *retention ratio*.

   a. It is the proportion of net income that is reinvested in the firm.

7. *Additional funds needed (AFN)* is the amount of external capital (interest-bearing debt and preferred and common stock) that will be required to acquire the needed assets.

B. The *AFN equation* shows the relationship of external funds needed by a firm to its projected increase in assets, the spontaneous increase in liabilities, and its increase in retained earnings. External financing requirements depend on the following:

1. Rapidly growing companies require large increases in assets, other things held constant, so sales growth is an important factor.

2. The amount of assets required per dollar of sales, or *capital intensity ratio*, has a major effect on capital requirements.

   a. Companies with higher assets-to-sales ratios require more assets for a given increase in sales, hence a greater need for external financing.

3. Companies that spontaneously generate a large amount of liabilities from accounts payable and accrued liabilities will have a relatively small need for external financing.

4. The higher the profit margin, the larger the net income available to support increases in assets, hence the lower the need for external financing.

5. Companies that retain more of their earnings as opposed to paying them out as dividends will generate more retained earnings and have less need for external financing.

C. A negative AFN indicates that surplus funds would be generated and available for investment.

D. The *sustainable growth rate* is the maximum achievable growth rate without the firm having to raise external funds.

   1. It is the growth rate at which the firm's AFN equals zero.

E. The AFN equation assumes that the A_0^*/S_0 ratio is a constant; however, if a firm's fixed assets are not operating at full capacity, then the calculation for the required level of fixed assets will need to be adjusted.

   1. *Excess capacity adjustments* are changes made to the existing asset forecast because the firm is not operating at full capacity.

   2. Full capacity sales are actual sales divided by the percentage of capacity at which the fixed assets were operated to achieve these sales:

$$\text{Full capacity sales} = \frac{\text{Actual sales}}{\substack{\text{Percentage of capacity at which} \\ \text{fixed assets were operated}}}$$

   3. The target fixed assets-to-sales ratio is equal to the current year's actual fixed assets divided by full capacity sales:

$$\text{Target fixed assets to sales ratio} = \frac{\text{Actual fixed assets}}{\text{Full capacity sales}}$$

   4. The required level of fixed assets is equal to the target fixed assets-to-sales ratio times projected sales:

$$\text{Required level of fixed assets} = \left(\frac{\text{Target fixed assets}}{\text{Sales}}\right)\left(\begin{array}{c}\text{Projected} \\ \text{sales}\end{array}\right)$$

   a. When excess capacity exists, sales can grow to the capacity sales with no increase whatever in fixed assets, but sales beyond that level will require fixed asset additions.

   b. Excess capacity can occur with other types of assets. However, as a practical matter excess capacity normally exists only with respect to fixed assets and inventories.

   c. Moreover, the L_0^*/S_0 ratio might be too low because the firm is underutilizing supplier credit and accruals.

   d. Because so many conditions can change, it is useful to go beyond the AFN equation analysis and examine *forecasted financial statements*. The forecasted financial statements will indicate how good or bad the firm's financial ratios are considering the assumptions made.

IV. **The AFN equation provides useful insights into the forecasting process, but this equation assumes that all of the company's key ratios remain constant, which is not likely to hold true. Therefore, it is useful to forecast the firm's financial statements.**

A. Examine projected sales growth and ratios over which management has control. These include, but are not exhaustive: operating costs-to-sales, receivables-to-sales, fixed assets-to-sales, and inventories-to-sales ratios, as well as the firm's debt and dividend payout ratios.

   1. Management would want to keep these operating ratios in line with industry and benchmark averages.

B. Other inputs that are not under management's control are required to create the forecasted financial statements. These include the firm's tax rate, its interest rate, common shares initially outstanding, and its initial stock price.

    1. The number of common shares will change depending on how much new equity financing is needed.

    2. On the basis of the forecasted financial statements the firm can review other operating ratios and projected stock price and make adjustments to its initial assumptions and inputs.

C. The forecasted income statement begins with the prior year's income statement and is adjusted based on the sales growth forecast.

    1. Depending on the operating cost ratio assumption, operating costs and forecasted EBIT are calculated.

    2. Interest expense is calculated based on the debt ratio and interest rate assumptions made earlier by management.

        a. Both the debt level and interest rate are needed to calculate the interest expense.

D. The forecasted balance sheet is calculated from the asset ratios that management examined at the start of this process.

    1. Management may decide to keep asset ratios constant from the prior year or change them depending on industry and benchmark analysis.

    2. Additions to debt and equity will depend on the sales growth rate, the various asset ratio assumptions, and the debt ratio assumption.

    3. The addition to retained earnings will depend on net income calculated in the forecasted income statement and the dividend payout ratio assumption.

E. Once the income statement and balance sheet have been forecasted, the firm's ratios and EPS can then be calculated.

F. An Excel spreadsheet model is used for this analysis.

    1. Changes to the forecasted statements can be reviewed under alternative scenarios.

    2. Changes to assumptions—growth rate and key ratios—can be easily made and the results reviewed.

    3. Changes to financing can be reviewed as well.

    4. Excel's "What If" Analysis tools such as Scenario Manager, Goal Seek, and Data Tables are useful.

V. **Regression analysis can be used to improve financial forecasts by investigating situations in which growth at the same rate as sales is not a good assumption.**

A. *Regression analysis* is a statistical technique that fits a line to observed data points so that the resulting equation can be used to forecast other data points.

B. Regression analysis is useful in excess capacity and economies of scale situations.

C. Plots of the actual data points against the regression line indicate how closely the analysis fits the data.

       1. The correlation coefficient is a quantitative measure of the relationship between the independent and dependent variables.

    D. Use of regression analysis can lead to improved financial forecasts and better information on which management can act.

VI.   **It is useful to examine specific asset ratios to get a better idea of the effects on the firm's financial position given various changes to these ratios.**

    A. We can look at the effects of modifying individual asset forecasts, such as inventories, receivables, and fixed assets by looking at individual ratios for these assets: inventory turnover, DSO, and fixed asset turnover ratios, to determine the additional free cash flow freed up by improvements in these ratios.

    B. Once a firm has developed a model to forecast its financial statements, it can do all types of special "what if" studies.

       1. The model can be used to analyze the effects of changing the dividend policy both on the statements and on the required AFN.

       2. The AFN equation can be modified to obtain a "quick and dirty estimate" as a preliminary estimate of AFN.

VII.   **The assumption of constant ratios and identical growth rates is appropriate at times, but there are times when it is incorrect. Web Appendix 16A gives a more detailed discussion about these situations.**

    A. Where *economies of scale* occur in asset use, the ratio of that asset to sales will change as the size of the firm increases.

    B. Technological considerations sometimes dictate that fixed assets be added in large, discrete units, often referred to as *lumpy assets*. This automatically creates excess capacity immediately after a plant expansion.

    C. Forecasting errors can cause the actual assets-to-sales ratio for a given period to be quite different from the planned ratio, resulting in excess capacity.

Self-Test

Definitional Questions

1. The most important element in financial planning is the _____ forecast.

2. If various asset categories increase, _____ and/or _____ must also increase.

3. As the dividend _____ ratio is increased, the amount of earnings available to finance new assets is _____.

4. Retained earnings depend not only on next year's sales level and dividend payout ratio but also on the _____ margin.

5. The amount of assets that are tied directly to sales, A_0^*/S_0, is often called the _____ intensity ratio.

6. A capital intensive industry will require large amounts of _____ capital to finance increased growth.

7. _____ funds _____ are funds that a firm must raise externally through borrowing or by selling new common or preferred stock.

8. The faster a firm's growth rate in sales, the _____ its need for additional financing.

9. _____ capacity _____ is defined as actual sales divided by the percentage of capacity at which fixed assets were operated to achieve those sales.

10. The _____ fixed _____-to-_____ ratio is equal to the current year's actual fixed assets divided by full capacity sales.

11. The _____ level of _____ assets is equal to the target fixed assets-to-sales ratio times projected sales.

12. Corporate _____ set forth the specific goals that operating managers are expected to meet.

13. A(n) _____ statement is a condensed version of a firm's strategic plan.

14. The corporate _____ defines a firm's lines of business and geographic areas of operation.

15. Corporate _____ are broad approaches developed for achieving a firm's goals.

16. The _____ ratio is equal to one minus the payout ratio.

17. A(n) _____ AFN indicates that surplus funds would be generated and available for investment.

18. _____ of _____ occur when a particular asset-to-sales ratio will change as the size of the firm increases.

19. Technological considerations sometimes dictate that fixed assets be added in large discrete units, often referred to as _____ assets.

20. The _____ growth rate is the maximum achievable rate at which the firm does not have to raise external funds. It is the growth rate at which the firm's AFN equals _____.

Conceptual Questions

1. An increase in a firm's inventory will call for additional financing unless the increase is offset by an equal or larger *decrease* in some other asset account.

    a. True
    b. False

2. If the capital intensity ratio of a firm actually decreases as sales increase, use of the AFN equation will typically *overstate* the amount of additional funds required, other things held constant.

    a. True
    b. False

3. If the dividend payout ratio is 100%, all ratios are held constant, and the firm is operating at full capacity, then any increase in sales will require additional financing.

   a. True
   b. False

4. The operating plan is the final element of the overall corporate plan; the heart of the operating plan is a set of projected financial statements.

   a. True
   b. False

5. Which of the following statements is *false*?

   a. When excess capacity exists, sales can grow to the capacity sales with no increase whatever in fixed assets, but sales beyond that level will require fixed asset additions.
   b. Financial planning should be done within the context of a well-articulated strategic plan.
   c. Because the AFN equation assumes that the firm's key ratios do not remain constant, both the AFN equation and the financial statement forecasting method would arrive at exactly the same AFN amount.
   d. Regression techniques can be used to improve financial forecasts by investigating situations in which growth at the same rate as sales is not a good assumption.
   e. The retention ratio is the percentage of net income that is retained; it is calculated as 1 – dividend payout ratio.

6. Which of the following would *reduce* the additional funds needed (AFN) if all other things are held constant?

   a. An increase in the dividend payout ratio.
   b. A decrease in the profit margin.
   c. An increase in the capital intensity ratio.
   d. An increase in the expected sales growth rate.
   e. A decrease in the firm's tax rate.

Problems

1. United Products Inc. recently reported the following balance sheet:

United Products Inc.
Balance Sheet as of December 31, 2011

Current assets	$ 5,000	Accounts payable	$ 1,000
		Notes payable	1,000
Net fixed assets	5,000	Long-term debt	4,000
		Common equity	4,000
Total assets	$10,000	Total liabilities and equity	$10,000

Sales in 2011 were $100,000. Business has been slow; therefore, fixed assets are vastly underutilized. Management believes it can double sales next year with the introduction of a new product. No new fixed assets will be required, and management expects that there will be no earnings retained next year. What is next year's additional funds needed (AFN)?

a. $ 0
b. $ 4,000
c. $ 6,000
d. $13,000
e. $19,000

Exhibit 16-1
American Pulp and Paper recently reported the following balance sheet (in millions of dollars):

American Pulp and Paper
Balance Sheet of December 31, 2011
(Millions of Dollars)

Cash	$ 3.0	Accounts payable	$ 2.0
Accounts receivable	3.0	Notes payable	1.5
Inventories	5.0		
Total current assets	$11.0	Total current liabilities	$ 3.5
Fixed assets	3.0	Long-term debt	3.0
		Common equity	7.5
Total assets	$14.0	Total liabilities and equity	$14.0

2. Refer to Exhibit 16-1. In 2011, sales were $60 million. In 2012, management believes that sales will increase by 20% to a total of $72 million. The profit margin is expected to be 5%, and the dividend payout ratio is targeted at 40%. No excess capacity exists. What is the additional funds needed (AFN) in millions of dollars for 2012 using the AFN equation?

a. $0.36
b. $0.24
c. $0.00
d. -$0.24
e. -$0.36

3. Refer to Exhibit 16-1. In 2011, sales were $60 million. In 2012, management believes that sales will increase by 20% to a total of $72 million. The profit margin is expected to be 5%, and the dividend payout ratio is targeted at 40%. No excess capacity exists. Using the AFN equation, how much can sales grow above the 2011 level of $60 million without requiring any additional funds? In other words, what is the firm's sustainable growth rate?

   a. 12.28%
   b. 14.63%
   c. 15.75%
   d. 17.65%
   e. 18.14%

4. Smith Machines Inc. has a net income this year of $500 on sales of $2,000 and is operating its fixed assets at full capacity. Management expects sales to increase by 25% next year and is forecasting a dividend payout ratio of 30%. The profit margin is not expected to change. If spontaneous liabilities are $500 this year and no excess funds are expected next year, using the AFN equation what are Smith's total assets this year?

   a. $1,000
   b. $1,500
   c. $2,250
   d. $3,000
   e. $3,500

5. Wilson Widgets Company has $500 million in sales. The company expects that its sales will increase 8% this year. Wilson's CFO uses a simple linear regression to forecast the company's inventory level for a given level of projected sales. On the basis of recent history, the estimated relationship between inventories and sales (in millions of dollars) is

$$\text{Inventories} = \$42 + 0.136(\text{Sales}).$$

   Given the estimated sales forecast and the estimated relationship between inventories and sales, what is your forecast of the company's year-end inventory turnover ratio?

   a. 3.33
   b. 4.68
   c. 1.57
   d. 2.44
   e. 3.50

6. Holden Industries has $3 billion in sales and $1.25 billion in fixed assets. Currently, the company's fixed assets are operating at 80% of capacity. What level of sales (in billions of dollars) could Holden Industries have obtained if it had been operating at full capacity?

   a. $3.25
   b. $4.50
   c. $3.75
   d. $4.80
   e. $5.23

7. Holden Industries has $3 billion in sales and $1.25 billion in fixed assets. Currently, the company's fixed assets are operating at 80% of capacity. What is Holden's target fixed asset/sales ratio?

    a. 33.33%
    b. 25.00%
    c. 10.50%
    d. 18.75%
    e. 41.67%

8. Holden Industries has $3 billion in sales and $1.25 billion in fixed assets. Currently, the company's fixed assets are operating at 80% of capacity. If Holden's sales increase 25%, how large of an increase in fixed assets (in millions of dollars) would the company need in order to meet its target fixed asset/sales ratio?

    a. $312.50
    b. $250.00
    c. $ 75.50
    d. $ 3.00
    e. $ 0.00

Exhibit 16-2

Crossley Products Company recently reported the following financial statements (in thousands of dollars):

Crossley Products Company
Balance Sheet as of December 31, 2011
(Thousands of Dollars)

Cash	$ 600	Accounts payable	$ 2,400
Receivables	3,600	Notes payable	1,157
Inventories	4,200	Accrued liabilities	840
Total current assets	$ 8,400	Total current liabilities	$ 4,397
		Mortgage bonds	1,667
		Common stock	667
Net fixed assets	7,200	Retained earnings	8,869
Total assets	$15,600	Total liabilities and equity	$15,600

Crossley Products Company
Income Statement for December 31, 2011
(Thousands of Dollars)

Sales	$12,000
Operating costs	10,261
EBIT	$ 1,739
Interest	339
EBT	$ 1,400
Taxes (40%)	560
Net income	$ 840
Dividends (60%)	$ 504
Addition to retained earnings	$ 336

9. Refer to Exhibit 16-2. Assume that the company was operating at full capacity in 2011 with regard to all items except fixed assets; fixed assets in 2011 were utilized to only 75% of capacity. By what percentage could 2012 sales increase over 2011 sales without the need for an increase in fixed assets?

   a. 33%
   b. 25%
   c. 20%
   d. 44%
   e. 50%

10. Refer to Exhibit 16-2. Now suppose 2012 sales increase by 25% over 2011 sales. Assume that the company was operating at full capacity in 2011 with regard to all items except fixed assets; fixed assets in 2011 were utilized to only 75% of capacity. Except for fixed assets, all asset ratios with respect to sales will remain constant. In addition, the operating cost and accrual ratios with respect to sales, the firm's tax rate, and dividend payout ratio will remain constant. Crossley cannot sell any fixed assets.

Develop a forecasted balance sheet and income statement. Assume that any required financing is borrowed as 30% notes payable and 70% bonds at an average interest rate of 12.5%. Finally, the firm wants to decrease its total debt ratio to 35%. The firm has 1,000 shares outstanding and its current stock price is $45. Common shares can be issued or repurchased at this price. What is the forecasted 2012 addition to retained earnings?

   a. $333.30
   b. $425.00
   c. $457.40
   d. $500.00
   e. $557.30

11. Refer to Exhibit 16-2 and Problem 10. What is the forecasted 2012 balance of common stock?

   a. $ 667.00
   b. $1,033.30
   c. $1,555.80
   d. $1,725.00
   e. $2,178.70

Exhibit 16-3

Tatum Toys recently reported the following income statement (in millions of dollars):

Tatum Toys
Income Statement for December 31, 2011
(Millions of Dollars)

Sales	$875
Operating costs	625
EBIT	$250
Interest	50
EBT	$200
Taxes (40%)	80
Net income	$120
Dividends (33.3%)	$ 40
Addition to retained earnings	$ 80

12. Refer to Exhibit 16-3. This year the company is forecasting a 20% increase in sales, and it expects that its year-end operating costs will decline to 65% of sales. Tatum's tax rate, interest expense, and dividend payout ratio are all expected to remain constant. What is Tatum's forecasted 2012 net income (in millions of dollars)?

    a. $ 75.75
    b. $151.50
    c. $225.25
    d. $190.50
    e. $300.00

13. Refer to Exhibit 16-3. This year the company is forecasting a 20% increase in sales, and it expects that its year-end operating costs will decline to 65% of sales. Tatum's tax rate, interest expense, and dividend payout ratio are all expected to remain constant. What is the expected growth rate in Tatum's dividends?

    a. 25.00%
    b. 33.33%
    c. 58.75%
    d. 15.50%
    e. 42.25%

14. Heuser Industries recently reported the following income statement (in thousands of dollars):

Heuser Industries
Income Statement for December 31, 2011
(Thousands of Dollars)

Sales	$6,000
Operating costs excluding depreciation	4,900
EBITDA	$1,100
Depreciation	500
EBIT	$ 600
Interest	250
EBT	$ 350
Taxes (40%)	140
Net income	$ 210

Looking ahead to the following year, the company's CFO has assembled the following information:

- 2012 sales are expected to be 15% higher than the $6 million in sales generated last year.
- 2012 operating costs excluding depreciation are expected to equal 80% of year-end sales.
- The ratio of depreciation to sales is expected to remain the same.
- Interest costs are expected to remain unchanged.
- The tax rate is expected to remain at 40%.

On the basis of this information, what will be the forecast for Heuser's 2012 net income (in thousands of dollars)?

    a. $175
    b. $333
    c. $125
    d. $215
    e. $288

Exhibit 16-4

Taylor Technologies Inc. recently reported the following financial statements:

Taylor Technologies Inc.
Balance Sheet as of December 31, 2011

Cash	$ 90,000	Accounts payable	$ 180,000
Receivables	180,000	Notes payable	78,000
Inventories	360,000	Accrued liabilities	90,000
Total current assets	$ 630,000	Total current liabilities	$ 348,000
		Common stock	900,000
Net fixed assets	720,000	Retained earnings	102,000
Total assets	$1,350,000	Total liabilities and equity	$1,350,000

Taylor Technologies Inc.
Income Statement for December 31, 2011

Sales	$1,800,000
Operating costs	1,639,860
EBIT	$ 160,140
Interest	10,140
EBT	$ 150,000
Taxes (40%)	60,000
Net income	$ 90,000
Dividends (60%)	$ 54,000
Addition to retained earnings	$ 36,000

15. Refer to Exhibit 16-4. Suppose that in 2012, sales increase by 10% over 2011 sales. Construct the forecasted financial statements. Assume the firm operated at full capacity in 2011. The firm would like to increase its total debt ratio to 45%, and 25% will be allocated to notes payable while 75% will be allocated to long-term debt. The firm's tax rate and dividend payout rate will remain constant, as will all other asset and accrual ratios. The firm has 75,000 shares outstanding and shares can be issued or repurchased for $30 per share. The average interest rate on all debt is 10%. What is the firm's 2012 forecasted net income?

   a. $61,111.80
   b. $68,000.00
   c. $77,662.20
   d. $83,417.40
   e. $88,789.20

16. Refer to Exhibit 16-4 and Problem 15. What is the firm's 2012 forecasted EPS?

   a. $1.15
   b. $1.23
   c. $1.33
   d. $1.50
   e. $1.62

Answers

Definitional Questions

1. sales
2. liabilities; equity
3. payout; decreased
4. profit
5. capital
6. external
7. Additional; needed
8. greater
9. Full; sales
10. target; assets; sales
11. required; fixed
12. objectives
13. mission
14. scope
15. strategies
16. retention
17. negative
18. Economies; scale
19. lumpy
20. sustainable; zero

Conceptual Questions

1. a. When an increase in one asset account is not offset by an equivalent decrease in another asset account, then financing is needed to reestablish equilibrium on the balance sheet. Note, though, that this additional financing may come from a spontaneous increase in accounts payable/accrued liabilities or from retained earnings.

2. a. A decreasing capital intensity ratio, A_0^*/S_0, means that fewer assets are required, proportionately, as sales increase. Thus, the external funding requirement is overstated. Always keep in mind that the AFN equation assumes that the assets-to-sales ratio is constant regardless of the level of sales.

3. a. With a 100% payout ratio, there will be no retained earnings. When operating at full capacity, all assets are spontaneous, but all liabilities cannot be spontaneous since a firm must have common equity. Thus, the growth in assets cannot be matched by a growth in spontaneous liabilities, so additional financing will be required in order to keep the financial ratios (the debt ratio in particular) constant.

4. b. The financial plan is the final element of the overall corporate plan; the heart of the financial plan is a set of projected financial statements.

5. c. This statement is false. The AFN equation assumes that the firm's key ratios remain constant. And, while the AFN equation is useful to arrive at a preliminary AFN amount, it is not likely that the projected financial statements would arrive at the same AFN. Forecasting financial statements is helpful when the firm has nonconstant ratios. All the other statements are true.

6. e. Answers a through d would increase the additional funds needed, but a decrease in the tax rate would raise the profit margin and thus increase the amount of available retained earnings.

Solutions

Problems

1. b.

    United Products Inc.
    Pro Forma Balance Sheet

Current assets $(0.05 \times S_1)$	$10,000	Accounts payable $(0.01 \times S_1)$	$ 2,000
Net fixed assets	5,000	Notes payable	1,000
		Current liabilities	$ 3,000
		Long-term debt	4,000
		Common equity	4,000
			$11,000
		AFN	4,000
Total assets	$15,000	Total liabilities and equity	$15,000

    With no retained earnings next year, the common equity account remains at $4,000. Thus, the additional funds needed (AFN) is $15,000 − $11,000 = $4,000.

2. b. None of the items on the right side of the balance sheet rises spontaneously with sales except accounts payable. Therefore,

    $$AFN = (A_0^*/S_0)(\Delta S) - (L_0^*/S_0)(\Delta S) - MS_1(1 - \text{Payout})$$
    $$= (\$14/\$60)(\$12) - (\$2/\$60)(\$12) - (0.05)(\$72)(0.6)$$
    $$= \$2.8 - \$0.4 - \$2.16 = \$0.24 \text{ million}$$

    The firm will need $240,000 in additional funds to support the increase in sales.

3. d. Note that g = Sales growth = $\Delta S/S_0$ and $S_1 = S_0(1 + g)$. Then,

    $$AFN = A_0^*g - L_0^*g - M[(S_0)(1 + g)](1 - \text{Payout}) = 0$$
    $$\$14g - \$2g - 0.05[(\$60)(1 + g)](0.60) = 0$$
    $$\$12g - [(\$3 + \$3g)(0.60)] = 0$$
    $$\$12g - \$1.8 - \$1.8g = 0$$
    $$\$10.20g = \$1.80$$
    $$g = 0.1765 = 17.65\%$$

4. c.
    $$0 = (A_0^*/S_0)(\Delta S) - (L_0^*/S_0)(\Delta S) - MS_1(1 - \text{Payout})$$
    $$0 = (A_0^*/\$2,000)(\$500) - (\$500/\$2,000)(\$500) - (\$500/\$2,000)(\$2,500)(0.7)$$
    $$0 = (\$500A_0^*/\$2,000) - \$125 - \$437.50$$
    $$0 = (\$500A_0^*/\$2,000) - \$562.50$$
    $$\$562.50 = 0.25A_0^*$$
    $$A_0^* = \$2,250$$

5. b. Sales = $500,000,000; g_{Sales} = 8%; Inv. = $42 + 0.136(Sales)

    $$S_1 = \$500,000,000 \times 1.08 = \$540,000,000$$

Inv. = $42 + 0.136(\$540) = \$115.44$ million

Sales/Inv. = $\$540,000,000/\$115,440,000 = 4.68$

6. c. Sales = $\$3,000,000,000$; FA = $\$1,250,000,000$; FA are operated at 80% capacity

Full capacity sales = $\$3,000,000,000/0.80 = \$3,750,000,000$

7. a. Sales = $\$3,000,000,000$; FA = $\$1,250,000,000$; FA are operated at 80% capacity

Full capacity sales = $\$3,000,000,000/0.80 = \$3,750,000,000$

Target FA/S ratio = $\$1,250,000,000/\$3,750,000,000 = 33.33\%$

8. e. Sales = $\$3,000,000,000$; FA = $\$1,250,000,000$; FA are operated at 80% capacity

Full capacity sales = $\$3,000,000,000/0.80 = \$3,750,000,000$

Target FA/S ratio = $\$1,250,000,000/\$3,750,000,000 = 33.33\%$

Sales increase = 25%; $\Delta FA = ?$

$S_1 = \$3,000,000,000 \times 1.25 = \$3,750,000,000$

There would be no increase in FA needed for sales up to $\$3,750,000,000$.

9. a. Full capacity sales = Actual sales/% of capacity at which FA were operated = $\$12,000/0.75 = \$16,000$

Percent increase = (New sales – Old sales)/Old sales = $(\$16,000 - \$12,000)/\$12,000 = 0.33 = 33\%$

Therefore, sales could expand by 33% before Crossley Products would need to add fixed assets.

10. c. From Problem 9 we know that sales can increase to 33% without an increase of fixed assets, so no new fixed assets are needed.

Part I. Inputs	Adjustable Inputs:			Fixed Inputs:	
	2011	2012			
Growth rate, g:	NA	25%		Tax rate (T)	40%
Operating costs / Sales:	85.51%	85.51%		Interest rate	12.50%
Cash/Sales:	5.00%	5.00%			
Receivables/Sales:	30.00%	30.00%		Shares out'ing	1,000
Inventories/Sales:	35.00%	35.00%		Price per share	$45.00
Accruals/Sales:	27.00%	27.00%			
Debt ratio:	38.87%	35.00%		FA/Sales:	48.00%
Payout ratio:	60.00%	60.00%			

Part II. Income Statements

	2011	Change	2012
Sales	$12,000.0	(1+ g)	$15,000.0
Operating costs (includes depreciation)	10,261.0	0.855	12,826.3
Earnings before interest and taxes (EBIT)	$1,739.0		$2,173.8
Less interest expense	339.0	See notes	268.1
Earnings before taxes (EBT)	$1,400.0		$1,905.6
Taxes	560.0	EBT(T)	762.3
Net income (NI)	$840.0		$1,143.4
Dividends	$504.0	NI(Payout)	$686.0
Addition to retained earnings	$336.0		$457.4

Part III. Balance Sheets

	2011	Change	2012
Assets			
Cash	$600	0.0500	$750.0
Accounts receivable	3,600	0.3000	4,500.0
Inventories	4,200	0.3500	5,250.0
Fixed assets (no new FA needed)	7,200		7,200.0
Total assets	$15,600		$17,700.0
Liabilities and Equity			
Payables + accruals (both grow with sales)	$3,240.0	0.2700	$4,050.0
Short-term bank loans	1,157.0	See notes	643.5
Total current liabilities	$4,397.0		$4,693.5
Long-term bonds	1,667.0	See notes	1,501.5
Total debt	$6,064.0		$6,195.0
Common stock	667.0	See notes	2,178.7
Retained earnings	8,869.0	$457.4	9,326.4
Total common equity	$9,536.0		$11,505.0
Total liabilities and equity	$15,600.0		$17,700.0

Part IV. Notes on Calculations

Assets in 2012 will change to this amount, from the balance sheet:		$17,700.0
Target debt ratio		35.00%
Resulting total debt: (Target ratio)(2012 Assets)		$6,195.0
Less: Payables and accruals		-$4,050.0
Bank loans and bonds (= Interest-bearing debt)		$2,145.0
Allocated to bank loans	30.00%	$643.5
Allocated to bonds	70.00%	$1,501.5
Interest expense: (Interest rate)(2012 Bank loans plus bonds)		$268.1
Target equity ratio = 1 – Target debt ratio		65%
Required total equity: (2012 Assets)(Target equity ratio)		$11,505.0
Retained earnings, from 2012 balance sheet		$9,326.4
Required common stock = Required equity – Retained earnings		$2,178.7
Old shares outstanding		1,000
Increase in common equity = 2012 Equity – 2011 Equity		$1,511.7
Initial price per share from input section		$45.00
Change in shares = Change in equity/Initial price per share		33.59
New shares outstanding = Old shares + Δ Shares		1,033.59
Old EPS = 2011 Net income / Old shares outstanding		$0.84
New EPS = 2012 Net income / New shares outstanding		$1.11

11. e. Refer to the balance sheet in the solution to Problem 10.

12. d.

Tatum Toys
Pro Forma Income Statement
(Millions of Dollars)

	2011	Forecast Basis	2012
Sales	$875	× 1.20	$1,050.00
Oper. costs	625	× 0.65 Sales	682.50
EBIT	$250		$ 367.50
Interest	50		50.00
EBT	$200		$ 317.50
Taxes (40%)	80		127.00
Net income	$120		$ 190.50
Dividends (33.3%)	$ 40		$ 63.50
Addit. to R/E	$ 80		$ 127.00

13. c.

Tatum Toys
Pro Forma Income Statement
(Millions of Dollars)

	2011	Forecast Basis	2012
Sales	$875	× 1.20	$1,050.00
Oper. costs	625	× 0.65 Sales	682.50
EBIT	$250		$ 367.50
Interest	50		50.00
EBT	$200		$ 317.50
Taxes (40%)	80		127.00
Net income	$120		$ 190.50
Dividends (33.3%)	$ 40		$ 63.50
Addit. to R/E	$ 80		$ 127.00

ΔDividends = ($63.50 – $40.00)/$40.00 = 58.75%

14. b.

Heuser Industries
Pro Forma Income Statement
(Thousands of Dollars)

	2011	Forecast Basis	2012
Sales	$6,000	× 1.15	$6,900
Oper. costs excluding depreciation	4,900	× 0.80 Sales	5,520
EBITDA	$1,100		$1,380
Depreciation	500	× 0.0833 Sales	575
EBIT	$ 600		$ 805
Interest	250		250
EBT	$ 350		$ 555
Taxes (40%)	140		222
Net income	$ 210		$ 333

15. d. Part I. Inputs

	Adjustable Inputs:				
	2011	2012		Fixed Inputs:	
Growth rate, g:	NA	**10%**		Tax rate (T)	**40%**
Operating costs / Sales:	91.10%	**91.10%**		Interest rate	**10.00%**
Cash/Sales:	5.00%	**5.00%**			
Receivables/Sales:	10.00%	**10.00%**		Shares out'ing	**75,000**
Inventories/Sales:	20.00%	**20.00%**		Price per share	**$30.00**
FA/Sales:	40.00%	**40.00%**			
Accruals/Sales:	15.00%	**15.00%**			
Debt ratio:	25.78%	**45.00%**		FA/Sales:	40.00%
Payout ratio:	60.00%	**60.00%**			

Part II. Income Statements

	2011	Change	2012
Sales	$1,800,000.0	(1+ g)	$1,980,000.0
Operating costs (includes depreciation)	1,639,860.0	0.911	1,803,846.0
Earnings before interest and taxes (EBIT)	$160,140.0		$176,154.0
Less interest expense	10,140.0	See notes	37,125.0
Earnings before taxes (EBT)	$150,000.0		$139,029.0
Taxes	60,000.0	EBT(T)	55,611.6
Net income (NI)	$90,000.0		$83,417.4
Dividends	$54,000.0	NI(Payout)	$50,050.4
Addition to retained earnings	$36,000.0		$33,367.0

Part III. Balance Sheets

	2011	Change	2012
Assets			
Cash	$90,000	0.0500	$99,000.0
Accounts receivable	180,000	0.1000	198,000.0
Inventories	360,000	0.2000	396,000.0
Fixed assets (grow with sales)	720,000	0.4000	792,000.0
Total assets	$1,350,000		$1,485,000.0
Liabilities and Equity			
Payables + accruals (both grow with sales)	$270,000.0	0.1500	$297,000.0
Short-term bank loans	78,000.0	See notes	92,812.5
Total current liabilities	$348,000.0		$389,812.5
Long-term bonds	0.0	See notes	278,437.5
Total debt	$348,000.0		$668,250.0
Common stock	900,000.0	See notes	681,383.0
Retained earnings	102,000.0	$33,367.0	135,367.0
Total common equity	$1,002,000.0		$816,750.0
Total liabilities and equity	$1,350,000.0		$1,485,000.0

Part IV. Notes on Calculations

Assets in 2012 will change to this amount, from the balance sheet:		$1,485,000.0
Target debt ratio		45.00%
Resulting total debt: (Target ratio)(2012 Assets)		$668,250.0
Less: Payables and accruals		-$297,000.0
Bank loans and bonds (= Interest-bearing debt)		$371,250.0
Allocated to bank loans, based on 2011 proportions	25.00%	$92,812.5
Allocated to bonds, based on 2011 proportions	75.00%	$278,437.5
Interest expense: (Interest rate)(2012 Bank loans plus bonds)		$37,125.0
Target equity ratio = 1 – Target debt ratio		55%
Required total equity: (2012 Assets)(Target equity ratio)		$816,750.0
Retained earnings, from 2012 balance sheet		$135,367.0
Required common stock = Required equity – Retained earnings		$681,383.0
Old shares outstanding (millions)		75,000
Increase in common equity = 2012 Equity – 2011 Equity		-$218,617.0
Initial price per share from input section		$30.00
Change in shares = Change in equity/Initial price per share		-7,287.23
New shares outstanding = Old shares + Δ Shares		67,712.77
Old EPS = 2011 Net income / Old shares outstanding		$1.20
New EPS = 2012 Net income / New shares outstanding		$1.23

16. b. Refer to Part IV of the solution to Problem 15.

$$2012 \text{ EPS} = \frac{2012 \text{ Net income}}{2012 \text{ Common shares}}$$
$$= \frac{\$83,417.40}{67,712.77}$$
$$= \$1.23$$

17

MULTINATIONAL FINANCIAL MANAGEMENT

Learning Objectives

1. Identify the primary reasons companies choose to go "global."

2. Explain how exchange rates work and interpret different exchange rate quotations.

3. Discuss the intuition behind interest rate parity and purchasing power parity.

4. Explain the different opportunities and risks that investors face when they invest overseas.

5. Identify some specific challenges that a multinational corporation faces and discuss how they influence its capital budgeting, capital structure, and working capital policies.

Overview

As the world economy becomes more integrated, the role of multinational firms is increasing. Although the same basic principles of financial management apply to multinational corporations as well as to domestic ones, the financial managers of multinational firms face a much more complex task. The primary problem, from a financial standpoint, is that cash flows must cross national boundaries.

These flows may be constrained in various ways, and, equally important, their values in dollars may rise or fall depending on exchange rate fluctuations. Consequently, the multinational financial manager must be constantly aware of the many complex interactions among national economies and their effects on international operations.

Outline

I. **A multinational, or global, corporation is one that operates in an integrated fashion in a number of countries. The growth of multinationals has greatly increased the degree of worldwide economic and political interdependence.**

   A. Companies, both U.S. and foreign, go "international" for seven primary reasons:

   1. Firms have moved their manufacturing facilities overseas to take advantage of cheaper production costs in low-cost countries.

341

2. Firms can avoid political, trade, and regulatory hurdles by moving production to other countries.

3. After a company has saturated its home market, growth opportunities are often better in foreign markets.

4. Many of the present multinational firms began their international operations because raw materials were located abroad and due to new technology.

5. Firms sometimes invest abroad rather than license local foreign firms in order to protect the secrecy of their production process, distribution system, or the product itself.

6. Firms go international so that they can diversify, and consequently, cushion the impact of adverse economic trends in any single country.

7. From the perspective of the supplier of inputs or services, it makes good business sense to follow customers abroad to retain the business.

B. Over the past 10 to 20 years, there has been an increasing amount of investment in the U.S. by foreign corporations, and in foreign nations by U.S. corporations.

1. These developments suggest an increasing degree of mutual influence and interdependence among business enterprises and nations, to which the United States is not immune.

II. **In theory, financial concepts and procedures are valid for both domestic and multinational operations. However, there are five factors that distinguish financial management as practiced by firms operating entirely within a single country from management by firms that operate globally.**

A. These factors complicate financial management, and they increase the risks faced by multinational firms. However, the prospects for high returns, diversification benefits, and other factors make it worthwhile for firms to accept these risks and learn how to manage them.

1. Cash flows will be denominated in different currencies, making exchange rate analysis necessary for all types of financial decisions.

2. *Political risk*, which is seldom negotiable and may be as extreme as *expropriation*, must be explicitly addressed in financial analysis. Political risk varies from country to country.

3. Economic and legal differences among countries can cause significant problems when the corporation tries to coordinate and control worldwide operations of its subsidiaries.

4. Financial models based on the traditional assumption of a competitive marketplace must often be modified to include political (governmental) and other noneconomic facets of the decision.

5. The ability to communicate is critical in all business transactions. U.S. citizens are often at a disadvantage because we are generally fluent only in English. At the same time, even within geographic regions that are considered relatively homogeneous, different countries have unique cultural heritages that shape values and influence the conduct of business.

III. **Every nation has a monetary system and a monetary authority. Moreover, if countries are to trade with one another, there must be some sort of system designed to facilitate payments between nations.**

A. The *international monetary system* is the framework within which exchange rates are determined.

1. It is the blueprint for international trade and capital flows.

2. The international monetary system ties together global currency, money, capital, real estate, commodity, and real asset markets into a network of institutions and instruments, regulated by intergovernmental agreements, and driven by each country's unique political and economic objectives.

B. There are some important concepts and terminology in the international monetary system.

1. An *exchange rate* is the number of units of a given currency that can be purchased for one unit of another currency.

2. A *spot exchange rate* is the quoted price for a unit of foreign currency to be delivered within a very short period of time.

3. A *forward exchange rate* is the quoted price for a unit of foreign currency to be delivered at a specified date in the future.

4. A *fixed exchange rate* for a currency is set by the government and allowed to fluctuate only slightly (if at all) around the desired rate, called the par value.

5. A *floating* or *flexible exchange rate* is one that is not regulated by the government, so supply and demand in the market determine the currency's value.

6. *Devaluation* or *revaluation of a currency* is the technical term referring to the decrease or increase in the par value of a currency whose value is fixed.

7. *Depreciation* or *appreciation of a currency* refers to a decrease or increase in the foreign exchange value of a floating currency.

C. At the most basic level, we can divide currency regimes into two broad groups: floating rates and fixed rates.

1. There are two main groups in the floating-rate category.

   a. A *freely-floating regime* occurs when the exchange rate is determined by supply and demand for the currency.

   b. A *managed-float regime* occurs when there is significant government intervention to control the exchange rate via manipulation of the currency's supply and demand.

2. Most developed countries follow either a freely-floating or a managed-float regime.

3. There are several types of fixed-exchange-rate regimes.

   a. The most extreme position is for the country to have no local currency of its own.

   b. A *currency board arrangement* occurs when a country has its own currency but commits to exchange it for a specified foreign money unit at a fixed exchange rate and legislates domestic currency restrictions, unless it has the foreign currency reserves to cover requested exchanges.

   c. A *fixed peg arrangement* occurs when a country locks its currency to a specific currency or basket of currencies at a fixed exchange rate. The exchange rate is allowed to vary only within ±1% of the target rate.

4. A majority of the world's countries employ a system that includes a fixed-exchange-rate arrangement along with occasional interventions.

5. While the most important currencies (as measured by volume of transactions) are allowed to float, and the international monetary system is often called a floating regime, most currencies are partially fixed but occasionally are manipulated in some manner.

IV.   Foreign exchange rate quotations can be found in leading print publications and websites.

A. Exchange rates are given in two different ways.

1. *American terms* is the foreign exchange rate quotation that represents the number of American dollars that can be bought with one unit of local currency.

2. *European terms* is the foreign exchange rate quotation that represents the units of local currency that can be bought with one U.S. dollar.

a. "European" is intended as a generic term that applies globally.

B. Alternatively, we can discuss exchange rates as being either direct or indirect quotations.

1. A *direct quotation* is the home currency price of one unit of the foreign currency.

a. For a person who considers the U.S. "home," American terms represents a direct quotation.

2. An *indirect quotation* is the foreign currency price of one unit of the home currency.

a. European terms represent indirect quotations to people in the U.S.

C. The *cross rate* is the exchange rate between any two currencies.

D. In this text, unless otherwise noted, we assume that the United States is the home country and thus that the U.S. dollar is the home currency.

V.   Importers, exporters, and tourists, as well as governments, buy and sell currencies in the foreign exchange market, which consists of a network of brokers and banks based in New York, London, Tokyo, and other financial centers. Most buy and sell orders are conducted by computer and telephone.

A. The rate paid for delivery of currency "on the spot" or, in reality, no more than two days after the day of trade is called the *spot rate*.

B. When currency is bought or sold and is to be delivered at some agreed-upon future date, usually 30, 90, or 180 days into the future, a *forward exchange rate* is used.

1. If one can obtain more of the foreign currency for a dollar in the forward market than in the spot market, then the forward currency is less valuable than the spot currency, and the forward currency is said to be selling at a *discount*.

2. If a dollar will buy fewer units of a currency in the forward market than in the spot market, then the forward currency is more valuable than the spot currency, and the forward currency is said to be selling at a *premium*.

VI.   Market forces determine whether a currency sells at a forward premium or discount, and the general relationship between spot and forward exchange rates is specified in a concept called interest rate parity.

A. *Interest rate parity* holds that investors should expect to earn the same return on security investments in all countries after adjusting for risk.

1. It recognizes that when you invest in a country other than your home country, you are affected by two forces—returns on the investment itself and changes in the exchange rate.

    a. Your overall return will be higher than the investment's stated return if the currency in which your investment is denominated appreciates relative to your home currency.

    b. Your overall return will be lower if the foreign currency you receive declines in value.

B. Interest rate parity is expressed as follows:

$$\frac{\text{Forward exchange rate}}{\text{Spot exchange rate}} = \frac{(1 + r_h)}{(1 + r_f)}$$

    1. Both the forward and spot rates are expressed in terms of the amount of home currency received per unit of foreign currency.

    2. r_h and r_f are the periodic interest rates in the home country and foreign country, respectively.

    3. If this relationship does not hold, then currency traders will buy and sell currencies—that is, engage in *arbitrage*—until it does hold.

C. Interest rate parity shows why a particular currency might be at a forward premium or discount.

    1. Notice that a currency is at a forward premium whenever domestic interest rates are higher than foreign interest rates ($r_h > r_f$).

    2. Discounts prevail if domestic interest rates are lower than foreign interest rates.

VII. Market forces work to ensure that similar goods sell for similar prices in different countries after taking exchange rates into account. This relationship is known as purchasing power parity (PPP).

A. *Purchasing power parity (PPP)*, sometimes referred to as the law of one price, implies that the level of exchange rates adjusts so that identical goods cost the same amount in different countries.

B. The equation for purchasing power parity is

$$P_h = (P_f)(\text{Spot rate}) \text{ or Spot rate} = \frac{P_h}{P_f}$$

    1. P_h is the price of the good in the home country.

    2. P_f is the price of the good in the foreign country.

    3. The spot market exchange rate is expressed as the number of units of home currency that can be exchanged for one unit of foreign currency.

C. PPP assumes that market forces will eliminate situations in which the same product sells at a different price overseas.

D. PPP assumes there are no transportation or transactions costs, or import restrictions, all of which limit the ability to ship goods between countries. In many cases, these assumptions are incorrect, which explains why PPP is often violated.

    1. An additional complication is products in different countries are rarely identical.

    2. Frequently, there are real or perceived differences in quality, which can lead to price differences in different countries.

E. The concepts of interest rate parity and purchasing power parity are critically important to those engaged in international activities.

    1. Companies and investors must anticipate changes in interest rates, inflation, and exchange rates, and they often try to *hedge* the risks of adverse movements in these factors.

    2. Parity relationships are extremely useful when anticipating future conditions.

VIII.   Relative inflation rates, or the rates of inflation in foreign countries compared with that in the home country, have many implications for multinational financial decisions. Relative inflation rates will greatly influence future production costs at home and abroad. Equally important, inflation has a dominant influence on relative interest rates and exchange rates. Both of these factors influence the methods chosen by multinational corporations for financing their foreign investments, and both have an important effect on the profitability of foreign investments.

A. A foreign currency, on average, will depreciate at a percentage rate approximately equal to the amount by which its country's inflation rate exceeds the U.S. inflation rate.

    1. Conversely, foreign currencies in countries with less inflation than the U.S. will, on average, appreciate relative to the U.S. dollar.

B. Countries experiencing higher rates of inflation tend to have higher interest rates. The reverse is true for countries with lower inflation rates.

C. Gains from borrowing in countries with low interest rates can be offset by losses from currency appreciation in those countries.

    1. The lower interest rate could be more than offset by losses from currency appreciation.

IX.   There exists a well developed system of international money and capital markets. It is important for both corporate managers and investors to have an understanding of international markets. These markets often offer better opportunities for raising or investing capital than are available domestically.

A. Americans can invest in world markets by investing in the stock of U.S. multinational corporations or by buying the bonds and stocks of large corporations (or governments) headquartered outside the United States.

    1. Investment by U.S. firms in foreign operating assets is called *direct investment*.

    2. Investment in foreign stocks and bonds is called *portfolio investment*.

B. There are three major types of international credit markets.

    1. *Eurocredits* are floating-rate bank loans, available in most major trading currencies, that are tied to LIBOR.

        a. Eurodollar deposits are the oldest example of a eurocredit.

        b. A *eurodollar* is a U.S. dollar deposited in a bank outside the U.S.

        c. Eurocredits exist for most major trading currencies.

    2. The eurobond market is the medium- to long-term international market for both fixed- and floating-rate debt.

    a. A *eurobond* is an international bond underwritten by an international syndicate of banks and sold to investors in countries other than the one in whose money unit the bond is denominated.

    b. This is a true international debt instrument and is usually issued in bearer form, so the names and nationalities of all investors are not recorded.

    c. Most eurobonds are not rated by one of the rating agencies.

    d. They can be issued with either a fixed-rate coupon or a floating-rate coupon depending on the preferences of the issuer, and they have medium- or long-term maturities.

3. Another type of international bond is a foreign bond.

    a. A *foreign bond* is a type of international bond issued in the domestic capital market of the country in whose currency the bond is denominated, and underwritten by investment banks from the same country.

    b. The only thing foreign about a foreign bond is the nationality of the borrower.

    c. Foreign bonds issued in the U.S. are sometimes called "Yankee bonds." Similarly, "bulldogs" are foreign bonds issued in London, and "samurai bonds" are foreign bonds issued in Tokyo.

    d. Foreign bonds can be either fixed or floating and have the same maturities as the purely domestic bonds with which they must compete for funding.

C. New issues of stock are sold in international markets for a variety of reasons.

1. Firms are able to tap a much larger source of capital than their home countries.

    a. Firms want to create an equity market presence to accompany operations in foreign countries.

    b. Large multinational companies also occasionally issue new stock simultaneously in multiple countries.

2. In addition to new issues, outstanding stocks of large multinational companies are increasingly being listed on multiple international exchanges.

3. In addition to direct listing, U.S. investors can invest in foreign companies through *American depository receipts (ADRs)*, which are certificates representing ownership of foreign stock held in trust.

    a. About 1,700 ADRs are now available in the United States, with most of them traded on the over-the-counter market.

    b. More and more ADRs are being listed on the NYSE.

X. **Investors should consider additional risk factors if they invest overseas.**

A. *Country risk* is the risk that arises from investing or doing business in a particular country.

1. It depends on the country's economic, political, and social environment.

2. Examples of country risk include the risk that property will be expropriated without adequate compensation in addition to risks associated with changes in tax rates, regulations, and currency repatriation.

B. *Exchange rate risk* is the risk that exchange rate changes will reduce the number of dollars provided by a given amount of a foreign currency.

C. Returns on a foreign investment depend on the in-country performance of the foreign security and on changes in exchange rates.

XI. **There are key differences in the capital budgeting analysis of foreign versus domestic operations.**

A. Cash flow estimation is much more complex for overseas investments.

1. Usually a firm will organize a separate subsidiary in each foreign country in which it operates.

2. Any dividends or royalties repatriated by the subsidiary must be converted to the currency of the parent company and thus are subject to exchange rate risk.

3. Dividends and royalties received are normally taxed by both foreign and home-country governments.

4. Some governments place restrictions, or exchange controls, on the amount of cash that may be repatriated to the parent company.

   a. This is done to encourage reinvestment of earnings in the foreign country, or to prevent large currency outflows, which might disrupt the exchange rate.

   b. *Repatriation of earnings* is the process of sending cash flows from a foreign subsidiary back to the parent company.

5. From the perspective of the parent organization, the relevant cash flows for foreign investment analysis are the cash flows that the subsidiary is actually expected to send back to the parent.

   a. The present value of those cash flows is found by applying an appropriate discount rate, and this present value is then compared with the parent's required investment to determine the project's NPV.

B. The cost of capital may be different for a foreign project than for an equivalent domestic project, because foreign projects may be more or less risky.

1. Higher risks might arise from two primary sources: (1) exchange rate risk and (2) political risk.

   a. An *exchange rate risk premium* should be added to the domestic cost of capital to reflect exchange rate risk.

   b. It is sometimes possible to hedge against exchange rate fluctuations, but it may not be possible to hedge completely, especially on long-term projects. If hedging is used, the costs must be subtracted from the project's cash flows.

2. A lower risk might result from the benefits of international diversification.

3. *Political risk* refers to potential actions by a host government that would reduce the value of a company's investment.

   a. It includes at one extreme the *expropriation* without compensation of the subsidiary's assets, but it also includes less drastic actions that reduce the value of the parent firm's investment in the foreign subsidiary, including higher taxes, tighter repatriation or currency controls, and restrictions on prices charged.

    C. Companies can take several steps to reduce the potential loss from expropriation.

       1. Finance the subsidiary with local capital.

       2. Structure operations so that the subsidiary has value only as a part of the integrated corporate system.

       3. Obtain insurance against economic losses due to expropriation.

          a. Insurance premiums would have to be added to the project's cost.

    D. Several organizations rate the *country risk*, which is the risk associated with investing in a particular country.

       1. These ratings are based on the country's social, political, and economic environment—which is its *business climate*.

XII. Companies' capital structures vary among the large industrial nations.

    A. After adjusting for accounting differences, evidence suggests that companies in Germany and the United Kingdom tend to have less leverage, whereas firms in Canada appear to have more leverage, relative to firms in the United States, France, Italy, and Japan.

       1. This conclusion is supported by the times-interest-earned ratio data.

          a. In general, firms with more leverage have a lower times-interest-earned ratio.

          b. The data indicate that this ratio is highest in the United Kingdom and Germany and lowest in Canada.

Self-Test

Definitional Questions

1. The _____ rate specifies the number of units of one currency that can be purchased for one unit of another currency.

2. Evaluation of foreign investments involves the analysis of dividend and royalty cash flows that are _____ to the parent company.

3. Some foreign governments restrict, or block, the amount of income that can be repatriated to encourage _____ of earnings in the foreign country.

4. _____ risk refers to potential actions by a host government that would reduce the value of a company's investment.

5. A dollar deposited in a bank outside the U.S. is often called a(n) _____.

6. Investment by U.S. firms in foreign operating assets is called _____ investment, while the purchase of foreign bonds and stocks by U.S. citizens or firms is called _____ investment.

7. _____ bonds are bonds sold by a foreign borrower but denominated in the currency of the country in which the issue is sold.

8. A(n) _____ corporation is one that operates in an integrated fashion in a number of countries.

9. A(n) _____ quotation is the home currency price of one unit of the foreign currency.

10. A(n) _____ quotation is the foreign currency price of one unit of the home currency.

11. _____ is the process that works to bring about an equilibrium among exchange rates.

12. A country with a fixed _____ exchange rate locks its currency to a specific currency or basket of currencies at a fixed exchange rate that is allowed to vary only within plus or minus 1% of the target rate.

13. The rate paid for delivery of currency, in reality, no more than two days after the day of trade is called the _____ exchange rate.

14. When currency is bought or sold and is to be delivered at some agreed-upon future date a(n) _____ exchange rate is used.

15. _____ rate _____ holds that investors should expect to earn the same return on security investments in all countries after adjusting for risk.

16. _____ power _____, sometimes referred to as the law of one price, implies that the level of exchange rates adjusts so that identical goods cost the same amount in different countries.

17. _____ are international bonds sold to investors in countries other than the one in whose money unit the issue is denominated.

18. _____ depository _____ are certificates representing ownership of foreign stock held in trust.

19. If a dollar will buy fewer units of a currency in the forward market than in the spot market, then the forward currency is more valuable than the spot currency, and the forward currency is said to be selling at a(n) _____.

20. The _____ rate is the exchange rate between any two currencies.

21. _____ of earnings is the process of sending cash flows from a foreign subsidiary back to the parent company.

22. Eurobonds are issued in _____ form rather than as registered bonds, so the names and nationalities of investors are not recorded.

23. If one can obtain more of the foreign currency for a dollar in the forward market than in the spot market, then the forward currency is less valuable than the spot currency, and the forward currency is said to be selling at a(n) _____.

24. Your overall return will be higher than the investment's stated return if the currency in which your investment is denominated _____ relative to your home country.

25. _____ occurs when a foreign government takes away assets within its boundaries without compensating the firm for those assets.

26. The international _____ system is the blueprint for international trade and capital flows.

27. _____ is the technical term referring to the decrease in the par value of a currency whose value is fixed.

28. _____ of a currency refers to an increase in the foreign exchange value of a floating currency.

29. _____ terms is the foreign exchange rate quotation that represents the number of American dollars that can be bought with one unit of local currency. For a person who considers the U.S. home, it represents a _____ quotation.

30. Foreign bonds issued in the U.S. are sometimes called _____ bonds.

31. _____ are floating-rate bank loans, available in most major trading currencies, that are tied to LIBOR.

32. _____ rate risk is the risk that relates to what the basic cash flows will be worth in the parent company's home currency.

33. _____ risk is the risk associated with investing in a particular sovereign nation.

34. Business _____ is a country's social, political, and economic environment.

35. A foreign project's higher risk could arise from two primary sources: _____ rate risk and _____ risk, whereas a lower risk might result from international diversification.

Conceptual Questions

1. Financial analysis is not able to take into account political risk.

   a. True
   b. False

2. Over the past 10 to 20 years, there has been an increasing amount of investment in the U.S. by foreign corporations, and in foreign nations by U.S. corporations. These developments suggest an increasing degree of mutual influence and interdependence among business enterprises and nations, to which the United States is not immune.

   a. True
   b. False

3. A foreign currency, on average, will appreciate at a percentage rate approximately equal to the amount by which its inflation rate exceeds the inflation rate in the United States.

   a. True
   b. False

4. The cost of capital is generally lower for a foreign project than for an equivalent domestic project since the possibility of exchange gains exists.

   a. True
   b. False

5. Which of the following statements concerning multinational cash flow analysis is *not* correct?

   a. The relevant cash flows are the dividends and royalties repatriated to the parent company.
   b. The cash flows must be converted to the currency of the parent company and, thus, are subject to future exchange rate changes.
   c. Dividends and royalties received are normally taxed only by the government of the country in which the subsidiary is located.
   d. Foreign governments may restrict the amount of the cash flows that may be repatriated.
   e. Expropriation occurs when a foreign government takes away assets within its boundaries without compensating the firm for those assets.

Problems

1. The "spot rate" for the Danish krone is 0.1263 U.S. dollar per krone. What would the exchange rate be expressed in krones per dollar?

   a.   0.1263 krone per dollar
   b.   3.1300 krones per dollar
   c.   7.9177 krones per dollar
   d.   79.1770 krones per dollar
   e. 255.2652 krones per dollar

2. One EMU euro can be exchanged for $1.0173 today. The euro is expected to appreciate by 10% tomorrow. What is the expected exchange rate tomorrow expressed in euros per dollar?

   a.   0.7750 euro per dollar
   b.   0.8500 euro per dollar
   c.   0.8936 euro per dollar
   d.   0.9830 euro per dollar
   e.   1.0813 euros per dollar

3. A currency trader observes that in the spot exchange market, one U.S. dollar can be exchanged for 114.35 Japanese yen or for 1.0611 EMU euros. How many euros would you receive for every yen exchanged?

   a.   0.00093
   b.   0.00928
   c.   0.034389
   d.   66.506724
   e. 107.76554

4. A deluxe refrigerator costs $1,300 in the United States. The same refrigerator costs 788 British pounds. If purchasing power parity holds, what is the spot exchange rate between pounds and the dollar? In other words, according to the spot rate calculated, how many pounds would you receive for every dollar exchanged?

   a.   0.5778
   b.   0.6375
   c.   0.6062
   d.   1.2349
   e.   1.6497

5. 6-month U.S. T-bills have a nominal annual rate of 8%, while default-free German bonds that mature in 6 months have a nominal annual rate of 6%. In the spot exchange market, one euro equals $0.9666. If interest rate parity holds, what is the 6-month forward exchange rate? In other words, how many U.S. dollars would you receive for every euro exchanged 6 months from now?

   a. $0.9760
   b. $0.9850
   c. $1.0000
   d. $1.0053
   e. $1.0100

6. Geneva Manufacturing Co. is a Swiss multinational manufacturing company. Currently, Geneva's financial planners are considering undertaking a one-year project in the United States. The project's expected dollar-denominated cash flows consist of an initial investment of $5,000 and a cash inflow the following year of $7,500. Geneva estimates that its risk-adjusted cost of capital is 15%. Currently, 1 U.S. dollar will buy 1.5078 Swiss francs. In addition, one-year risk-free securities in the United States are yielding 5.50%, while similar securities in Switzerland are yielding 3.25%.

    If this project were instead undertaken by a similar U.S.-based company with the same risk-adjusted cost of capital, what would be the net present value and rate of return generated by this project?

    a. $1,578.85; 50%
    b. $1,521.74; 15%
    c. $1,500.00; 25%
    d. $1,521.74; 50%
    e. $1,578.85; 25%

7. Geneva Manufacturing Co. is a Swiss multinational manufacturing company. Currently, Geneva's financial planners are considering undertaking a one-year project in the United States. The project's expected dollar-denominated cash flows consist of an initial investment of $5,000 and a cash inflow the following year of $7,500. Geneva estimates that its risk-adjusted cost of capital is 15%. Currently, 1 U.S. dollar will buy 1.5078 Swiss francs. In addition, one-year risk-free securities in the United States are yielding 5.50%, while similar securities in Switzerland are yielding 3.25%. What is the expected forward exchange rate one year from now? [Hint: Remember that the "home" country is Switzerland.]

    a. 0.9787 SF per U.S. $
    b. 1.2500 SF per U.S. $
    c. 1.5555 SF per U.S. $
    d. 1.3333 SF per U.S. $
    e. 1.4756 SF per U.S. $

8. Geneva Manufacturing Co. is a Swiss multinational manufacturing company. Currently, Geneva's financial planners are considering undertaking a one-year project in the United States. The project's expected dollar-denominated cash flows consist of an initial investment of $5,000 and a cash inflow the following year of $7,500. Geneva estimates that its risk-adjusted cost of capital is 15%. Currently, 1 U.S. dollar will buy 1.5078 Swiss francs. In addition, one-year risk-free securities in the United States are yielding 5.50%, while similar securities in Switzerland are yielding 3.25%. If Geneva undertakes the project, what is the project's net present value and rate of return for Geneva?

    a. 2,000.00 SF; 46.80%
    b. 2,084.76 SF; 46.80%
    c. 2,084.76 SF; 45.75%
    d. 1,857.85 SF; 40.00%
    e. 2,000.00 SF; 45.75%

9. You are considering the purchase of a block of stock in Gallic Steel, a French steel producer. Gallic just paid a dividend of 1.5244 euros per share; that is, $D_0 = 1.5244$ euros. You expect the dividend to grow indefinitely at a rate of 15% per year, but because of a higher expected rate of inflation in Europe than in the United States, you expect the euro to depreciate against the dollar at a rate of 5% per year. The exchange rate is currently 0.9830 euro per one U.S. dollar. For a stock with this degree of risk, including exchange rate risk, you feel that a 20% rate of return is required. Assuming that the constant growth model may be used, what is the most, in dollars, that you should be willing to pay for the stock?

   a. $16.21
   b. $18.75
   c. $20.90
   d. $25.33
   e. $30.00

10. You are considering the purchase of a block of stock in Gallic Steel, a French steel producer. Gallic just paid a dividend of 1.5244 euros per share; that is, $D_0 = 1.5244$ euros. You expect the dividend to grow indefinitely at a rate of 15% per year, but because of a lower expected rate of inflation in Europe than in the United States, you expect the euro to appreciate against the dollar at a rate of 1% per year. The exchange rate is currently 0.9830 euro per one U.S. dollar. For a stock with this degree of risk, including exchange rate risk, you feel that a 20% rate of return is required. Assuming that the constant growth model may be used, what is the most, in dollars, that you should be willing to pay for the stock?

   a. $33.33
   b. $35.00
   c. $38.75
   d. $43.60
   e. $46.78

Answers

Definitional Questions

1. exchange
2. repatriated
3. reinvestment
4. Political
5. Eurodollar
6. direct; portfolio
7. Foreign
8. multinational
9. direct
10. indirect
11. Arbitrage
12. pegged
13. spot
14. forward
15. Interest; parity
16. Purchasing; parity
17. Eurobonds
18. American; receipts

19. premium
20. cross
21. Repatriation
22. bearer
23. discount
24. appreciates
25. Expropriation
26. monetary
27. Devaluation
28. Appreciation
29. American; direct
30. Yankee
31. Eurocredits
32. Exchange
33. Country
34. climate
35. exchange; political

Conceptual Questions

1. b. Political risk must be explicitly addressed by international financial managers.

2. a. This statement is correct.

3. b. The foreign currency will depreciate if its inflation rate is higher than that of the United States.

4. b. The cost of capital is generally higher because of exchange rate and political risks.

5. c. Dividends and royalties received will generally also be taxed by the U.S. government, but the total taxes paid to both governments will not exceed that which would be paid had the earnings occurred in the United States.

Solutions

Problems

1. c. The exchange rate for krones per dollar would be the reciprocal of the exchange rate of dollars per krone: 1/(0.1263 dollars per krone) = 7.9177 krones per dollar.

2. c. Today: 1 EMU = $1.0173. Tomorrow: 1 EMU = $1.0173 × 1.1 = $1.1190, or 1/1.1190 = 0.8936 euro per dollar.

3. b. $1 = 114.35 Japanese yen; $1 = 1.0611 EMU euros; Euros/Yen = ?

   Cross rate: $\dfrac{\text{Dollar}}{\text{Yen}} \times \dfrac{\text{Euros}}{\text{Dollar}} = \dfrac{\text{Euros}}{\text{Yen}}$

   Note that an indirect quotation is given for the Japanese yen; however, the cross rate formula requires a direct quotation. The indirect quotation is the reciprocal of the direct quotation. Since $1 = 114.35 Japanese yen, then 1 yen = $0.00874508.

   $\dfrac{\text{Euro}}{\text{Yen}} = 0.00874508 \times 1.0611 = 0.00927941 \approx 0.00928$ euro per yen

4. c. $P_h = (P_f)(\text{Spot rate})$
   $1{,}300 = (788)(\text{Spot rate})$
   $\dfrac{1{,}300}{788} = \text{Spot rate}$
   Spot rate $= \$1.6497$ per pound

   This is a direct quotation. However, the problem asks for how many pounds would you receive for every dollar exchanged, an indirect quote. To obtain the answer, take the reciprocal of 1.6497 =

1/1.6497 = 0.6062 pound per 1 U.S. dollar.

5. a. $\dfrac{\text{Forward exchange rate}}{\text{Spot exchange rate}} = \dfrac{(1 + r_h)}{(1 + r_f)}$; $r_h = \dfrac{8\%}{2} = 4\%$; $r_f = \dfrac{6\%}{2} = 3\%$; Spot rate = \$0.9666

$$\frac{\text{Forward exchange rate}}{\$0.9666} = \frac{1.04}{1.03}$$

(1.03)(Forward exchange rate) = \$1.0053
Forward exchange rate = \$0.9760

6. d. If a U.S.-based company undertakes the project, the rate of return for the project is a simple calculation, as is the net present value.

NPV = -\$5,000 + \$7,500/1.15 = \$1,521.74

Rate of return = \$7,500/\$5,000 – 1 = 50%

Alternatively, using a financial calculator input the following data: CF_0 = -5000; CF_1 = 7500; I/YR = 15; and solve for NPV = \$1,521.74 and IRR = 50%.

7. e. According to interest rate parity, the following condition holds:

$$\frac{\text{Forward exchange rate}}{\text{Spot exchange rate}} = (1 + r_{Swiss})/(1 + r_{US})$$

Forward exchange rate/1.5078 = (1 + 0.0325)/(1 + 0.0550)
Forward exchange rate/1.5078 = 0.9787
Forward exchange rate = 1.4756 SF per U.S. \$

8. b. First, we must adjust the cash flows to reflect Geneva's home currency, which is the Swiss franc. However, the forward exchange rate must be calculated first to arrive at the exchange rate one year from now. (The spot rate has been given in the question.)

$$\frac{\text{Forward exchange rate}}{\text{Spot exchange rate}} = (1 + r_{Swiss})/(1 + r_{US})$$

Forward exchange rate/1.5078 = (1 + 0.0325)/(1 + 0.0550)
Forward exchange rate/1.5078 = 0.9787
Forward exchange rate = 1.4756 SF per U.S. \$

Year	CF (\$)	ER	CF (SFrancs)
0	-5,000	× 1.5078 =	-7,539.00
1	7,500	× 1.4756 =	11,067.32

Using the Swiss franc-denominated cash flows, the NPV and appropriate rate of return can be found.

NPV = -7,539 SF + 11,067.32 SF/1.15 = 2,084.76 Swiss francs

Rate of return = 11,067.32 SF/7,539 SF − 1 = 46.80%

Alternatively, using a financial calculator input the following data: $CF_0 = -7539$; $CF_1 = 11067.32$; I/YR = 15; and solve for NPV = 2,084.76 SF and IRR = 46.80%.

9. a. First, the valuation equation must be modified to convert the expected dividend stream to dollars: $D_t = D_0(1 + g)(ER)$, where ER = exchange ratio. ER = 1/0.9830 today, but if euros depreciate at a rate of 5%, it will take more euros to buy a dollar in the future. The value of ER at some future time (t) will be

$$ER_t = \frac{\text{Dollars}}{\text{Euros}} = \frac{1}{0.9830(1.05)^t}$$

Therefore, D_t in dollars may be calculated as follows:

$$
\begin{aligned}
D_t \text{ (in dollars)} &= (1.5244 \text{ euros})(1 + g)^t (ER_t) \\
&= \frac{\$1.5244(1.15)^t}{0.9830(1.05)^t} \\
&= \frac{\$1.5508(1.15)^t}{(1.05)^t} \\
&= \$1.5508\left(\frac{(1.15)}{(1.05)}\right)^t \\
&= \$1.5508(1.0952)^t
\end{aligned}
$$

Thus, if the dividend in euros is expected to grow at a rate of 15% per year, but the euro is expected to depreciate at a rate of 5% per year against the dollar, then the growth rate, in dollars, of dividends received will be 9.52%. We can now calculate the value of the stock in dollars:

$$\hat{P}_0 = \frac{D_1}{r_s - g} = \frac{\$1.5508(1.0952)}{0.20 - 0.0952} = \frac{\$1.6984}{0.1048} = \$16.21$$

10. e. First, the valuation equation must be modified to convert the expected dividend stream to dollars: $D_t = D_0(1 + g)(ER)$, where ER = exchange ratio. ER = 1/0.9830 today, but if euros appreciate at a rate of 1%, it will take more dollars to buy a euro in the future. The value of ER at some future time (t) will be

$$ER_t = \frac{\text{Dollars}}{\text{Euros}} = \frac{1(1.01)^t}{0.9830}$$

$$D_t \text{ (in dollars)} = (1.5244 \text{ euros})(1 + g)^t \left(\frac{(1.01)^t}{0.9830}\right)$$

$$= \left(\frac{\$1.5244}{0.9830}\right)(1.15)^t(1.01)^t$$

$$= \$1.5508(1.1615)^t$$

Thus, the euro dividend is expected to increase at a rate of 15% per year, and the value of these euros is expected to rise at the rate of 1% per year, so the expected annual growth rate of the dollar dividend is 16.15%. We can now calculate the stock price:

$$\hat{P}_0 = \frac{D_1}{r_s - g} = \frac{\$1.5508(1.1615)}{0.20 - 0.1615} = \frac{\$1.8012}{0.0385} = \$46.78$$